To
Mary, Maia,
My mother and father,
and
My grandparents

Truth is the shattered mirror strown
  In myriad bits: while each believes
His little bit the whole to own.
            —Haj Abdu. El-Yazdi
                Quoted in Lasky 1945, found in the
                files of the President's Materials
                Policy Committee, Truman Library.

CONTENTS

LIST OF FIGURES

LIST OF TABLES

LIST OF ABBREVIATIONS

DD — Declassified Documents Microfiche, Carrollton Press, Washington, D.C.
DDEL — Dwight D. Eisenhower Presidential Library, Abilene, Kansas
FRUS — *Foreign Relations of the United States*. Washington, D.C.: U.S.
    Department of State.
HSTL — Harry S Truman Presidential Library, Independence, Missouri
JFKL — John F. Kennedy Presidential Library, Boston, Massachusetts
JPRS — Joint Publication Research Service
MEIMO — *Mirovaya Ekonomika I Mezhdunarodnye Otrosheniya* (journal of the
    Soviet Institute of World Economics and International Relations)
NARS — National Archives and Records Service, Washington, D.C.
PRO — Public Record Office, Kew, England
SShA — *SShA: Ekonomika, Politika, Ideologiya* (journal of the Soviet Institute of
    the United States and Canada)

FOREWORD

In the modern history of international relations, the struggles of industrial states over the control of basic raw materials have provided a recurrent theme. The urge of industrialized nations to capture secure sources of raw materials was a major factor in the competition of European powers as they carved up Africa during the last decades of the nineteenth century; it figured in the motives of Germany and Japan in the great wars of the twentieth century; it pitted Britain, France, and the U.S. against one another during the 1920s in arcane political maneuvers over the middle East; and it occupied center stage in the 1970s as members of the Organization of Petroleum Exporting Countries attempted to control the world market for oil.

> — Raymond Vernon, *Two Hungry Giants — The United States and Japan in the Quest for Oil and Ores*, (Cambridge, Mass.: Harvard University Press, 1983), p. 1.

US and Soviet interests focus to a large degree on the less-developed countries, many of which are resource rich.... The resource supply patterns ... demonstrate why access to these regions is important to the US and its allies, and how the Soviet Union, by intrusion therein, gains political and economic leverage against the West.

> — Organization of the Joint Chiefs of Staff, *United States Military Posture FY1984*, (Washington, D.C.: U.S. Government Printing Office, 1984), p. 9.

A centerpiece among popular conceptions about the determinants of U.S. foreign and military policy since World War II, fed by some forty years of pronouncements by our political and military leaders, is the notion that a great industrial nation must be prepared to use military force to defend its access to foreign sources of raw materials. U.S. troops went to Korea in 1950, Americans were told, not merely to

contain the Communist tide for fundamental geopolitical and ideological reasons, but also to prevent the loss to the West of Korean
tungsten, Malaysian tin and rubber, New Caledonian nickel, and
Indonesian oil. Similar explanations were periodically offered to the
public in the 1960s for the growing U.S. military involvement in
Vietnam. And the key U.S. interest driving our willingness to use
military force in the Middle East, we have been assured by every
administration from Truman's to Reagan's, is to maintain Western
access to the two-thirds of the world's petroleum reserves that underlie
that troubled region.

Indeed, it has been frequently asserted or implied by official and
unofficial analysts alike that a systematic program to deprive the West
of assured access to Third World resources has been a major pillar of
Soviet foreign policy for decades, accounting for the pattern of Soviet
involvement in the Middle East and Southwest Asia, in Southeast Asia,
in Africa, and even in Central America. (This hypothesis has stressed
denial of Western access more than acquisition of Soviet access because
the Soviet Union possesses within its own territory the richest and
most diverse mineral endowment of any country in the world.) This
"Resource War" theory of Soviet strategy has been on the wane in the
academic community for some time, but it continues to exert a hold on
the popular imagination and—one could deduce from a perusal of
official speeches and writings on foreign and defense policy—on the
thinking of at least some of our political and military leaders.

The aim of protecting access to resources has been used not only as
an explanation of particular U.S. military actions or preparations for
such action, but also—not surprisingly—as a rationale for the kinds of
military forces we need to procure and maintain. Until relatively
recently, for example, the case for a 600-ship navy was argued largely
in terms of the requirements for protecting far-flung U.S. resource
interests, including, of course, the maintenance in wartime of secure
"sea lines of communication" by which these resources would travel to
the U.S. defense-production complex to be transformed into war
materiel. And the Rapid Deployment Force, later less provocatively
renamed the Central Command, was a Carter administration innova-
tion intended to underline the U.S. commitment to use force to protect
Middle Eastern oil resources.

Has the problem of access to resources really played the central role
in shaping U.S. foreign and military policy in recent decades that
popular perceptions and many official pronouncements attribute to it?

Or have resource issues been secondary rather than primary factors, given prominence in official statements more for their ready acceptance by the public than for their real weight in policy choices? To the extent that policymakers and military leaders have believed their own statements about the need to defend access to foreign resources, what have been the sources of those beliefs in analysis or experience? Does preparing to fight over resources make any sense militarily or economically? Is the role of resources in international relations — and the chance of actual military conflict over access to resources — growing or shrinking with time?

Clearly, the answers to these questions are of more than just academic interest. They relate, after all, to the sensitive issue of "truth in advertising" in official explanations of U.S. foreign and military policy; to the validity of suppositions underlying those policies by the people who formulate them; to the nature of the military forces the United States needs to buy; and to the possibilities for avoiding major military conflicts in the years ahead. Of course the answers are not easily uncovered, for these issues lie at the center of a tangled web whose strands include geology and technology, economics and politics, domestic and international relations, subjective perceptions versus "objective" realities, and the proper interpretation of historical experience in a changing world.

No one is yet in a position, in my view, to sort all of this out completely and persuasively, and Dr. Lipschutz, in this book, does not attempt quite so sweeping a task. But his exceptionally thorough and perceptive examination of the role of resources in the foreign policies of the United States, the United Kingdom, and the Soviet Union in the post-World War II period has shed more light on the essence of the matter than any other work of which I am aware. That essence is found in the intertwining, in official thinking and decisionmaking about the role of resources in international affairs — of ideology with analysis, of ideal interests with material ones, of ends with means, of historical influences with contemporary realities, and of motivation with rationalization.

Dr. Lipschutz's success in illuminating this tangle is attributable in part to a two-pronged approach to the historical part of the work, in which he not only recounts what the countries *did* in their foreign policies vis-a-vis resources but also draws heavily on archival sources (many of them only recently declassified) to explore what the policymakers *believed* about these issues at the time. The other key ingredient in the success of this work is the ambitious and compelling theoretical framework Lipschutz has fashioned from diverse strands of international relations theory, political economy, and political philosophy; the construction of this synthesis is an impressive exercise in the mastery and integration of several vast and difficult bodies of literature, but most important is that the result makes wonderfully good sense.

To compress rather shamelessly a richly textured and subtle argument, I would say that Lipschutz shows the popular conceptions about the role of resource access in international relations to be not so much plain wrong as hugely oversimplified. This is to say, first of all, that while resources unquestionably have played a role in the foreign and military policies of modern industrial states, the role has usually been a secondary one, enmeshed in more fundamental causes and effects. Rather than being the primary aims of policies or the fundamental sources of conflicts, resources have more often either (a) become important for sustaining war efforts undertaken for other reasons, or (b) been used for the exercise of leverage in support of policies having nothing to do with the resources themselves, or (c) served as (at best oversimplified) rationalizations, for consumption by publics and legislatures, in support of policies and conflicts with much more elaborate origins.

Even in those instances where leaders appeared to *believe* that access to resources was of central, policy-determining importance, analysis generally was lacking to show that the resource stakes really justified the military investments and risks undertaken to protect those stakes, or to show that no cheaper and safer alternatives to defending access to the resources militarily were available. Indeed, it is Lipschutz's provocative and persuasively argued hypothesis that leaders in these circumstances have acted more out of deep-rooted perceptions and convictions about how great powers should behave (for example, protecting certain "property rights") than out of rational assessment of objective needs for particular resources.

It is not hard to see, in any case, where leaders (and publics) could get the idea that it is in the nature of a great power to acquire and protect access to foreign resources, and that even going to war over such access is within the realm of reasonable state behavior. This idea permeates the literature of foreign relations and international conflict all the way back to Thucydides, and Dr. Lipschutz in his own research had no trouble finding some two hundred books, articles, and reports written on this theme in just the period since World War I. Certain elementary facts about mineral resources, moreover, seem at least broadly consistent with the proposition: First, many such resources are unquestionably essential both to the economic prosperity and to the military strength of any nation; second, the extent to which different nations are endowed with their own deposits of these resources is wildly uneven; and, third, constrictions in the international flow of certain resources whose extraction is concentrated in only a few countries have, from time to time, indeed generated significant economic disruption.

Yet, as already hinted, there is scarcely a study to be found that supports with analysis or examples the notion that trying to defend resource access militarily, or simply preparing to try to do so, actually pays off. Almost always the costs of military action — or military preparations — are extremely high, the chances of succeeding in a military venture to protect access to a threatened resource are extremely low, and the alternatives to protecting access are much more promising. (There is also a striking circularity, as Lipschutz has pointed out elsewhere, in the idea that a country must build a large military force in order to defend access to the resources needed to build a large military force.)

Many readers may be inclined to regard as a compelling counterexample the case of Middle Eastern oil since the 1970s — a situation in which, after all, both Secretary of State Henry Kissinger and President Jimmy Carter threatened at least implicitly to use nuclear weapons if necessary to protect access to the resource. For despite the high costs and risks of U.S. preparations to intervene militarily, and of the (so far rather limited) interventions themselves, and despite the slim chances of keeping the oil flowing if a determined adversary inside or outside the region really wanted to shut it off, it may appear that the alternatives to trying to protect access have been nonexistent — thereby presenting U.S. leaders with no other choice than shaping our foreign policy in the region around the need to protect a crucial resource.

I would argue, on the contrary, that this example (which, having been extensively analyzed by others, does not play a particularly large role in Dr. Lipschutz's book), supports rather than undermines the thesis that resource considerations usually are — and almost always should be — secondary rather than primary factors in shaping foreign and military policies. For while Middle Eastern oil comes closer than any other example to being indispensable enough and irreplaceable enough to justify preparing to fight to protect access, the case still is not persuasive; when one examines the matter closely, oil does not in fact seem to be the primary reason for U.S. military involvement in that region.

It is revealing, first of all, that in the mid-1980s U.S. oil imports from the Middle East accounted for only 14 percent of our total oil imports, 4 percent of our total oil consumption, and 1.7 percent of our total energy use — scarcely enough on its own to warrant going to war to protect it. (At the peak of our oil-import dependence, in 1977, the flow from the Middle East accounted for 17 percent of our oil consumption and about 8 percent of all our energy use, higher fractions than today's but nonetheless much easier to replace or conserve than to defend by force.) Of course, the dependence of Western Europe and Japan on Middle East oil is greater than our own — amounting in the mid-1980s to almost 40 percent of Japan's energy and 12 percent of Western Europe's — and this circumstance seems to some the central reason for regarding the Middle East as a core strategic interest of the United States. But it is instructive that the Western Europeans and Japanese themselves, who are after all the ones most directly at economic risk from this dependence, have been far less enthusiastic about maintaining a major Western military presence in the Middle East than has the United States. Instead they have preferred to build fuel-frugal cars and nuclear reactors, while assuming — I think correctly — that a complete cutoff of Middle East oil is extremely unlikely under almost any circumstances: after all, it would not be in the interest of the countries in the region, nor even in the interest of the Soviet Union, which needs food and technology from a prosperous West at least as much as the West needs Middle East oil.

All this is not to say that considerations of oil have played no role in the attitudes and policies of the major industrial powers toward the Middle East; they *have* played a role, but for the most part not the biggest one. The United States, in particular, does what it does in the Middle East because of a constellation of convictions and interests (a "strategic synthesis" in Lipschutz's terms), which includes not only conceptions about the importance, vulnerability, and defendability of the oil, but also the venerable philosophy of "containment" of the Soviet Union in general geopolitical terms; a culturally and historically grounded commitment to the viability of the state of Israel; and — intertwined with the rest — a sense of how a great power should define and protect its interests if it wishes to remain a great power. Oversimplifying just a bit, one could say that we are in the Middle East more to protect our status as a superpower than to protect access to oil for oil's sake.

I should add, underlining Lipschutz's point about the largely secondary role of resource issues in the recent past, that there do not seem to be any other mineral resources with the potential to exert in the future even remotely as much influence over international affairs as oil has done in the last twenty years. To be sure, there are a number of "strategic" metals and ores—perhaps most importantly, from the U.S. standpoint, chromium, cobalt, manganese, and the platinum group metals—that are currently essential in both the defense and nondefense sectors of modern industrial economies and that are found in attractive concentrations and quantities mainly in the Soviet Union and a few countries in Africa. And a longer list of essential minerals for the supply of which the United States relies heavily on imports, mostly from the Third World, is easily compiled: in addition to the "big four" already mentioned, more than two-thirds of U.S. consumption of columbium, strontium, bauxite, tin, titanium, nickel, zinc, and tungsten (among others) come from imports. But none of these resources, and no combination of them that is controlled by a small or politically cohesive group of nations, even approaches the economic value or potential for short-term economic disruption that attaches to oil.

Much confusion has arisen about these matters through a persistent failure of publics and policymakers alike to distinguish between dependency and vulnerability. Dependency on imports for critical minerals is widespread and immediately quantifiable; but to be vulnerable requires, in addition to dependency, a politically realistic possibility of being cut off, a lack of possibilities for alternative foreign or domestic supplies (including stockpiles and recycling), the absence of options for substitution, and the expectation of significant impacts from doing without. For years the annual *Posture Statement* of the U.S. Joint Chiefs of Staff contributed to the confusion by presenting, early in its treatment of the challenges to which our military must be responsive, a table of mineral dependencies without any accompanying discussion of the additional factors germane to vulnerability. The fact is that only very rarely are all those factors aligned so as to produce an acute vulnerability. (Even in the case of oil the vulnerability proved to be much less over the medium term than had been widely supposed; diversification of supply, substitution, and conservation turned out to be remarkably effective.) Where the vulnerability *is* genuine, one can add, there is rather little reason to think that use or threats of force will help much.

The main focus of Dr. Lipschutz's detailed analyses and supporting archival material about these matters in *When Nations Clash* is on the two-decade period between the end of World War II and 1965. The conclusions he draws and the model he develops of the interaction between ideal and material interests, however, have much broader applicability; they shed much light on the role of resources in international relations today, and indeed on what it may be in the future. In this connection, it is worth emphasizing here what seem to me to be some particularly important trends that have been altering the way international resource issues are perceived by specialists and policymakers alike.

One such trend is the rather rapid diminution of the once predominant role of the United States in global consumption of mineral resources. In the early 1950s (the time of the famous Paley Commission report, *Resources for Freedom*), it was a commonplace observation that the United States accounted for about 50 percent of the world's annual consumption of mineral resources. (Some actual U.S. shares in 1950 were: crude oil, 63 percent; nickel, 62 percent; bauxite, 47 percent; iron ore, 42 percent; copper, 38 percent; coal, 25 percent.) But by 1965, when the earlier figure was still being widely quoted, a more representative number would have been 25 or 30 percent; and by 1985 it had fallen still further: 27 percent for oil, 14 percent for nickel, 12 percent for bauxite, 8 percent for iron ore, 15 percent for copper, and 18 percent for coal. This transition resulted in part from rapid and sustained economic growth in other parts of the world, and in part from a shift away from heavy, materials-intensive industries in the United States. In any case, the consequence has been that reliable raw materials supply is no longer so much a special interest of the United States as it is a universal interest of a far-flung industrial civilization.

A second trend, albeit a generally slower one, has been geographic diversification in the sources of supply of critical minerals, in terms of both the pattern of extraction worldwide and the distribution of purchases by the United States. The most pronounced example by far has been petroleum, in which the Middle East share of world production plummeted from nearly 40 percent in the mid-1970s to about 20 percent in the mid-1980s, with increases in Mexico, the North Sea, and China, among others, making up the difference. More gradual reductions in the dominance of the biggest producing regions have been

evident over the same period for cobalt, nickel, bauxite, and a number
of other strategic minerals. These tendencies are limited, to be sure, by
the realities of the distribution of the richest deposits; but the oil
experience should have taught us that when the economic or political
costs of the usual sources of supply rise too sharply, other sources
previously considered uneconomic may come into play.

The alternatives include not only lower grade deposits of material
that are more widely distributed than the high-grade ones, but also
recycling (albeit only in the case of nonenergy resources), conservation
(in the form of optimizing applications to obtain increased functional
benefits from each kilogram of material), and substitution of more
abundant materials capable of performing the same functions. Recycling has been gradually increasing for many critical resources, despite
a number of technical and institutional obstacles. Increases in efficiency of use of critical minerals have also been steady, if gradual, and
would accelerate sharply if constrictions of international flows (or even
serious threats of constrictions) added to the motivations. Finally,
remarkable advances in materials science have been expanding the
possibilities for substitution, ranging from changing the composition
of particular alloys (replacing scarce ingredients with more abundant
ones conferring the same properties) to replacing metals altogether in
some applications with ceramics and composites made from universally available materials.

These favorable trends in the strategic resources picture do not
mean there are no potential problems and dangers. The minerals that
pose the biggest potential difficulties are precisely those whose production is most concentrated in a few countries of questionable
reliability, for which lower grade deposits are far from economical, for
which recycling possibilities are limited, and for which no substitutes
in the most critical applications are yet in sight. (Platinum-group
metals and chromium are probably the most difficult cases.) Even for
a somewhat longer list of minerals, the development of lower grade
deposits, the expansion of recycling, the introduction of conservation
measures, and the conversion of manufacturing processes to use substitutes would tend to be too slow to permit escape from the economic
impacts of politically imposed supply cutoffs in the short run. And in
a longer term perspective, it is certainly possible that depletion of the
richest resources of some key minerals — and rising environmental
burdens of extracting and harvesting others — will outrun the offsetting
effects of technological improvements, increasing the role of raw

materials in the real cost of living in an industrialized world. (In the case of energy, it has become increasingly likely that the most intractable problems — and the greatest threats to international stability — will come not from the economics or politics of supply but from large-scale environmental and social "side effects" of energy sources, such as climate change by carbon dioxide from fossil fuels and the spread of nuclear bomb materials by nuclear energy technology.)

In any case, most of the relevant trends support the proposition that the secondary role played by resource-supply questions in governing the formation of political and military policies in the postwar period, as described by Lipschutz in this book, is more likely to shrink further in the near future than to blossom into a primary role. The single most important reason for that judgment is the growing reality — and the growing acceptance and hence stability — of global economic interdependence. The international flows of energy, nonfuel minerals, food, manufactured goods, technology, money, and information have grown so large, so multifaceted, so ubiquitous, and so mutually indispensable that the idea of any country or group of countries waging systematic economic warfare against others by restricting a subset of these flows is becoming less plausible all the time.

This insight seems to have reached even those unnamed laborers in the trenches of strategy articulation who write the annual statements on U.S. military posture in the organization of the Joint Chiefs of Staff. In the last few editions, the prominence given to critical minerals has shrunk noticeably, being confined largely to passing mention in lists of U.S. interests in various parts of the Third World plus a brief discussion of the implications of the materials needs of our military establishment (emphasizing stockpiling and maintenance of sea lines of communication in wartime). In place of the previous, rather heavy-handed emphasis on access to resources in the opening sections of the posture statement, there are now more sophisticated summaries of U.S. interests stressing the maintenance of a political climate favorable to economic cooperation and interdependence in general.

I consider this modest sign of greater realism about resource access issues in the U.S. military establishment to be very encouraging, and for the same reason that I consider Ronnie Lipschutz's book to be as important as it is informative. The point is that the roots and aims of our foreign and military policy are much too important to allow them to be misrepresented or misunderstood, least of all by the people in charge of formulating and executing those policies. There is no reason

we should end up going to war over resources, but that insight really becomes helpful only when publics, opinion leaders, and policymakers all understand it.
John P. Holdren

John P. Holdren is a professor and vice chair of the Energy and Resources Group at the University of California, Berkeley. He is also chairman of the Executive Committee of the Pugwash Conferences on Science and World Affairs, vice chair of the Committee on International Security Studies of the American Academy of Arts and Sciences, and a former chairman of the Federation of American Scientists.

ACKNOWLEDGMENTS

In *The Eighteenth Brumaire of Louis Bonaparte*, Marx (1926:23) wrote:

> Hegel says somewhere that, upon the stage of universal history, all great events and personalities reappear in one fashion or another. He forgot to add that, on the first occasion, they appear as tragedy; on the second as farce.

When I began the research for this book in 1983 (as a doctoral thesis), the United States was just coming out of a period of hysteria about events in the Persian Gulf and potential Soviet threats to Western supplies of oil. As I write these words, in mid-1988, we seem to be coming to the end of another cycle of hysteria. To be sure, as any student of psychoanalysis might point out, even hysteria has "real" causes. But, as often as not, it becomes fixated on other things and obscures those original causes. In this study, I have attempted to uncover some of those causes and to shed light on their meaning. Whether I have been successful will be for others to judge, but I am in any event bound to thank those who have pointed me in various directions in an effort to assist me in this arduous task. All responsibility for what follows rests, of course, with me.

I owe a particular debt of gratitude to my doctoral thesis committee — John Holdren, Gene Rochlin, and Robert Price — for their suggestions, criticisms, and ideas, usually offered at critical points in the course of my research and writing. Others who have aided me — either wittingly or unintentionally—include (in no particular order) Ernst Haas, Barton Bernstein, Diane Clemens, Stephen Krasner, George Breslauer, Gregory Grossman, Benny Miller, Greg MacLauchlan, Michael Maniates, Derrick Tucker, Ethan Kapstein, Jonathan Marshall, Peter Gleick, Jonathan Stern, Alex Pravda, Louis Turner, Andrew Deng, Claudia Vaughn, Kate Blake, Ken Conca, Kent Anderson and, in general, everyone associated with the University of California Institute on Global Conflict and Cooperation and the Energy and Resources Group.

I greatly appreciated the help of the staffs of the various archives in which I worked—the Kennedy, Truman, and Eisenhower Presidential Libraries, the National Archives and Records Service, and the Public Record Office—and the library at the Royal Institute of International Affairs in London, and the encouragement and help of Carol Franco and Carolyn Casagrande at Ballinger. I am also grateful for the gracious hospitality of my family in London.

Finally, there are two people without whom I would never have arrived at this point: Mary, whose love and support over the past six years made this book possible, and Maia, whose kicks and tricks motivated me to work that much harder.

The research for and writing of the thesis preceding this book were made possible by a series of grants and dissertation fellowships from the University of California Institute on Global Conflict and Cooperation (IGCC) and the Social Science Research Council/MacArthur Foundation Program in International Peace and Security. The revision of my thesis for publication was made possible by a grant from the IGCC and a postdoctoral fellowship from the University of California-Berkeley MacArthur Interdisciplinary Group in International Security Studies.

Berkeley, California
November 1988

1 INTRODUCTION
Raw Materials and the Tracks of Interests

In the context of modern world politics, it is often held that only an economically and militarily powerful state can exert significant influence in international affairs and that only through continued economic prosperity can such influence and control be maintained (Calleo and Rowland 1973:10; Gilpin 1975:37; Russett 1983:384–85; Kennedy 1987). A dynamic economy, according to this wisdom, depends on uninterrupted inputs of essential energy and mineral resources that, if not available domestically, will be sought elsewhere. A shortage or cessation in the flows of these resources or access to them (or even threats to access) may, it is thought, undermine the economic well-being of a state and, as a consequence, reduce its influence in world affairs, its ability to exert control over events beyond its borders, and perhaps even its prospects for survival.

Many analysts consider denial of access to strategic and critical raw materials to have been a major instigator of wars, both large and small (see, for example, Emeny 1934; Szuprowicz 1981; Deese 1981; Russett 1981/82). Thus, in a book published by the Stockholm Peace Research Institute in 1986, the problem of competition for resources was characterized as follows (Westing 1986:1):

> Global deficiencies and degradation of natural resources, both renewable and non-renewable, coupled with the uneven distribution of these raw materials, can lead to unlikely — and thus unstable — alliances, to national rivalries, and, of course, to war.

1

Certainly, if one takes the popular, policy, and academic literature as a guide, a linkage between access to critical resources and international conflict is strongly suggested, and the importance of adequate supplies of raw materials to national power and wealth seems axiomatic. One need only consult virtually any standard text on foreign policy or international politics published since World War II to come away convinced that assured control of raw material supplies is essential to national security (see, for example, Morgenthau 1967; Noble 1975; Aron 1966). The number of publications on the subject suggests the hypothesis to be one worthy, at least, of investigation. I have identified at least 200 articles, books, and studies on the topic written between the end of World War I and the present, and this list could, without doubt, be greatly enlarged (for comprehensive bibliographies see Lipschutz 1985; Prestwich 1984; Andor 1985).

It pays to be cautious, however, in addressing the relationship between the twin problems of strategic material resources and international peace and security. States go to war in response to a variety of actual or perceived threats. These threats may involve the material bases of wealth and power, such as energy and mineral resources. But states may also go to war on behalf of ideas and principles that have very little to do with material interests.[1] Often, the causal link between material and ideal interests is unclear, and a conflict ordinarily described as a "resource war" may have been triggered, in fact, by other factors.

This is a study of the relationship between access to fuel and mineral resources and the foreign policies of modern states. It addresses two related questions: Do states go to war in order to gain access to strategic resources? Are the foreign policies of states influenced significantly by efforts to gain access to such resources? The central thesis of this book is that the conventional wisdom regarding the relationship between access to strategic raw materials, international conflict, and foreign policy is incorrect, or at least incomplete.

In this study, I argue that attention only to material factors in an analysis of the role of strategic resources in international politics fails to provide a complete picture of the issues underlying conflicts and wars over resources. Ideal interests are at least as important. The

[1]Throughout this study, I use the term "material" in two different senses: The term "raw materials" refers to such things as hard rock minerals, agricultural commodities, and petroleum. The term "material interests" refers to tangible, physical factors or capabilities, such as power, wealth, and property, etc.

material interests of a state are reasonably easy to define; the ideal interests are not. We can look to the behavior of that state in the international arena, and the formulation of a state's foreign policies, however, to deduce what those ideal interests might be. Furthermore, we can explain many of the inconsistencies in, and some of the failures of, state policy by reference to the clash between ideal interests and material ones.

WHAT IS THE ARGUMENT?

Strategic materials are those natural resources and commodities — hard rock minerals, agricultural products, petroleum-based goods — that are thought to be essential to the national security and economic stability of an industrialized state.[2] Because such materials are distributed globally in an uneven and unequal pattern — a consequence of geology, geography, politics, and environment — many states lack reliable domestic or secure foreign sources (see, for example, Barnet 1980; U.S. BOM 1981; Bullis and Mielke 1985). This pattern of distribution, when combined with the vagaries of international politics, has led many analysts to conclude that numerous international conflicts and wars have been triggered by one state's need for such resources and another state's attempts to deny them to the first. There exists a tendency in much of the literature, therefore, to regard the question of access to resources as one involving only the material concerns of states, such as military capabilities or economic output, and to treat impending or potential shortages of supply as a *prima facie* cause for alarm and action. Although some statistical analyses do suggest a correlation between shortages of resources (as inputs to gross industrial capabilities) and the belligerence of a powerful state denied them, the causal link between the variable and the outcome is weak (Lipschutz 1987: ch. 3).

Modern industrialized states tend to define their interests in a pervasive fashion, often going beyond what is necessary to maintain security and sustain society. Powerful states, to a much greater extent than weaker ones, are able to shape the international environment in which they exist (Keohane 1984), and they do so with a certain set of beliefs and objectives in mind. These beliefs and objectives — which, *in*

---

[2]Criteria for evaluating whether a material is critical or strategic are discussed in (U.S. CRS 1981; Maull 1984; Lipschutz 1987: ch. 2, app.).

toto, might be called the "national myth" (Haas 1985, 1986) — reflect interactions between forces external to the state or society, and those internal to the state itself. A national myth, in effect, sets an "agenda" for behavior in the international realm.

One consequence of a powerful state's efforts to impose its objectives on its international environment is that behavior may come to be determined by precedent, custom, or ideology, rather than by a rational assessment of needs (Rosenau 1986). Consequently, threats to security may be perceived even when basic sources of power and well-being are not objectively threatened. These perceptions may be used, in turn, as justification for an expansive foreign policy. In this context, the requirements of "national security" — the elements necessary to national survival — may become elaborated into far-reaching conceptions of the "national interest" — those factors essential to maintaining the *status quo.* In other words, the explanations for foreign policy may become idealized and, at times, detached from more basic material concerns.

This is not to say that power is irrelevant or that the natural endowment of a state is meaningless in the formulation of foreign policy. But the way in which a state approaches the problem of survival within a given international environment may be as much an idiosyncratic function of nonmaterial factors as a rational response to material ones. For those states large and powerful enough to have a significant impact on the international system, the deliberate manipulation of that system may often be channeled and explained by elaborate formulas and theories — ideologies and schemas — rooted in historical causes and events (Larson 1985:50–57). Access to raw materials can come to play a crucial role in justifying resulting actions and policies. The material and ideal elements are, consequently, not easily disentangled.

In a broad sense, the ideal interests of a state are encapsulated in what I call "organizing principles" and the material interests in what I call "ideas." Both organizing principles and ideas may be thought of as means-ends guides to action, but whereas ideas are grounded in empirical experience (Odell 1979:64), organizing principles are not: They posit, instead, a relationship between individual action and ideal objectives. In Weberian terms, ideas are a manifestation of "practical rationality," while organizing principles are a reflection of "theoretical rationality" (see Kalberg 1980). In all we do as individuals, we observe, decide, and act on the basis of a combination of ideas and organizing principles. The balance between ideas and organizing principles — and success in action — rests on the balance between individual idealism and material constraints. The same is true with respect to national decisionmakers and the states they represent.

In the international arena, this balance of material and ideal desires is reflected in what I call "property rights" systems — systems of rules, customs, norms, and laws that specify relationships between actors as well as actors' interactions with their political, economic, and physical environments (see Chapter 2). Such systems are often idiosyncratic in that they arise from the preferences and ideal and material interests of a single, powerful state.[3] To the extent that they are accepted by many or all states, property rights systems are similar to or identical with international regimes (see, e.g., Ruggie 1983). It is not necessary, however, that property rights systems be as clearly defined or accepted as regimes (see Chapter 3).

The attempt to impose a broad-ranging property rights system on the international area — and to see it develop into a full-fledged regime — can be regarded as one of the main goals of a state's foreign policy and may be called a "strategic synthesis" (Milward 1977: 19–23). Access to strategic raw materials plays a subsidiary, although an important, role in the formulation of a strategic synthesis. Conflicts and wars arise when national conceptions of legitimate property rights — that is, the strategic syntheses of states — clash in the international arena. In this context, problems of resource scarcity and distribution are, more often than not, the symptoms of such a clash, rather than the cause (see Chapter 4).

The post-World War II foreign policies of the United States, the United Kingdom, and the Soviet Union may be understood in terms of strategic syntheses incorporating ideal *and* material interests. For each state, acquisition of secure sources of supply and protection of flows of strategic raw materials provided a means to be used in the fulfillment of the strategic synthesis, rather than an end of that strategy. In the case of the United States, raw materials played a role in defining geopolitical threats, in pursuing an international system of economic liberalism, and in advocating global pluralism and political liberalism (Chapter 5). In the case of the United Kingdom, raw materials provided the material justification for the pursuit of an ideal

[3]This is less true of negotiated regimes (such as the UN Convention on the Law of the Sea), in which bargaining among participants plays a central role.

goal—the maintenance of the British Empire and Great Power status (Chapter 6). For the Soviet Union, raw materials provided a means—even though not a very successful one—of expressing disapproval of the political actions of trading partners and ideological allies (Chapter 7).

The degree of success or failure in the pursuit of a strategic synthesis is, ultimately, a function of the balancing of organizing principles against ideas. To the extent that ideas originate in empirical success, they may be used to generate further success. To the extent that organizing principles lead to failure, they may be discarded in favor of other principles or even empirically based ideas. Success or failure rests on the power of a state—in economic, diplomatic, and military terms—to implement its strategic synthesis in the international arena. Within the small subset of all states considered here, the pursuit of ideal interests was and is practiced universally, but pragmatism and capabilities determine whether ideal interests are achieved and protected (Chapter 8).

In addition, a *caveat* may also be in order here: Success in the pursuit of ideal interests can, over the long term, prove more detrimental to a state than failure in the short term. Why is this so? The international system is constantly changing, and international success depends on a state's ability to deal with and adapt to those changes. This requires flexibility and the successful application of ideas. A state that succeeds in pursuing its ideal interests at one time may be slow to change its behavior when it becomes necessary to do so, and suffer great losses as a result.

IN PURSUIT OF MATERIAL AND IDEAL INTERESTS

What is the nature of the difference between material and ideal interests? In a puzzling passage that is often quoted, Max Weber wrote (quoted in Gerth and Mills 1946:200):

> Not ideas, but material and ideal interests, directly govern men's conduct. Yet, very frequently the "world images" that have been created by "ideas" have, like switchmen, determined the tracks along which action has been pushed by the dynamic of interest.

It is possible, for heuristic purposes, to make a distinction between those matters that involve our physical condition and well-being and over which we may exercise purposive, directed control, and those matters that involve our perceptions and desires and are less amenable to instrumental action. The former may be called "material" interests, the latter, "ideal" ones. Material interests may be said to relate to the way the world is or might be; ideal interests, to the way the world should or ought to be. The conflict between *what is* and *what ought to be* is one of the primary governors of human conduct.

The tension between material and ideal interests, and their interaction, is especially visible in political action, as politics is the art of the possible rather than the preferable. Nonetheless, decisionmakers do have preferences, even in the face of limited possibilities, and they do act to fulfill those preferences. When preferences and outcomes can be unambiguously tied to measurable, physical goals, the logic of action is presumably clear and "rational." We may call these goals "material." Situations also arise in which preferences and outcomes cannot be linked to such measurable goals and in which the logic of action is unclear. In such circumstances, actors may be characterized as behaving in an "irrational" or "nonrational" manner, even though they may be acting out well-formulated programs and schemes. We may call these types of goals "ideal." Material and ideal goals are not, of course, entirely disassociated; there is overlap between the two and they may be pursued simultaneously, as I shall show later in this study.

A problem arises in trying to understand these two types of goals in that the conventional methods and models of political science may not be adequate for investigating the relationship between them. In particular, political science and political economy do not generally allow for a real distinction between material and ideal interests. The realist approach to international conflict begins and ends with power, arguing that, in the anarchic international system, capabilities and not intentions are paramount. In the parlance of the realists, "outcomes are a function of the distribution of power in the system" (Krasner 1983b:356). There are clearly problems with this formulation for, as the economist R.G. Hawtrey pointed out more than fifty years ago, "Ostensibly . . . power is only an instrument of welfare, though the means tend to be exalted into an end" (1930/1952:99). What power-based analyses never clearly define is "power for what purpose?"

Conversely, studies with an economic orientation see actors as motivated by preferences and self-interest, attempting to maximize or satisfice some ill-defined utility function (for a discussion and critique, see Thompson and Tuden 1959). Given that few people believe actors to be totally rational utility-maximizers (or even satisficers), we are left to explain outcomes that seem to be contrary to self-interest.

The study of wealth and power by themselves provides few clues as to the meaning of ends. What the power and interest approaches to international relations tend to ignore or downplay is the role of beliefs, values, culture, and history as important forces in motivating action. As David Laitin (1986:x) has put it: "Instrumental action implies goal-oriented behavior; but only a theory of culture can tell us what goals are being pursued."

The strategic materials policies of modern states should be a particularly fruitful realm in which to explore the distinction between material and ideal interests, particularly as they are related to national security and the national interest. On the one hand, analysis of the *flows* of these resources into an industrialized economy allows us to assess objectively (that is, deductively on the basis of logical reasoning and empirical data) the effects of shortages on a state and, by extension, to measure the impact on national security and material conditions within that state. On the other hand, the study of the announced *policies* of that state allows us to determine inductively decisionmakers' understanding of the nation's interests and ideals — that is, their perceptions of what threatens national security and is essential to the nation's material needs.

Standard microeconomic approaches to foreign policy suggest that strategic minerals policies *should* derive largely from objective, or material, interests. As Stephen Krasner (1978) has demonstrated, the logical-deductive assessment does not always match the empirical-inductive one. The task before us, therefore, is to explain this discrepancy. Krasner appeals to ideology. In this study, I rely on the twin concepts of material and ideal interests.

AN ALTERNATIVE ANALYTICAL APPROACH

How might one investigate the questions posed earlier in this chapter? Three models of action and behavior are prominent in political science and political economy: liberal/interest-group; realist-mercantilist; and Marxist (see Krasner 1978: ch. 1 for a more detailed exposition). Among the central questions at issue in these three approaches are:

Who acts? In response to what? Power? Interests? Class? Is the state distinct from society? Is government the passive recipient of societal pressures? Is the state the handmaiden of corporate interests, or does it act to preserve the system? I assert that no one of these models is applicable at all times; their utility is very much a function of time, place, and circumstance, and one model may more accurately describe one situation than another. Applicability is contingent, not universal (Craib 1984:60).

What I offer here, and apply, is an analytic framework based on the contrast between material and ideal interests as understood within a broadly defined conception of property rights (elaborated in Chapter 2). Within this framework, history becomes important in that it explains how relationships between actors are based not only on power, interests, and economics but also on past actions and events as well as customs and institutions. Unlike materialist theories of human action, this framework provides space for nonmaterial motivations and objectives. The tools of the three conventional models are not discarded; instead, they are used as heuristic devices for interpreting history. Under this approach, the foreign policies of states, insofar as they recognize or deal with raw material problems, can be seen as a mix of material *and* ideal factors. This analytical approach can be broadly described as *historical sociology*. Historical sociology, in this instance, is not a theory or model of foreign policy; rather, it is a method of description.

Why is history so important? History both directs and constrains. It directs through decisionmakers' interpretations of the past (May 1973; Jervis 1976: ch. 6; Neustadt and May 1986), as well as through the ways in which the national myth reifies the past. It constrains through both precedent and customary practice (Rosenau 1986:861–70). But this does not mean that history is deterministic. In a paraphrase of Marx, Reinhard Bendix suggests that it is the problem of reconciling biography with history that is of concern; that is, it is the nature of the relationship between history and human action that is critical. He writes (Bendix 1984:49), "Men make their own history; but they make it under given conditions, and they become entangled thereby in a fate which is in part the result of other men having made their own history earlier." In other words, as in classical physics, to explain the state of the political system at a particular time, we need to know something about it at earlier times. By the same token, we can influence the trajectory of the system, but not all describable future states are physically possible.[4] While we lose the parsimony of a model with one or a few variables, a method rooted in history introduces a richness and an element of dynamic change that is largely absent from the other models.

METHODS

How do we go about applying the method of historical sociology to an analysis of the relationship between strategic materials policies and the foreign policies of states? To begin with, we must understand the origins of those policies. Public policies, both foreign and domestic, are subject to and carriers of a great deal of institutional inertia. Policies and preferences evolve out of and are shaped in response to both societal and foreign pressures. Institutions are created and rules are legislated to implement those policies. Institutions are difficult to create, resistant to change, and hard to destroy (Goldstein 1986). Logic and rationalism do not often carry the day in the face of history. As any policymaker will testify, it is not enough to be right, you also have to win.[5] And it is much easier to win if the weight of history and precedent are on your side, because existing institutions and rules channel and direct policies by defining what is allowed and what is not. John Thompson (1984:135) has written that:

> As constellations of social relations and reservoirs of natural resources, specific institutions form a relatively stable framework for action and interaction; they do not determine action but *generate* it in the sense of establishing, loosely and tentatively, the parameters of permissible conduct.

The explanation of a policy at a particular point in time must acknowledge the influence of policies and events at an earlier time. Policies do change in response to changing material conditions in the surrounding political and economic environment, but they sometimes

[4]The analogy is not exact; there are too many variables to predict precisely the state of the system at some future time.

[5]I owe this observation to a member of the staff of the U.S. National Security Council, interviewed in Washington, D.C., in June 1986.

change very slowly. Even when altered, policies often retain many of the essential elements of previous ones in the same issue area. At the same time, it must also be recognized that some conditions, related to geography and geology, or the perception of those conditions, can remain relatively fixed, regardless of changes in the political and economic environment.

From the perspective of the student of politics, this creates some difficulties. It is not always possible to pinpoint the origins and causes of particular policies because they may be contingent on previously existing conditions and policies. To give one example, although U.S. policy in the Middle East following World War II was conditioned heavily by the presence of massive quantities of oil in the Persian Gulf region, other elements influenced the eventual form of that policy. These included physical factors, such as depletion of Western hemisphere reserves; domestic political factors, such as state-corporate relationships and the influence of interest groups; and foreign factors, such as U.K.-U.S. competition, regional and internal pressures on local regimes, and geopolitical competition with the Soviet Union (see, for example, Louis 1984; Painter 1986).

The outcome of U.S. policy in the region has not necessarily been what one might have predicted on the basis of the selection of a limited set of variables. Presumably, one could rank these factors in order of their importance, thereby isolating the most important, and one could also account for particular elements by application of one or more of the three models of political science described earlier. But simplification does not always provide illumination. The superiority of the historical sociological method does not lie in its ability to explain outcomes in a parsimonious fashion but, rather, in its presentation of the richness and complexity of policy deliberations and decisions.

In this study, I have tried to utilize and combine what I believe are the most useful elements of each method or model. Thus, interest groups can have a significant influence on foreign policy, particularly in issue areas where policy is poorly developed or decisionmakers lack expertise. Power does play a critical role in policy formulation and outcomes, but it does not always carry the day. A state is autonomous to the extent that it successfully creates and maintains a benign and protected environment within which a society may reproduce itself. Finally, history is important: We do not wake up each morning to face the new day with a clean slate.

I have used two analytical methods here. The first is to try to discern long-term trends in the relationships of states to the global political economy of strategic materials. These trends manifest themselves in what I have called (after Milward 1977), for lack of a better term, "strategic syntheses," that are really policies of economic, political, and military "imperialism." For this purpose, I have used contemporaneous secondary sources as well as more recent historical studies.

The second method involves the analysis, where possible, of declassified archival policy documents relating to strategic materials (this has obviously not been possible with respect to Soviet policy). Such documents have been used traditionally for historical reconstruction; their use for sociological and other forms of analysis is less common (Larson 1985; Hunt 1987; see also Gaddis 1982). Although declassified documents cannot provide the complete context of an event, they can offer a "window" into decisionmakers' minds. They reflect decisionmakers' perceptions and explanations of a problem, and they indicate, in certain circumstances, the evolution of a consensus in high policy circles. Presumably, declassified documents also provide more truthful insight into the motivations for action than do statements issued for public consumption (although the differences between the two are often surprisingly small). Finally, such documents demonstrate that, when similar situations occur at different times, similar responses may be forthcoming (Rosenau 1986).

In the historical portion of this study (Chapters 4 through 7), I have focused on two different periods: 1919 to 1939, and 1946 to 1965. (I have omitted World War II because I am interested in the role of access to raw materials in establishing the conditions leading to war, and not in their actual role in the prosecution of that war.) The first period, between the two World Wars, was characterized by a great deal of economic and political instability in the international system. The "raw materials problem" was highly prominent during that twenty-year period and has often been described as a major cause of World War II (see Chapter 4). In any case, the interwar period had a major impact on the postwar policies of the remaining Great Powers.

The second period, which encompasses the period of greatest conflict in the Cold War, was characterized by U.S. hegemony and developing bipolarity in international politics. Raw materials figured prominently, although not exclusively, in the strategic calculations of U.S., British, and (presumably) Soviet decisionmakers (see Chapters 5,

6, and 7). There are three benefits to studying this period, rather than a more recent or contemporary one: First, more information is available about that period, primarily from declassified sources and, second, time provides the advantage of both hindsight and perspective. Finally, this twenty-year period is not so distant that its influence on current policies is difficult to discern.

THE PLAN OF THIS BOOK

Chapter 2 provides an analytic framework for understanding the general problem addressed in this study, and Chapter 3 develops this framework in greater detail, based on a broad concept of "property rights." Chapter 4 summarizes the historical evolution of the "raw materials problem" as a prelude to Chapters 5 through 7, which analyze the strategic resource policies of the United States, the United Kingdom, and the Soviet Union during the period from approximately 1946 to 1965. Chapter 8 returns to the general problem of distinguishing between material and ideal interests, and present conclusions and some thoughts about the policy relevance of this work.

2 THE DOMESTIC CONTENT OF INTERNATIONAL DESIRE
Property Rights, Organizing Principles, and the Foreign Policies of States

In Chapter 1, the concepts of "property rights" and "organizing principles" were introduced. I use the term "property rights" here to encompass a variety of systems of rules governing interactions within societies as well as between states. These systems may exist in the international realm as a set of fixed concrete rules or laws, or merely as tacit understandings between or among actors. "Organizing principles" may be thought of as means-ends guides that posit a relationship between individual action and ideal objectives. They are applied as operational templates to instrumentally map out desired courses of action, with the expectation that a particular effect will follow from a specific cause. Organizing principles are related to property rights in the sense that a specific set of the latter — for example, rights pertaining to a liberal trade system — may embody one or more of the former — in this case, what actions must be taken to achieve and maintain such a system.

Because the fundamental issue involved in the strategic materials problem is that of control, the question of property rights — how they are defined, and what they mean — is a useful starting point for this discussion. Property rights are often studied and defined only in an economic context, and ordinarily with respect to domestic political and economic systems. Here, I will expand the conventional definition to include those "political" and "economic" property rights that are a manifestation of state sovereignty.

Political property rights are those that inhere to autonomous political units, such as nation-states (or governments), as a consequence of control of or authority over territory. These types of property rights can be defined on two levels: in relation to other states and in relation to individuals. Property rights in relation to other states most often (but not always) have the form of international law. Property rights in relation to individuals are simply the law of the land (whichever land that happens to be).

As noted in Chapter 1, the attempt by a state to impose a broadly-ranging property rights system on the international arena — and to see it developed into a set of interlinked regimes — can be regarded as one of the main goals of a state's foreign policy, and may be called a "strategic synthesis" (Milward 1977: 19–23). Access to strategic raw materials plays a subsidiary, albeit an important, role in the formulation of such a synthesis. Conflicts and wars arise when national conceptions of legitimate property rights — that is, the strategic syntheses of states — clash in the international arena. In this context, problems of resource scarcity and distribution are, more often than not, the symptoms of underlying disagreements, rather than the cause of conflict. This chapter develops in greater detail the concepts of "property rights," "organizing principles," and the "strategic synthesis." In later chapters, these concepts are applied to specific case studies.

DEFINING "PROPERTY RIGHTS"

What, exactly, are "property rights"? Property rights delineate the right of actors to behave in particular ways in various arenas, establish liability for actions (Demsetz 1967:347; Keohane 1984:87), and convey rights to ownership and exploitation of physical goods. Property rights also can be defined in terms of systems of rules, customs, norms, and laws that specify relationships between actors (people, groups, states) and between actors and their political, economic, and physical environments. Property rights express an idealized version of the relationship of actors to the material conditions of their environment (on this, see also Oakerson 1985).

Closely analogous to "property rights" is "regime," as the term is used by students of international political economy. "Regimes," according to them, are defined as "principles, norms, rules, and decisionmaking procedures around which actor expectations converge in a given issue area" (Krasner 1983a:1). The term "regime" is generally applied, however, to a specific issue area and not used in the broader sense I use "property rights" here. Furthermore, as Richard Ashley (1980:273–74) points out, regimes can exist without the conscious recognition or acknowledgment of the participants. "International law" is also too restrictive, while "political culture" is too broad, although both terms are relevant.

Property rights as used here are not variables in the ordinary sense of the term. Although they do change over extended periods of time, they cannot be measured or compared in any conventional sense. Rather, they provide a context within which the meanings of actions can be interpreted. Property rights may be seen as a set of rules and rights that channel and constrain perceptions and behavior, or alternatively, as filtering mechanisms that, by explaining what is allowed and what is not, provide meaning to actions. Property rights systems, when projected into the international arena, allow us to understand what Bruce Andrews (1984:321) has phrased so felicitously "the domestic content of international desire." In addition, because conceptions of property rights are value- and ideology-based, a theory of conflict that incorporates a property rights framework is necessarily a cognitive one. Unlike cognitive theories based on individual perception and interpretation (Jervis 1976) or group dynamics (Janis 1982), however, a property rights framework is rooted in history and social culture (Demsetz 1967: 347; Andrews 1975; Larson 1985) as well as in power and interests.

Rules of Property, Rules of Eligibility, Rules of Access

Property rights as defined here are embodied in two distinct categories of rules: those having to do with eligibility and those having to do with possession or distribution. Rules of eligibility define access to rights, while rules of possession or distribution define access to goods (a similar point is made, albeit in a somewhat different form, by d'Arge 1981:5). That is, an actor's access to property is contingent not only on the observation of basic rules regarding acquisition, but also on fulfillment of certain qualifications that convey the *right* to participate in the distribution of property. Anatole Rapoport (1974:176) has distinguished between conflicts that are issue-oriented — they are resolvable without changing the basic structure of relations — and those that are structure-oriented — they cannot be resolved without changing the structure of interaction (see also Krasner 1985). The difference between rules of eligibility and rules of distribution or possession can be understood in the same way.

At the international level, political property rights may be defined either in terms of generally prevailing international norms that specify eligibility and the rights of actors, or they may be open to dispute and, hence, largely idiosyncratic to individual states. In the former case, a "regime" may be said to exist. Although actors may enter into disputes over the distribution of property (or resources), a regime establishes an accepted set of participant characteristics and rules under which disagreements can be negotiated (the United Nations Convention on the Law of the Sea is an example of such a regime; see Oxman 1985). If an explicit regime does not exist, the very basis of whatever system of rules or norms exists may be challenged by dissatisfied actors.

In issue areas where well-defined political property rights do exist, or where efforts are made to find international acceptance of particular sets of rules, the resulting definitions often are outgrowths of domestic ones (see, e.g., Andrews 1975). Thus, the system of international property rights operative during the nineteenth century was modeled on the domestic norms and values of Great Britain and, after World War II, U.S. rules formed the basis for international interactions (Ruggie 1983; Lipson 1985). The exclusive spheres of influence established by Nazi Germany and envisioned by Imperial Japan prior to World War II can be understood in similar terms. In each case, a dominant state wielded its political and economic power in order to reduce uncertainty in the international environment and to extend its value system beyond national borders, as such a program was thought to enhance domestic social welfare.[1]

Participation in an international system of property rights, or a regime, requires being *eligible* to participate prior to gaining *access* to the distribution system. Although it is true, as Lindblom observes

---

[1]The universe of possible cases is not, of course, limited to these. More generally, the theory of hegemonic stability posits the cyclical rise and fall of great powers, each of which attempts to establish such a system of regimes within a well-defined territory or empire (see, for example, Avery and Rapkin 1982; Keohane 1984; Kennedy 1987).

(1977:26), that property is "a set of rights . . . to refuse use of them to others", among other things, the right to refuse use is different from the right to participate in the system that determines use.

A domestic example of the distinction between rules of eligibility and rules of access may be found in the regulations dealing with intercollegiate sports. The body governing such sports activities within the United States (the National Collegiate Athletics Association or NCAA) is empowered to establish qualifications that athletes must fulfill in order to participate in NCAA-sanctioned events. These rules are quite arbitrary; after all, what is sacred about maintaining a particular grade point average?[2] In theory, however, they must be observed. The failure to meet eligibility requirements often leads to conflict and the suspension of schools from competition in certain sports. Different set of rules governs the way each particular sport is played, and the manner in which points are scored by participants in the game, but in order to acquire points an athlete and his or her school must first be eligible to participate.

Consider another example. In some rural areas, especially in the Third World, land ownership is determined by one's membership in a community. Use of the land is governed by rules of usufruct that often are based on familial lineage or some other hereditary characteristic. Land cannot be alienated through sale in a free market. An individual from another village or another country may be able to acquire temporary rights to use land, but he or she is ineligible to own property. In other words, the right to acquire or transfer property depends on first meeting certain eligibility requirements (for a detailed discussion of variations on rural land tenure schemes, see Bruce 1986:1–12).

Property rules of eligibility involve structure, whereas rules of possession involve issues or processes. This means that conflicts over resources, when and where they occur, have their origins not only in the rules regarding distribution of resources but also in basic definitions of the right to participate in the distribution of resources. Both

---

[2]An illustrative example of this point may be found in a 1988 newspaper report that explains why NCAA Division I schools have refused to adopt the same stricter athletic eligibility requirements adopted by Division II schools. According to the writer: "A chief argument against the rule was that different schools have different grading standards. Opponents also said the rule would discriminate against athletes who are willing to enroll in more difficult courses" (*San Francisco Chronicle* 1988:D5).

sets of rules are normally encoded in domestic law. Rules of distribution or possession are usually encoded in international law or international regimes; the rules of eligibility often are not. Furthermore, during periods of weak or nonexistent international regimes, national definitions of rules tend to take precedence. Given this distinction, it is possible to interpret (and, perhaps, to predict) certain types of conflicts over resources as the result of actors' conflicting conceptions of what constitutes legitimate economic and political property rights in a given issue area or arena. In situations where disputes over rules of eligibility develop, war is a potential outcome.

Economic versus Political Property Rights

As I noted earlier, property rights can be seen as either "political" or "economic" in nature. Political property rights govern relations between actors, for example, a state and its citizens. Economic property rights govern relations between actors and material goods or objects. On the one hand, therefore, political property rights define what a state or government may do with respect to territory, society, and population (Hawtrey 1930/1952:16):

> Each Government possesses in virtue of its sovereignty over its various territories rights which are really rights of property. It has the power to delegate out of these rights concessions and similar privileges to private people.

Political property rights allowed to the population of a state derive either from the authority of the sovereign, state, or government or, alternatively, from custom, norm, or common law. Such rights include not only entitlement (i.e., eligibility) to "real property" but also relate to things such as an individual's rights to control over his or her body, rights in relationship to others, and so forth. Furthermore, the state has been granted the right to define rules of eligibility for its inhabitants, such as qualifications for citizenship, for ownership of real estate, and for voting.

"Economic property rights," on the other hand, refer to the more conventional concepts used in the economic and political literature. In this case, it is assumed that rules exist or can be legislated to make assignments of property, and the function of government is to assign property rights where such assignments have not been previously made. By extrapolation, therefore, the residual functions of government with respect to property rights are two: (1) to protect them where they have been assigned, whether in a domestic or foreign context, and (2) to adjudicate, on the basis of established rules, where conflicts arise over assignment.

As noted earlier, however, political property rights are somewhat different from economic ones in that they do not necessarily convey rights to ownership of private property or exploitation of physical goods. State sovereignty over national territory—which may or may not include ownership (see Lipson 1985:77; Shaw 1986)—may be considered such a right (Hawtrey 1930/1952:18). Territorial exchanges or extra-territorial agreements between states are practical applications of property rights conveyed by sovereignty. The integrity of national territory—often called "national security"—is a primary political property right.

How are property rights extended outside of the domestic realm? In the international sphere—that is, where states are the primary actors— the establishment of political property rights is often considered problematic for at least three reasons: (1) There exists no overriding international authority to impose definitions; (2) information is costly and held unequally by different actors; and (3) the costs of determining property rights through negotiations or other means, or establishing institutions for defining those rights, are very high (Keohane 1984:87). Such property rights as do exist have developed via historical evolution (for example, diplomatic immunity), precedent (laws of maritime passage), imposition by a hegemonic power (base rights, treaty ports), or international negotiations (UNCLOS, the United Nations Convention on the Law of the Sea). Consequently, although issues may resemble each other in general terms, the appropriate sets of property rights that are applicable from case to case may differ greatly, if they exist at all.

International law, international organizations, and international regimes are mechanisms that explicitly define basic property rights at the international level (Conybeare 1980; Lipson 1985; Krasner 1985:5).[3]

[3] In this case, property rights may also be seen as a set of implicit rules or tacit understandings intended to regulate actor behavior, although these are frail reeds on which to stand in the international arena.

Such institutions arise only where there exists basic agreement between states on rules, principles, and norms. Where these do not exist, there may result what Krasner (1985:5) calls "structural conflict." Structural conflict can develop into actual physical conflict, particularly when "basic national values" are threatened (Keohane 1984:39). In formal terms, structural conflict can be described by an inversion of the Coase theorem; that is, the transaction costs involved in the compromising of values (property rights) and lack of sufficient information about the minimum requirements of other actors combine to create a conflictual situation (Keohane 1984:87). In the international sphere, therefore, the foreign policy of a state may be seen as a program to protect property rights as defined by that state in both the international and domestic contexts.

Demsetz (1967:348) argues that economic property rights develop only when the costs of externalities become so large that there is a benefit to internalizing them. In this instance, an "externality" may be understood as a cost to parties arising from both imperfect information and high transaction costs.[4] In the international economic and political arenas, the externality problem may be dealt with in one of three ways. First, a more powerful party may force on others a particular division of property through territorial conquest or aggression (hegemony). In this case, the costs are absorbed by the victims. Alternatively, the more powerful party may choose to absorb some of the costs as an inducement to others to follow a particular definition of property rights (cooptation). Finally, a number of parties may negotiate over the distribution of costs and the appropriate set of rules governing access to property (cooperation). The resulting agreement is either based on, or constitutes, a set of norms or rules defining international property rights. Thereafter, property rights reflect the prevailing international structure of power and wealth and define fundamental social values until such time as that structure is changed either by revolution, reform, or war.

Some economists are more optimistic than others about the possibilities of arriving at mutually agreed-on sets of internationally accepted rules in the absence of precedent, coercion, or incentives. A

---

[4]In classical economics, an externality is understood to be a cost or benefit for which the producer or consumer does not pay, such as pollution. When the cost of the pollution to the consumer exceeds the benefit to the producer, there arises an incentive to eliminate it, but this is prevented by lack of information regarding the distribution of costs and benefits and the high cost of negotiating a solution (Fisher 1981:166–69).

number of microeconomists, following Coase (1960), believe that the market, left to itself, is the most efficient means of internalizing externalities and maximizing equity. They argue that "bargaining and mutual adjustment" can lead to rules (Keohane, 1984:86). The evidence for this belief is provided by what Conybeare (1980:314) calls the "evolution of international externality law," which, he asserts,

> [I]llustrates the ability of states operating in a *market exchange environment* to develop a system of property rights and liability rules consistent with global welfare, in the absence of any overarching supranational IO [international organization] directly intervening to force states to internalize the effects of externalities [emphasis added].

The only task left to the state, according to Conybeare (1980:311), is to "assign property rights to the party with higher transaction costs."

In Conybeare's system, rules seem to be self-evident — they are the rules of the market — and power is of no consequence. Thus, he writes (1980:325, emphasis added),

> A higher propensity to deny the *rule of law* (euphemistically called the principle of "self-help" in international law) and to resort to coercion is a characteristic distinguishing international from domestic politics.

There is a need, he continues, to prohibit the use of force in the interest of the maintenance of international property rights (1980:327). How such a rule is to be enforced in the absence of an overriding authority is left unclear. As a result, this statement leads the reader to conclude that someone must establish at least *one rule independent of the market.*

The microeconomic approach proposed by Conybeare ignores certain other important points. The very existence of a "market exchange environment" implies a set of established and broadly accepted rules. Adherence to the rules of the market, as well as to international law (and organizations and regimes), arises out of a perception that such arrangements serve national welfare by reducing uncertainty in a state's general environment, including threats of coercion of one state by another.

By the same token, however, the international arrangements applicable in a particular issue area may not reflect the actual preferences of a state that adheres to those arrangements. The outcome may be, at best, a utility-satisficing one (Bueno de Mesquita 1981: ch. 2), and the utility realized may be sufficiently low to impel a state to break away from an international arrangement or to collaborate with others to change the rules. Keohane's critique of the application of Coase's theorem (and Conybeare's argument) centers on a similar set of points. Keohane (1984:87) points out that in the real world, none of the conditions required by the theorem — "a legal framework establishing liability for actions . . . ; perfect information; and zero transaction costs" — exists. Indeed, the absence of these conditions is what leads to conflicts between states.[5]

Property rights are not only legislative constructs, however, as suggested by the foregoing discussion. They can also be seen as historical and cultural artifacts, arising out of custom and the structure of society. In particular, rules of eligibility are often derived from customary rules, as in the case of English common law. Demsetz (1967:347) writes:

> Property rights are an instrument of society and derive their significance from the fact that they help a man form those expectations which he can reasonably hold in his dealings with others. These expectations find expression in the laws, customs, and mores of a society. An owner of property rights possesses the consent of fellowmen to allow him to act in particular ways. An owner expects the community to prevent others from interfering with his actions, provided that these actions are not prohibited in the specifications of his rights.

Thus, at the domestic level the development and application of property rights incorporate not only interests and authority, but also socio-cultural rules and values. Concepts of ownership arise out of economic *and* political relationships within a society, and the principles used to explain those rights reflect and justify the existing social structure and the distribution of wealth and power within that society. In different societies and states, the explanations for the distribution will be different and the definitions of property rights will differ. Often, these explanations become part of a national ideology or myth.

In addition, property rights, such as they are, are never fixed permanently because a central purpose of them is the "rationalization

---

[5]The international externality problem arose traditionally because the absence of regulations led to a situation in which states threatened the security and economic well-being of each other (the so-called security dilemma; Jervis 1978) but were unable to bear the transaction costs of communicating and reaching agreements. The solution to this problem was to establish spheres of influence. In the post-World War II era, the advent of nuclear weapons and the globalization of the market system may have shifted the externality problem from a zero-sum situation, in which one state's loss is another's gain, to a commons problem, in which potential costs and benefits are seen as accruing simultaneously to all states.

and maintenance of social relations" (Lipson 1985:32) at both the domestic *and* international levels. Therefore, observes Lipson (1985:32):

> [C]hallenges [to property rules] are important because . . . they do not have fixed meanings of decontextualized significance. Rather, [the rules] . . . are continually reproduced and redefined in the dispute process as the actors use or resist existing standards.

Krasner (1983b:363) writes: "If sovereignty is the constitutive principle of the international political system, property rights are the constitutive principle of the international economic system" (although his distinction is appropriate only to the extent one disconnects politics and economics). Hawtrey (1930/1952:8) notes that "The public safety is the paramount law, and before such measures all private rights must give way. Private rights of property are overridden by the [state's] power of requisition."[6]

This power or right can extend to the assertion of control over property owned by foreign citizens or foreign states. The justification for expropriation or nationalization may be economic or political. In either case, the act of taking becomes an assertion of state power with multiple meanings because, according to Lipson (1985:30):

> Expropriation . . . is more than just the assertion of state control over some portion of the domestic economy. It is a powerful and evocative expression of sovereign authority against outside powers and, most often, a rejection of subordinate status within an international hierarchy. Action and representation are thus intermixed.

Therefore, to the extent that "national interests" are seen as essential to the maintenance of sovereignty or protection of national territory, they, too, may be thought of as political property rights (often, a state's political interests are thought to be congruent with its economic interests, and thus require the protection of private property owned by its citizens outside of the national territory).

---

[6]An expression of this notion may be found in an article about the efforts of Lawrence Livermore National Lab to acquire land in California's Central Valley for an experiment related to the Strategic Defense Initiative. According to the author of the piece (Dowie 1986:24):

> [Livermore physicist Richard] Briggs says the government will invoke a higher principle than property rights if it decides to lay claim to the ranchers' land. "I do believe, as do many people in the federal government, that this program is vital to national security."

In Chapter 3, I will return to the concept of property rights and apply them specifically to the problem of conflict over resources. The following section turns to the notion of "organizing principles" and defines their relationship to property rights systems.

DEFINING "ORGANIZING PRINCIPLES"

"Organizing principles," as noted earlier, may be thought of as means-ends guides that posit a relationship between individual action and ideal objectives. They are applied as operational templates to instrumentally map out desired courses of action, with the expectation that a particular effect will follow from a specific cause. Organizing principles are related to property rights in the sense that in pursuit of a specific set of the latter — for example, rights pertaining to a liberal trade system — an actor will behave on the basis of one or more of the former — in this case, what actions must be taken to achieve and maintain such a system. Organizing principles can also be seen as reflective of a "theoretical rationality" that underlies national objectives (Kalberg 1980; Haas 1986). As a result, they are worth exploring in greater detail.

The objectives of a nation — the codification of national purpose — do not spring up overnight. Decades, and even centuries, are required for the national purpose to develop, and even as it evolves, it is modified and revised. At some point, the essential core ideas can become obscured, overgrown by the glosses and marginalia of successive generations of politicians, policymakers, and publicists. To focus only on the consequences of national purpose — on outcomes — in both domestic and foreign policy terms, is to miss and misunderstand the meaning of that purpose (Laitin 1986:x). Only by returning to the origins of influential ideas, themes, and institutions can we explain many of the patterns of behavior that confound more ahistorical approaches characteristic of conventional academic research. In this instance, such an analysis involves elucidating and explaining the organizing principles underlying the perceptions and behavior of decisionmakers. Through the study of the behavior patterns of decisionmakers and the tracing of continuities of policy over extended periods of time, it becomes possible to determine which ideas and organizing principles continue to have influence, why they persist, and how they affect action.

The influence of ideas, themes, and institutions in actor behavior and the formulation of policies has often been given short shrift by political science and other disciplines. This may be due to the fact that such phenomena are difficult to "observe" or "measure." It may be a reflection of the positivist belief that the determinants of behavior can be isolated and analyzed in some absolute sense or as Kal Holsti (1986:643) has written, it may be that academics "prefer authoritative outcomes . . . [and], like the policymakers [they] often criticize, are uncomfortable with conceptual or theoretical grey areas."

Over the past two decades, in any case, political scientists have preferred to focus on more easily observed variables as determinants of actor behavior, namely maximization of power and pursuit of economic self-interest (see, e.g., Krasner 1978; Waltz 1979; Gilpin 1981; Keohane 1984; for a critique applied to public administration, see Thompson and Tuden 1959). This is not to say, of course, that cognitive elements in perception and action have been ignored. A number of studies dealing with the importance of cognitive factors in individual behavior, such as perceptions, beliefs, and experiences, have been undertaken, but these studies have, by and large, focused on the cognitive "process" rather than on its "content" and on the way in which belief systems develop. The unit of analysis in such studies has typically been individuals (Steinbruner 1974; Hermann 1976; Jervis 1976; Steiner 1983; Larson 1985), small groups (Janis 1982), presidential administrations (Clough 1983), governments (King 1972), or states (Snyder and Diesing 1977). On a societal level, however, where belief systems originate, cognitive elements and their meanings have been largely disregarded. Ideas, themes, and institutions often have their roots in social and political culture, and they continue to have major influence on policymakers long after the originators or founders have passed on (see, for example, Clough 1983: ch. 2; Goldstein 1986; George 1969 applies this notion to "Bolsheviks").

As a result, what is conspicuously lacking in most analyses of foreign policy are the antecedents to policy formation—the underlying "organizing principles" used to account for particular phenomena and to devise appropriate responses. The neo-Marxist literature posits the existence of such principles but ascribes them to forces exogenous to social and political culture (see, for example, Frank 1982). Consequently, in the

Marxist model such principles become universal influences on behavior. The more mainstream literature dealing with cognitive determinants treats them as instrumental elements of a legitimation process, to wit (Clough 1983:28):

> An [American] administration's ability to maintain domestic support for its politics depends upon its success in legitimating those policies by relating them to an overarching symbolic framework grounded in widely held beliefs pertaining to foreign policy such as political ideologies and strategic presumptions.

But this assumes that rationalization often follows decisions or action. In reality, decisions and actions are often directed or modified by the "symbolic framework" posited by Clough. Organizing principles are thus more appropriately seen as "soft" structural elements that both constrain and direct behavior. They are used instrumentally to map out courses of action, they possess explanatory power, and they relate cause and effect.

As noted earlier, organizing principles are ordinarily applied not as ideals or theories but rather as operational templates. For example, with respect to U.S. foreign policy formulation, it has been assumed that the implantation of liberal democratic forms in a developing state must necessarily lead to operating democracies, and that the adoption of Marxist forms of governance necessarily leads to major shifts in regional, and hence global, balances of power as a result of "bandwagoning" (that is, the "domino" theory). The overriding U.S. goal in applying these principles has been that of "order"—at home and abroad—by means of which the world could evolve to a better state (for a contemporary explication of the application of several of these principles, see Shipler 1986).

There are two advantages to exploring such principles: First, as Bruce Andrews (1984:323) suggests, they allow us to more clearly understand the origins of national perceptions and behavior. Ordinarily, he writes,

> The domestic social relations that lie behind the broad purposes of policy are hidden; both official rhetoric and orthodox analysis transport them almost outside of history and the process by which the social and material life of society are reproduced. The record of the nation's policy becomes a chronology of fixations rather than an unfolding of society's desires.

Second, there is, as Andrews indicates, the question of history. Ideas and interests do not spring full-blown from new situations; older ideas are elaborated and older interests refined and redefined to take account of changing circumstances. Although it is often convenient to ascribe the origins of policies and actions to major world events or certain political principles, such as World War II or balance-of-power politics, deeper layers of meaning can always be found and traced to earlier times.

But why talk about organizing principles? Why not explain the causes of policies, and policy failures, in terms of interests and power, the common currency of international politics? All behavior is motivated by some conception of cause and effect, by some explanation of how the world works. Organizing principles, as applied in this study, are both explanatory — they suggest how the world ought to be — and causal — they express the processes that must be implemented if the ideal is to be realized (Geertz 1964 explores this for ideology). Furthermore, they are based on historical experience, particularly the national experience. Hence, they are the idealized projection of a nation's successful history into and onto the world.

Because they are rooted in history, these principles cannot be extracted from case studies without reference to prior historical experience. In addition, they remain operative for long periods of time, and function as the context within which events are understood and actions are taken. They are, therefore, "soft" constraints, defining the limits of permissible actions (Thompson 1984:135). Acceptable interpretations and actions must remain within the bounds of these principles if the policymaker is to retain credibility with his or her peers *and* if policies are to be implemented successfully. Even then, success is not guaranteed, for outcomes are frequently unpredictable.

Policy formation is not, of course, a simple matter, particularly when domestic and foreign issues become intertwined. Problems that appear relatively "pure" at first glance often turn out to be entangled with other, seemingly unrelated issues. Describing the raw materials policy of a state is a fairly straightforward matter. Discerning where such a policy fits into the broader strategic synthesis is more difficult. As asserted earlier, access to strategic materials is rarely, if ever, an end in itself, but it may be utilized as a means of achieving other ends. Indeed, raw materials strategy may come, at times, to be determined by these other ends, even if apparently irrational policies result.

The problem of the tension between material and ideal interests is one addressed throughout this study. What follows from the preceding discussion, and the earlier parts of this chapter, is a recognition that the strategic syntheses, embodied property rights, and organizing principles of different states may, at times, be incompatible with one another, with conflict, and even war, the result.

STRATEGIC SYNTHESES AND FOREIGN POLICY

If one thinks about the nature of the state in the twentieth century, it does appear that a major factor in the accumulation of national power—including economic and industrial strength—has been reliable access to raw materials (see Lipschutz 1987: ch. 3 for a review of the literature on this point). The issue of concern here is how a state might acquire these materials. Geopolitical theory, which underlies a good deal of thought about strategic materials, maintains that the only sure way to obtain them is through territorial control. This must, of necessity, flow from military strength and its threatened or actual application (Emeny 1934; Strauss-Hupè 1942; Gyorgy 1944; Spykman 1944; Parker 1985; Zoppo and Zorgbibe 1985).

A military strategy focused on the conquest of territory is not, however, the only one available to a state. Even if the needed raw materials are found within the national territory, there may exist incentives to import them. Conversely, even a state lacking certain raw materials may decide to forgo foreign trade in the pursuit of other goals. Although a strategy may be internally or externally oriented, in either case it should be understood as one component of a broader set of foreign policy goals. Without going too deeply at this point into the postulated rationales for these strategies (see Boulding and Mukerjee 1972; Wright 1976; Milward 1977; Kennedy 1987 for discussions), in this century every industrialized state has developed some strategy—either intentionally or by default—for acquiring raw materials. These strategies are not independent from broader foreign policy objectives, of course, but they do reflect the general organizing principles of the foreign policies of a particular state.

In a theoretical sense, there are two approaches to the raw materials problem: autarky and dependence (this can be applied more generally to foreign trade, as well). At one extreme, pure autarky represents complete self-sufficiency, that is, no imports of any raw materials of strategic significance. At the other extreme, pure dependence implies little or no self-sufficiency with respect to strategic raw materials.[7] Each approach carries different implications for the foreign policy of a state. A policy of autarky means that a state need pay no attention to any other state, except where direct military threats are concerned, for the autarkic state cannot be manipulated or coerced by threats of interrupted supplies. Furthermore, the autarkic state can act without regard for the concerns of any other state (Karber and Menzel 1975). A policy of dependence means that a state must take into account not only the response of other states to its actions, but also the possibility that other states may decide, for one reason or another, to cut off trade with it in strategic materials.

Raw materials strategy is a function of geography as well as politics and economics, and it is in this respect that control of sources of raw materials may become important to broader foreign policy objectives. Autarky is contingent on having both the raw materials base and the industrial infrastructure needed to eliminate external dependence. A foreign policy driven by those forms of geopolitical theory that stress secure control of resources must necessarily focus on sovereignty over territory. If the resources are not to be found within the national territory, they must be sought elsewhere. Because economic "sovereignty" does not ensure security in a time of crisis, political or military control must be sought (see, for example Leith 1925, 1939, 1940; U.S. Military Academy 1947; see also Chapter 4).

Hence, only a state in control of a reasonably large territory, and in possession of the necessary resources, can have even the remotest possibility of achieving self-sufficiency. A strategy of autarky can be quite expensive, both in terms of economic as well as opportunity costs. Autarky requires exploitation of the domestic resource base and, perhaps, its premature depletion. Self-sufficiency may also mean passing up access to foreign technology and innovations, as well as less costly commodities and trading opportunities. A state may have to do without goods supplied by other states, or it will have to acquire these in some other fashion. An autarkic state is likely to be neomercantilist or to construct a relatively closed sphere of influence (Milward 1977: ch. 5; Gilpin 1977, 1981). In an effort to prevent cultural penetration,

---

[7]I use the term "dependence" here in a sense different from that of "dependency." Dependence means intentional reliance on others; dependency means structured subservience to others.

it may be xenophobic and difficult to "see into." Although autarky does not require authoritarianism or a centrally planned economy, the empirical data base (admittedly not very large) does suggest a correlation between economic and political "closure" (Buzan 1983:52–53).

Dependence represents a strategy opposite to that of autarky. A state may be highly or completely dependent on external trade, markets, and raw materials (Japan is an example of such a state; see Bobrow and Kudrle 1987). Sensitivity to events occurring outside the national territory may be high, and national integrity and sovereignty will be complex functions of military, political, and economic variables. Furthermore, the costs of dependence must be reckoned rather differently from those of autarky. Direct economic costs associated with dependence are likely to be lower, and access to foreign goods, technology, materials, and markets may well provide additional economic benefits as well as reduced opportunity costs. Although the security of raw materials supplies might be less sure than under an autarkic policy, this might be compensated for through more flexible diplomatic policies and greater sensitivity to the concerns of other states (Kennedy 1983a; Rosecrance 1985; Bobrow and Kudrle 1987).

In addition, the degree of control over activities within the state's territory that is required by dependence is much lower than it is in the case of autarky. In the real world, states fall somewhere between these two extremes. If the set of possible strategies is sketched on a spectrum ranging from autarky to dependence with respect to raw material supplies, it is possible to place, very roughly, real states along that spectrum as shown in Figure 2–1.

Autarky and dependence are clearly connected to territory and sovereignty. The autarkic state zealously protects its territory and

Figure 2–1. Raw Materials Strategies in the Twentieth Century

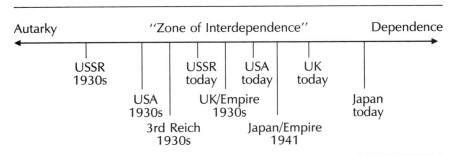

sovereignty in both a physical and psychological sense. Dependence on others equates to loss of sovereignty, and keeping out foreign influences fosters national culture and the nation-state. The dependent state relies on its diplomatic relations with other states and their good will, as well as the viability of its national culture, to maintain its identity and security. Although the borders of such a state are very permeable, national sovereignty is not at risk because it is conceptual rather than territorial. Rosecrance (1985) distinguishes between these two extremes by calling one a "territorial" state and the other a "trading" state.

As possibilities, autarky and dependence represent only one variable in the "strategic synthesis" (Milward 1977:19–23). A second variable has to do with whether a strategy has a military, political, or economic rationale. A military strategy places a premium on national security and territorial control and involves the conquest and occupation of territory in order to obtain raw materials and other advantages. This strategy is probably most similar to classical mercantilism (Gilpin 1977, 1981). A political strategy, while including elements of military coercion, focuses on diplomacy in order to achieve desired ends. It may also involve the creation of satellites or satrapies in order to ensure that these ends are achieved (Gallagher and Robinson 1953; Monroe 1981:15; Cox 1983:175 n.22). An economic strategy is aimed at maximization of welfare and utilizes superior economic resources in order to achieve desired ends (Block 1977: 86–92; Gardner 1980; Kennedy 1981:262; Buzan 1983: ch. 5; North and Choucri 1983:455–57; Pollard 1985; Bobrow and Kudrle 1987). Once again, although there are no pure cases, one of the three elements is normally dominant in the foreign policy of a state. Table 2–1 shows the six strategies that result, along with some examples. Although this table does not represent the complete universe of possibilities, it does provide a useful means of categorizing national policies with respect to the raw materials problem, as is discussed in the following chapter.

SUMMARY

This chapter introduced the concepts of "property rights," "organizing principles," and "strategic synthesis," and their relationship to one another. Property rights are more than mere rules of ownership; they are rules of interaction between actors and between actors and

Table 2–1. Raw Materials Strategies and the "Strategic Synthesis"

	Autarky		Dependence
	Internal	*External*	
Strategy			
Military	Mercantilism	Sphere of influence (Third Reich; Japanese sphere, pre–WW II)	Empire (France; Belgium, post–WW II)
Political	Isolationism (PRC-1960s; Kampuchea/Khmer Rouge)	Ideological bloc (USSR & East Europe)	Protectionist bloc (Empire preference; British Commonwealth)
Economic	Import substitution (Brazil, energy)	Customs union (Zollverein, 1800s; European Common Market)	Liberalism (British system of "free trade"; GATT)

their political and economic environments. They function as expected, accepted, or agreed-on sets of rules governing interactions. Systems of property rights are similar to the concept of "regimes" as used in the political economy literature, although they may be less formally constituted than regimes.

Organizing principles are rules of action, as opposed to interaction. They specify in a general way what an actor must do in order to achieve a desired end. They also enable an actor to organize incoming information in an internally consistent manner that allows him or her to formulate a response. Organizing principles are often formulated in such a way as to support the systems of property rights advocated by a state. In this sense, if the rules represent structure, organizing principles reflect the cognitive content of systems of rules in that they indicate ways of maintaining the coherence of a system.

Finally, a strategic synthesis represents the coming together of property rights and organizing principles within a broad strategy of foreign policy. Operating in the international realm, with its varying systems of rule and regimes, a state will try to chart a long-term course toward its desired material and ideal objectives. Property rights, to some degree, represent social constraints on the anarchic impulse; organizing principles, the means of navigating past these constraints, and the strategic synthesis, the fusion of world view with world realities.

3 PLAYING BY THE RULES
Applying a Property Rights Framework to the Analysis of Conflict Over Resources

In Chapter 2, it was proposed that conflicts over resources could be seen as growing out of disputes over two different types of "property rights." Some property rights—generally associated with the concept of "ownership"—are simply rules of distribution. They specify how goods are to be divided up (or at least, how an actor goes about obtaining a share of a good). Other property rights—often associated with the concept of "sovereignty"—involve specific rules of eligibility that an actor must meet in order to participate in the distribution of goods. Consequently, disputes over the rules of eligibility—which some call "structure-oriented" (Rapoport 1974; Krasner 1985)—are much more fundamental than disputes over rules of distribution. This chapter develops further the distinction between these two types of property rights and analyzes case studies of conflict over resources in order to determine whether such a distinction makes any sense.

TYPOLOGIES OF PROPERTY RIGHTS

"Economic Orders"

As pointed out in Chapter 2, in issue areas where well-defined political property rights do exist, or where efforts are made to find international acceptance of particular sets of rules, the resulting definitions often are outgrowths of domestic ones. In order to understand the relationship between a strategic synthesis and property rights, we need to look at the range of property rights systems that are available to a state, how they are applied, and how they might come into conflict.

Krasner (1985:66–67) has proposed a spectrum of government-property relationships (which he calls "economic orders") that explicitly define ideal cases and implicitly define different possible sets of domestic as well as international political property rights. His two variables are based on whether resources are allocated by the market or in an authoritative fashion, and whether ownership of property is public or private. This leads to the four cases shown in Table 3–1. In addition, the ideal cases also suggest related sets of political property rights defining the relationship of a state to domestic society. These sets run the gamut from rampant individualism to highly circumscribed centralization. In between lie a variety of mixed cases, for example, authoritarian corporatism or social democracy, in which the political property rights of state, social groups, and individuals vary. Krasner (1985:66) notes that "Any actual economic system will be a mix of these types with different transactions falling into different categories."

Table 3–1.   "Economic Orders."

Principle of Allocation	Type of Ownership	
	Private	Public
Market	"Free enterprise": private ownership; rights to alienate property reside fully with owner	"State capitalism": public ownership; allocation of resources at discretion of managers of property
Authoritative	"Paternalism": property owned by private actors but cannot be alienated	"Redistribution": property owned by state; uses dictated by state

Source: Krasner (1985:66–67). This table is reproduced by permission of the University of California Press.

The important points arising from these four cases are, first, that the domestic characteristics of a state may determine its bargaining position in international arenas and, second, that international arrangements (regimes, organizations, laws), more often than not, reflect the economic and political ability of one or more actors to impose a particular set of rules on that realm (in the hegemonic or cooptative senses described in Chapter 2). Thus, says Krasner (1985: ch. 1), the fundamental conflict between North and South reflects the enormous difference in power and capabilities between the two groups of states. This asymmetry is not limited to economic and military power but includes as well the power to impose on the South a particular set of rules governing rights, eligibility, and rules. What is at issue, therefore, is not simply the question of dividing property and resources between North and South, but deciding who determines the rules of eligibility.

The remainder of this section elaborates typologies of property rights that can be applied across a broad set of raw material and other, similar resources. Because the categories delineated by Krasner in Table 3–1 deal only with the broadest characteristics of states, they do not address finer distinctions that might lead to conflicts between states. For example, even though both the United States and Japan would fit in the same box in Table 3–1, differences over definitions of reciprocal property rights are at the heart of their current trade disputes. These differences depend not only on configurations of power and interests, or idiosyncratic national politics and definitions of property rights unique to each state, but also on a state's willingness to "play by the rules" and accept certain restrictions on its sovereign rights.

Playing by the Rules

The last point above leads back to the distinction made in Chapter 2 between the rules of eligibility for access to property and the rules of distribution of property. Assume that a reasonably well-defined set of property rights does exist with respect to some international issue area (say, for example, rules of foreign investment; this model also could be applied to other disputes). What position might a state take with respect to the rules of eligibility for such an issue area? A state might support the rules of eligibility in a general sense but be dissatisfied with its share of property and agitate for a different distribution. Conceivably, a state might even decide to challenge the distribution of property (this is one conventional interpretation of World Wars I and II; the "have-nots" wanted more). More basic disputes might arise over the rules of eligibility. A state might support or oppose these rules, doing so on either rational or nonrational grounds. Four ideal cases result from such distinctions:

1. A state might support the rules on economic grounds as representing the best means of maximizing its national welfare;
2. A state might support the rules of eligibility on political/ideological grounds, as being "right" or "natural," even though such a position might be maintained only at considerable cost to its welfare or security;
3. A state might oppose the rules on economic grounds, arguing that they are stacked in such a way as to put it at an economic disadvantage; or
4. A state might oppose the rules on political/ideological grounds, arguing that they are in conflict with its basic belief system (and hence a threat to security).

Table 3–2 shows the matrix of possiblities arising from these four cases, along with some specific examples. Of the four elements in Table 3–2, the box on the lower right is the only one that appears to lead unequivocally to conflict (although not necessarily to war), with this result following only if the actors in that box choose to challenge the system. (More conventionally, the states falling into this box might be thought of as "non-status quo" states.)

Table 3–2 does not take into account state-to-state conflicts over rules applicable to specific issue areas. In some international issue areas, as I noted elsewhere, strong sets of agreed-on rules do not exist and national definitions may take precedence. Many conflicts ordinarily grouped under the rubric of "resource conflicts" center on areas where definitions of property rights are weak or nonexistent (as in the commons) *or* focus on differing interpretations of strong property rules (as in sovereignty disputes). Table 3–3 categorizes specific economic and political property rights on the basis of relative "strength."

Defining property rights in terms of relative strength allows me to construct a hierarchy of property rights. The table suggests, as might be expected, that political property rights are generally "stronger"

Table 3–2.   Playing by the Rules.

Basis for Position	Attitude toward Rule Set	
	Support	*Oppose*
Economics	Case 1 Utility-satisficer, maximize return, but might want a bigger piece of the pie (Present-day Japan; Pre–WW II United States)	Case 3 Rules provide unfair advantages to states with wealth, power, capabilities; want in on the action ("New international economic order")
Politics/ Ideology	Case 2 Less interested in economic return than in support because it is "right" (pre–WW II United Kingdom; present-day United States)	Case 4 Rules are "wrong," not just unfair; must be completely changed (pre–WW II "have-nots"; Soviet Bloc, postwar)

than economic ones or, rather, that infringement on a state's political property rights is likely to engender a quicker or stronger response than a challenge to economic ones. In recent decades, the international rights of states have been stronger than those of individuals or corporations, although this has not always been the case (Lipson 1985:38–44) and may not be true in the future. Table 3–3 also suggests two other relevant variables: the actor(s) involved and the "space" within which the property right is asserted. Thus, the two salient dimensions (or variables) in this argument are the "strength" of the property right and the "space" in which the right is operative.

Table 3–4 shows a matrix of "strength" versus "space." For the most part, a state will intercede on behalf of a subnational actor only if a sufficiently strong political property right is threatened (although this

Table 3–3. A Hierarchy of Property Rights.

Relative Strength	Type of Property Right	Relevant Actor
Very strong	Territorial integrity	State
	National sovereignty	State
	Private "real" property	Citizen, company, state
	Other private property	Citizen, company, state
Strong	Usufruct property	Citizen of tribe/village
	Communal property	Village
	Property of nonnational	Person, company, state
	Military base	State
	"Freedom of the seas"	Person, company, state
	Shared resources	State
Moderate	Diplomatic immunity	State
	Mineral concessions	Person, company
	Rules of investment and compensation	Person, company, state
Weak	Trade and market rights	Person, company
	Public goods	Person, company, state
	Commons	State

may be much less true today than it was thirty to fifty years ago). The dominant property rights, as might be expected, have to do with national integrity, or "territory," and national authority, or "sovereignty."

Dyadic Conflicts over Property Rights

The distinction between rules of eligibility and rules of distribution, and the differing perspectives on the relationship between these two concepts and national security and interests, may lead to conflict between states. A comparison of the relative "strength" of the property rights being defended by two states in conflict therefore provides some insight into the nature of that conflict, as well as into it might be resolved. Note that Table 3–4 applies only from the perspective of a single state. For each given issue in which two or more states are

Table 3–4. A typology of property rights.

Operative Space	Strength		
	Strong	Moderate	Weak
In the national territory	Sovereignty/state integrity	Private property, state property	Property of nonnationals
In the territory of other states	Military bases, shared resources	Treaty rights, property, concessions, diplomatic immunity	Right to trade, enter markets
In the global commons	Maritime free passage	Resources shared on common borders	Public goods, global resources

involved, the relevant matrix element differs. That is, for a given situation, a property right that is strong from the perspective of one state may be weak for the second. Depending on the relative strength of the property right and space within which it is operative, the responses of the states involved will vary. The four ideal outcomes are shown in Table 3–5; several examples also follow below.

1. Strong (State 1) versus Strong (State 2).   If a strong property right is at stake for both states, conflict is a likely outcome. A military base controlled by a one country in the territory of another may be an issue of "national interests" for the former but a problem of sovereignty for the latter. These are both strong property rights, but sovereignty is stronger than the "national interest" by consequence of spatial differentiation (such as the former U.S. listening posts in Iran or military bases in the Philippines). In the international arena, and in foreign policy terms, national sovereignty and integrity are fundamental. Actions by other states that are seen as threatening this basic property right are likely to give rise to conflict. "National interests" can also be interpreted in terms of sovereignty and integrity, but at one remove. Where two states have an interest in a third state or territory, and

Table 3–5. Relationship of Dyadic Perceptions of Property Rights to Conflict.

| | State 1 | |
	"Strong"	*"Weak"*
State 2 "Strong"	National sovereignty versus national interests—strong conflict likely; base rights; colonialism (United States/Japan in Asia, 1930s; Falklands/Malvinas War)	Economic goals versus national interests; State 2 reasserts right to property in State 1 (United Kingdom/Iran; nationalization of AIOC, early 1950s)
"Weak"	National sovereignty versus economic interest; renegotiation of contract or withdrawal by State 2 (United States/Cuba, 1960; United States/Panama, Canal, 1970s)	Economic interest versus economic interest; not conflictual; can be resolved on basis of existing rules (United States/United Kingdom over oil, 1920s; United States/Bolivia, tin, 1952; Oil nationalizations)

conflicting definitions of property rights, the two may come into conflict and even engage in war (such as Southeast Asia prior to World War II and the Falklands/Malvinas war).

2. Weak (State 1) versus Strong (State 2). State 1 may choose to challenge a strong property right under which another is present. In this case, State 2 may choose to reassert its right to be present, perhaps allowing minor contractual adjustments. Property rights allowed to the State 2 with respect to State 1 may be deemed by the former to be causally linked to "national security," even though such a linkage may be doubted on logical-deductive grounds, and the assertion of economic sovereignty or interests by State 1 may be seen as threatening to the security of State 2. State 1, on the other hand, may wish only to assert some form of nominal control over the disputed property, or to renegotiate the terms of the contract. Under such circumstances, and depending on the assessment of relative costs and benefits of action or withdrawal, State 1 may provoke a hostile reaction by the State 2 *if* the latter sees the costs of not reacting as too high (for example, the nationalization of the Anglo-Iranian Oil Company in 1951; the Suez Crisis in 1956).

3. Strong (State 1) versus Weak (State 2). In this case, State 2's perception of the strength of property rights is weaker than that of State 1, leading to ejection of or withdrawal by the former (United States/ Cuba, 1960). Alternatively, if State 2 sees the costs of reacting as being too high, the understanding between the two may be renegotiated in such a way as to give State 1 greater or eventual sovereignty (United States/ Panama, over the Canal treaty; United Kingdom/People's Republic of China, over the return of Hong Kong). Changes in host country laws regarding mineral concessions, and the nationalization of such concessions, may be seen in this light. For State 1, principles of sovereignty may be at stake; for State 2, weaker economic rights are involved. Although this has not always been true, in recent years State 2 (the "guest") has usually yielded to State 1 (the "host") on such matters, as long as strongly defined national security issues have not been involved.

This type of outcome also illuminates the separation between economic and security issues. If such separation did not exist, Western countries might well have intervened in the Persian Gulf when the price of oil was raised so precipitously by OPEC in the 1970s. In the absence of clear evidence that price hikes, or even the 1973 oil embargo, were sufficiently damaging to Western security to justify violation of the sovereignty of the Arab OPEC countries, very little happened, or was even possible. This suggests that, in terms of the distinction between conflict over eligibility and distribution, the oil crisis was of the second type.

4. Weak (State 1) versus Weak (State 2). This is not an overtly conflictual case; disputes normally can be resolved through existing rules of distribution and associated mechanisms for negotiation. Where the rules of such cross-national property rights are well defined and adhered to by both states — for example, in a situation in which a contract with clearly defined rights and terms exists — little overt conflict occurs (unless disagreement develops over the terms of or the values implicit in the contract). Where states have moderately strong conceptions of property rights but with costs or gains difficult to determine, such as with respect to littoral fisheries, the outcome is likely to be determined on the basis of estimates of the relative costs to parties involved. In such a case, these costs are likely to be a function of the extent to which the issue impinges either on extra-territorial threats to security (for example, food for Japan) or to interests (such as the economic well-being of some interest group), and the availability of information regarding the potential distribution of costs and bene-fits. Conflict is probable only if the host country attempts to reduce its costs as much as possible by denying rights of distribution to other countries (such as in a "cod" or "tuna" war).

In issue areas where two or more parties have weak conceptions of property rights, the potential for conflict may be dependent on the divisibility of the resource. The only areas in which this set of uncertain conditions occurs regularly is with respect to commons resources (Wijkman 1982). Even here, one can distinguish between those issue areas where sovereignty is potentially divisible (Soroos 1982) and those where it is not. Thus, the issue of sovereignty in Antarctica, postponed for twenty-five years by an international treaty concluded in 1959, is said by some to be one of the next major areas of conflict due to the resources thought to exist there (Shapley 1986; Mitchell 1988; see, however, Shabecoff 1988 on the proposed interna-tional treaty for exploiting Antarctic resources). But the potential for conflict there must be considered remote. Only the states of the Southern hemisphere can be said to have at stake any sort of strong security-related property right there, although territory has also been claimed by several "Northern" states. In the final analysis, however, Antarctica cannot be considered vital to the national security or territorial integrity of any individual state.

Although the deep seabed could, in theory, be divided among states, the assertion of absolute control would be a difficult proposition even for the most powerful navy. The UN Convention on the Law of the Sea, opened for accession in 1982, represents an attempt to define property rights for the sea and seabed (and the refusal of the United States to ratify the Convention has to do with a conflict over the rules of eligibility for exploitation of the seabed). Finally, some common resources, such as the atmosphere, are entirely indivisible, and the notion of ownership is very weak and diffuse. Changes in atmospheric composition could, however, have enormous costs in terms of climatic change, and it is not inconceivable that conflict might arise as a result of such changes (Myers 1987; Gleick in press).

The distinction between "strong" and "weak" property rights does not result from some implicit quality of the resource to which the term is applied. Rather, the distinction reflects the relative current importance of political as opposed to economic property rights. What Tables 3–3 and 3–4 show is that political property rights, such as national sovereignty, are stronger than economic ones, such as private property and rules of investment. This has not always been the case. Just as the strength of property rights may vary across space, they may also change over time as a result of changing political configurations, interests, and norms.

Thus, on the one hand, colonialism, as a particular type of internationally accepted property right, is virtually extinct, as are treaty rights of the type imposed on the Ottoman and Chinese empires. On the other hand, a fairly strict definition of national sovereignty, in relation to national territory, has evolved only since World War I and has gained widespread acceptance (with numerous exceptions) only since World War II (Bilder 1977:391). It is also conceivable that a new type of property right, having to do with the treatment of the global commons, may eventually gain ascendancy over national sovereignty (see, e.g., Soroos 1986). It is possible to graph in qualitative terms a changing hierarchy of international economic and political property rights (see Figure 3–1).

Do any data exist to support the trends suggested here? One can find some general agreement in the literature that, during this century, there has been a shift from conflict over territory to political and ideological conflict and competition (Buzan 1983:59). In a study of the "Stakes of Conflict," Dowty and Kochan (1976) found a distinct change in "operational objectives" of states at war before and after World War II. Between 1714 and 1945, conflicts over possession of territory — primarily involving European states — were found to be major objectives in 53 to 77 percent of dyadic conflicts. Since the end of World War II, the major operational objective of states in war has shifted from territorial to "political" control, the latter being found important in 66 to 85 percent of dyadic conflicts (Dowty and Kochan

Figure 3–1. The Changing Hierarchy of Economic and Political Property Rights.

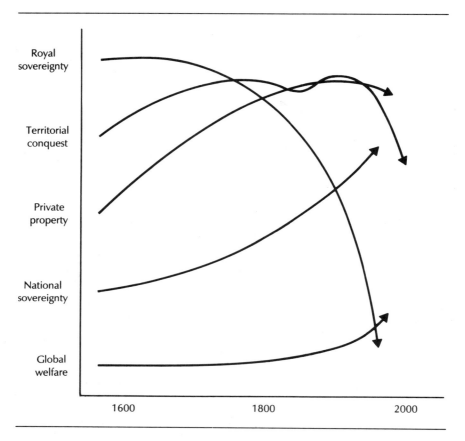

1976:26). This implies that the nature of conflict has shifted from a focus on the distribution of property—possession of territory—to the rules of eligibility—who legitimately exercises sovereignty within a territory, and on what basis.[1]

Recent studies of the pattern of expropriation of foreign property during the twentieth century suggest a somewhat different trend in that, over time, the goals of host countries have shifted from political and ideological to economic. Prior to about 1965, most acts of expropriation included all economic sectors and were motivated by ideology

[1]More broadly, the Cold War might be interpreted as a manifestation of this shift.

(such as Soviet Union in 1917 and Cuba in 1960). After 1975, states tended to nationalize, rather than expropriate, with their acts being more economically oriented and aimed at particular sectors or firms (Kobrin 1980, 1984, 1985; Lipson 1985:98–99). Even states formerly hostile to foreign investment, such as the Soviet Union and Ethiopia, have revised their laws to encourage such investment (see, for example, Nelson and Kaplan 1980:155–56), as long as it does not threaten national sovereignty. This does not mean that challenges to the rules of eligibility have disappeared completely. It does suggest that many host countries have found it possible to achieve national objectives within the existing sets of property rights and rules.

These two sets of findings are not, however, inconsistent with each other. Applying the distinction between rules of eligibility and distribution, and recognizing that there exists a difference between sovereignty and jurisdiction (Lipschutz 1987:133–36), the data suggest that conflicts over control of territory increasingly fall into the eligibility/sovereignty category, while those over property ownership increasingly fall into the distribution/jurisdiction group. Furthermore, even when an eligibility conflict does occur within a state, leading to the installation of a new government that may be ideologically hostile to the old one, the new leaders often take great pains to assure foreign investors that their properties are not at risk.

CASE STUDIES OF PROPERTY RIGHTS AND CONFLICT OVER RESOURCES

Is the framework provided above useful in analyzing conflict over resources? That is, does it provide any insight into the structure of confrontations between states and their causes? Is it a useful predictor of future conflict over resources? Does the framework clarify or merely restate the obvious? I provide here four brief case studies of conflict over mineral resources that may serve to illuminate distinctions between rules of eligibility and rules of distribution: the "struggle" for control of Middle East oil after World War I; the competition for hegemony in Asia prior to World War II; the confrontation over the Iranian nationalization of the Anglo-Iranian Oil Company in the early 1950s; and the conflict in the Congo during the early 1960s.

"Oil Eyes": The Struggle for Control of Middle East Oil, 1918–28

At the end of World War I, an oil scare hit the United States. Warnings of the imminent depletion of U.S. petroleum sources had been in the air since the middle part of the decade. A post-war decline in domestic production, combined with an increase in imports from Mexico, suggested to U.S. policymakers that a time of U.S. dependence on foreign supplies might not be far off (O'Brien 1974; Stivers 1982:194–99). From the perspective of policymakers the main question was: where would these new foreign deposits be found? U.S. oil companies were also interested in this question. They wanted new sources of oil to supply their foreign subsidiaries and did not want to be left out of participation in any new discoveries for fear that uncontrolled competition might destroy the market (Stivers 1982:194–99). Both Mexico and Russia were engulfed in revolutionary turmoil and, hence, not entirely reliable sources. The only potentially large remaining deposits were in the Middle East, and it was to these that all oil eyes turned.

World War I had demonstrated both the military importance of petroleum and the preeminence of U.S. supplies. The strategic implications of these two points were lost on no one, least of all the British, who depended on the United States for more than 70 percent of their oil consumption (McBeth 1985:15, 93). In fact, until World War I very little oil was produced within the territories of the British Empire. Following the war, the just-acquired British territories and mandates in the Middle East appeared to be prime locations for new discoveries of oil. Given the decline in domestic output, from the U.S. perspective it appeared as though the United States might become "absolutely dependent on foreign countries, especially on the British Empire and other sources under British control, for oil supplies and consequently for her existence as a powerful industrial and maritime nation" (FO 371/4585 Des. 989 Geddis (A.) to Lord Curzon, 7/20/20, quoted in McBeth 1985:56). A State Department trade advisor warned that the British were "leaving no stone unturned to gain control of all oil properties on the surface of the earth ... " (Office of the Foreign Trade Advisor to Phillips, 7/3/19, DS 467.11 St 25/34, quoted in DeNovo 1963:170).

Of course, the British held similar views of U.S. objectives. They argued that newly found oil fields in Central and South America would be "swallowed up by the U.S. Standard octopus" (ADM 137/2826 Additional Naval Assistant to First Sea Lord, Director of Trade Division, Admiralty, "Oil Fuel Supply-Memorandum from the Strategic Point of View," 9/26/18, quoted in McBeth 1985:23), and that U.S. control of British supplies gave the former the power to put the United Kingdom "in an impossible position should they desire to be unfriendly" (POWE 33/12 Cadman, "Memorandum," 5/25/18, quoted in McBeth 1985:20).

Consequently, following the end of the war, Great Britain embarked on a deliberate policy of exploring for new sources of oil within the Empire so as to reduce its dependence on foreign-controlled sources and companies. From the British point of view, it was essential that any oil production within the Empire be under *British* control (Royal Dutch Shell was not considered British because majority control was in the hands of "unreliable" Dutch investors). To this end, since 1904, it had been official policy to allow only British companies to have access to Crown lands within the Empire. According to the Foreign Office (POWE 33/353 Colonial Office, "Memorandum. British Control of Oil Mining Companies," June 1923, quoted in McBeth 1985:2, emphasis added):

[T]he Crown insists on the corporation [seeking a concession] being registered in the British dominions and having its head on British soil, on its having a British manager and a majority of British directors, and a majority of its shareholders being British subjects. *Foreign capital is not excluded, only foreign control.*

The U.S. policy on access to foreign mineral concessions was embodied in the concept of the "Open Door." Enunciated by Secretary of State John Hay in 1899, the Open Door was at first applied only in China. Later, it came to be understood as implying nondiscriminatory treatment of private economic endeavors and investments by foreign nationals in territories under the control of another state (McBeth 1985:80 n.14). The British policy on concessions was clearly in opposition to that of the United States, and so the stage was set for conflict between the two powers.

Soon after the end of World War I, Britain began to apply its policy of discrimination against nonnationals seeking oil within its Mandatory territories in the Middle East. Geologists from the Standard Oil Company of New York (Socony) were denied access to the company's prewar concessions—granted by the now-vanished Ottoman authorities—in the British mandate in Palestine (DeNovo 1963:169). The British justified this action by arguing that the "occupying authorities should do nothing to compromise the freedom of future authorities in developing mineral resources [within the Mandates]" (DeNovo 1963:174). By contrast, in Mesopotamia (later Iraq), the British tried to prevent the entry of U.S. companies on the grounds of the "sanctity of international contracts," in this case a concession granted to the Turkish Petroleum Company in 1914 by the same now-vanished Ottoman authorities (DeNovo 1963:184).

The U.S. attitude toward the British position was that, although not a member of the League of Nations, as a co-victor in the war the United States was entitled to a say in the governance of the Mandates. In particular, in keeping with Article 22 of the League of Nations covenant, the United States maintained that the principle of the Open Door should be applied in all Mandatory territories (DeNovo 1963:184; Stivers 1982:46–47). The impasse between the two powers was complicated further by an agreement between Britain and France that gave the latter a share in Mesopotamian oil in return for permission to build a British pipeline through the French mandate in Syria to the Mediterranean (DeNovo 1963:176–77).

Although the specific terms of access for U.S. companies were debated for a number of years, the cutting of the knot came about because the oil in hand proved more influential than the oil in the ground. In 1920, the U.S. Congress approved a bill that forbade the leasing of oil concessions on federal lands to nationals of countries that practiced discrimination against nonnationals within their territories (O'Brien 1974: ch. 6; McBeth 1985:57–58). This law, and similar ones passed by various state legislatures, was clearly aimed at the British and Dutch, both of whom practiced such discrimination. Although the federal bill did not apply to privately held property, some of the state laws did.

Furthermore, because the United States remained Britain's primary supplier of oil, the latter's assurance of continued supplies was placed in growing jeopardy as bills were introduced in Congress to embargo exports of U.S. petroleum (McBeth 1985:62). Ultimately, the British capitulated to U.S. pressure, granting an interest in the Turkish Petroleum Company to a consortium of U.S. companies (DeNovo 1963:196–97). Although more disagreements were to follow, and Britain continued to depend on the Western Hemisphere for the bulk of its oil supplies until after the end of World War II, the principle of equal access was established as the basis for division of the petroleum resource.

Within the property rights framework presented earlier, how is this episode to be interpreted? First, the "struggle" for the control of oil centered both on the rules of eligibility and on the rules of access or distribution of property. The British policy of discrimination against nonnationals represented a set of eligibility rules somewhat different from the Open Door policy of the United States. As noted above, however, the norm of nondiscriminatory access was part of the League of Nations Covenant, to which the United Kingdom was a signatory (of course, as a nonsignatory the United States theoretically could have been denied access to the Mandates). The conflict was not over fundamental rules of eligibility — or total exclusion of one party from another's territory — as was the case at the same time in Mexico and Russia (Lipson 1985: ch. 3; O'Brien 1974) but, rather, over the size of each individual country's share of the resource and control of that share.

The British attempted to ensure control of a sizable share by limiting the terms of distribution of the resource. The United States, by protesting loudly and threatening to change the rules of eligibility for access to *its* oil supplies, was able to pressure a change in the British policy and to gain a piece of the Middle Eastern action for U.S. companies. Furthermore, the conflict involved relatively weak conceptions of property rights within what were essentially colonial territories. At stake were economic interests (although both countries saw the issue in terms of national power and security), but once the problem of discrimination was settled, the existing system of rules proved adequate to negotiate an agreement. The British never intended to establish a completely exclusionary regime within the Mandates. Hence, short of the United States' actually cutting off exports of petroleum to Britain in order to prove the point, it is extremely unlikely that the two countries would have come to blows over the oil issue.

The "Arbiter of Asia": the Struggle for Hegemony, 1931–41

The War in the Pacific did not begin in 1941 with the bombing of Pearl Harbor. Nor did war break out, as is commonly believed, because of Japan's "industrial hunger for essential minerals" (Browne 1986:20). Rather, the roots of the conflict must be sought in the foreign economic and political policies of two expanding nations and their conflicting visions of an appropriate future for Asia. Both the United States and Japan were relative latecomers to Great Power status, and both saw Asia as important to their self-image. As Herbert Feis (1950:3) so poetically put it:

> Japan, from its seat on the small island of Honshu, wanted to be the arbiter of Asia and the Western Pacific. The wish throve in poverty and pride, finding company in thoughts which made it seem just. The Japanese people came to believe that the extension of their control over this vast region was both natural and destined; that the other people living there needed the guardianship of Japan as much as Japan needed them. The Japanese armies sailed across the China seas under a banner which proclaimed peace, justice and partnership for all. The bayonets were merely to expel the devil who would not understand their true intentions.

For the United States, a not too dissimilar picture could be drawn. Arkira Iriye (1967:19–20) has written that, "[In the nineteenth century, the U.S.] image of China and Japan had been totalist in that they had pictured the Chinese and Japanese as standing at a particular stage of development and susceptible to wholesale transformation." The instrument of that transformation was to be U.S. morality and ideals.

China was of particular concern to Americans. It engendered a vast and confused mixture of interests and desires among businessmen, politicians, and missionaries. For the United States, to put it most bluntly, the 400 million Chinese represented a giant Market — a market for political ideas, for Christianity, and for trade. Although China never lived up to U.S. expectations in this regard — in 1939 less than 3 percent of U.S. exports went to China (Marshall 1975:4) — the image required that China be open to cultural, political, and economic penetration. In the international environment of the 1930s, it is not surprising that a clash occurred over East Asia. For the Japanese, national autonomy was at stake; for the Americans, something less was at issue, although that something grew in importance as time passed.[2]

Economic and political nationalism were powerful motivating forces throughout the decade, and Japan drew on these currents in devising its foreign policy. Beginning with the invasion and conquest of Manchuria in 1931 — an act vociferously protested by the Western powers in stern diplomatic notes — Japan sought to construct the Great East

[2]Iriye's (1967:326) observation in this regard is germane. He writes: "After all, national security is an idea. By talking about the nation's survival, one is talking not only of its physical existence but also what it stands for."

Asia Co-Prosperity Sphere, an autarkic bloc within which economic and political functions would come under its monopoly control. Asia would supply the raw materials and food for metropolitan Japan and the markets for Japanese industry. In return, Japan would educate Asia in politics and culture. The Western powers would be excluded from any more than a residual role within this sphere of influence (Iriye 1967:207–211; Milward 1977:165–68).

From the perspective of the United States and the European colonial powers, Japanese activities in China represented a blatant effort to revise the rules of eligibility for participation there and were in direct contradiction to those principles represented by the policy of the Open Door. As noted earlier, the Open Door had its nineteenth century origins in a series of limited diplomatic initiatives by the United States, but by the 1930s it had been transformed into a policy not only of seeking equality of trade and nondiscrimination but also one of providing support for "Anglo-Saxon principles and traditions" in China (Dulles 1946/1967:106). During that decade, writes Irvine Anderson (1975:60 n.35) in his study of U.S. oil policy in East Asia:

> [The] exact phrase, "the principle of the Open Door," recurs frequently enough in Anglo-American diplomatic correspondence to suggest a value almost as completely internalized as "the right of self-defense."[3]

But the relative positions of Japan and the United States — particularly with respect to China — were quite different. On the one hand, unlike Southeast Asia, China was never very important to the United States or Europe in terms of either resources or markets (although Korea and China were sources of tungsten and various other critical materials such as hog bristles; see Emeny 1934; Staley 1937). On the other hand, from Japan's perspective, it was clear that its freedom to act in the region was severely constrained by the potential economic leverage possessed by the other Great Powers. In 1939, for example, 80 percent of Japan's imported petroleum and petroleum products came from the United States, and most of the rest was supplied by the Royal Dutch Shell and Standard Vacuum operations in the Netherlands East Indies (Anderson 1975:4).

Thus, the Western interpretation of the Japanese program of expansion in East Asia settled on what seemed the most logical and visible objective: minerals and raw materials. That Japan was gradually

---

[3]Given the degree to which economics and military security concerns became fused in the 1930s, this observation should come as no surprise.

forced into this position by the increasingly stringent sanctions imposed on it was not lost on U.S. policymakers (Feis 1950:41); it simply made no difference to U.S. and British policy. Long before 1941 the Japanese saw their failure to carve out a niche in the world as threatening their nation's security, and so they were willing to defy greater power. Conversely, until 1941 the United States never felt its national security or territorial integrity to be threatened sufficiently to react violently or compromise deeply held principles. Throughout the 1930s, because only rather weak U.S. economic interests were at stake in Asia, the same was thought to be true of Japan. The appropriate responses were, therefore, diplomatic protests and economic sanctions. The real surprise at Pearl Harbor was not the attack. Instead, it was the intensity of Japanese feeling as reflected in what proved to be such a rash move over the long run (see Russett 1967 for an interesting analysis of the Japanese action and the threat to U.S. security).

The conflict in Asia can be interpreted in two ways. First, the Japanese deliberately chose to challenge the legitimacy of the system of property rights enshrined in the Open Door and the unequal treaties imposed by the Great Powers on China. In place of the existing "liberal" system—liberal only for the European powers, not for China—Japan wished to install one with rules of eligibility that would have excluded other states from any more than nominal access to China. In turning to economic nationalism, as did Germany in Europe, Japan sought to reduce the power of other states over her by denying them rights within a limited sphere of influence. This was not simply a question of dividing up China; rather, it was a matter of changing the rules of eligibility as they applied to Asia. Ironically, Japan's failure in this regard may have been due more to the way in which she tried to achieve this change than in the policy itself, because both the United States and Great Britain also engaged in limited forms of economic nationalism in the 1930s (see Chapter 4).

Second, the property rights exercised by the Western powers in Asia were mostly economic ones, at least in principle, and not very strong. Japan was welcome to participate in China on the basis of this system of rules, although she would have been at an economic and political disadvantage in doing so and would have remained subject to Western influence. The Western powers did not act to oppose Japan's efforts to change the rules until they began to perceive threats to *their* national security.

Honor and the "Free World": The Nationalization of Anglo-Iranian, 1951–54

In May 1951 the government of Iran nationalized the British-owned Anglo-Iranian Oil Company (AIOC). This action was not totally unexpected. For some time a special committee of the *Majlis*, the Iranian parliament, had been studying the question of Iranian relations with the AIOC. The nationalization was the culmination of disagreements between the government of Iran and the AIOC over the terms of a concession granted to the latter in 1933 (PRO 1951a; Krasner 1978:120; Keddie 1981:132–33). The specific dispute began over the question of royalties — Iran was dissatisfied with the company's offer to renegotiate percentages — but quickly grew into a full-scale confrontation over national sovereignty versus economic control and ownership. When Prime Minister Razmara, an opponent of nationalization, was assassinated in March 1951, it became clear that the issue had become a domestic litmus test for political survival in Iran.

In April 1951 the Shah appointed a new prime minister, Mohammed Mossadeq. Mossadeq had been instrumental in getting the *Majlis* to study the nationalization issue. In principle, he was not opposed to negotiations with the AIOC over revising the terms of the oil concession, but his freedom to maneuver was constrained by domestic pressures. Added to this were two complications: (1) During the same month, the AIOC ceased royalty payments to Iran, and (2) the British government began to impose economic sanctions on Iran. For the Iranians the dispute with Britain became a matter of honor, as much as anything else. In response to the growing British pressures, the Iranian government moved to eject British technicians and take over the AIOC's operations (Painter 1986:176).

For the British, however, the Iranian challenge involved not only questions of ownership of property and contractual rights, but also international stature and, by extension, British national security. The AIOC represented Great Britain's largest overseas investment and provided the country with significant amounts of foreign exchange, an important factor given its persistently dismal balance of payments following World War II (PRO 1951a; Painter 1986:174). In fact, the British felt so strongly about the issue that they moved troops into position throughout the Middle East and Persian Gulf in preparation for the occupation of the oilfields and the Abadan refinery (Painter

1986:175). From Paris, Ambassador David Bruce cabled the U.S. State Department to explain that it was neither the oil nor the radicalization of Iran that really concerned the British. Rather, they desired to "preserve what they believe to be the last remaining bulwark of Brit solvency; that is, their overseas investment and property position" (HSTL 1951a) (the British themselves admitted as much; see PRO 1951b).

The U.S. perspective—or, rather, perspectives, for there were several—was different. For U.S. policymakers, broader concerns were at stake. The U.S. Government made it clear to all parties involved that it strongly opposed the Iranian nationalization (Painter 1986:174). Nonetheless, out of fear that radicalization of the Iranian government might provide opportunities for Soviet infiltration or intervention, U.S. policymakers framed the conflict in terms of the security of the "Free World." At a Cabinet Meeting in June 1951, Secretary of State Dean Acheson (HSTL 1951b) cautioned that, "Developments in Iran are very bad. [The] British made a generous offer but it was turned down cold and Iran took over British oil property . . . . This will probably result in a revolution in Iran." The goal of the State Department therefore became the successful mediation of an agreement that would give the Iranians what they sought without forcing the British out of Iran (that is, changing the rules of distribution but not eligibility). Failing this, however, other measures might have to be taken. In a 1952 memo on "The Progressive Threat to the U.S. Position in Foreign Oil," consultant Walter Levy wrote (quoted in Painter 1986:172):

> The question arises . . . whether in a situation where a vital power position of the United States is at stake, it can afford to apply the normal and traditional laws of sovereign self-determination to the control of underdeveloped countries over the oil in their soil.

The U.S. Joint Chiefs of Staff saw the problem in global geopolitical terms. Warning that a failure to resolve the impasse would threaten the "position and prestige of the United Kingdom in the Middle East and possibly throughout the entire world," they asserted that "events in Iran cannot be separated from the world situation" (NARS 1951a:3). They concluded (NARS 1951a:4) that,

> Strictly from the United States military point of view, Iran's orientation towards the United States in peacetime and maintenance of the British position in the Middle East now transcend in importance the desirability of supporting British oil interests in Iran.

Finally, the oil companies felt the future of their investments in the region to be in jeopardy. In October 1951 (HSTL 1951c), in a meeting between Secretary of State Acheson, George McGhee, Assistant Secretary of State for Near Eastern, South Asian, and African Affairs, and the heads of Esso, Socal, Gulf, Socony-Vacuum, and Texaco, the latter:

> [E]mphasized the very grave consequences of giving the Iranians terms more favorable than other countries. They expressed the opinion that if this were done the entire international oil industry would be seriously threatened. *The opinion was offered that even the loss of Iran would be preferable to the instability which would be created by making too favorable an agreement with Iran.* Other representatives pointed out that not just the oil industry was involved but indeed all U.S. investment overseas and the concept of the sanctity of contractual relations [emphasis added].

To which the Secretary replied (HSTL 1951c):

> [W]e would keep in mind the points they brought forth although we must, of course, give consideration at the same time to the other factors involved in the situation, including the consequences of the loss of Iran to the free world.

The adequacy of oil supplies was never an issue from the U.S. perspective, although the British were quite worried about this (PRO 1951c:16–17). A National Intelligence Estimate prepared by the U.S. Central Intelligence Agency (CIA) in January 1951 estimated that "The amount of crude oil and refined products now exported from Iran could be derived from other areas by small increases in crude-production and by fuller use of available refining capacity." The CIA thought, however, that the loss of other Middle East sources would create much more serious problems (HSTL 1951d:1).

Ultimately, it was agreed by all Western parties that Iranian oil should be shut out of world markets. U.S. policymakers expected that the resulting decline in oil revenues to the Iranian government would to make it more willing to strike a deal with the British. The major oil companies, in cooperation with the U.S. Petroleum Administration for Defense, and under an antitrust exemption granted by the Department of Justice, implemented an embargo on Iranian oil. Replacement supplies were provided to consumers from other sources in both the Eastern and Western Hemispheres. In an effort to keep Iranian oil off the market, the oil companies even brought suit in the World Court to stop Iran from selling oil, arguing that it belonged to them (Painter 1986:179–80).

But the sanctions had an effect opposite the one intended, increasing internal pressures on Mossadeq to break with the West. State Department officials then began to worry that economic deterioration might lead to instability and a leftist coup against the government. Negotiations between the Iranian government and the AIOC, nursed along by the United States, continued until the end of the Truman administration in early 1953, albeit with no success. By this time, various individuals in both the United States and Britain had concluded that ordinary diplomatic methods were not going to resolve the crisis.

Beginning in late 1952, plans were laid by the CIA and British intelligence to remove Prime Minister Mossadeq, who was seen (probably unfairly) as the main obstacle to a settlement (Painter 1986:189) and thought to be coming increasingly under the influence of the *Tudeh* (Communist) Party. In August 1953, in an effort to assert his own authority, the Shah attempted to replace Mossadeq with a member of the conservative opposition. When this effort failed, the Shah fled the country. Soon thereafter, a countercoup orchestrated by the U.S. and British intelligence agencies forced Mossadeq from office and brought the Shah back to Iran (Roosevelt 1979; Keddie 1981:138–41; Painter 1986:191–92).

While negotiations continued until the end of 1954, in principle the impasse was resolved with the ousting of Mossadeq because his successor agreed to negotiate a settlement of the dispute on the basis of "accepted principles of international intercourse" (Painter 1986:191–92). The nationalization was rescinded, but in order to mollify Iranian antagonism toward the British, and to get Iranian oil back into the market in large quantities, a consortium of oil companies was established to run the Iranian oil operations. This agreement held for another two decades, until the Shah expropriated the multinationals' oil properties in the 1970s (Painter 1986:192–98).

How can this conflict be interpreted in terms of a property rights framework? The oil itself was not irreplaceable, and Iran *qua* Iran was not of paramount importance in the general scheme of things (except to Iran). But from the perspective of Great Britain and the United States, the issues at stake were much more significant than the fate of a single Middle Eastern country. There were three major players in the Anglo-Iranian crisis (four, if one counts the oil companies, but they were of lesser importance and played along with the U.S. government), each with a different set of property rights at stake.

Although Iran asserted its right of sovereignty over the AIOC's oil concession, its main concern was the distribution of profits. It used the explicit threat of nationalization, and perhaps the implicit threat of radicalization (changing the rules of eligibility), to try to force the AIOC to increase royalties, but the AIOC and the British government adamantly refused to make any concessions to Iran. The British did want their property back, although as David Bruce noted, they could have survived the loss of oil and revenues, albeit with some hardship. It was the loss of position, prestige, and solvency that counted most. Thus the *British-Iranian* dispute falls into the category of strong (State 1) versus strong (State 2) conflicts over property rights. When Iran asserted the right of sovereignty, Britain tried to reassert her right to remain in Iran.

From the perspective of the United States, however, the Anglo-Iranian dispute was one that was in principle resolvable through negotiations (a "weak-weak" conflict), even though oil company executives were not at all happy with the notion of granting Iran terms more favorable than those allowed other oil-producing states.[4] U.S. policymakers feared the implications of the "loss" of Iran to Communism and the resultant threat to U.S. national security. Seeing the world in terms of a seamless, geopolitical web, they could not help but believe that events in Iran, if left uncontrolled, could have global consequences, with a concomitant threat to U.S. national security. The dispute could not be allowed to continue indefinitely. As Walter Levy had pointed out in his memo, very strong property rights appeared to be at stake, and this provided the justification for covert action against the Iranian government.

Chaos and Communism: the Congo Crisis, 1960–63[5]

On June 30, 1960, the Belgian colony of the Congo (today called Zaire) became an independent state. On July 5, units of the *Force Publique*, the

[4]Actually, the British did not even want to give Iran the 50–50 deal granted to Venezuela several years earlier because they could not afford the loss of tax revenues resulting from such an arrangement (PRO 1951d:2). It is of some interest to note that, according to Louis (1984:69), the notion of a 50–50 split may have had its origins in an offer by the Soviet Union during its abortive attempt to coerce petroleum concessions from Iran between 1944 and 1946.

[5]Much of the material in this section is taken from an unpublished paper I have written on the Congo Crisis (Lipschutz 1986a).

national army, mutinied over their pay and living conditions. Within several days, the Congo began to come apart. Belgian forces were redeployed throughout the country in an effort to suppress the mutiny. Many Congolese thought Belgium was intervening to reestablish control over the country. On July 11, the mineral-rich province of Katanga, with covert support from Belgium, seceded from the new state. Within ten days of the first mutinies, the United Nations, in an action with major material and political backing from the United States, intervened in the Congo to restore order, replace the Belgians, and suppress the Katangan secession. Even so, conditions gradually degenerated to the point that, by the end of August, a full-scale civil war seemed imminent (for general histories, see Hoskyns 1965; Young 1965; Weissman 1974; Kalb 1982; Mahoney 1983).

The growing chaos in the Congo was of great concern to the Western powers, notwithstanding its remoteness from traditional centers of strategic conflict. Lying in the center of Africa, the country was thought by many to be of critical geopolitical importance. What happened in the Congo was likely to affect the stability not only of the surrounding area but of the entire continent, as well. A 1957 National Security Council policy paper on "Africa South of the Sahara" (DDEL 1958a:2) stated:

> The strategic value of Africa South of the Sahara stems principally from the area's geographic location athwart alternative air and sea routes to the Far East, and from its strategic materials. In the event of war or loss of Western access to sea and air routes through the Middle East, control of sea and air communications through Africa South of the Sahara would be extremely important. Recent events increasingly jeopardize our sea and air lanes through the Middle East, thereby increasing the strategic significance of Africa South of the Sahara. From bases in certain areas of Africa South of the Sahara, the Communists could pose a serious threat to communications in the Atlantic, the Indian Ocean, and the Red Sea, as well as our important North African strategic facilities, the Mediterranean littoral, and the flank of NATO.

Although the U.S. investment in the Congo was relatively minor — less than $20 million in 1960, out of a total of $500 million in all of Africa — it was growing rapidly (DDEL 1958a:3; Weissman 1974:31–39). The United States' European allies already had major, long-established stakes in the region. Belgium's Union Minière du

Haut Katanga (UMHK), for example, produced a number of strategic minerals and held a direct investment in the Congo of $2 to $3 billion (DD 1962a). British corporations held major properties in neighboring Northern Rhodesia (now Botswana) and Tanganyika (Tanzania). The French also had major political and economic investments in the vicinity of the Congo. Not the least important was the fact that Katanga and the neighboring province of South Kasai together produced some 7 percent of the world's copper, 70 percent of its cobalt and industrial diamonds, 9 percent of its tin, and a considerable fraction of its uranium (PRO 1945a:9, 11; FRUS 1950a:1842; DD 1960a:5; Kalb 1982:349; Helmreich 1986). Northern Rhodesia was also a major source of minerals, as were the colonies farther to the south.

What was the problem in the Congo? The Congolese were largely unable to agree on a political basis for the new state. Congolese society was organized primarily along ethnic and tribal lines, and most of the political parties in existence were sectarian rather than broadly representative (Hoskyns 1965:5; Weissman 1974:18–19). The Katangan secession was rooted in both economic and ethnic concerns and was encouraged by various Western interests, as were secessionist movements in other provinces. Only one party, led by Prime Minister Patrice Lumumba, appealed to a broad section of the populace (Weissman 1974:18–19, 33), and Lumumba was very early on tagged as a radical. He was suspected of having ties to the Belgian Communist Party, and thought to be under the influence of hard-core Marxists, if not one himself (DD 1960b, 1960c).

Although the Congolese wished to exercise their right to national sovereignty, they were in broad disagreement as to the exact meaning of the term. A coherent, unified government was never established under the terms of the *Loi Fondomentale* left by the departing Belgians. The Congolese state itself was not a direct threat to Western investment. Instead, what most terrified Western decisionmakers was the specter of a successful alliance between a Congolese faction rebelling against the "central government" (such as it was) and the Soviet Union, with all that such a victory seemed to imply. But the balance of interests was not the same for every Western state.

For the British, Belgians, and French, the primary concern was protection of their investments in the "Cape to Katanga" mineral belt. In meeting after meeting with the Europeans, U.S. policymakers found enormous resistance to their proposals for dealing with the civil strife in the Congo (see, for example DD 1961a, 1961b, 1962b). The French refused outright to cooperate in reintegrating Katanga into the Congo. The British and Belgians were reluctant to allow the United Nations to use military pressure to end the secession, fearing that any effort to end it by force would lead to the torching and destruction of the European-owned mines and factories. They discussed these concerns in the language of the "Communist threat," as did the Katangans themselves, but the particular coloration of local politics was not as important as the investments.

The Americans, having little direct economic stake in the Congo, painted the conflict in global terms. Explaining the goals of U.S. policy to the Subcommittee on Africa of the House Committee on Foreign Affairs in 1963, a State Department official testified (Cleveland 1963:19):

> I think the immediate gain [in the Congo] is in terms of stability in this part of the world . . . . I am not sure I can separate our material gains from our need to have a peaceful world to do business in . . . . [Q]uite apart from the business that American businessmen may do in Africa . . . every major threat to local peace and security in one region of the world risks exploitation by the Communists, risks a confrontation between us and the Communists, and risks escalation to a world war.

In essence, the goals of U.S. policy were, so to speak, to keep three balls in the air. First, it was necessary to establish a democratic, "middle-of-the-road" government that reflected popular support and respected the rules of international intercourse (Lipschutz 1986a:47). Second, Katanga must be reintegrated into the Congo for the sake of the health of the latter's economy and in order to prevent a "radical" solution that might give the upper hand to leftist factions in the struggle for power and threaten Western stakes in the country. Third, Soviet influence was to be kept to an absolute minimum. All of this was to be done without offending or alienating the European allies.

Curiously, however, the specter of Soviet involvement largely remained just that, even though the threat was invoked repeatedly by Western policymakers. Soviet intervention in the Congo never reached the level feared by the Americans and was limited mostly to the provision of arms and equipment to left-leaning factions that moved in and out of the Central Government several times between 1960 and

1965. In addition, the Soviet Union was generally supportive of the United Nations effort in the Congo, although it opposed a number of U.S. initiatives connected with that intervention.

The establishment of a viable government in Leopoldville also proved very difficult. Although success seemed at hand in 1963, the fragile coalition nursed along by the United States gradually crumbled, and a stable government was not established until 1965 when General Joseph Mobutu stepped in and declared himself president. Furthermore, the reintegration of Katanga came about almost by accident in early 1963 when UN forces overcame the Katangan gendarmes in a largely unplanned and unintended action. The greatest irony in the entire drama may be that, several years after assuming command of the Congo (and renaming it "Zaire"), Mobutu himself nationalized all foreign mining investments.

The Congo Crisis does not fall clearly into any of the categories of conflict discussed earlier in this chapter; it is a mixed case. As in the case of Iran, the Americans painted the issue publicly as one of Western security — that is, national security versus Congolese sovereignty under a radical ("Communist") regime. The real conflict, however, took place between the supporters of Congolese unity under a pro-Western government — certain U.S. policymakers — and the champions of Katangan independence — other U.S. and European interests and various European governments. The precise political composition of the Congolese government was of secondary concern, as long as it was not radical. In the African context, Katangan independence had no standing as a political property right: it was based on ethnic solidarity and the economic interests of foreign investors, neither of which formed the basis for the granting of independence to African colonies or was considered grounds for national secession.

Ultimately, economic property rights, although of great concern to the European states, ranked below their national security. Because European security was perceived to be dependent on U.S. support and the United States linked that security to the outcome in the Congo, the Europeans had to be engaged in any solution to the Congo crisis. The United States could probably have walked away from the Congo, but in the early 1960s the pull of the seamless geopolitical web was still very strong. Political property rights and threats to rules of eligibility proved stronger than economic ones.

CONCLUSIONS AND SUMMARY

The concept of "property rights" explains why, when, and where conflicts over raw materials take place. Property rights are not laws — although they can be — and they are not regimes — although they often are embedded in regimes. Property rights incorporate both the material and ideal interests of states; they rationalize the order of things and act as instrumental rules for maintaining that order. Property rights are, in Bruce Andrew's words, "domestic rules" projected into the international arena (Andrews 1975:525). Their successful propogation is, of course, a function of state power, among other things, but their application often comes about only as the result of a process of negotiation between states. When an internationally accepted regime exists in an issue area (and, as I noted earlier, regimes may be implicit, as well as explicit), conflict is muted, and war does not occur. When a state tries to impose its own idiosyncratic set of property rights into an international arena, in the face of opposition from other states, conflict is likely to occur, and war is possible.

Of the two types of property rights, eligibility defines one's right to participate, whereas distribution has to do with one's share of the proceeds. Conflict can occur over distribution, but the right to participate in distribution implies one's acceptance of the rules of eligibility. Implicit in this rule structure are means for resolving such conflict. Conflict over eligibility implies a rejection of the rules of eligibility, and there are no mechanisms short of war to resolve such disagreements. The "raw materials problem" between the two world wars (discussed in the following chapter) and the U.S. conflict with Communism after World War II were symptomatic of a basic disagreement over the rules of eligibility. More recent conflicts have focused primarily on the rules of distribution, although in many instances, Western policymakers have chosen to portray these disagreements as more fundamental.

What does this suggest for the future? To predict whether conflicts over resources are likely to occur, we have to look at the broader context within which such a conflict might take place. If a breakdown of the international economic and political system were to take place over the coming decades, as some have suggested (Russett 1981/82), conflict over material resources might very well develop. In the absence of direct challenges to the rules of eligibility embodied in the existing system, however, conflict leading to war is not very probable.

4 TO HAVE AND TO HAVE NOT
Raw Materials Strategies and the Foreign Policies of States

Chapter 3 introduced a framework for analyzing resource conflicts that was based on a broadly defined concept of "property rights." This chapter develops in greater detail the notion of "raw materials strategies" and describes their relationship to international property rights systems and the broader foreign policies of states.

The tendency in much of the literature on the subject of raw materials access and conflict is to address the problem as one involving political strategy (the cultivation of client states) or military strategy (the conquest of states) or economic strategy (the creation of linkages of dependency and interdependency). In fact, a foreign policy is ordinarily comprised of elements of each, although one element is normally dominant in the "strategic synthesis" that characterizes the general direction of foreign policy (Milward 1977: ch. 2). Each type of strategic synthesis, furthermore, treats the property rights question in a somewhat different way. Each type of strategic synthesis also consists of a mix of material and ideal interests.

What differs among states is the balance between the political, economic, and military elements. When there is general agreement among states on what constitutes a legitimate mix of strategies, a "regime" may be said to exist. When such agreement breaks down — as during the period between the two world wars — the result is conflict over property rights. Thus, as has been suggested, it is a mistake to see access to raw materials as a major driving force in foreign policy formulation. More frequently, such access is ancillary to broader foreign policy goals that have to do with the protection of territory and sovereignty and particular cultural beliefs and values.

This chapter first discusses the way in which concepts of international property rights have changed over the past century, particularly with respect to strategic and other raw materials. This history provides an insight into the way conflicts over eligibility, as well as over distribution, have taken place. Next, the concepts and strategies outlined in Chapter 2 and the general relevance of property rights in international politics are further examined by focusing on the raw materials policies of the Great Powers during the period between the two world wars. There are two reasons for this exercise. First, it helps clarify the distinctions between the different approaches to raw materials strategies and place these approaches in the broader context of national foreign policies. Second, the interwar period provides the historical backdrop and institutional basis for the postwar policies of the United States, the United Kingdom, and the Soviet Union. The failures of the 1930s became, in some sense, the benchmarks for reaction after the war. Thus, although World War II changed the fundamental structure of international relations and provided useful lessons in strategy to the three states, the ideological and institutional patterns of postwar policymaking, particularly with respect to raw materials, were established during the interwar period.

THE EVOLUTION OF INTERNATIONAL PROPERTY RIGHTS

The evolution of international property rights since the nineteenth century reflects, in part, the increasingly important role of the sovereign nation-state in defining and defending those rights. The rise of the state system led to the transfer of sovereignty, first to the crown and then to the bureaucratic state (Kennedy 1987:31–41). In some states, such as Great Britain, where the middle class gained a major degree of political power, economic property rights became largely distinct from political ones, whereas in others, such as Russia, the two remained fused (although Imperial Russia cycled back and forth; see Shaw 1983:138). In the international sphere, since at least the middle of the nineteenth century, periods of the primacy of economic property rights (that is, "economic liberalism") have alternated with the primacy of political and military property rights ("economic nationalism"). This cycling, among other things, seems to have strongly influenced the degree of conflict between states over access to resources, since the two approaches have different rules of eligibility.

The international property rights regime of the nineteenth century was underwritten by Britain, the dominant economic and political power of the time, and it fell to Britain to see that laws protecting the rights of foreigners, their property, and their investments were observed.[1] Under the British system of free trade and naval protection, furthermore, every European state was, at least in theory, equally free to engage in similar economic activities in foreign countries. Conflicts between European states over property did occur, but these disputes generally centered not on eligibility but rather on distribution and access (for example, the partition of Africa in 1884 and subsequent conflicts over jurisdiction). Toward the end of the nineteenth century, the regime supported by Britain began to break down under the pressure of economic depression and competition and as other European states sought to project their value systems into the international realm in order to protect their domestic societies.

In the Western Hemisphere, the United States took on the role of enforcing the British liberal system of property rights. The British had relied on the threat of combined action by several European states to deter economic nationalism in the Latin American states. The United States, however, pursued a different path. The United States sought to prevent European states from actively intervening on behalf of their nationals, but also recognized that it possessed neither the economic clout nor the control of sufficient foreign investment to coerce Latin American states by itself without resort to force. Therefore, the United States undertook to intervene directly in order to protect the property rights of all foreign investors (Lipson 1985:63–64; see also Howland 1929, Angell 1933, and the definitive assertion of this right, as expressed by U.S. Secretary of State Philander Knox in FRUS 1912:581–95).

World War I marked something of a turning point in terms of the dominance of economic property rights. One consequence of the war

---

[1]Kindleberger (1975) asserts that Britain's reasons for adopting a free-trade regime in the nineteenth century were ideological and not rooted in material interests. Others, of course, would dispute this contention.

was the strengthening and extending of political property rights—those related to national territory and sovereignty—along with the weakening of economic property rights—particularly those related to foreign private investment. The Bolshevik Revolution, building on the Russian tradition of a state-centered economy and cultural self-sufficiency, proceeded to alter dramatically the "potential relationship between the state and private property" (Lipson 1985:69) and to redefine rules of eligibility within the new Soviet state. Prior to 1918, according to Charles Lipson (1985:69–70):

> [The] rules were based on a nearly absolute right of property, subject only to narrowly bounded eminent domain procedures. As enforced by the major European powers, traditional international law guaranteed foreigners complete property rights and protected them from the breakdown of local government or isolated acts of expropriation-by-fiat. Practice and expectations were thus convergent. The Soviet expropriations were unique because they resulted from neither turmoil nor executive decree, but from the redefinition of the social character of the state.

Elsewhere, the Mexican Revolution of 1917 redefined the relationship of the state to the national territory, asserting that it was the "nation that owned the land within its borders" (Lipson 1985:77) and not individuals. In Turkey, the government embarked on a nationalistic program of state-led development under which the state became a major property owner, thereby setting a pattern for others to follow. After 1918, political property rights acquired growing primacy over economic ones, and this process culminated in the intense economic and political conflicts of the following decades.

However one might choose to interpret the gradual decline of international cooperation during the interwar period, the fact of that decline is recorded in fundamental changes in the system of property rights, particularly with respect to rules of eligibility. For many of the great powers—Germany, Japan, Italy, and the Soviet Union, in particular, but also Great Britain, France, and even the United States—political property rights, manifested by economic nationalism, began to take precedence over economic ones. Economic rights relating to investment, property, and markets as they existed under the rules of the old property regime came to be viewed as a Trojan horse that might be used to reduce national sovereignty and independence and to threaten national values. Political property rights were thus asserted by some states in order to limit economic ones available to others.

In a sense, World War II may be seen as a conflict over rules of eligibility — that is, the conditions of state participation in the international system. The Axis Powers sought to establish closed, hegemonic spheres of influence within which other states would have few or no rights. Up to a point, the Allies were willing to accept such spheres (the British established a somewhat exclusive "sterling zone," for example). But the effort to incorporate into these spheres states that had no desire to be absorbed raised the more fundamental issues of national sovereignty and integrity, and war resulted.

Following World War II, the United States, in concert with Great Britain, attempted to reconstitute the liberal free trade regime of the nineteenth century within an internationalized liberal political structure. The theory behind this effort, expounded most resolutely by individuals such as Roosevelt's Secretary of State, Cordell Hull, was that unfettered trade between nations — unfettered by "politics," that is — would be the surest path toward peace (Welles 1942; Clayton 1946; Gardner 1980). As expressed in documents such as the Atlantic Charter, the Open Door policy would be expanded to encompass the entire world. States, working together through the United Nations (led, of course, by the United States), would guarantee peace and ensure the necessary environment for market rationality to operate in relative freedom. The rules of economic intercourse would be embodied in institutions such as the International Trade Organization (ITO), the World Bank, the International Monetary Fund, and the Bretton Woods monetary system, with rules of eligibility precisely defined. In Richard Gardner's words (1980:12):

> The [American] post-war planners were united in their determination to break completely with the legacy of economic nationalism and economic isolationism.... They recognized that the United States, despite its comparative self-sufficiency, had a very great stake in the economic well-being of the rest of the world, not only because it needed foreign markets for the produce of its factories and farms, but because it needed a healthy environment on which to base its efforts at world peace.

(On this point see also Painter 1986:128–29.) Or as Susan Strange (1983:340) has described the effort:

> In this vision, Washington was the center of the system, a kind of keep in the baronial castle of capitalism, from which radiated military, monetary, commercial, and technological as well as purely political channels carrying the values of American polity, economy, and society down through the

hierarchy of allies and friends, classes and cultural cousins, out to the ends of the earth.

The implementation differed from the vision (Ruggie 1983). In the late 1940s and early 1950s, the political world was a disorderly place. Nationalism was on the rise and decolonization was getting underway. The U.S. effort to maintain a liberal system of international property rules was frustrated, to some degree, by the political and economic nationalism that accompanied decolonization. Why? Colonialism carried with it the supposition that metropolitan values—political, economic, and cultural—would be diffused into native societies. New states would develop along the lines of the older ones, eventually becoming either English or French or Belgian in form. With this would come a strong commitment to metropolitan values, and strong economic, cultural, and political links to the colonial power. In other words, the rules of eligibility would remain largely the same.

In practice, decolonization led to an entirely different set of outcomes. Nationalism, as it developed, presupposed the legitimacy of *national* systems of values (from wherever they originally derived) that might or might not be liberal (Haas 1986:729–34). It was not sufficient to be rid of the colonizers; it was also necessary to eliminate all overt vestiges of the colonial legacy in order to construct the new state. More often than not, nationalists rebelled against the values of the metropolitan state, replacing them with other systems in which property rights, and the relationships of states to their societies, were defined differently. When independence did not bring with it expected economic and political benefits, many states began to look for means to gain control over their economies. Expropriation and nationalization of the properties of Western multinationals—the disavowal of the post-war system of economically based property rights—were thought to be one means of achieving this end.

The erosion of the U.S.-supported regime of international property rights has been documented in the pattern of takeovers of foreign investments during the post-war period. Depending on how one interprets the data and defines expropriation,[2] roughly 80 percent of foreign takeovers of U.S. firms since World War II took place between 1967 and 1976 (Lipson 1985:98–99). As noted in Chapter 3 (pp. 48–9),

[2]"Expropriation" refers to the modification of individual property rights by a state in the exercise of its sovereignty, (that is, wholesale takeover), often without compensation. "Nationalization" refers to state assertion of ownership or control of property, usually with compensation (Webster's 1970).

prior to 1965 most expropriations were total — the acts of radical governments such as Cuba. After 1975, expropriations became more selective, aimed at particular industries or firms (Kobrin 1980, 1984, 1985). In addition, nationalization became a legitimate act for any type of government — conservative or radical — as evidenced by examples such as Chile and Zaire.

The responses of both multinationals and industrialized states to the changing environment for property rights is suggestive of the extent to which the postwar regime has eroded. Although the United States has tried to maintain its position on the sanctity of private investment and noninvolvement by government, other states, such as Japan, have encouraged and aided the diversification of foreign joint investment in extractive and material-processing industries (Vernon 1977; Puxty 1979; Bobrow and Kudrle 1987). Multinational firms have responded to this changing environment in a number of ways, by signing management contracts, accepting minority ownership as a condition of doing business, and investing in joint ventures. In the mining industries, investment has been directed to "secure" countries, such as Canada and Australia (Manners 1978; Govett and Govett 1978). It has also been suggested that what is important to corporate decisionmakers is not the particular national investment policies of a country as much as the stability of those policies over the longer term (Bilder 1977:410; Price 1984). In this respect, the rules of eligibility under "Marxist" regimes may, somewhat ironically, be more stable than under market-oriented ones and therefore present better long-term investment climates.

RAW MATERIALS IN THE INTERWAR PERIOD

I have suggested that the various conflicts of the period between the two world wars — economic and political, as well as military — can be interpreted as consequences of "structural conflict" over sets of property rules (Rapoport 1974; Krasner 1985). The tendency in most historical accounts and analyses of the period is to focus on the specific conflicts — the jockeying for strategic advantage, the disagreements over international economic structure, the friction between political systems. These accounts generally ignore a much more fundamental struggle over what might today be called an intersecting set of global regimes but that, at the time, had to do with the very structure of international politics.

This structural conflict was reflected, to some degree, in the so-called raw materials problem, which occupied a good deal of the time and energy of diplomats and decisionmakers during the 1920s and 1930s (probably as much as was expended during the 1970s). As noted earlier, the raw materials strategies of the Great Powers cannot and should not be seen in isolation from or independent of the broader foreign policy goals of the period. Rather, the strategies were elements of an effort to establish political, economic, and social stability in what was then, and continues to be, a rapidly changing world. To the extent that industrialization and growth undermined domestic and international stability, even while providing the apparent means of restoring that stability, the effort was doomed to failure. Furthermore, to the degree that trade (dependence) and self-sufficiency (autarky) were pursued as two means to the same end, even though fundamentally incompatible, conflict may have been inevitable.

The raw materials problem was only one facet of a fundamental dilemma involving the relationship between economy and security, expressed in the contradiction between free markets and state intervention and regulation. Achieving a sound and stable material base remained problematic throughout the 1920s and into the 1930s. The economic nationalism of the period was intertwined with several great panics over access to particular resources and was accompanied by efforts to exert greater state control over various raw material markets. World War I impressed on the leaders of the industrial powers the notion that control of raw materials was the key to national power. Thus, the French Senator Henri Berenger announced definitively in 1919, "Who has oil has empire!" (quoted in Tramerye, 1924:10), and a decade later, R.G. Hawtrey, professor of international economics at the Royal Institute of International Affairs, wrote (1930/1952:59):

> The War of 1914–18 was a conflict between the British and German coal fields. The French and Belgian coal fields were out of action from the beginning, but in the end the American coal field, which is bigger than any, intervened.

It seemed imperative to policymakers that each great power acquire sovereign control over assured sources of industrial commodities if national greatness were to be guaranteed.

The interwar period was characterized by alternating periods of great scarcity and great surplus in commodity markets, a consequence of the general economic conditions of the times. With the onset of the

Depression, efforts to exert control over markets and the business cycle shifted more and more from economically oriented strategies—raw material cartels and producer-consumer agreements—to political and military ones—decoupling from the international economic system and consolidating territorial "spheres of influence" within which the governments concerned could regulate both economy and security. These territorial strategies brought in their wake conflict over the structure of property rights within those regions.

In 1935, the German Minister of Finance, Count von Krosigk, warned (quoted in RIIA 1936:8):

> If we fail to obtain through larger exports the larger imports of foreign raw materials required for our greatly increased domestic employment, then two courses only are open to us, increased home production or the demand for a share in districts from which we can get our raw materials ourselves.[3]

The colonial powers were not entirely unsympathetic to this position, but they maintained that a solution to the problem did not rest on the transfer of territory. In a debate on the issue in the Assembly of the League of Nations during the same year, Sir Samuel Hoare summed up the British position as follows (quoted in RIIA 1936:12, emphasis added):

> The fact remains that some countries, whether in their native soil or their colonial territories, do possess what appear to be preponderant advantages, and that others, less favoured, view the situation with anxiety. Especially as regards colonial raw materials it is not unnatural that such a state of affairs should give rise to fear lest exclusive monopolies be set up at the expense of those countries that do not possess colonial empires . . . . *The view of His Majesty's Government is that the problem is economic rather than political and territorial.* It is the fear of monopoly—of the withholding of essential colonial raw materials—that is causing alarm. It is the desire for a guarantee that the distribution of raw materials will not be unfairly impeded that is stimulating the demand for further enquiry . . . . I suggest that emphasis in the terms of reference should fall upon free distribution of such raw materials from colonial areas, including protectorates and mandated territories, among the industrial countries which require them, so that the fear of exclusion or monopoly may be removed once and for all.

Others saw the problem somewhat differently, but still focused on the distribution of raw materials as the central concern. In an address at the University of Wisconsin in 1938, C.K. Leith (1938:434), a

---

[3]Von Krosigk's argument was a bit disingenuous, as German strategy was aimed at decoupling from the international economy (Milward 1977:153–54).

prominent U.S. geologist and an advisor on minerals policy to the Army and Navy Munitions Board, warned that:

These nations [Germany, Italy, Japan] have announced by word and deed that there can be no permanent peace until natural resources have been redistributed among nations. This demand is sometimes camouflaged by political objectives based on historical and racial considerations and the general desire for national prestige. In the last analysis, however, the acquirement of larger supplies of raw materials is a basic prerequisite to the accomplishment of these ends, and the dictators at least are frank to say so. Minerals are not the only raw materials sought, but they are the spearpoint of the demand.

But agreements over the distribution of natural resources were not exactly what Germany was after, since it was bound to pursue a strategy of territorial control and autarky as opposed to an economic one of trade and dependence. In a study written after the outbreak of World War II, entitled "The League of Nations and Raw Materials — 1919–1939," K.W. Kapp (1941:52) wrote:

By linking the raw materials problem with her colonial claims Germany apparently tried to create the impression that her raw materials difficulties were due to the territorial changes caused by the Treaty of Versailles. Actually, Germany's former colonies never produced any substantial amount of raw materials and her insistent requests for their return merely served the purpose of giving Germany's claims at least in some quarters a modicum of justification, while at the same time concealing wider and more far-reaching territorial demands.

The irony of the German demands was that, during the 1930s, production of practically all raw materials outstripped consumption (RIIA 1936:34). Markets were glutted and prices were low. It was true that within their national territories, Germany, Italy, and Japan did not possess certain raw materials whereas, within their colonial empires, Britain and France did. But it was also true that, in 1937, colonial territories generated only about 3 percent of world production of commercially important raw materials (Henderson 1939:4). Although many major producers of such commodities were linked politically to Great Britain — for example, South Africa and Australia — they were not colonies in the legal sense of the term and therefore not available to be transferred to the Axis powers.

Furthermore, most raw materials were available to those countries that could pay for them. It was the lack of foreign exchange, brought on by the collapse of trade, that impeded countries from acquiring these same commodities. The reasons for this shortage of currency varied. By the mid-1930s, Germany and Italy had responded to the general economic crisis brought on by the Depression by establishing stringent exchange controls on economic transactions. This was done to maintain a high exchange value for their currencies, to establish restricted trading areas within Europe, and to avoid a repeat of the inflationary disasters of the early 1920s (RIIA 1936: 33–35; Milward 1977:7–8). A high exchange value reduced the competitiveness of their goods in an already weak international economy, and this left the Axis powers short of the sterling, dollars, and francs needed to purchase raw materials in open markets. Japan, while not artificially supporting its currency, found its traditional foreign markets devastated by the Depression and, hence, its foreign exchange position to be very weak. Because to rejoin the international economy might upset domestic economic stability in Germany and Italy as a result of a new inflation, the only alternative was to expand the domestic economy beyond national borders, a process that knew no limits and, ultimately, reinforced and was reinforced by military power (RIIA 1936:35; Knorr 1943:385).

The establishment of economic spheres of influence generally failed to lead to the degree of autarky desired. In 1938, the states and territories within the Japanese sphere — China, Hong Kong, Indo-China, Burma, Malaya, Thailand, the Netherland East Indies, and Kwantung — supplied less than 38 percent of the raw materials required by Japan and purchased just over one-half of Japan's exports (Whyte 1941:35; Milward 1977:32–33). Japan continued to be highly dependent on supplies of raw materials from the United States — particularly oil — until the outbreak of the War (Anderson 1975:4; Milward 1977:31; Vernon 1983:89–91). Even Germany, with a deliberate policy after 1933 of restricting imports of manufactures and exports of raw materials and foodstuffs (Hirschmann 1945/1980:38; Milward 1977:29), as late as 1938 continued to acquire 31 percent of its imports and to send 37 percent of its exports to "richer" countries (a decrease from 42 percent and 49 percent, respectively, in 1929) (Hirschmann 1945/1980:37). As Leith (1938:440) observed, "The acquirement of Abyssinia,

Austria, Manchuria, and large parts of China and Czechoslovakia have done little to meet the mineral requirements of the "have-not" nations." Thus, although the autarkic strategies of Germany, Japan, and Italy did reduce somewhat the level of imports of raw materials and other goods, they did not serve to eliminate entirely Axis dependence on the colonial powers and others.

From the perspective of the "have" nations (as the United States, Great Britain, and France were often called), the autarkic policies of the "have-nots" were seen as direct threats to the residual legitimacy of the international economy and to the formers' efforts at economic reconstruction. Because autarky was admitted to be essential to the territorial strategies of the "have-nots," these programs came to be seen as a threat to the peace. It became customary, of course, to refer to the heavy U.S. dependence on rubber and tin from Southeast Asia, and the potential threat of denial of these commodities posed by Japanese expansionism in the region (Marshall 1975), but the fact remains that a strategy of denial was followed by the United States in the closing years of the 1930s and not by Japan (Milward 1977: ch. 9).

In addition, even had Japan occupied tin- and rubber-producing areas during the 1930s, it could never have consumed their output of raw materials. Just prior to the war, for example, Japan imported 8,000 to 10,000 tons of tin per year, while the conquered regions produced some 150,000 tons per year. At the same time, new technology had reduced U.S. consumption of tin by one-third (Fox 1974:199). In Europe, most of the countries under Germany's economic domination were important to Great Britain for their role in trade and not as sources of raw materials. Those European states that did constitute important sources of agricultural and raw material resources continued to remain important trading partners of Great Britain (Hirschmann 1945/1980:113).

Notwithstanding their opposition to the economic policies of Germany and Japan, both Great Britain and the United States pursued general policies that were, if anything, weaker versions of the autarkic strategies of the Axis states. Following the end of World War I, and throughout the 1920s, there were continuing discussions about establishing closer political and economic relations between Great Britain and the Dominions, mandates, and territories of the British Empire (Hancock 1943; Kennedy 1981:201, 335). Although these discussions never progressed very far, the Empire always represented a central element of British foreign policy in political, economic, and military terms. Great Britain represented the most important export market for almost all of the Empire's territories, and after the onset of the Depression and the collapse of the international economy, Britain looked more and more toward the Empire as its rightful sphere of trade and influence.

Such a role was natural. These territories all traded in sterling, did their banking in London, and constituted an important source of "invisible" income for Britain, both in terms of services and foreign exchange earnings. In 1932, the Dominions and Great Britain signed the Ottawa Agreement, which established a system of relatively weak "Imperial preference" in British Empire trade. Essentially a customs union, the Ottawa Agreement was intended to reduce or eliminate duties on the import and export of Imperial goods into and out of Great Britain and to increase duties on traded goods originating outside the Empire. In theory, such preference would lead to stabilized markets within the Empire for both commodities and finished goods.

As a result of Imperial preference, between 1931 and 1936 imports from the Empire into Great Britain increased from 29 percent to 39 percent (as a fraction of total imports), while exports to Empire countries and territories increased from 44 to 49 percent (as a fraction of total exports) (RIIA 1938:9).[4] Later in the decade, the British also established the so-called Sterling Bloc, which limited the convertibility of the pound sterling. All of the Imperial territories, plus a number of other countries such as Argentina and Egypt, agreed to maintain their balances of sterling in London. This gave Britain a certain degree of leverage over how those pounds would be spent while helping to maintain its balance of payments.

In effect, therefore, the British strategy was to use political and diplomatic means to maintain the flow of goods and raw materials between the home islands and the Empire. The Ottawa Agreement (whether or not it was effective) and the Sterling Bloc may be thought of as elements of a political approach, rather than an economic one, because the strategy rested on political intervention in the operation of markets — through treaties, agreements, and various political arrangements — and relied to a large degree on the weight of historical and sentimental ties between the core and periphery of the Empire.

[4]Hirschmann (1945/1980:113–14) suggests this was due more to the effects of the Depression on world trade than to the efficacy of the Agreement .

By contrast, the strategy of the United States emphasized economic power to a much greater degree. In general, U.S. diplomacy throughout the interwar period was concerned mostly with economic and commercial opportunities and ensuring that U.S. business got its fair share of overseas markets. While it is true that the Hawley-Smoot Tariff of 1932 represented a political effort to protect domestic markets, the U.S. commitment to the Open Door overseas reached obsessive levels. The Open Door, stated most simply, required equal access for all countries to the markets of all countries and no discrimination against anyone where trade was concerned. But there was a loophole in this admirable sentiment: Under the Open Door, tariffs were not forbidden and were not considered to constitute discriminatory protection. Hawley-Smoot was acceptable because it discriminated equally against everyone; Imperial preference was not because it discriminated selectively.

The Open Door principle, when followed, was thought to have almost mystical powers. In 1938, the U.S. government sent a note to Japan in which it explained, once more, the benefits of an Open Door in China (quoted in Wellington Koo 1939:22):

> This country's adherence to and its advocacy of the principle of equality of opportunity do not flow solely from a desire to obtain the commercial benefits which naturally result from the carrying out of that principle. They flow from a firm conviction that observance of that principle leads to economic and political stability, which are conducive both to the internal wellbeing of nations and to mutually beneficial and peaceful relationships between and among nations; from a firm conviction that failure to observe that principle breeds international friction and ill will, with consequences injurious to all countries, including in particular those countries which fail to observe it; and from an equally firm conviction that observance of that principle promotes the opening of trade channels, thereby making available the markets, the raw materials and the manufactured products of the community of nations on a mutually and reciprocally beneficial basis.

Notwithstanding the rhetoric, the United States relied largely on economic muscle and influence to get its way. The U.S. market remained quite large, even in the depths of the Depression, and this tended to draw in raw materials, particularly from the Western Hemisphere and the Far East. Conversely, these regions were seen as the natural markets for U.S. goods.

Thus, when the Japanese began to close the door in the Far East, the U.S. reaction was to focus on the economic issues at stake. Under a discriminatory regime as might be established by Japan, the United States would no longer have the continued access to the markets and goods to which it had become accustomed. Furthermore, it might have more difficulty in purchasing raw materials (although there is little evidence to suggest that this would have been the case, as Japan continued to need dollars). Ultimately, it might be said that, when all of the issues at stake in the Far East were laid on the table — and given the U.S. isolationism of the period — only the raw materials problem remained prominent, and this captured more and more attention as the decade progressed.

The Soviet strategy, if one can be said to have existed during this period, was a selective one. Although the Soviet Union did export a variety of raw materials to the West between the two world wars, it imported virtually none, relying mostly on production from within its national territory. Furthermore, the xenophobia of the 1930s tended to keep the Soviet Union a closed realm in both political and economic terms. Not until the outbreak of the war — with the losses of industrial regions and sources of raw materials to the Germans and the start of Lend-Lease — did the Soviets deviate markedly from a policy of high self-sufficiency. Eventually, the onset of the Cold War led to a return to this policy.

The outbreak of World War II had two consequences. First, it put to the test the policy of territorial autarky pursued by Germany and, to a lesser extent, Japan (Milward 1977). Second, the war temporarily derailed the U.S. and British strategies, as they were forced to adopt mercantilist policies in order to ensure continued and secure supplies of industrial raw materials needed to prosecute the war. Germany and Japan managed to fight for a remarkably long time on fairly limited supplies of raw materials (Mason 1949; Milward 1977), but in the end, it was the superior *industrial* base of the Allies that defeated the Axis.

Policies of autarky and spheres of influence as viable national strategies were largely laid to rest in the wake of the Allied victory (except, perhaps, with respect to the Soviet Union). What the war did not destroy in the victorious nations was the philosophical underpinnings of the prewar strategies, or what might be called the collective cognitive framework of decisionmakers. The experiences of the 1930s, followed by those of the war, seemed to verify a number of theories —

military, economic, and political—that explained how the world worked, how states interacted, the relationship between domestic political structures and a state's foreign policies, and so on. These theories were linked to real, material concerns but, at the same time, were (and remain) animated by strong ideal elements.

The sum of these material and ideal interests represented a "strategic synthesis" that encapsulated the purposes and goals of the state in the post-war world. These syntheses were not put down on paper; they were not part of a master plan for global hegemony or world domination. Rather, they were the end result of a concatenation of experiences, as well as beliefs and ideals, that came to be codified in the "world views" and "schemas" utilized by national decisionmakers. For the United States, affected most deeply by the economic experience of the Depression and the geopolitical events of World War II, the postwar synthesis came to focus on the establishment of a benign international system within which economic and political liberalism could flourish. The United Kingdom, bowing to U.S. power, paid lip service to U.S. ideals but was more concerned with maintaining the territorial integrity of the British Empire, in some form. The Soviet Union, insulated to a large degree from the effects of the Depression but most concerned that the experiences of the war never be repeated, sought to establish a relatively self-sufficient territorial bloc as a means of protecting itself from the rest of the world. Ultimately, these three syntheses came into conflict with one another, producing the tensions and crises of the period we call the "Cold War."

RAW MATERIALS, STRATEGIC SYNTHESES, AND FOREIGN POLICIES

The final section of this chapter, elaborates on the form, content, and application of these "strategic syntheses": How these principles were formulated by decisionmakers in the United States, the United Kingdom, and the Soviet Union and how they were put into action through "organizing principles." This section provides the basis for the next three chapters of this study, which delve more deeply into the relationship between the raw materials policies and strategic syntheses of the three states following World War II.

The United States

A central, and recurrent, difficulty in formulating a rational materials policy for the United States has been that of conflicting objectives. Strategic minerals are most commonly seen as vital inputs into the industrial capacity of the state and, by extension, its defensive capabilities. At a basic material level, therefore, the goals of a sensible policy might seem self-evident. There are, however, major contradictions embedded in even this single objective—to wit, that establishing secure sources of supply may entail costs that could prove even more deleterious to the national economy than those associated with the risks of insecure supplies.

Curiously, the United States finds itself tempted by the ideal extremes of autarky and dependence, and this has created a recurring dilemma for policymakers. On the one hand, autarky has been a theoretical possibility because, for many decades, the United States was almost entirely self-sufficient with respect to industrial raw materials. This golden past still beckons to some. On the other hand, interdependence has come to be seen as a vital element of the United States' political and economic foreign policies. Indeed, without such a goal of interdependence there would be no good reason for the economic and political policies pursued by successive U.S. administrations since the end of World War II.

In the U.S. case, these conflicting objectives have extended beyond straightforward concerns about industrial capabilities to include others, such as depletion of domestic supplies, relative prices of domestic and foreign sources, viability of domestic producers, the politics and stability of producer governments, the stability of markets, and the needs of the military planners. Any effort to describe the evolution or objectives of U.S. strategic materials policy thus depends on one's perspective (Halperin 1974:20–21).

A variety of material and ideal interests have been commingled to form a rather complicated and sometimes incoherent policy. Table 4–1 lays out the range of objectives one finds manifested in U.S. policymakers' deliberations over strategic raw materials policies. Both material and ideal interests are of concern with respect to each element of foreign policy—military, political, and economic—where strategic raw materials are concerned. In other words, the manipulation of raw materials policies has been seen as providing a means

Table 4–1. Relationship of Interests to Aspects of U.S. Raw
Materials Policies.

	Military	Political	Economic

Material interests	Strategic planning
	Denial of access
	Adequacy of
	  supplies
	Security of
	  facilities
	Mobilization
	  planning
	Strategic stockpile
		Trade sanctions
		Foreign
		  investment
		Purchasing
		  arrangements
		Sharing
		  agreements
			Cost of supplies
			Domestic
			  producers
			Business cycle
			Stockpile size

Ideal interests	Geopolitical
	  containment
	National security
		Support friendly
		  governments
		Undermining of
		  enemies
		Political liberalism
		National security
			Economic
			  liberalism
			Market stability
			Economic
			  prosperity

to material as well as ideal ends in the military, political, and economic realms.

It is also possible to invert this matrix in order to highlight broader
foreign policy goals and perspectives. One can then ask where strategic
raw materials fit. Three broad principles or perspectives emerge from
this exercise: (1) a deterministic geopolitical doctrine; (2) a "free-
market" economic doctrine; and (3) a liberal political doctrine. Briefly,
these three doctrines incorporate the following beliefs:

1. *Geopolitical determinism*: imputation of political significance to
    geographic features; evaluation of the importance of states on the
    basis of location and resources; assumptions about the nature of
    the geographic expansion of states;

2. *"Free-market" economics*: free trade between nations; equal access to raw materials and markets; capitalist economic systems within states and between states on the international level;
3. *Political liberalism*: national sovereignty; one-state, one-vote; pluralist democratic political systems within states; opposition to "radical" or populist forms of nationalism.

These principles have not been pursued consistently over the post-World War II period, but as is shown in Chapter 5, they have been central ideas in policymaking. Their application can be seen to a greater or lesser degree in declassified State Department and White House policy papers and cable traffic for particular areas of the world.

One should not get the idea that this "policy trinity" has been formulated in any coherent form or fashion. These three doctrines were present in policymaking in the form of organizing principles. To a significant extent, the attempt to attain these idealized goals was reflected in the more prosaic and mundane problems of everyday life. The overarching goal of U.S. foreign policy — if, indeed, there was one — was, as noted earlier, the creation of a hospitable global political and economic environment for the propagation of U.S. values, this being thought the "best" way to preserve peace (Gardner 1980; Strange 1983:340). Anti-Communism can therefore be seen as a reaction to alien values — a different set of "rules of eligibility," if you will — and "containment" as not just a military strategy but also an ideological one.

Thus, for U.S. policymakers, raw materials policy was not only of relevance to domestic prosperity and security but also germane to the pursuit of global prosperity and security. With respect to the policy trinity, raw materials were crucial in a number of ways. Geopolitical doctrine saw raw materials as a military objective. Economic doctrine saw the stability of commodity markets as essential to a smoothly functioning and prosperous Free World economy. Political doctrine saw the support of friendly governments through foreign aid programs essential to international order, and these three doctrines were interlinked in sometimes contradictory and confusing ways.

A good example of the way in which these three grand doctrines were commonly fused together can be found in a 1951 State Department memorandum on "Point 4 and Raw Materials Development" (HSTL 1951e).[5] The memo is worth quoting at length because it presents so carefully the image of connectedness (HSTL 1951e; emphasis in original):

> The objective of the Point 4 program is the evolution of strong, self-reliant, democratic and freedom loving nations able and willing to cooperate with each other and with the United States in building a strong, peaceful and free world . . . .
>
> The strength of the free world comprises economic strength, political strength and military strength. The Point 4 program builds *economic* strength *directly* by increasing production of food, materials and other products needed for civilian and military consumption; by building healthier bodies; by training labor, management and civil servants, and in other ways contributing to the productivity of existing resources and the development of new resources . . . .
>
> *Indirectly*, Point 4 contributes to *political* strength by building the confidence of peoples in their own future, in their governments,. in the effectiveness of democratic institutions, and in the friendship of the United States. Indirectly also, Point 4 contributes to *military* strength by aiding the production of strategic materials, the development of strategic transportation facilities, the development of greater economic self-sufficiency (thus reducing wartime needs for transportation); by building a healthier, stronger manpower reserve; and by bettering economic and social conditions that might otherwise threaten internal security. It thus serves as a powerful positive force resisting Communist penetration . . . .
>
> The objectives of Point 4 are peaceful, for strengthened economies and better living conditions are inherently desirable and in the interest of all countries in time of peace. Their value is not limited to peacetime, however. Strength is even more necessary in wartime. Aid activities that speed up economic development strengthen the free world and serve both emergency security needs and the long-run peacetime goals stated by the President in his Point 4 proposal.

Ultimately, this type of circuitous reasoning was applied to all parts of the world. The material interests — the security and prosperity of the United States — were linked to the ideal interests — an image of how the world should be — and the ideal interests were made essential to the realization of the material ones. These interests, in turn, were embedded in a matrix of rules of eligibility and property that were seen as

[5]Point 4 was an economic and technical aid program for developing states, first announced by Truman's in his 1949 inaugural address (Pollard 1985:205–09).

being in opposition to those advocated by Communism. The global strategy was both political and economic, but the binding together of the "Free World" was to come about primarily through economic linkages and not political ones.

Following World War II, U.S. policymakers eschewed rhetorically the political interventions into "free markets" represented by arrangements such as commodity stabilization agreements and restricted customs unions. But the United States was not above the political manipulation of markets or support of customs unions (such as the European Common Market) if certain ends, both ideal and material, could thereby be achieved. That is, although military power was instrumental to U.S. foreign policy, that power was a means to a stable international environment within which both political and economic liberalism could thrive. Global economic liberalism was seen as the ultimate end of that stable environment. Of course, many compromises were made along the way, with the result that the ideal goal has never been reached (and would probably be impractical, in any event) (Ruggie 1983). In all likelihood, few policymakers probably ever expected that the ideal could be reached. But to use Weber's terminology once again, the ideals acted as the "switchmen" for the policy (Gerth and Mills 1946:200).

The United Kingdom

The choice between autarky and interdependence came early to Britain. Although foreign trade had always been an important component of British foreign policy, until the 1830s it pursued a protectionist strategy as regarded the production of food, reflected in the so-called Corn Laws, which were part of the Navigation Acts. These laws, passed in the heyday of British mercantilism, were designed to keep out imports of grain from the Continent and North America. The reasoning behind the laws had been that self-sufficiency in food production was necessary to the security of the realm. Tariff barriers against imports also ensured, conveniently, the survival of domestic agriculture in the face of cheaper foreign supplies of food.

There were, however, disadvantages to such protectionist barriers, having to do with the ongoing process of industrialization. The Corn

Laws kept the price of basic foodstuffs high, thus requiring that workers be paid a wage sufficient for basic survival. Although repeal of the laws eliminated domestic self-sufficiency, it also lowered food prices, which allowed a reduction in workers' wages and in the cost of British manufactures. This was adduced to be advantageous to trade (Polanyi 1957).

The end of the Corn Laws was one of the first acts in the British-led era of liberal "free trade." Although international trade in the mid-nineteenth century was never as "free" as often depicted (Kindleberger 1975; Stein 1984), the British decision to reduce tariff barriers on certain goods represented a conscious and deliberate step toward a policy of dependence on foreign commodities and markets. For an island nation like Britain, which possessed both economic and military power but which already in the 1800s faced a declining domestic resource base, this was an eminently sensible strategy. In the long run, however, the pursuit of this strategy may have proved Britain's undoing as an imperial power.

For the United Kingdom, the post-World War II environment was not the same as that facing the United States. It may have been one of Britain's great misfortunes that the Empire emerged largely intact from the war, at least in conceptual terms, for this meant that the political/territorial strategy of the prewar period was not discredited entirely (Gallagher 1982; Kennedy 1983b:29). In a time of growing poverty, and lacking the financial resources available to the Americans, political and diplomatic currency were the only factors that remained in "surplus," so to speak, and Britain used these diplomatic strategies for gaining desired, and frequently economic, ends.

Writing of an earlier period in British history, Elisabeth Monroe (1981:15) observed that in order to protect the Empire, "the British desire and technique was to create friendly buffer states by means of influence exercised through trade treaties, loans, friendly advice, and pressure by ambassadors or gunboats if necessary." Although their touch was lighter after World War II, British policymakers continued to use these techniques. But neither the Empire nor the Commonwealth that followed were sustainable as organic political and economic units, and they were militarily indefensible, too. The overwhelming problem facing the British was not that the United States was opposed to the retention of certain territories within the colonial system (HSTL 1948a; Verrier 1986:43), or that the Soviet Union was bound and determined to see the end of the Empire, but, rather, that World War II set in motion a process of decolonization that could not be stopped.

British foreign policy during the period following World War II was, therefore, motivated by a set of ideal and material arguments that stood as justification for the territorial/diplomatic strategy it pursued. Although for an island nation with limited resources, raw materials were demonstrably more critical than for an insular, continental country like the United States, access to and control of strategic materials loomed much less strongly in the policy formulation process of the former than in that of the latter. To put it another way, every British schoolboy knew that the Empire supplied vital raw materials to the British Isles (although even this might be arguable), but the Empire was much more than just a source of commodities. The Empire *was* Britain, and vice versa, and this provided a critical underlying rationale for foreign policy (Kennedy 1983b).

The geopolitical determinism that is so strong in U.S. policy documents is therefore also present in the British ones, but the formula is stated with much less conviction. The difference between the two was that the British *did* have territories to protect, whereas the United States had, for the most part, only interests. Only with respect to British policy in the Middle East do raw materials and geopolitics emerge as strongly intertwined themes, and even there, economic concerns take precedence.

Indeed, although both U.S. and British policymakers were deeply concerned about economic issues in the postwar world, the focus of this concern emerges as a major divide between the two states. For U.S. policymakers, global prosperity was seen as the key to a peaceful world. For British policymakers, national prosperity was *the* central concern because only an economically strong Britain could maintain its military commitments, and hence its prestige, around the world (Abadi 1982).[6] By comparison, the spread of economic or political liberalism was of minor importance in the scheme of things. In a period of general economic decline, the objective of achieving national prosperity proved much more daunting.

---

[6]Or as Anthony Eden, the foreign minister, warned in 1952: "[O]nce the prestige of a country has started to slide there is no knowing when it will stop" (PRO 1952a:2).

The rush for empire prior to World War I and the protectionist strategies of the Depression were essentially part of the same phenomenon. Both were territorially based strategies for establishing predictable stability in the economic and political realms. Today we might call these strategies "limited regimes," in the sense that they applied to specific, geographically defined areas of the world. All of the Great Powers of the early twentieth century followed such strategies — some more than others — and those Powers that survived the two world wars continued to practice them, albeit in different form. The British Empire/Commonwealth was (and is) a political association of very diverse states united only by virtue of having once been part of Great Britain's diplomatic/territorial strategy of empire. At one time, Britain had hopes of realizing major economic benefits from this political union and continued to pursue its policy of political association during the period 1945 through 1956 (approximately). The Suez debacle demonstrated the weakness of its strategy in the face of U.S. economic might and Soviet military power.

The argument has been made that, following World War II, Britain overextended herself far beyond what was possible given the resources available to it (Abadi 1982; Kennedy 1987) and that the emotional commitment to Empire (or to its former self) was the source of the repeated economic crises of the postwar period. But oil and trade were so important to Britain's economic position that to give them up was unthinkable, and no alternative strategy seemed available. W.R. Louis (1984: pt. I) has suggested that it was the policy of the British Labour Party, in power from 1945 to 1951, to liquidate the Empire and replace it with something more in keeping with the times (such as the Commonwealth). There was no intention, however, of giving up formal political and economic ties with former Imperial territories, and this, as shall be seen in Chapter 6, proved to be Britain's undoing.

The Soviet Union

The Soviet Union represents a somewhat special case. As the second greatest military power in the world, possessing the third largest economy, the Soviet Union demands attention as a major actor in global politics and economics. This is particularly true with respect to the production, consumption, and sale of raw material and energy commodities. Although the Soviet Union has never been completely independent of world markets, for many decades it was virtually self-sufficient in terms of a number of important mineral commodities. Thus, a relatively high degree of autarky with respect to strategic materials was possible.

Some have argued that the Soviet Union has traditionally pursued autarkic policies for both ideological and material reasons (PRO 1947a:3) while others have seen the high degree of self-sufficiency as a consequence of socialist industrialization (Pisar 1970:188–89) or Western-inspired economic warfare (DDEL 1956a). Yet others have argued that the Russian cultural tradition of insularity is responsible for the pursuit of autarky (Ulam 1981). Whatever the reason, many outside observers have viewed self-sufficiency as one of the great strengths of Soviet economic development (Overton 1983) because it appears to have reduced the USSR's sensitivity to external politics. Over the past several decades, the relative isolation of the Soviet Union from the world economy meant that its impact on world supplies and demand for raw materials was, for the most part, small or nonexistent.

In attempting to account for and explain the Soviet policy of autarky, insofar as it exists, there are at least two possible explanations. First, the goal of self-sufficiency may have its origins in ideology. Second, self-sufficiency may be a consequence of environmental opportunities and/or constraints. In either case, the original rationales for pursuing the goal may have disappeared long ago, but the "stickiness" of institutions and practices is such that policies often continue to be pursued long after they have become inefficient or pointless.

Soviet trade and strategic policies have been motivated by both explanations. Ideologically, self-sufficiency was pronounced by Lenin and Stalin as a necessary element in the building of "socialism." In 1920, Lenin told the Eighth Congress of Soviets that the rapid resumption of trade would allow the Soviet Union to purchase the machinery necessary to "achieving economic independence of the capitalist world" (quoted in Smith 1973:25). Several years later, Stalin told the Fourteenth Congress of Soviets (quoted in Smith 1973:25) that

> We must build our economy in order that our country will not become an appendage to the capitalist system, in order that we will not be included in the overall system of capitalist development as a second class undertaking, in order that our economy will grow not as a second class undertaking of capitalism but as an individual economy in its own right, based primarily on the internal market which is based on the union of our industry with the peasant economy of the country.

In 1935, M.M. Zhirmunski (1935:8, quoted in Smith 1973:15) wrote that

> The explanation of the nature of Soviet export trade must be sought not in comparison with the foreign trade of capitalist countries, but in the specific tasks of a state which is building socialism in the midst of capitalist encirclement.

At the same time, the experiences of the period between 1918 and 1920, when the territory under the control of the Bolshevik government was blockaded by the Western Allies, indicated to the Soviet leaders the risks of depending upon external sources of goods and markets. These risks were repeatedly brought home again and again. In 1930 and 1931, seven countries (France, Belgium, Hungary, Rumania, Yugoslavia, Canada, and the United States) passed antidumping legislation designed to prevent the Soviets from undercutting other producers of commodities and goods in world markets. The subsequent history of Western export controls only served to underline the risks of an interdependent trade policy (Adler-Karlsson 1968; Holloway 1984:106).

Practical factors also determined the evolution of trade policy and the trend toward autarky. As a geographically large, land-oriented power, with a vast resource base, a strategy of self-sufficiency was a natural policy to follow. By the end of the first five-year plan, most industrial raw materials were being produced domestically, so imports were, logically, eliminated (Smith 1973:16). At the same time, Soviet leaders and planners recognized the importance of selective imports of necessary goods and materials. This strategy was pursued most forcefully during the period of the "New Economic Plan" under Lenin as a means of building socialism. In the 1920s, large concessions in such basic materials as petroleum and manganese were granted to foreign concerns and individuals (Fischer 1927:164–67). These were, however, revoked later in the decade, leading to various efforts by the West to retaliate with economic sanctions.

By the 1930s, it was recognized that foreign trade could not be halted entirely, but it could be limited. The Stalinist program of industrialization gave further impetus to a policy of autarky in trade and development. Soviet trade policy thus came to be determined by the needs of the economy as determined by central planners and not by any mechanisms related to markets. The export policy of the Soviet

Union was thus pronounced to be "in the quantity necessary for the flow of imports or for the payment of obligations on imports of the past year" (Commissariat on Foreign Trade 1935:10, quoted in Smith 1973:17).

Although, as noted above, the reasons given for a policy of high self-sufficiency were often derived from ideology, the need to maintain centralized and close control over industrial inputs and outputs also led to this end. Samuel Pisar (1970:188–89) noted in 1970, writing from the perspective of fifty years of Soviet development, that

> [I]t would be somewhat simplistic to blame the autarky syndrome on entirely theoretical factors. In large measure it has become a facet of ingrained methodology. As an approach, the notion of economic self-sufficiency makes the planner's task much easier, his forecasts much more controllable. Bureaucratic conservatism renders him reluctant to submit to the imponderables of a less regimented environment of exchanges, particularly in the area of resource allocation. Instead of attempting to bend official doctrine to the practical needs of the economy, his instincts impel him to use it as a shield against exposure to the variable, the uncertain, the adventurous.

(On this point, see also Smith 1973:12–13.)

This strategy did not change following World War II. In the years immediately after the end of the war, the Soviets concentrated on consolidating their hegemony in Eastern Europe. Practice in the region was, by and large, an extension of "socialism in one country," and self-sufficiency continued as a central element in the Soviet strategic synthesis. Not until the death of Stalin in 1953 did a major change in this policy take place, a shift that was, in Elizabeth Valkenier's words (1983:3), "[P]art and parcel of an all-out political offensive aimed at encouraging the developing countries to nibble away at the territorial, strategic, political, and economic domain of the West." Policymakers in the West became alarmed that the Soviets might achieve major economic gains in newly independent areas at the expense of the West. But, the real goal of this offensive was "not to expand trade so much as to score political victories" (Valkenier 1983:5). Soviet entry into commodity markets was thus primarily a means of gaining influence with others—much as the United States used its economic leverage toward the same end—and the policy of high self-sufficiency was, as a result, modified but not abandoned.

The case for an ideological and political interpretation of Soviet raw materials policy, as opposed to an economic one, thus remains mixed. To be sure, ideology and politics have been important elements in commercial operations, and remain so today. As well, the military needs and strength of the Soviet Union have also determined the tendency toward autarky and a selective import policy. Economic pragmatism should not be overlooked as an important motivator of Soviet trade relations and practices, however. The fact that Soviet trade has been state-controlled for many decades simply means that it is possible to coordinate these elements, unlike the case in the West where trade decisions are often beyond the control of governments. As a result, "resource diplomacy" has been a tool readily available to the Soviet Union to influence other countries and to express Soviet displeasure at certain events. As will become apparent in Chapter 7, however, the restricted nature of Soviet trade in resources has limited the circumstances in which this tool can be applied successfully.

SUMMARY AND CONCLUSIONS

There are different strategic syntheses open to a state, within which raw materials play a role. A state may choose to be economically self-sufficient but, in the ideal case, this requires close control over territory and economy. Conversely, a state may choose a path of dependence or economic intercourse and rely on internationally accepted property rights regimes to protect its access to raw materials. This has been the generally accepted approach taken by Great Britain and the United States over much of the past century. Even when there is general agreement about the structure of international property rights regimes, however, states may pursue different strategies for achieving broader political and economic goals. When these "strategic syntheses" diverge too widely between states, conflict may result. Property rights regimes may also break down in times of international stress, as was the case in the 1930s, leading to structural conflict over property rule sets and, perhaps, war. If war comes, however, it is the result of fundamental disagreements over basic national strategies, of which raw material policies are only one small part.

During the period between the two world wars, the autarkic strategies of the Axis powers, which envisioned the establishment of closed spheres of influence, came into structural conflict with the more liberal strategies of the United States, Great Britain, and other Western powers. The result was global war. (These strategies did not, however, offend the Soviet Union — at least not until Germany sought to pursue autarky into Soviet territory.)

Following World War II, the liberal strategy of the United States — based on open markets and political liberalism — clashed with the more territorially oriented strategy of the United Kingdom. This conflict was finally resolved at Suez, in 1956. The U.S. strategic synthesis also came into conflict with the nonliberal strategy of the Soviet Union, predicated on economic and political autarky within a defined sphere of influence. This basic incompatibility established the conditions for the Cold War. (Again, it is of interest to note that, notwithstanding their abhorrence of Communism, the British were much more willing to strike economic deals with the Soviet Union than was the United States.) In the following three chapters, these syntheses, and the conflicts that resulted, are described in greater detail.

5 RESOURCES FOR FREEDOM
Raw Materials and United States Foreign Policy

In early 1951, in the middle of the Korean War, President Truman summoned William S. Paley, the founder and head of the CBS radio and television networks, to a meeting. According to Paley's recollection (1979:203), Truman was "very intent, very serious":

> In that even-toned, flat voice, he told me that a full survey of our mineral and energy resources was essential for the nation. The government needed to look ahead and see what the future demands on our natural resources were going to be, what shortages could be expected, and finally, what the government should do about it. It was an important job and he wanted me to take it.

Paley took it.

The onset of the Korean War and the accompanying rearmament triggered an economic boom in both the United States and its European allies. For a period of time, as demand outstripped supply, critical raw materials became scarce. Industrialists grumbled as prices rose, defense analysts warned of the dangers of strategic materials shortages, and the United States' allies found themselves shut out of international markets. Something had to be done. Truman, in his often uncanny way, did do something: He appointed a prominent, outspoken individual to head a major study of the raw materials problem and to make recommendations to the government. Thus was born the President's Materials Policy Commission (PMPC)—known forever after as the "Paley Commission."

The Commission worked at top speed and in June 1952 issued its final report, a glossy, five-volume study, entitled *Resources for Freedom*. At the very beginning of the report, the Commission warned that the present situation was fraught with danger (PMPC 1952:1):

> The United States, once criticized as the creator of a crassly materialistic order of things, is today throwing its might into the task of keeping alive the spirit of Man and helping beat back from the frontiers of the free world everywhere the threats of force and of a new Dark Age which rise from the Communist nations. In defeating this barbarian violence moral values will count most, but they must be supported by an ample materials base. Indeed, the interdependence of moral and material values has never been so completely demonstrated as today, when all the world has seen the narrowness of its escape from the now dead Nazi tyranny and has yet to know the breadth by which it will escape the live Communist one — both materialistic threats aimed to destroy moral and spiritual man. The use of materials to destroy or preserve is the very choice over which the world struggle today rages.

Notwithstanding the purple prose of its introductory paragraphs, the central premise of the study was (and remains, even today) surprisingly pedestrian. According to the Commission (PMPC 1952:3):

> The over-all objective of a national materials policy for the United States should be to insure an adequate and dependable flow of materials at the lowest cost consistent with national security and with the welfare of friendly nations.

What is of greater interest for the purposes of this study is the basic philosophy laid out by the authors of *Resources for Freedom*: That an adequate materials base is meaningless without the appropriate ideals to back up policy.

This chapter and the ones that follow turn from a general discussion of access to strategic raw materials and conflict to the question of how access to such materials has influenced the formulation of foreign policy in the United States, the United Kingdom, and the Soviet Union. As will be seen, raw material supplies often represent the tangible, material aspect of policies whose objectives may be quite complex and contradictory. U.S. raw materials policy during the height of the Cold War (roughly 1946–65) was virtually *always* a rather confusing mix of material objectives and ideal desires. Archival sources are drawn on to show how raw materials policy, embedded in the three organizing principles of U.S. foreign policy described in Chapter 4, reflected both material and ideal interests. A brief concluding section discusses the relevance of the historical material to the present.

PURPLE PROSE AND POLICY

The Paley Commission report was intended to influence policy in a number of areas related to raw materials policy: the strategic stockpile, international materials distribution, defense, and the problem of unstable markets. It was expected that the National Security Resources Board (NSRB)—a little-remembered counterpart to the National Security Council (NSC) (Hobbs 1954: ch. 7)—would be the lead agency on a new national materials policy. The NSRB issued a policy paper based on the recommendations of the Commission (U.S. NSRB 1952), but the incoming Eisenhower administration dismantled the board, preferring to develop its own policies. These, as it turned out, did not deviate markedly from those proposed by the Paley Commission (DDEL 1953a).

Then, as well as thirty-five years later, the lurid language is gone, but the basic conclusions reached by the Paley Commission regarding an appropriate raw materials policy remained and remain very much the same. Public Law 96–479, the National Materials and Minerals Policy, Research and Development Act of 1980 (quoted in U.S. OTA 1985:116), declares that

> [I]t is the continuing policy of the United States to promote an adequate and stable supply of materials necessary to maintain national security, economic well-being and industrial production with appropriate attention to a long-term balance between resource production, energy use, a healthy environment, natural resources conservation, and social needs.

More recently, in May 1985, the Congressional Office of Technology Assessment (OTA) advocated pursuit of a similar policy and added that a combination of three technical approaches—greater diversity of sources, decreases in demand, and development of substitute materials—could further reduce the uncertainties associated with strategic materials supplies (U.S. OTA 1985:3).

The conclusions and recommendations of the OTA study to reduce U.S. sensitivity to shortages of strategic raw materials do not differ greatly from those offered by the Paley Commission in 1952 (nor, for that matter, from a number of other similar studies conducted between

100 WHEN NATIONS CLASH

the 1920s and the present): stockpiling, conservation, recycling, substitution, diversification of foreign suppliers, better coordination of
information, and so on. Thus, according to the OTA, the United States
is capable of reducing national vulnerability to strategic mineral shortages if—and this is a big "if"—it is willing to implement the policy
recommendations of the OTA study and preceding ones. But if past
experience is any indicator of future practice, the OTA study will be
ignored, forgotten, and left on the shelf to collect dust with its
predecessors. Indeed, it has been the experience of many similar panels
commissioned by presidents to offer technical policy advice that their
conclusions are either politically untenable or ideologically unpalat-
able and therefore are ignored (Wolanin 1975).

Although *Resources for Freedom* has been cited frequently as the
definitive postwar study of raw materials policy (Ascher 1978:33–34),
its long-term impact on policymakers cannot be judged to have been
very great. In this respect, the Paley Commission did not suffer a
unique fate because it was not the first to consider the problem of a
national materials policy (Meyer and Riley 1985). With respect to
policy change in this issue area, the difficulty lies not so much in the
inappropriateness of recommendations as in the contradictions that
would and do arise during their implementation. Reducing U.S.
vulnerability to uncertainties in international markets and politics
leads not only to greater security but also, logically, to a reduction of
influence with other states, an effect that paradoxically may serve to
decrease security. This dilemma, which remains essentially unresolv-
able, began to develop in earnest after World War I, when it became
apparent to policymakers that the depletion of domestic sources of raw
materials meant that foreign sources would have to be found and
exploited (O'Brien 1974; Huddle 1976).

Following the experiences of World War II, in which raw materials
seemed to play such an important role (see, for example U.S. BOM
1940; U.S. Military Academy 1947; Mason 1949; Hurstfield 1953), the
notion that neither war *nor* peace could be conducted without adequate
flows of oil and minerals became firmly fixed in the minds of both U.S.
policymakers and the public. Clearly, this was true where the conduct
of war was concerned (but, see Mason 1949 and Milward 1977 on how
Germany managed to fight for five years on very limited supplies of
raw materials). Peacetime, however, represented a different problem,
as we shall see.

In 1946, determined not to be caught unprepared again, Congress passed the Strategic and Critical Materials Stock Piling Act, which, focusing on U.S. dependence on imported minerals, created a program that mandated the purchase and stockpiling of certain materials as well as research and development into ways to extend supplies and find substitutes (Huddle 1976:655). Nonetheless, during the five years following the end of World War II, strategic materials policy remained relatively unfocused and disorganized. To be sure, there were programs for stockpiling, programs for acquiring raw materials overseas (included as part of the Marshall Plan and Point Four), and programs for defense mobilization in the event of a national emergency. All of these were related to the unfolding Cold War. But at any one time the number of agencies involved in different aspects of strategic raw materials acquisition was legion, making coherent coordination very difficult.

The Munitions Board (and its various mobilization agency successors) was concerned primarily with the status of the strategic stockpile. The State Department was responsible for both foreign trade policy and relations with producer and consumer countries. The National Security Resources Board (followed by a myriad of alphabetic agencies such as ODM, OCDM, OEP, FEMA, and so on.[1]) concerned itself with defense mobilization and emergency planning, the National Security Council with grand strategy, and various branches of the military with strategic planning.

After the outbreak of the Korean War, agencies such as the Defense Materials Procurement Agency and the Petroleum Administration for Defense also became involved in the raw materials problem. In 1950, according to the Legislative Reference Service of the Library of Congress, "at least 16 executive agencies and 11 congressional committees" had a hand in the strategic stockpiling program, as did twelve interagency commodity committees, twelve industry advisory committees and twenty-eight unspecified subcommittees (U.S. LRS 1950: 126–27; see also FRUS 1949a for one agency's story, NARS 1951b for a report on stockpile administration, and Snyder 1965 for a detailed history of the stockpiling program).

Notwithstanding all of this help, in 1950 the head of the Munitions Board still found it necessary to inform Congress that "The stockpile program is now in the middle of its fourth year of a projected 5-year

[1]Respectively, the Office of Defense Management, the Office of Civilian and Defense Mobilization, the Office of Emergency Planning, and the Federal Emergency Management Agency.

program. Yet it is still many years away from completion" (quoted in U.S. LRS 1950:127). The strategic stockpiling program failed to alleviate widely held concerns about materials security, and access to strategic materials rapidly became a basic explanation for U.S. involvement overseas, perhaps because decisionmakers thought that the public would not support foreign ventures based wholly on values or ideology.

In 1947, for example, in a draft of the speech announcing what came to be known as the "Truman Doctrine," presidential advisor Clark Clifford wrote (HSTL 1947a:13, 1947b:11),

> If by default, we permit free enterprise to disappear in the other nations of the world, the very existence of our own economy and our own democracy will be gravely threatened . . . . [The eastern Mediterranean] is an area of great natural resources which must be accessible to all nations and must not be under the exclusive control or domination of any single nation. The weakening of Turkey, or the further weakening of Greece, would invite such control.

Although this passage was deleted from the final text, its spirit remained intact, as indicated subsequently by U.S. policies in the region. What is not clear in retrospect, however, is the degree to which access to resources was the *main* interest at stake in the eastern Mediterranean. Similarly, access to raw materials was used as one of the rationales for the Marshall Plan, Point Four, military aid to developing countries, and other similar programs (Pollard 1985: ch. 9). But there were other equally important concerns underlying foreign policy, all linked together. It is during this period of the Cold War that one can see the three organizing principles described earlier — geopolitical determinism, free-market economics, and political liberalism — coming together in U.S. foreign policy and reflected in raw materials strategy.

THE POLICY TRINITY AND ITS IMPLEMENTATION

Geopolitical Determinism and Raw Materials

U.S. geopolitical thought had its roots in the naval theories of Alfred Thayer Mahan (1893; 1895), but geopolitical determinism did not truly gain influence until World War II (Parker 1985: ch. 7). By the time George Kennan sent his famous telegram from Moscow to the

State Department in 1946, proposing a strategy of containment of the Soviet Union, geopolitical determinism had become firmly embedded in U.S. policymaking (see also FRUS 1950b; Gaddis 1982: ch. 2; Parker 1985: ch. 8).

Geopolitical determinism was more than just a tool of strategy, however. It also accounted for the sources of national power, explained how states expanded, and why political and military crises took place. Thus, in a 1951 meeting with a group of Congressmen, General Eisenhower could assert that France's efforts to defeat the Vietminh in Indochina were critical because of the colony's location "on the Southeast Asian sea routes and also at the crossroads of the paths that lead into India" (quoted in Cook 1981:108; see also Eisenhower to Winston Churchill on this in PRO 1954a). A French withdrawal was unthinkable, for if it occurred (quoted in Cook 1981:108), "[The Communists] would be pushing in through Burma — already a hotbed of unrest and trouble — pushing on down to rubber, tin, tungsten, the Sumatra oil. Then you begin to see a picture that is terrible."

The U.S. military's view of the world was predicated on a geopolitical framework within which strategic raw materials played a vital role. Within the confines of military planning, the long-term objectives of the enemy could only be two: the capture of militarily important pieces of property or the acquisition of vital raw materials needed to conduct war.

As a consequence of this geopolitically determinist view, virtually every strategic planning document produced by the U.S. National Security Council, the State Department, or the various offices of the Defense Department included a standard piece of boilerplate, inserted to outline the geopolitical consequences for U.S. security were a particular bit of territory to fall into the hands of the enemy. For example, NSC 84, "The Position of the United States with Respect to the Philippines" (HSTL 1950a:2–3), warned that

> From the viewpoint of the USSR, the Philippine Islands could be the key to Soviet control of the Far East inasmuch as Soviet domination of these islands would, in all probability, be followed by the rapid disintegration of the entire structure of anti-Communist defenses in Southeast Asia and their offshore island chain, including Japan. Therefore, the situation in the Philippines cannot be viewed as a local problem, since Soviet domination over these islands would endanger the United States military position in the Western Pacific and the Far East.

Or consider a 1950 State Department assessment (FRUS 1950c:1589), according to which:

> "Black" Africa is important for the supply of strategic materials that may have to be obtained there in the event of war or where other sources of supply are denied to us. These strategic materials must not only be made available to the United States but must be denied the enemy. Thus the strategic value of Africa is increasing. In the event of war, an air route across Central Africa to the Middle and Far East would become very important as an alternative for the North African route. In addition our Navy would no doubt require bases and/or ship repair and supply facilities [throughout Africa].

Military planning, therefore, came to rest on two objectives: preventing the loss of vital territories, including those with strategic raw materials, to the enemy, and developing the mobilization base for fighting a war, should that become necessary. But these two objectives were not the responsibility of the same agencies within the government. War plans were developed by the military; defense mobilization by various civilian agencies. The key question was to determine which areas could realistically be kept within the Western defensive perimeter during peace and in the event of war.

This problem was particularly acute with respect to the oil of the Middle East. Much has been written in recent years about military strategy and the long-term U.S. commitment to the Middle East and Persian Gulf (see, for example, Kuniholm 1980; Painter 1986; Epstein 1987), but it is important to note that for decisionmakers the geopolitical significance of the region has almost *always* outweighed the importance of the oil.[2]

The geopolitical centrality of the Middle East dated back to the nineteenth century and the "Great Game" played by the British and Russian Empires with respect to British trade and communication links to India (Abadi 1982:xiv). Oil became a concern only during the

---

[2]As the head of the Near East Branch of the U.S. Office of Strategic Services during World War II wrote in 1947 (Speiser 1947:165, quoted in Rubin 1980:131–32):

> It is idle to speculate, as is often done, which . . . element in the region's renewed prominence is the most important: location, communications or oil? Is the United States interested in the oil alone while Russia wants oil plus warm-water ports, and Britain all three of these factors and such added political and economic advantages as might be included? The fact is that none of these precious articles is stored in a separate locker, each by itself; they are all interlocked. They cannot be readily sundered (for a similar argument, see also p. 162, below).

first decades of the twentieth century as the British navy converted its warships from coal. Middle Eastern oil became a focus of commercial competition in the 1920s and again in the late 1940s (World War II was fought largely on the basis of oil from the Western Hemisphere; see Painter 1986:19, 96). But it was only with the onset of the Cold War, in 1946 and 1947, and the initial implementation of containment in the "Northern Tier," that the Middle East came to assume an extraordinary strategic significance in the minds of U.S. policymakers (although the area had never lost its significance for the British) (Kuniholm 1980; Louis 1984; Painter 1986).

The presence of oil served mainly to focus attention on the region, magnify its importance, and provide a material basis for intervention. Even so, the United States showed a surprising reluctance to commit military forces to defense of the region, preferring to leave this responsibility to the British (PRO 1950a; NARS 1952a). The U.S. Navy did not officially consider the Middle East to be critical to the conduct of a war until 1950 (PRO 1950b). Furthermore, the relative importance of the strategic resources of the Gulf was belied to some degree by Anglo-U.S. plans to destroy and abandon the oilfields in the event of war rather than let them fall into Soviet hands (see pp. 107–109, below).

The problem of defense mobilization was also clearly linked to the access/denial question in that, unless the United States were to become entirely self-sufficient with respect to raw materials, wartime access to secure sources would be required. In September 1948, the chairman of the Munitions Board, T.J. Hargrave, lobbied President Truman for increased stockpile appropriations for this purpose. He wrote (HSTL 1948b:2) that

> A further reason for expediting the [stockpile] program now is that if a national emergency should occur, we would avoid the necessity of protecting certain sea lanes, the loss of material and shipping, and the possible occupation by military force of some of the sources of these materials. The savings in cost, in lives, and of the diversion of effort would alone justify the increased appropriations at this time.

Although the logic of the argument was sound, it seemed to contradict one of the underlying rationales of the Truman Doctrine. In addition, Hargrave's perspective was, perhaps, too isolationist, for it implied a substantial retreat from forward positions around the world. But his argument did point out the difficulties of maintaining such extended positions in the event of war.

The strategic problem never, it seems in retrospect, really improved. Two or three years later, according to Horst Mendershausen, an analyst working for the Paley Commission, even the Joint Chiefs of Staff were not sanguine about the prospects of retaining seemingly vital areas if war should break out (HSTL 1952a:50, emphasis in original):

> In May, 1950, JCS considered *militarily inaccessible*: Turkey, Iran, Afghanistan, Burma, Thailand, Malaya (excluding the Singapore neighborhood), Indo-China, Hong-Kong, and Korea, at the beginning and during the war; and all of the continental Western Europe and the rest of the Middle and Near East during the war. (China was not mentioned in that statement.) In September, 1950, JCS notified MB [Munitions Board] of the inaccessability [sic] of China, and in February, 1951 JCS shifted Spain and Portugal into the accessible column and called parts of North Africa "partly accessible." Most of Europe and the Middle East are still considered military inaccessible in wartime.

Thus, for planning purposes, much of the Eastern Hemisphere was immediately written off. This sharpened the need for stockpiles as well as access to resources in Latin America and southern Africa. The actual requirements for defense mobilization rested on assumptions concerning the duration of a war. Between 1947 and 1960, this period was decreased from five to three years, as the recognition that a nuclear war was unlikely to last very long began to penetrate the minds of decisionmakers and military planners. Once this new fact of life was acknowledged, the problem became one of how to get rid of stockpile excesses without disrupting world markets or destabilizing friendly governments.

Oil and the Middle East. How critical was Middle East oil to the military security of the West during the Cold War? Undeniably, the oil first became important to Europe during reconstruction in the late 1940s (although even then there were warnings against undue reliance on Middle East oil; see U.S. DOI 1947:82), and it came to represent a real strategic concern after the mid-1950s. But U.S. military planners were always faced with a dilemma in assessing the strategic importance of the oil: Increased consumption of Middle Eastern oil would lead to a condition of strategic vulnerability, while exploitation of Western Hemisphere oil meant depleting strategically secure supplies. Following the end of World War II, there was a very real concern that the United States might (once again) be running out of oil and this, among other things, motivated the development of Persian Gulf sources (Painter 1986:97–99).

At the same time, the adequacy of U.S. supplies was not seen as a constraint on European recovery (U.S. DOI 1947:47, 81–82; President's Commission on Foreign Aid 1947:191–97).[3] It was the conservation of Western Hemisphere supplies that impelled the Joint Chiefs of Staff to view the security of the ARAMCO (Arabian-American Oil Company) concession in Saudi Arabia as critical to U.S. security, not a recognition that Persian Gulf oil was essential to the conduct of a world war (HSTL 1949a:9; NARS 1950a:2–3; Etzold and Gaddis 1978:315–23). In any event, by the end of the 1940s a condition of somewhat tight markets had turned into a glut, and efforts were being made to restrict imports of cheap foreign supplies (Painter 1986:100).

Notwithstanding the state of the oil market at any given time, some U.S. policymakers took the view that it would be better to destroy the Persian Gulf oil fields than to let them fall into Soviet hands, a view held in spite of a 1948 CIA report (HSTL 1948c:5), that concluded that "the occupation of Continental Europe and the Near East, in fact, would not yield immediate economic support to the Soviet Union for a much greater military effort than the Soviets alone could mount at the present time." Nonetheless, beginning in late 1947 or early 1948, the subcommittee on the Middle East of the State-Army-Navy-Air Force Coordinating Committee (SANACC), a planning body whose functions were eventually subsumed by the National Security Council, began to formulate SANACC 398/4, a plan called "Preparation for Demolition of Oil Facilities in the Middle East" (NARS 1948a).[4]

---

[3] As both the Interior Department and the President's Commission on Foreign Aid observed, somewhat paradoxically (U.S. DOI 1947:81; President's Commission on Foreign Aid 1947:191),

Our exports of petroleum and its products to Europe cannot be considered to constitute a drain on our natural resources, because we are producing all the petroleum we can efficiently with our present equipment and reserves, and would not produce less even if we should export less.

[4] SANACC 398/4 is interesting for another reason, as well. It and its successive revisions (NSC 26, NSC 176/5401, NSC 5714) are one of two NSC policy series documents considered so sensitive that their titles remained classified as of 1986 (Tilly 1986). According to a list of Eisenhower administration NSC documents in the Kennedy Presidential Library, NSC 5714

The program developed by the SANACC subcommittee was necessitated by the desire of the U.S. Joint Chiefs to ensure the destruction of the oil facilities in the event of war. They reasoned that "the allies cannot expect to hold the Middle East oil fields against a determined attack by the USSR" (NARS 1948a:21). They may have been influenced in this view by Dutch efforts to destroy oil wells in the Netherland East Indies in 1942 (Anderson 1975:119; Turner 1983:34), as well as the unsuccessful British attempt to accomplish the same in Rumania early in World War II (PRO 1946a:14, 17). The subcommittee therefore took on the task (NARS 1948a:21, emphasis in original)

> To determine the officials who should be empowered to issue, and who should be responsible for the issuance of, the necessary orders for:
>
> (a) The timely and proper abandonment of oil producing wells in the Middle East, and
> (b) The destruction of refining, loading, and transportation facilities in the Middle East by demolition;
>
> and further to determine the circumstances under which the programs in *a* and *b* should be implemented.

The plans for abandonment would be developed in cooperation with the British and would include the oil fields of eastern Saudi Arabia, Bahrein, Iran, Kuwait, and Kirkuk (NARS 1948a:22; HSTL 1949a; Etzold and Gaddis 1978:321).

The subcommittee recognized that abandonment could not occur overnight and that (NARS 1948a: 22)

> A 30–60 day period will be required to abandon properly the oil wells. With properly trained and directed crews and the necessary materials, a few hours would be required effectively to destroy the refining, loading and transportation facilities of the oil fields by demolition.

The authors of the document acknowledged that "Such plugging might create the impression that the West intends to abandon the Middle East" (NARS 1948a:24) but concluded that if war seemed imminent the National Security Council should assume the responsibility of deciding whether to go through with the plan (NARS 1948a:25).

---

continued to remain in force until at least August 1962, although by then it had been given the more prosaic title "Protection and Conservation of Middle East Oil Resources and Facilities" (JFKL 1962a).

The authors also recognized the extreme sensitivity of the program and the need to keep it secret (NARS 1948a:25–26):

> The responsibilities of implementing this demolition program are so great that an officer of the armed services with suitable background and technical experience should be stationed in Saudi Arabia. He should be both authorized and required to implement the demolition program . . . . In order to prevent speculation, he should also be assigned other duties which will furnish a logical pretext for his presence in the area.

Not even the Saudis were to be made aware of the program, except at the "discretion of the Secretary of State" (NARS 1948a:27).

SANACC 398/4 was, according to declassified records, first discussed by the National Security Council on June 4, 1948. At that meeting, the political implications of an abandonment program were raised by Undersecretary of State Robert Lovett (subsequently appointed Secretary of Defense), who was concerned that "first, the slightest implication that we propose to withdraw from this area would throw out seven years of work and, second, that it might indicate a change in policy" (HSTL 1948d).[5] Nonetheless, on January 1, 1949, the NSC adopted the document without change, as NSC 26/2 (HSTL 1949b), and Truman approved it three days later (HSTL ND).

NSC 26 continued to undergo review and revision throughout the remainder of Truman's presidency (HSTL 1950b). In 1951 formal responsibility for the implementation of NSC 26 was shifted to the CIA (HSTL 1951f, 1951g). During the Eisenhower administration, oversight for the program was assigned to the Operations Coordinating Board of the NSC, although operational responsibility remained with the CIA (DDEL 1953b). A memo for the Secretary of Defense from the Joint Chiefs of Staff, to be used by Eisenhower in a 1958 meeting with the Shah of Iran, noted that, if the continued availability of Middle East oil in a general war could not be ensured, U.S. policy would be "to deny [those resources] . . . to the enemy" (DDEL 1958b:1). This would be accomplished, presumably, with the help of the eight Special Forces Teams assumed to be placed in the Middle East prior to "D-Day" (DDEL 1958b:3) (on the feasibility of a nuclear defense of Iran, see Epstein 1987: ch. 2,3).

---

[5]Although given the extreme secrecy of the plan, who was to know enough to draw this conclusion?

But the general U.S. attitude about the importance of Middle East oil changed under Eisenhower. Whereas the Truman Administration tended to view the problem in strategic terms, the Eisenhower Administration adopted a perspective more rooted in economic concerns, thereby discounting somewhat the military significance of the oil. A draft of a 1955 Cabinet Committee report on "Energy Supplies and Resources Policy," drawn up by representatives of the Office of Defense Mobilization and the Departments of State, Treasury, Defense, Justice, Interior, Commerce, and Labor (DDEL 1955a:2) stated that

> The Task Force, after consideration, reached the conclusion that over-all energy supplies, assuming adequate incentives to development and a healthy economic climate generally, will be adequate, not only for economic growth, but also for at least the first year or two of full mobilization, should that become necessary any time during the next ten years.

Although this paragraph was omitted from the final version of the report, the implication remained that Middle East oil could be sacrificed at the start of a war, should such a drastic step appear necessary.

When oil supplies to Europe were cut off during the Suez Crisis, their replacement by Western Hemisphere oil only served to underline the availability of alternative supplies in the event of an emergency. In the late 1950s and early 1960s, in any case, the issue was cost, and not security of supply. As the president of Standard Oil-New Jersey emphasized in a 1959 speech on "Middle East Nationalism", "The accumulation of experience should in time make Arab nationalists realize that — vital though it is — the oil of the Middle East is not indispensible, nor does it have an inherent priority status" (Rathbone 1959:7). This attitude had official status, as well. In a Briefing Note for a National Security Council meeting in 1960 set to discuss NSC 5820/1, "US Policy Toward the Near East" (DDEL 1960a:2), the author wrote that the revised document was

> [M]ore realistic in that it continued to place denial of the area to Soviet domination as of paramount importance, while downgrading somewhat the relative importance of Near Eastern oil and removing the implication that the U.S. acting alone would be prepared to use force to maintain Western access to it.

Although parallels with the present situation should not be drawn too strongly, the implications of this historical recitation are clear. As early as the late 1940s, the dilemma facing U.S. policymakers was that although Middle East oil was essential to economic prosperity it was less critical to a military strategy that had to assume the nonavailability of the oil in time of war. Throughout the following decades, and into the 1970s, this continued to remain true. Even Harold Brown, President Carter's Secretary of Defense, seemed to acknowledge this point in 1979 when he explained that it was the United States' reliance on foreign trade, and not any credible military threat to material resources, that necessitated the establishment of a Rapid Deployment Force (RDF; later renamed the "Central Command) (Halloran 1980). Indeed, part of the stated rationale for the RDF was that it was needed to protect sources of U.S. raw materials from any threat, internal or external to the producing state (U.S. CBO 1983b:4).

Internal instability in foreign states is not easily controlled or dealt with, as recent experience in the Middle East has demonstrated. External threats present even greater problems. Whether the Joint Chiefs of Staff, in their secret planning, hold the view that Persian Gulf oil is or is not essential to the conduct of a conventional war in the Middle East is unclear, but the Carter Doctrine—the promise to intervene by any means, including with nuclear force, to protect Persian Gulf oil—is, in a sense, an empty threat.[6] It disregards the difficulties of maintaining the flow of oil by military means and it relies primarily on nuclear weaponry to deter "outside forces" from trying to gain control of the Persian Gulf (Holdren 1986; but see also Epstein 1987, who argues that conventional forces could be effective in defending Iran from the Soviets). In the event of a Soviet thrust into Iran (whatever the motive), even against opposition from both local forces and the U.S. Central Command, the United States might very well have to sacrifice the Persian Gulf oil fields rather than see them fall under the enemy's control. This illuminates the dilemma associated with declaring vital an interest that might be gotten along without and is almost impossible to protect.

Defense Mobilization. Even as one leg of geopolitical strategy rested on denying to the Soviets access to certain critical parts of the world,

---

[6]Current U.S. Navy analysis "shows the straits [of Hormuz] could be closed for about 2 months without . . . impacting . . . warfighting capability." (Brooks 1986:68). If this length of time refers to a general war, it seems an optimistic assessment of the duration of conflict. If it means a local war, sufficient oil supplies should be available from other sources outside of the Gulf.

or at least depriving them of the use of strategic resources, another leg was based on the continued control or availability of territory and resources in other parts of the world (see, for example, NARS 1953a). Until late 1949, defense mobilization was not a pressing issue, and U.S. possession of the atomic bomb was thought sufficient to protect Western Europe and the Middle East from the Soviets (Rosenberg 1979; Gaddis 1982: ch. 3). Hence, there was little need to undertake the exercise of determining which parts of the world would remain strategically secure in the event of war. Certain regions were considered vital for economic reasons, but their loss in the event of war was seen as a virtual certainty. The start of the Korean War in June 1950 rapidly changed mobilization and planning assumptions for three reasons.

First, the outbreak of hostilities was widely seen as a prelude to general conflict in Asia and elsewhere (FRUS 1951a; Wells 1981:40; Gaddis 1982:109–10), and this meant that some parts of the world would, in fact, no longer be accessible. Second, and of greater importance, the rearmament program that followed the onset of war placed enormous demands on the materials supply system, creating spot shortages that were thought by some to be related to political events at large (Hamilton 1963: ch. 8). Finally, prior to 1950, the outbreak of general war with the Soviet Union was considered likely, albeit at some indefinite point in the future. The Soviet atomic bomb quickly changed this calculus, and defense mobilization planning was thereafter predicated on the notion of a "D-Date" — the time at which the Soviets would have sufficient atomic weapons and delivery capabilities to launch a devastating attack against the United States (DDEL 1953c). Cold War mobilization thus required that the United States be able to respond rapidly in the event of such an attack (DDEL 1954a).

The conceptual shift wrought by the Soviet bomb can be seen in an assessment by W. Stuart Symington, who, at different times during the Truman Administration, filled the posts of Secretary of the Air Force, head of the Reconstruction Finance Corporation, and chairman of the National Security Resources Board (NSRB). In a memo to President Truman (Symington 1951:1–2), he wrote,

> In the past, there had been time to arm, and there had been a wealth of manpower and materials. Accordingly, it had been safe for the United States to neglect its military posture until war appeared probable. Mobilization could then be accomplished fairly rapidly, but with enormous waste in both men and materials. . . .

The lessons of World War II, along with subsequent very rapid technical progress in this atomic age, showed all too clearly that there was for the future no sanctuary in the nation's boundaries against the sudden attack of a possible enemy. . . . It also became clear that the United States could no longer afford the luxury of taking years to rearm. The boundaries of our nation had become comparable to the boundaries of European states, in effect, arbitrary lines drawn on a map. Any future defense structure, therefore, had to be created and had to function with this fundamental difference constantly in mind.

The actual shift to a partially mobilized base created enormous problems for military planners. Whereas it was relatively easy to plan for the loss or denial of territory or resources, it was much more difficult to predict or ensure their availability. Discounting particular parts of the world as potential sources of raw materials in wartime carried the implication of their being "lost" even before the start of conflict. Brave words about global responsibilities and missions could not hide this fact, as even the Joint Chiefs were occasionally forced to admit (NARS 1950b).

Assumptions about the length of a general war also influenced planning. Based on prior experience, the Truman administration thought five years the most probable length of a future war. As it became clear that long conventional wars were not likely to become global, and nuclear wars would not last very long, the planning assumption was reduced to three years (DDEL 1958c). Some individuals thought that even this was too long, as Eisenhower complained in a 1956 entry in his diary (DDEL 1956b).

Although defense mobilization in the 1950s consumed vast amounts of resources and personnel in a variety of programs and tasks, two stand out because of their relationship to strategic raw materials and foreign policy: (1) the strategic stockpile and (2) NSC 29, the program on the "Security of Strategically Important Industrial Operations in Foreign Countries" (HSTL 1952b). Neither of these programs was, strictly speaking, a military one, but both were considered essential parts of the defense program. In implementation, moreover, both highlighted the inherent contradictions between material and ideal interests.

During the 1945–46 debate over funding for a strategic stockpile, the Army-Navy Munitions Board and the Interior Department, in cooperation with domestic mining interests, lobbied Congress to continue wartime subsidies to U.S. producers of certain minerals, arguing that this was necessary to preserve domestic production capacity. Most of the minerals of concern were available more cheaply from foreign sources. The State Department generally favored low-cost imports for reasons of political and economic policy (Pollard 1985:200). In the event, Congress included a "buy American" provision in S.752, the Stockpile Act, that required purchases to be made from domestic sources whenever possible. Truman reluctantly signed the bill in the interests of getting stockpiling legislation (HSTL 1946a), but even with this provision, many materials could not be obtained domestically and had to come from abroad. The problem was, of course, that flows from foreign sources might be disrupted in the event of a crisis.

A good example of this difficulty was provided by the Soviet embargo of shipments of manganese and chromium (very little of which were produced domestically) to the United States. In December 1947 and January 1948, the U.S. Commerce Department proposed broad controls on the export of strategic items to the Soviet Bloc (Jentleson 1986:54–56). These rules went into force in March 1948. Because the Soviet Union was then supplying 22 percent of the manganese and 45 percent of the chromite ore consumed in the United States, various agencies and individuals were sensitive to the possibility that the Soviets might retaliate with their own embargo on strategic items (HSTL 1948e; NARS 1948b). As a consequence (NARS 1949a:1, emphasis in original),

> It was generally agreed [by the agencies involved] that items of the highest strategic character should be denied the U.S.S.R. Orbit, but that important items should continue to be cleared as a form of unspoken *quid pro quo* to guard against a reprisal embargo on manganese.

In the event, the Soviets did reduce shipments of manganese to the United States but did not halt them completely until December 1948. By then, the United States had begun to look for alternative supplies from Brazil, India, and the Gold Coast (NARS 1949a:2) and was able to replace the embargoed Soviet shipments.

Ultimately, planning for stockpile objectives and the implementation of defense mobilization became intimately tied up with three, somewhat contradictory, efforts: (1) assessing the reliability of foreign sources, (2) balancing the requirements of both programs, without unduly affecting markets or the civilian economy, and (3) preparing for the next war. The first two efforts were complicated by the fact that the war plans of the Joint Chiefs of Staff were, from the mobilization point of view, considered impossible to support. In a May 1950 memo to Symington, an NSRB staffer complained about the difficulties of mobilizing for the Joint Chiefs' two then-current war plans. One, called "OFF-TACKLE," was an emergency plan for immediate war. The other, "STRAIGHT-EDGE," was a three-year plan for a so-called "shooting war (NARS 1950c):

> STRAIGHT-EDGE is dated January 20, 1950, and is a revision of JCS 1752/22, produced by JCS in 1948. The latter, 1752/22, was a three-year plan which was rejected by the Munitions Board in June 1949 as not feasible. In general its requirements were almost double the capacity of the national economy to meet them.

When war did come in Korea, it was not the one envisioned by the Chiefs, and mobilization proceeded on a largely ad-hoc basis (Yoshpe 1953:103–04; Vawter 1983).

The Korean War did, however, generate broad support for the development of industrial mobilization capabilities that, it was thought, would be required in a general conflict with the Soviet Union. The war highlighted, once again, what were thought to be serious U.S. vulnerabilities in the raw materials area. As a result, new life was breathed into the strategic stockpile. In 1951, the Defense Department and Office of Defense Mobilization advocated self-sufficiency in strategic and critical materials in order to be able to prosecute a five-year war and asserted (FRUS 1951b:208) that

> The stockpile of strategic and critical materials is a national stockpile, not just a military stockpile. It is a blood bank of materials to be called upon in a time of national emergency when the supplies of those critical materials may be cut off at the very moment when we need them most.

Sinister forces were thought to be behind the Korean War and the developing conflict in Indochina, forces not unlike those that supposedly goaded the Japanese into World War II. In briefing notes prepared for Truman's January 1952 meeting with Prime Minister Churchill, the president was advised to say (only if the point were raised by the prime minister) (HSTL 1952c) that

> In my opinion, it is essential that we prevent by all practicable means the expansion of the Communists into any part of Southeast Asia. The fall of

Indochina would immediately weaken the position of Burma, Thailand and Malaya. Communist control of these areas would mean not only the loss to us of 70% of the world's natural rubber and 50% of the world's tin, but also it would mean turning these valuable resources over to the Soviet Union.

Eisenhower held similar views on the threat to the region (PRO 1954a; Cook 1981:108).

It is true that some materials, such as tungsten, were in very short supply for a time during the Korean War. These shortages came about mostly as a result of increased demand. But part of the reason for the tungsten shortage lay in a reduction of imports from China, which, historically, had been a major supplier of the metal to the United States. Korea had not been an important exporter of tungsten to the United States, although as a result of the war, by 1952 South Korea had become the largest single source, replacing mainland China (U.S. BOM 1952).

Mainland China would have been, it seems, only too willing to continue shipments of tungsten to the West, were it not for the latter's efforts to impose sanctions against the former. Toward the end of November 1950, Secretary of State Acheson told Secretary of Commerce Sawyer that the United States should halt virtually all shipments of goods to the People's Republic of China, beyond those listed in the U.S. export control lists, in order to punish the Chinese. In their conversation (HSTL 1950c),

> Secretary Sawyer said that actually very little of importance had been going to China, while we had been getting important amounts of tungsten from them, and were getting some wool and tin. 85% of our shipments to China in the last six months had been cotton; nothing of any military importance had been shipped . . . .
> Mr. Acheson suggested that the matter should be talked over with Mr. Symington, since tungsten was involved. Secretary Sawyer did not seem to think that this was necessary, and he said he thought that the Chinese would continue to ship tungsten, since they have been shipping it to us, even after we had drastically cut down on shipments to China.

In the final analysis, it is difficult to find evidence that U.S. policy in eastern Asia during the Cold War was driven explicitly by the need for strategic raw materials, although this has been implied by some

(Cumings 1987–88), particularly with respect to the conflict in Vietnam (see the skeptical comments on this in Barnet 1972:159–60; see also PRO 1952b for British reports on U.S. preclusive buying of tungsten in Korea).

Rational planning for defense mobilization depended, as noted earlier, on what materials were available and from what sources. Throughout the late 1940s, efforts were made to determine which countries should have priority for receiving military aid from the United States. In SANACC 360/11, "Military Aid Priorities," the SANACC Subcommittee for Rearmament attempted such an exercise. "Stripped of its essentials," the Subcommittee tried to answer the question (FRUS 1949b:264, emphasis in original):

> To what country or combination of countries, and in what priority, should United States military aid be accorded to enable them to further the security interests of the United States by military, political, or economic action.

On the basis of combined military and political factors, Europe and the Near and Middle East received highest priority, followed by countries in the Far East and Western Hemisphere, with southern Africa given the lowest priority. The reasoning behind this ranking seems to have been largely strategic; there is no indication in the document that sources of essential raw materials were given major consideration in the exercise (FRUS 1949b:262–63).

In 1947, the Munitions Board asked the Joint Chiefs to define those areas that would still be accessible in time of war. The Joint Chiefs, in turn, assigned this task to the Joint Strategic Survey Committee, which wrote off major portions of the world (JCS 626/3 in Etzold and Gaddis 1978:311–13). These findings were, in turn, used by the NSRB to see whether existing war plans were feasible under then-current strategic assumptions. The NSRB found a number of bottlenecks, having mostly to do with the production of materials such as copper and aluminum, but was unable to resolve the problem prior to the outbreak of the Korean War, when it was forced to turn to short-term planning (HSTL 1951h:1–2).

Because it was not obvious what sources of raw materials would remain accessible during a general war, in 1948 the National Security Council initiated NSC 29, "Security of Strategically Important Industrial Operations in Foreign Countries" (HSTL 1952b), perhaps in response to a Central Intelligence Agency study of the "Vulnerability to Sabotage of Petroleum Installations in Venezuela, Aruba, and Curaçao" (ORE 31–48). The latter study warned (HSTL 1948f:1) that

> Oil wells in Venezuela and refineries on the adjacent Netherlands West Indies islands of Aruba and Curaçao offer one of the most remunerative targets for industrial sabotage of the Western Hemisphere. . . . Political conditions are generally favorable in both areas, but both areas have particular points of vulnerability to sabotage, especially by trained agents.

NSC 29 and its successor (NSC 163) were programs for assuring that particular installations would remain in operation at all times (NARS 1953a:1):

> The security of strategically important industrial operations in foreign countries is important to the national security of the United States. U.S. efforts aimed at maintaining, and where feasible, improving, the security of its most important and vulnerable foreign sources of supply, should be continued.

These installations included cobalt mines in the Belgian Congo, nickel mines in Canada and Cuba, bauxite mines in Surinam and Trinidad, copper mines in Chile, and petroleum sources in Curaçao, Venezuela, Aruba, and Indonesia (NARS 1953a:3–5). The United States also made major investments in a number of industrial operations judged essential to national security (HSTL 1952b:1–2; FRUS 1952–54a). Furthermore, the CIA was directed to conduct, when requested, "intelligence appraisals of the nature and extent of the threat of sabotage to the security of each of the listed facilities; and, in exceptional circumstances . . . [to] conduct covert surveillance of such facilities" (NARS 1953a).

The efforts of the Truman administration to establish a basis for defense mobilization were not followed as enthusiastically by the Eisenhower administration. Although Eisenhower held very strong opinions regarding geopolitical strategy and the role of raw materials in world politics, his views seem to have been rooted more in political and economic considerations than strictly military ones (a bit ironic, perhaps, considering his military background; see, for example, DDEL 1951a, 1951b; Cook 1981:91). He favored the maintenance of a strategic stockpile as a hedge against uncertainty, but he also believed that the type of partial mobilization favored by the Truman administration was too expensive to continue (hence, the "New Look"; see Gaddis 1982: ch. 5, 6). He also thought that the "defense" of the Free World was more dependent on the present peace than on a future war. In his statement to the Cabinet on the FY1954 budget, delivered in April 1953 (DDEL 1953c:5), he explained that

> The new policy drops emphasis on getting ready for a global aggresion [sic] by some specified D-date. Implicit in that concept are very heavy expenditures until that specified D-date. Then, if war does not come at the time toward which all the expenditures have been made, what course of action should thereafter be followed. To continue the build up will involve unnecessary expenditure. Suddenly to cease the build up may bring on a major economic recession and begin a military deterioration. . . .
> Instead, this policy is premised on the concept of a "floating D-day" — a maintenance of forces and materiel that can be paid for without breaking our backs and that can be lived with over the years ahead.

Notwithstanding his concern about "busting" the budget, Eisenhower's apparently high level of economic consciousness did not extend to putting limits on the growth of the strategic stockpile. He liked particularly the notion of stockpiles and always advocated their maintenance and further buildup. In 1953, based on the advice of the Joint Chiefs of Staff (DDEL 1954b:60–61), a Cabinet Stockpiling Subcommittee recommended that "the United States discount by 100 per cent all foreign sources of supply during wartime and that present stockpile goals be increased to compensate for that amount" (DDEL 1954c). In a Cabinet discussion of this idea (DDEL 1954d:3),

> The President expressed his gratification at such a method which would avoid last minute and ineffective actions. He added that in any event critical shipping facilities should not have to be utilized in wartime for transporting materials which could be stockpiled in advance.

The president defended stockpiling as a "capital investment rather than an outright expenditure" (DDEL 1954c), in the face of dissension from Secretaries Humphrey and Wilson, respectively of Treasury and Defense, who believed that stockpile objectives ought to be reduced. Humphrey thought "the policy of strengthening America by stockpile operations [was] . . . in the long term, a very bad one" (DDEL 1954e).

Sentiment in the Congress and the Cabinet nonetheless came down in favor of stockpiling.

In 1956 the Cabinet discussed reducing from five years to three the planning assumption regarding the length of a future war. This, in turn, would imply a downward revision of stockpile objectives (DDEL 1956c). Eisenhower strenuously opposed such a change. He felt that a stockpile would provide the basis for industrial reconstruction in the aftermath of a thermonuclear war (DDEL 1957a). As he continued to argue throughout his term of office (DDEL 1959a:5),

> [T]hings like copper were much more desirable to hold on to even than the gold that is buried at Fort Knox. . . . [T]he supplies of these things were necessarily limited and eventually the day would come when these things would be very much needed. . . . [Nonperishable materials] . . . could be considered as money in the bank.

In the end, the president's view prevailed, and the United States was left with large surpluses of strategic materials, some of which were useless for industrial purposes (Huddle 1976:656). But that was an economic problem left to later administrations to resolve (JFKL 1961a; Huddle 1976:656).

Generally speaking, the twin problems of denial and access were ones that could never be resolved entirely, except in the event of an actual war. Two geopolitical strategies were possible, and both were pursued. One strategy sought to assess which parts of the world might remain accessible in the event of war; the other simply wrote off foreign sources of raw materials. One was based on dependence (albeit a limited form); the other on autarky.[7] The indeterminate nature of the Cold War meant that military planners could never be quite sure for what contingencies they were planning. Efforts to create a base for defense mobilization in anticipation of a future war created bottlenecks in industry and competition for supplies of foreign materials and goods, and threatened to bust the budget. Self-sufficiency and the "New Look" were much more appealing in that they made defense less beholden to the domestic and international economies. But the ideal goal of self-sufficiency in military matters continued to run up against material realities. As shall be shown, this basic contradiction manifested itself in the political and economic spheres, too.

---

[7]These two strategies were roughly parallel to although hardly identical with the internationalist and isolationist strains in U.S. politics (see U.S. Senate 1954; NARS 1954a; U.S. Senate 1959).

Politics and Raw Materials

When U.S. policymakers surveyed the world scene after 1945, they found disorder everywhere. The chaotic state of the world was ascribable, in part, to the destruction wrought by the war. It was also a consequence of the disintegration and collapse of the old world order controlled by numerous Great Powers, each with its own colonial empire. That order was being replaced by a new one, based on self-determination and national sovereignty. In 1948, the CIA observed (HSTL 1948a) that

> The growth of nationalism in colonial areas, which has already succeeded in breaking up a large part of the European colonial systems and in creating a series of new, nationalistic states in the Near and Far East, has major implications for US security, particularly in terms of possible world conflict with the USSR. This shift of the dependent areas from the orbit of the colonial powers not only weakens the probable European allies of the US but deprives the US itself of assured access to vital bases and raw materials in these areas in the event of war.

Throughout the 1940s and 1950s, and well into the following decade, U.S. policymakers found themselves in a bind with respect to decolonization. On the one hand, it was the policy of the United States to encourage the breakup of the colonial empires and the establishment of independent states. On the other hand, the United States opposed the kinds of radical nationalist movements that invariably developed in reaction to old colonial mores. Often as not, nationalism was linked in the minds of U.S. policymakers to Communism as well as geopolitical threats to national security. The U.S. solution to the problem posed by radical nationalism was to encourage in newly independent states the kind of centrist, politically liberal system found in the United States (on this, see, for example, Packenham 1973; Lipschutz 1986a). States with such political arrangements, it was believed, were much more likely than radical ones to ally with the West. They would become dependent, as well, on U.S. largesse for their security. In this schema, therefore, raw material flows, U.S. foreign investment, and economic warfare became important elements in the effort to sell political liberalism.[8]

[8]This did not mean then, or today, that U.S. policymakers placed the implantation of politically-liberal systems above all other goals. This was an ideal interest that could be sacrificed easily in the name of geopolitical considerations.

Ironically, the United States bore much responsibility for encouraging the sort of nationalist movements that, even today, seem to constantly bedevil U.S. policymakers. In a 1948 NSC memorandum on "French North Africa" (FRUS 1948a:684), this contradiction was already recognized:

> U.S. wartime propaganda was in part responsible for the recent spur to North Africa [sic] nationalism and for the present unrest in the area. The Atlantic Charter declared that the American and British Governments "respect the right of all people to choose the form of government under which they live." Descriptions of the Charter and of the Four Freedoms were extensively spread among the native inhabitants at the time of the Allied landings in order to create a favorable atmosphere for our forces. There is strong evidence that President Roosevelt, during the Casablanca Conference of 1943, personally encouraged the Sultan to hope for American support in throwing off French control and in preparing Morocco, possibly under a joint U.S., British and French protectorate, for independence some years hence.

The recognition that nationalism might represent a force that could not be stopped, and that wartime and other propaganda might have contributed to its spread, did not bring an *understanding* of the process. There was instead a tendency to see nationalism as a phenomenon linked to geopolitics.

For example, in discussing the Anglo-Iranian crisis in 1951 with U.S. Secretary of State Acheson and Paul Nitze of the State Department's Policy Planning Staff, British Ambassador to the United States Sir Oliver Franks suggested that "[T]he U.S.S.R. tactic was to permit nationalism to develop and then to come in behind and capture the nationalism after it had taken over" (HSTL 1951i:2). Continued Sir Oliver (apparently an adherent of the 1919 School of Thought) (HSTL 1951i:4):

> [T]he breakup of the Turkish empire left a power vacuum. This happened so recently in history that the Kipling type of technique was not then appropriate. The influence of the universities has offset the economic benefits which have been brought to the area. The U.S. talks about more and more money which just disappears in the sand. No one has found out how one exercises the necessary degree of control in the power vacuum which exists. The universities are the acid in the situation. These chaps now have ideas. The same problem exists in Cairo.

Franks's assessment of the Iranian situation must have impressed Acheson, for several months later he told Max W. Thornburg, an advisor to the State Department on oil policy (HSTL 1951j:1), that

> [T]he present situation in Iran is probably due to Western ideas which have been started in that country, but which the Iranians are unable for various reasons to carry through. As a result, there are a good many "unemployed intellectuals" who have picked up the theme of nationalization and are pressing it without an adequate understanding of how to bring it about in an orderly manner or how to use it for the real benefit of the country.[9]

Ultimately, all explanations of nationalism were reduced to the lowest common denominator of Communism, and the United States found itself defending the old colonial order. A 1952 State Department memo on "NATO and the Arab World" (NARS 1952b:5) was typical in explaining that

> We cannot turn on a switch and halt the flood of Arab nationalism overnight, particularly as we have allowed it to come so far. But is [sic] must be checked in order that we are not impeded in the super struggle. Our moral support to France and Great Britain would do much to discourage dissidents who now believe the US is on their side. We cannot afford now to replace an established order with the instability of "independence" . . . The Arab must understand that we are faced with a mortal struggle in which we are already giving our blood and resources. In unifying, European nations are in addition giving up a measure of their sovereignty. Arab independence movements cannot take precedence over this effort.

(Many Arabs were not terribly inclined to accept such reasoning; see p. 171, below for one reaction to such "Free World" rhetoric.) It did not, therefore, require a great conceptual leap to equate nationalism with Communism for, as President Eisenhower noted in a 1953 entry in his diary (quoted in Cook 1981:176),

---

[9]Compare this to a British view of Chinese nationalism in 1927 (PRO 1924, quoted in Louis 1971:116 n.14):

> The Chinese student is the result of the zeal of the foreigner for bringing the Chinese up to modern requirements, and I think the very large bulk of the foreigner now regrets his arrival . . . . The student, usually a wretched half-baked creature who argues like a small child without fear of correction, has no solid basis of education to help him. He picks up a smattering of foreign learning, which enables him to pose without difficulty as a superior being among his own people, who therefore fear him, whilst before the foreigner he realises his inferiority, causing him a loss of face and turning him to antiforeign feelings at heart.

Nationalism is on the march and world Communism is taking advantage of that spirit of nationalism to cause dissention [sic] in the free world. Moscow leads many misguided people to believe that they can count on Communist help to achieve and sustain nationalistic ambitions. Actually, what is going on is that the Communists are hoping to take advantage of the confusion resulting from the destruction of existing relationships and in the difficulties and uncertainties of disrupted trade, security and understandings, to further the aims of world revolution and the Kremlin's domination of all people.

Although the connection between the fear of nationalism and concern over strategic materials might not, at first glance, seem obvious, the internal logic was clear to U.S. policymakers. Nonradical, Western-leaning states would do nothing to upset either supply or investment arrangements with the United States. Thus, it was in the U.S. interest to support such governments. Similarly, because of the supposed geopolitical threats posed by radical governments, it was in the interest of the United States to deny support to them. This principle was applied not only in Europe but throughout the world. In one form or another, it underlay the Marshall Plan, Point Four, Mutual Security Assistance, and the various stockpiling programs implemented during the 1950s (Pollard 1985: ch. 9).

Point Four, first announced by Harry S. Truman in his inaugural address in 1949, was intended to provide developing countries with the technical knowledge, management skills, and capital thought necessary for economic development and, hence, political stability. By demonstrating the virtues of capitalism and political stability, it was believed that these states would make firm commitments to political liberalism and would therefore remain firmly in the pro-Western camp (Pollard 1985:205–09; see also Baldwin 1966; Packenham 1973). Point Four never lived up to original expectations, mostly because it was poorly funded and a stepchild among foreign assistance programs. Furthermore, it was such an odd mixture of ideal and material interests that its prospects for success were probably questionable from its inception. For example, according to a 1951 NSC memo (HSTL 1951k:3),

Point IV activities could be expected to aid in exploration of new sources of strategic materials, to strengthen economies of underdeveloped countries important to the United States defense effort, and to elicit cooperation and good will toward the United States from the governments and peoples of such countries.

And (HSTL 1951k:2–3)

> Point IV is not only a significant economic program, but also must be regarded as an important political and psychological measure on the theory that economic progress and better living conditions, as well as the cooperative methods of technical assistance at the "village level" by which these results are sought, will promote political stability and popular morale, create attitudes favorable to the United States and render the people of the underdeveloped countries less susceptible to communist subversion.

But perhaps one should not be misled by the apparent idealism of these paragraphs; real industrialization on the Western pattern was not necessarily an objective of such aid programs. In an early draft of a paper written for the President's Materials Policy Commission, entitled "Security and Political Assumptions," a staffer suggested (HSTL 1951*l*:2) that "By preserving the specialized economies of such areas as Malaya, we may not only aid our own materials position but also reduce the potential value of the areas to the Soviets should they ever seize them."

The Eisenhower administration was, in a way, more direct in its policies toward Third World development and strategic resources. Instead of dressing up aid programs in altruistic language, the Eisenhower approach was to focus directly on the manipulation of raw materials as a means of exerting political influence over developing countries. The rearmament and defense mobilization programs of the Truman administration laid the groundwork for such an approach because they encouraged the expansion of raw material production around the world. In a number of instances, U.S. government purchases of raw materials and commodities became a major source of revenue to producing states. The glutted markets and depressed commodity prices of 1953 and 1954 led to drops in the income of these states, which was seen as a threat to their political stability, insofar as it existed. In a 1953 study prepared for Eisenhower's Commission on Foreign Economic Policy, Raymond Vernon (DDEL 1953d:2) wrote that

> For most countries, access to foreign markets and foreign sources of raw materials are vital aims because the jobs and well-being of their people and the tenure of the political parties in power often depend on the success with which these aims are achieved.

Consequently, although intervention into commodity markets was abhorrent to the free-market ideology of the administration, the quest for political stability sometimes made it more expedient to ignore certain ideals. In 1953, the Eisenhower administration decided to participate in negotiations for an International Tin Agreement, an action that Treasury Secretary Humphrey strongly opposed (as he did all commodity agreements). In explaining the Administration's decision, Secretary of State Dulles wrote to Humphrey (FRUS 1952–54b:1016) that

> [V]iolent commodity price fluctuations which are felt by the underdeveloped areas, and indeed by many of our important allies in Western Europe . . . could not but have the most adverse affect on our foreign relations, especially with Asia and Latin America . . . . [A]n extended period of distressed [tin] prices would be a serious threat to our interest in economic and political stability in Bolivia and strategic areas of Southeast Asia and the Belgian Congo.

Following a tour of South America in the summer of 1953, Dr. Milton Eisenhower, the president's brother, proposed extensive U.S. efforts to improve the standard of living in the region. Among his recommendations was one proposing the purchase of minerals for the strategic stockpile as a means of stabilizing international commodity prices and, hence, supporting the governments of Latin America (Eisenhower 1953; DDEL 1954d:3; Cook 1981:258). But this was too much for some government officials, who felt it would be tantamount to taking long-term responsibility to intervene in commodity markets. One State Department official criticized Eisenhower's proposal (NARS 1953b:1) on the grounds that it would

> [A]cknowledge that we have an obligation to maintain the prices of stockpile commodities whether we need them or not and whether we have had anything to do with stimulating their production in the first place. Worse than that, it would create a perpetual obligation to continue to do so, for foreign producers in the future could argue strongly that they had invested their money on the basis of the United States undertaking to support prices.

The administration remained of two minds on this problem. On the one hand, there was some sentiment to engage in the support of commodity prices, but such a program would require appropriations from Congress for funds with which to purchase the raw materials. On the other hand, this action might undercut domestic producers and create, as well, a constantly growing stockpile of commodities that would have to be stored, maintained, and kept out of markets. At the same time, the United States already had a domestic commodity problem of its own: a surplus of agricultural goods. Although these could be sold to other countries, they generally were paid for in nonconvertible, local currencies and not dollars, which were, in turn, in short supply.

The favored solution to the dilemma was barter trade, which would solve both the domestic and foreign problems simultaneously (or so it was believed). Under the terms of Public Law 85, passed by the Eighty-first Congress in June 1949, the Commodity Credit Corporation was authorized to trade surplus agricultural commodities for foreign raw materials (NARS 1952c:7). In 1954 Congress passed the Agricultural Trade Development and Assistance Act (Public Law 480), which allowed the government to use foreign currencies received from the sale of surplus agricultural goods to purchase strategic materials abroad (DDEL 1955b). In this way, both domestic political and foreign policy needs were met.

The materials acquired by barter were put not only into the strategic stockpile but also into two supplemental stockpiles. By 1956 barter transactions of this type had become the single largest source of strategic materials (Bidwell 1958:44–45), and by the end of the decade huge surpluses of various commodities were in hand (DDEL 1959b:4). The problem then became one of how to dispose of the excesses without disrupting international markets. President Eisenhower, as noted earlier, was always reluctant to get rid of stockpiled commodities, but by 1959 the surplus problem had become acute. When the president visited Chile in 1960, President Alessandri "expressed to him the very great concern over the impact of our [the United States'] copper stockpile on world copper markets" (DDEL 1960b). Although Eisenhower assured him that the United States would never dump the copper, the surpluses continued to hang over commodity markets.

The Kennedy Administration made a greater attempt to balance its material concerns with its idealistic goals, at least where raw materials were concerned. According to a 1961 estimate, there were some $3.5 to $4 billion of excess materials in the three stockpiles (Boutin 1964:42). The Defense Department, under the tutelage of Robert McNamara, was particularly eager to sell off the surpluses. Once again, however, the difficulty of balancing contradictory objectives was discovered. President Kennedy ordered the Office of Emergency Planning (OEP) to conduct two studies, one to determine what should be done with the excess materials, and the other to consider the relationship of the stockpile to broader political and economic goals. Kennedy asked that "[c]onsideration . . . be given to the problems of our domestic minerals industry and to the international consequences of our programs of acquisition and disposal" (quoted in Huddle 1976:656).

Together, the two studies recommended that surpluses be sold off with due consideration of the effects of such sales on markets and the economies of developing countries. They warned, however, that there existed "the possibility that in a mobilization situation short of war, sources of raw materials may be denied to us" (JFKL 1962b:4). The OEP favored retention of the stockpile as a guard against blackmail by what it called "guided revolutions" (Huddle 1976:656). But in the context of broader foreign policy objectives, the political importance of strategic materials was necessarily minor. The existence of large stockpiles eased the fears of "blackmail" by developing countries and reduced the salience of the mineral issue (Kaysen 1986; see also JFKL 1962c, 1963a, 1963b; Lipschutz 1986a). The Kennedy administration therefore engaged in a program of disposing of certain minerals in surplus, such as tin, with a careful eye toward the effects of such sales on markets and the political stability of producing countries (JFKL 1962d:2, 1962e).

Where the Kennedy Administration did show a high degree of querulousness was with respect to Soviet oil sales to Western Europe. Its campaign against Soviet oil represented a classic mingling of material and ideal interests. In the early 1960s the Soviet Union sought to increase trade relations with Western Europe through the sale of petroleum at below-market prices (Jentleson 1984:641) (this episode is also discussed in Chapter 7). The Western response to the Soviet "oil offensive" was, in retrospect, predictable (with a familiar resonance in the 1980s, as well). As had been the case with Iran in 1951, the major oil companies were more concerned about their investments than the threat of Communism. Unlike 1951, however, the fears of the majors paralleled those of the U.S. government. The oil companies were extremely worried that Soviet penetration of their markets in Europe might lead to loss of revenues, while the administration was concerned that undue reliance by the Europeans on Soviet oil might open them to pressure and blackmail. The material interests of the oil companies and the ideal interests of the United States thus converged.

In Congressional debate, Senator Kenneth Keating (R-N.Y.) warned of a "Communist oil war" (quoted in Jentleson 1984:639), while Senator Hubert Humphrey (D-Minn.) called Soviet activities in the oil market "one of the major threats that face us . . . perhaps even more dangerous than the military offensive threat" (quoted in Jentleson 1984:640). Congress and the Kennedy administration, for ideological reasons, worked to limit the Soviet Union's ability to export oil to Europe, through embargoes on equipment and supplies. At the same time, the major oil companies, for economic reasons, worked against Soviet penetration of Western markets by lowering the price of their oil and offering "sweetheart" deals to U.S. allies. Eventually, both the United States and the majors reasonably successful in accomplishing their aims (Jentleson 1984; see also Stent 1981), although the Soviets managed to capture significant market shares in several countries, such as Italy. Somewhat ironically, the price war in which the majors engaged to halt the Soviets was conducted without the approval of the oil-producing nations, who reacted by establishing the Organization of Petroleum Exporting Countries (OPEC) (Jentleson 1984:641).

By contrast with often confused and ill-defined programs of political support, policies of economic warfare were often much more carefully planned. It may be that policymakers thought they better understood the relationship between economic sanctions and the collapse of political structures than that between economic support and political stability.[10] Whatever the reason, economic warfare took two forms: the undercutting of governments judged to be unfriendly to the United States, and the imposition of sanctions and trade controls against the Soviet Bloc.

The classic cases of economic warfare against unfriendly governments are well known—Iran, 1951–53 (Krasner 1978:119–28; Painter 1986: ch. 8); Guatemala, 1954 (Krasner 1978:279–82; Cook 1981: chs. 6–7; Immerman 1982); Cuba after 1960 (Krasner 1978:286–91; Welch 1985: ch. 3); Chile in the early 1970s (Petras and Morely 1975; Krasner 1978:298–313) and, more recently, Nicaragua—as are the supposed conditions necessitating such action (on sanctions, in general, see Hufbauer and Schott 1985; Baldwin 1985). The anti-Communist, antinationalist formula usually adduced as the explanation for such economic warfare (Reagan 1987) has been a necessary but not sufficient condition, for

[10]Although the Reagan administration's unsuccessful campaign of economic sanctions against Panama in 1988 suggests empirically that policymakers' beliefs are unreliable guides to action.

there have also occurred counterexamples. The sanctity of U.S. foreign investment (Cook 1981: ch. 6; see also Balsier 1985) has also been important, but not essential. What largely has determined U.S. policy on economic warfare was (and continues to be) geopolitical determinism. To be sure, geopolitical theory has often been linked to the spread of Communism, as we have seen, but it has been the deterministic element in the theory that has underlain the judgement of whether a particular government has "threatened" the security of the United States.[11]

For example, U.S. subversion of the Arbenz government in Guatemala in 1954 was, at the time, ascribed to the nationalization of U.S. banana plantations (not of any particular strategic value) and the growing influence of Communists, of whom there were demonstrably very few (Cook 1981: chs. 6–7). The critical issue seems to have been, as it had been many times before and has been since, the relative proximity of the country to the Panama Canal (LaFeber 1979; Cook 1981:255), and the likelihood that a successful revolution in one state might lead to similar events in others (Painter 1986: ch. 6).

One counterexample to the pattern was Bolivia. In 1951 the Bolivian government demanded an increase in royalties from U.S.-owned tin mines in that country, this in the midst of the Korean War, when traditional sources in Southeast Asia appeared to be gravely threatened. A State Department mission sent to Bolivia reported "rather explosive conditions" there as a result of economic problems (HSTL 1951m). In a meeting on the Bolivian tin situation in July 1951, Stuart Symington, by then head of the Reconstruction Finance Corporation and concerned with raw material supply rather than raw material politics, expressed the opinion that "[T]he problem of buying tin and the problem of preserving the Bolivian economy ought to be treated separately." To this, Secretary Acheson replied that "[W]e could not determine tin prices just on political considerations, but we could not ignore political considerations either" (HSTL 1951m).

In 1952 the Bolivian government was overthrown in a nationalist revolution. By then, Acheson had become somewhat less sanguine

[11]In this respect, the U.S. economic "squeeze" placed on Panama in 1988 as a means of forcing General Noriega from office provides a classic example of economic warfare to protect geopolitical "interests" (but see the newspaper column by Harry Summers (1988) effectively refuting the geopolitical argument).

about the situation. In a Cabinet meeting in April 1952, he warned (HSTL 1952d) that

> The current revolution in Bolivia is serious. It is financed and supported by Peron. The American owned tin mines will probably be nationalized which will cause great repercussions in our relations with Bolivia and other Latin American countries.

Although the political ideology of the Peronist movement in Argentina was never clearly right or left, Acheson's comment suggests an implicit concern that long-term U.S. interests might be threatened by revolutionary activities in Bolivia, particularly if they set an example throughout the region. In the event, the revolution was not opposed by the United States, and nationalization proceeded without incident. U.S. investors were promptly and adequately compensated. It has been argued that the United States did not attempt to subvert the new Bolivian government because there was no evidence of Communist involvement in the revolution (Krasner 1978:282–85; see also Alexander 1958). Although this may have been one factor, it is also true that Bolivia, by itself, was not considered to be of great geopolitical significance. The same cannot be said, at least in terms of geopolitical theory, of Guatemala, Cuba, Iran, or Chile.

A second type of economic warfare practiced by the United States centered on controls on trade with the Soviet Bloc. Although these controls covered many different commodities and products (Adler-Karlsson 1968; Mastanduno 1985), certain strategic materials were included in the restrictions. The controls originated in late 1947 and early 1948 as an element of the developing policy of containment. A memo written at the time by the executive secretary of the National Security Council to the Secretary of Commerce explained the rationale for such a program (HSTL 1947c: app. A):

> One of the primary objectives of the United States' foreign policy is the revival of a working economy in the world as a necessary step toward the establishment and maintenance of world peace. The United States Government has offered to cooperate with any government that is willing to assist in the task of recovery. Sixteen European countries have voluntarily joined in the development of a European recovery program, and have requested US assistance. The USSR and its Eastern European satellite nations have refused to join (and in fact actively opposed) this program.

This opposition to European recovery constitutes a threat to world peace and, in turn, to U.S. security.

In 1947, Soviet Bloc trade with the European Recovery Program (ERP—Marshall Plan) countries amounted to $1.4 billion (HSTL 1947c:7, app. B), while in 1949, after the imposition of controls, the value of traded goods was $1 billion (HSTL 1950d). Most of these imports were considered essential to the recovery of Western Europe and could not be obtained from other sources without the expenditure of scarce dollars. Hence, a central goal of limiting trade with the Soviet bloc (HSTL 1947c: app. B) was

> [A] selective control under which certain key commodities are denied export licenses from the United States [and ERP nations] to the Soviet Bloc . . . [while] our restrictions on trade should not cause the Soviet Bloc to limit the strategic materials which they have been supplying to us.

In 1950, the assorted U.S. efforts to restrict East-West trade were pulled together in the eponymously-named Battle Act (Adler-Karlsson 1968:28-30; Jentleson 1986: ch. 2) which declared it to be U.S. policy to (DDEL 1959c)

> [E]mbargo to nations threatening the security of the United States all shipments of (A) arms, ammunition, implements of war, and atomic energy materials, and (B) petroleum, transportation materials of strategic value, and items of primary strategic significance used in the production of arms, ammunition, and implements of war . . . . The Act calls for mandatory termination of all U.S. military, economic, and financial assistance to countries which ship category (A) items to the Soviet Bloc.

The Battle Act was used periodically to threaten recalcitrant nations with punishment, such as a cutoff of U.S. economic or military aid, if they failed to stop dealing with the Soviet Bloc in certain goods. But the effectiveness of such threats was mixed, and the United States often found it necessary to compromise with its allies on revisions to the export control lists so as not to alienate them (DDEL ND).

Another element in the program of economic warfare against the Soviet Bloc was one that had been tried against Nazi Germany with wolfram (tungsten) and uranium during World War II: preclusive buying. Throughout much of the Cold War period, the United States and Britain cooperated in an attempt to corner world supplies of uranium and thorium through the activities of the Combined Development Trust, even though this did not prevent the Soviet Union from developing an atomic bomb (Gowing 1974; Helmreich 1986). In the late 1940s, the United States and Great Britain, along with a number of other states, also worked together to prevent the Soviets from purchasing tin on world markets (see Chapter 7, below). In 1952, the National Security Council asked the Economic Defense Advisory Committee to prepare a study on the feasibility of a coordinated program of preclusive buying (FRUS 1952–54c:854). The National Security Resources Board also prepared a number of studies on preclusive buying of strategic commodities (NARS ND).

A large program of preclusive buying was never implemented, but some efforts were made to redirect production of certain raw materials toward the West. For example, in 1952 it was reported in NSC 104/2, "Implementation of U.S. Policies and Programs in the Economic Field Which May Affect the War Potential of the Soviet Bloc" (HSTL 1952e), that

> Action has been taken to investigate projected expanded Finnish cobalt production involving a new process, with a view to purchases for the United States Government stockpile. If agreement is reached as to price, specifications, and other important technical details, the arrangement will result in precluding possible Soviet purchases.

Sometimes such strategies backfired. Preclusive buying of tungsten from South Korea during the Korean War, along with the embargo on imports from China, simply meant that fewer supplies were available to U.S. allies in international markets (PRO 1952b; Bidwell 1958:54–55). This often created considerable political friction.

Generally speaking, export controls and efforts to restrict East-West trade did not prove as effective as had been hoped, due to a combination of European resistance, circumvention of regulations, and availability to the Soviets of alternative supply routes and sources. In addition, the volume of trade in strategic items never became very large, in part because of the restrictions. Hence, the Soviets never found themselves suddenly cut off from critical sources of materials and technology.

As the 1950s wore on, there were repeated debates about whether to drop trade controls entirely. Britain, in particular, favored major changes in the control lists (see the files in DDEL ND). The United States responded by arguing that the gains in trade that might result would amount to no more than $350 million, a quantity that would be of importance only to Japan or to individual firms. Ironically, the small size of potential gains was due to (DDEL 1956a:1) "The relative self-sufficiency of the Bloc's economy [which] is the result of years of Soviet policy directed toward autarky [and] stimulated to some degree by over five years of Western trade controls." The whole notion of trade controls has been premised, until the present day, on the assumption that Western technology and goods were required by the Soviet Bloc if the latter were to build up its economic and military capabilities. A secondary argument has been that significant Western dependence on trade with the Soviet Bloc would open up the West to all sorts of "economic blackmail" (see, for example, DDEL 1955c, 1960c; Jentleson 1984). In practice, controls may have had an effect opposite the one intended (on this point, see Valkenier 1983:40).

Some U.S. policymakers in the 1950s and 1960s also worried about the "example effect" that the Soviets might have on developing countries and the possibility of reverse economic warfare. They viewed economic nationalism in Third World countries as tantamount to a transition to socialism (and, by implication, Communism). As Joseph Rand of the Council on Foreign Economic Policy explained to Chairman Joseph Randall in a memorandum (DDEL 1958d), "Nationalism, in many cases, is inimical to our foreign economic policy" because

> Nationalism . . . created a receptivity to communist blandishments. With its feverish desire to accomplish an overnight transition from a medieval to a modern economy, nationalism may more readily accept the Soviet argument that aspirations for rapid industrial expansion can best be achieved through communism.

Indeed, to the extent that the Soviets were able to industrialize and prosper without excessive dependence on the West, they set an example for the developing states of the world. This worried Eisenhower's advisors, who warned (DDEL 1956d:2–3) that

> The steady transition of the USSR from a relatively undeveloped to a highly industrialized economy, provides the economic basis for the foreign economic policy toward underdeveloped countries being evolved by the present Soviet leadership. This policy may have the dual purpose of using the current needs and capabilities of the Soviet economy to promote the broader and longer range political and strategic aims of the USSR in world affairs.

Such warnings reflected concern over what was called at the time the Soviet "economic offensive" — an effort launched by Premier Khrushchev in May 1957 that sought to prove the superiority of the

Soviet system through economic rather than military competition —
and fears of what forms that offensive might take (DDEL 1958e; see
also JFKL 1961b). In a 1958 Cabinet meeting, Secretary of State Dulles
(DDEL 1958f:1–2)

> [C]ited the advantage that a Communist dictatorship has over a "profit"
> economy through dumping goods or providing them at a price below cost
> so as to eliminate competitors and dominate various national markets.

At another Cabinet meeting, CIA Director Allen Dulles asserted
that "[T]he Free World faces quite a dangerous situation in the Soviet
capacity to dislocate established markets" (DDEL 1958g). This capacity was described in detail in a memorandum on "Soviet Economic
Penetration" (DDEL 1958e), according to which,

> We have to consider the impact of these Communist activities on the
> Western-fashioned economic system of private enterprise, the operation of
> which depends on profits. Since the Sino-Soviet system operates without
> regard to profits and can channel the efforts of its people into international
> economic warfare, the consequences of such all out warfare by this
> industrialized totalitarian state would obviously be serious.

Among the activities open to the Soviets were "manipulation and
disorganization of staple markets such as wheat, cotton, metals and so
forth" (DDEL 1958e) and the "[e]ffects of possible large-scale Sino-
Soviet barter deals for raw materials, eliminating for the raw material
countries the risks inherent in free markets which fluctuate sharply in
terms of prices and volume.[12]"

In November 1960, Admiral Arleigh Burke, chief of Naval Operations (and later chairman of the Joint Chiefs of Staff under Kennedy),
wrote to President Eisenhower's National Security assistant, Gordon
Gray, expressing concern over "the increase in Soviet commerce with
the free and uncommitted nations of the world" (DDEL 1960c:1).
Burke warned that

> Unless the United States and the other western powers can thwart such
> [economic] moves, the semblance of Soviet ability under communism to
> produce and sell more cheaply than we can under the capitalistic system
> may have very serious consequences in our struggle to convince the
> peoples of the world that democratic principles and free enterprise are
> better and more efficient than dictatorship and communism.

[12] Although this strategy was tried, the Soviets themselves found that it did not work (see pp.
208–209 in Chapter 7, below).

Such concerns were not limited only to the business-oriented Eisenhower administration. In 1961 an official in the State Department's Bureau of African Affairs warned G. Mennen Williams (JFKL 1961b:8) that

> If we cannot stabilize our demand [for commodities], we must deal with its consequences, if our political objectives are not to be frustrated. The Soviets can mass purchase over a period of years. One can easily remember Nazi economic penetration which was based on stable prices and stable markets.

These fears were no doubt fed by Soviet activities in the tin and oil markets during the late 1950s and early 1960s (see Chapter 7). In 1957 the Soviets began to sell massive amounts of tin, apparently acquired from the Chinese in barter deals, on the world market, with disastrous effects on prices (DDEL 1958h). This continued until 1958, when the Soviets were asked by the International Tin Council to limit such sales, a request with which they complied. One analyst of the tin industry has observed that the details of Soviet motives in selling tin from 1957 to 1960 are not known. There was little evidence of price-cutting, and it is unclear, at least to him, whether it was malice or stupidity that led them to continue selling in the face of declining prices (Fox 1974:295). As recounted earlier, the Soviets also made efforts to gain a market share in petroleum sales to Western Europe during the same period. But the kinds of mass purchases and economic penetration so feared by U.S. policymakers never materialized, mostly because the Soviets lacked the goods and technology that developing countries wanted. The fear of an "economic offensive," with its political implications for the developed and developing worlds, finally petered out in the mid-1960s.

Economics and Raw Materials

U.S. economic doctrine encompasses a series of beliefs and policies that date back to the late 1800s. What began in the closing years of the nineteenth century as the "Open Door" policy in China as a means of ensuring U.S. access to Chinese markets, eventually evolved after World War II into the wholesale adoption—at least on the rhetorical level—of English-style international economic liberalism and free trade. Fundamental to this organizing principle was the idea that economic liberalism was an engine of historical progress and freedom. In his biography of John Foster Dulles, Townsend Hoopes (1973:286) describes this belief as the notion that

> American economic and technical superiority rested in large part on the *moral* superiority of the free enterprise system. Only men operating in political freedom could achieve spectacular industrial progress. And as political freedom and economic progress were interdependent partners, it followed that emerging nations, given a choice, could not fail to choose allegiance with the West.

What began therefore as a means of competing with other, more powerful industrial nations in the world economy gradually evolved into a self-contained doctrine linking economic and political principles. As suggested by the summary of the Point Four program presented in Chapter 4 (p. 86), economic doctrine was an essential part of the strategic "triad" of policy goals. Although some revisionist historians have fastened on the expansion of capitalism and markets as the underlying or overriding motivating force of postwar U.S. foreign policy (Kolko 1969; Bernstein 1970; Williams 1972; Cotman 1978), this is a view that tends to consider only one part of the overall strategic synthesis.

U.S. policymakers have been good liberals, in both the political and economic sense, with an abiding belief in a curiously fuzzy and circular form of economic determinism. Without economic prosperity, went the refrain, peace was impossible, and without capitalism, free trade, and open markets, prosperity was impossible – QED (Welles 1942; Clayton 1946; Gardner 1980; see also Ronald Reagan as quoted in Hall 1988). As Secretary Acheson told President Truman in 1950 (HSTL 1950e:1),

> The expansion of trade is an indispensable part of our total effort to create strength and unity in the free world. Free trade, economic development and foreign assistance form together the economic instrument through which we hope to build up the military strength of the free countries and offer to their people the hope for economic progress on which that strength greatly depends.

The corollaries to this theorem had to do with the relationship between the conditions bred by poverty and the appeal of nationalism and Communism, and the need for global peace and security if U.S. business were to prosper.

During the Eisenhower administration, economic development was seen as intimately tied to political stability. Economic aid and trade became adjuncts of defense policy; indeed, the "low politics" of trade were often treated as virtually inseparable from the "high politics" of defense (Kaufmann 1982). In his wartime memoirs, Eisenhower (1948:476–77, quoted in Kaufmann 1982:12) proposed a sort of economic "domino theory" that claimed

> Wherever popular discontent is found or group oppression or mass poverty or the hunger of children, there Communism may stage an offensive that arms cannot counter. Discontent can be fanned into revolution, and revolution into social chaos.

This theory, among others, became very important to Eisenhower's foreign policy. The connection between the organizing principles of geopolitical determinism, political liberalism, and economic liberalism can also be seen in a 1963 statement—cited in Chapter 4 but repeated here to make the point—by Harlan Cleveland (1963:19) (later JFK's Assistant Secretary of State for International Organization Affairs) to the Subcommittee on Africa of the House Committee on Foreign Affairs:

> I am not sure I can separate our material gains from our need to have a peaceful world to do business in. I am more and more impressed with the fact that the state of American business is crucially dependent on maintaining a reasonable level of peace and security around the world . . . . [Q]uite apart from the business that American businessmen may do in Africa . . . every major threat to local peace and security in one region of the world risks exploitation by the Communists, risks a confrontation between us and the Communists, and risks escalation to a world war. And a world war is about the worst and biggest thing that could happen to American business.

That such beliefs became entrenched principles is not surprising, given prevailing views that the causes of World War II were rooted in the economic problems of the 1930s.

In the second half of the 1940s and throughout the 1950s, the United States functioned as a global economic "balance wheel." The prosperity of the world came to depend on it, and vice versa. In the aftermath of the war, this role was inevitable, given the size of the U.S. economy relative to the rest of the world, but U.S. policymakers held fast to this economistic perspective long after it had ceased to be very functional. Although the prosperity of the Western world in the 1950s and 1960s seemed to validate the liberal economic determinism of the U.S. government, the correlation does not prove causation. What *was* demonstrated is that cooperation within an established economic regime — where rules of eligibility and participation are broadly accepted — is conducive to economic intercourse. The particular form of the regime may lead to greater or lesser absolute levels of benefits to all concerned, but overall welfare is generally improved. After all, even the Eastern European states, operating within a decidedly nonliberal economic system, are materially better off today than they were forty years ago.

Within the general economic doctrine adhered to by U.S. policymakers, flows of strategic raw materials were important in several respects. First, there was the ever-present problem of matching supply with demand and ensuring access to available sources overseas. Second, there was a growing concern over the sanctity of U.S. investments abroad. Finally, there were questions of domestic subsidies and foreign barter for building up the strategic stockpiles.

Following the end of World War II, there developed a generalized fear that the United States was running short of various raw materials, such as petroleum, copper and iron ore, in part because supplying the war effort had placed such a tremendous drain on domestic sources. The commitment to European recovery only served to exacerbate concerns over future supply because it was not clear from where would come the raw materials required for reconstruction. Furthermore, as inevitable supply-demand imbalances linked to the business cycle began to appear, and given the atmosphere of the developing Cold War, there was some thought that inimical political forces might be involved in the shortages. This was particularly true after 1950.

The surge in demand for raw materials associated with the Korean War led to high prices and spot shortages of various commodities. Although these shortages were correctly attributed by policymakers to the pressures of rearmament (PRO 1950c:1; Mason 1952), such explanations did little to stem the fears and bad feelings held by producers and consumers (Just 1951; Mather and Meyerhoff 1951). A number of strategic materials were rationed, further exacerbating the supply situation. In addition, U.S. allies sometimes found themselves shut out of markets by the U.S. government, which itself was looking for materials needed for the mobilization effort.

For example, in January 1951 the chairman of the Munitions Board, John D. Small (NARS 1951c:1), told the General Services Administration that

> In view of the extremely critical situation in the Far East, it is imperative that your most vigorous efforts be directed toward the purchase of all the rubber and other materials on the purchase program originating in Indonesia, Malaya, Thailand, and French Indo China that you can find. The matter of price should be of no consequence in your re-doubled efforts to acquire the maximum amount of these materials. This includes preclusive buying.

Curiously, the basis for this order, as explained by Mr. Small, was that two days earlier (NARS 1951d:1–2)

> [H]e had received indications from the White House . . . that on the basis of information supplied by sources in the State Department, there was a real danger of losing a good part of Southeast Asia in the very near future. He said that in addition he had been advised by General Bradley to move very promptly in this field and he said further that General Bradley possessed some information which was in the hands of only six people in the government, which appeared to warrant the most energetic possible action to remove all strategic and critical materials from the area.

In a series of hurried meetings, Small's order was countermanded by State Department officials, but the episode provides an example of the kinds of pressures and rumors loose in the marketplace that later led the head of the Defense Production Administration to complain (Fleischmann 1952:297) that "The United States, in the midst of a tremendous mobilization effort, is short of aluminum and has also been unable to buy tin at what we consider a reasonable price in world markets."

Ironically, U.S. demands on world supplies for stockpiling purposes were thought to be one cause of the spot shortages of certain materials. These shortages, which had a particularly severe effect on the British economy, were discussed at the summit meeting between President Truman and Prime Minister Attlee in December 1950 (HSTL 1950f). Out of this meeting came an agreement to establish an "International Materials Conference," with representatives from twenty-seven nations, to consult on the problem of supply, demand, and distribution (Liebhafsky 1957; Bidwell 1958:54–55). Although this arrangement allayed some complaints that the United States was cornering the bulk of world supplies, it did little to actually increase their availability, and it created domestic dissatisfaction, too. Writing in 1958, Percy Bidwell (1958:57) observed that

> In shifting from a policy of isolation to one of international collaboration, the Truman administration aroused strong opposition in Congress. Certain members complained that insufficient allocations of copper and other minerals had caused unemployment in fabricating industries and had unduly restricted the civilian economy. Curtailment of supplies, they said, had interfered with stockpiling and had obstructed the nation's war effort. Behind these objections, and others of a more specious character, there lurked a deep-seated suspicion of foreign countries and a reluctance to collaborate with them in economic matters.

(See U.S. Senate 1954; NARS 1954a for specific complaints and allegations of this nature.)

Another consequence of the supply/demand problems attendent to rearmament was the establishment of the President's Materials Policy Commission (PMPC) under William Paley. Various accounts, as well as archival materials in the Truman Library, fail to clarify the precise combination of forces that motivated the establishment of the Commission. According to one historian, W.R. Hamilton, the idea origi-nated with W. Stuart Symington, who was seeking new functions to revitalize the National Security Resources Board (to which he had been appointed chairman) (Hamilton 1963:43–46).[13]

In late 1950, according to Hamilton, Symington discussed with Paley the idea of such a study, and the latter apparently had very clear suggestions regarding the structure and goals of the project. In his memoirs, however, Paley claimed that Symington, his neighbor and golfing partner, first raised the idea soon after the outbreak of the Korean War. During the following months, wrote Paley, Symington pressured him to take on the job (Paley 1979:202–03). Initially, Paley demurred, claiming to know nothing about minerals or mining (al-though this was, apparently, not entirely true). He maintained this pretense until he was summoned to Truman's office. According to Hamilton (1963:43), there was no public or congressional pressure to establish such a commission, but the problem of raw materials supplies

---

[13]In the files of the chairman of the NSRB (Symington), I found an undated document with the title "Outline of Report." The document obviously refers to the report of the Paley Commission. Whether it predates the start of the Commission's work is unclear from its contents (NARS 1951e).

was not an invisible one, particularly since the government formally imposed rationing of certain materials not long after the outbreak of the Korean War.

The commission began its work with at least some thought that the spot shortages were as much a result of geologic as economic scarcity (Wolanin 1975:100), and that East-West competition for raw materials was bound to be an important factor in the future (HSTL 1951*l*:1, 1951n). Neither of these assumptions was developed in detail for the final report. An attempt to compare the relative materials positions of the United States and the Soviet Union was dropped, apparently for lack of time (HSTL 1951o), and, in the words of the NSRB, all that the Commission was really able to establish was that the United States had "settled solidly into the position of consuming more materials than we produce" (U.S. NSRB 1952:1).

The commission completed its work in the summer of 1952. Its central recommendation (or, perhaps, "recognition" is a better word) was the maintenance of the *status quo* even as it warned that, over the following twenty-five years, the United States would become increasingly dependent on foreign sources of raw materials. The PMPC was never expected to do more than recommend policy, but as a highly visible presidential commission, it *was* expected to suggest how to resolve an increasingly intractable dilemma: How to face a world in which the United States seemed to be as dependent on others as others were on her. During the materials shortages accompanying rearmament, this dependence suggested a long-term threat to political and economic security.

Alas, the shortages disappeared at about the same time *Resources for Freedom* hit the streets. By 1952, time and markets had caught up with the PMPC, and (Huddle 1976:655)

> [A]s the Korean War subsided, mobilization programs tapered off, stockpile goals began to be achieved, and demand for materials eased. The mining industry, tuned to expanded wartime demands, found itself once more producing surpluses.

In 1953 a new administration took office, and it chose to ignore the Paley Commission's work. Instead, Eisenhower commissioned a blanket review of foreign economic policy, of which raw materials supply and security was only one part (DDEL 1953d, 1953e). The conclusions reached in these new studies were the same as those of the PMPC, of course (compare HSTL 1951*l* with DDEL 1953e, for example), but they were reached by the new president's advisors and were therefore thought to be of greater validity.[14]

The experiences of the period from 1950 to 1952 — roughly the peak of the Korean War — only served to underline to U.S. policymakers the economic difficulties associated with operating as the balance wheel of the global economy. During periods of economic expansion, U.S. demand for raw materials drew even marginal sources into the market. High prices meant good times for both domestic and foreign producers. Under various aid programs, the United States encouraged the development of foreign sources of strategic materials (Pollard 1985: ch. 9). Unfortunately, when the good times came to an end, as they always did, markets would become glutted, and price cutting by both foreign and domestic producers would ensue. Because domestic mineral sources were almost always high-cost, they would be driven out of business first. Hence, there was always pressure on Congress and the president to implement protectionist measures. But even foreign producers suffered during bad economic times and, as noted earlier, the decision to support or cast them adrift posed a never-ending foreign policy problem.

The examples of oil during the Truman administration and lead and zinc during the Eisenhower administration are instructive in this regard. During and immediately following World War II, U.S. policymakers thought it essential for U.S. companies to participate in the development of Middle East oil for reasons of both security and economic competition (Painter 1986: ch. 4–5). Toward the end of the 1940s, the Truman administration came face to face with the economic consequences of this policy. Whereas oil supplies had been tight during the first few years after the war, and U.S. policymakers feared a lethal drain on Western Hemisphere reserves, by 1949 a glut of foreign oil came floating toward America's shores. Domestic producers, fearing a flood of cheap imports, demanded restrictions (HSTL 1949c).

The oil majors, conversely, faced with stiff competition from so-called sterling oil and restrictions on what they could sell for dollars in the British Empire and Commonwealth (HSTL 1950g; Kapstein

[14]As Michael Shafer has pointed out, each administration believes it has discovered something new in U.S. dependence on foreign sources of raw materials (Shafer 1982:155), but each Administration must eventually reconcile itself to this fact of life.

1983),[15] saw their foreign markets threatened and looked to the United States as a market into which they could bring Middle East oil (Painter 1986:99–101). Because the stability of Great Britain depended on the health of sterling, which was none too robust (HSTL 1949d), the United States was reluctant to place too much pressure on Britain to change its rules.

In a memo to Truman, dated (ironically) June 26, 1950, W. Stuart Symington outlined the various arguments for and against import restrictions, and summed up the overall dilemma (or trilemma) (HSTL 1950h:3):

> There is a third point of view which requires consideration — the effect of restriction of oil imports on American interests abroad. In my opinion, such restrictions, unless substantiated by serious harm to the domestic oil industry, would do violence to our efforts to promote the expansion of international trade, to the purposes underlying the President's Point-Four program, and to various reciprocal trade agreements now in effect. It would invite retaliatory measures on the part of foreign governments, specifically Venezuela. The political situation in the Middle East, dependent upon economic well-being, might be seriously injured.

Somewhat miraculously, the Korean War broke out that very day, resolving the problem for the moment. But the petroleum shortage/surplus problem arose again in the latter half of the decade, thereby leading the Eisenhower administration to impose import quotas and to follow a policy of "drain America first" (see Bohi and Russell 1978; Keohane 1984:174–77).

A similar set of problems confronted the Eisenhower administration with respect to domestic mineral production when it took office in 1953: a mining industry that was severely hurt by the flood of cheap mineral imports accompanying the now-glutted market, and the continuing problem of what to do about the stockpile. At the same time, the administration wrestled with the business cycle and the strategic implications of economic interdependence. Eisenhower and his advisors believed, as noted earlier, that political stability in developing

---

[15]The "dollar-sterling" problem arose from two facts: First, sterling was not convertible into dollars and, second, many countries had sterling but no dollars. Hence, any currency generated by sales by U.S. oil companies in sterling areas could not be changed into dollars. Furthermore, because the UK wanted to retrieve sterling held by foreign countries, so as to reduce its monetary obligations, British oil companies could undersell "dollar" oil (see HSTL 1949d, 1950g; Kapstein 1983; Keohane 1984:159–67; Painter 1986:160–65).

nations required economic stability in commodity markets. Thus, on the one hand, he followed the advice of Secretary of State Dulles in opposing higher domestic tariffs on imports of lead and zinc (FRUS 1952–54d), warning that such barriers against trade could result in Mexico's turning Communist (Kaufman 1982:39).

On the other hand, the Eisenhower administration was strongly oriented toward business, and the problems bedeviling domestic mineral producers would not go away. A memo from the president to the director of the Office of Defense Mobilization, on long-term mineral stockpile objectives, attempted to resolve the contradictions by recommending support for domestic producers, acquisition of strategic minerals in exchange for surplus commodities, foreign purchase of materials at "advantageous prices," and minimization of interference with "normal producer-consumer relationships of regular trade" (FRUS 1952–54e). Trying to reconcile these varying and sometimes conflicting goals proved enormously difficult.

Western mining interests demanded that something be done. In 1953 and 1954 a Congressional investigation into the strategic materials situation was undertaken (U.S. Senate 1954) under the leadership of the isolationist and anti-British Senator from Nevada, George Malone (for his anti-British sentiments, see his article on "Twentieth Century Trade Wars" in U.S. Senate 1959). The congressional committee, parroting the position of the American Mining Congress, demanded that the government provide increased assistance to domestic producers in order to increase self-sufficiency, recommended increased depletion allowances, and urged acceleration of the stockpiling program. The committee also roundly denounced any sort of economic interdependence where minerals were concerned (Bidwell 1958:42; see Penn State 1979:349–50 for excerpts from the Mining Congress' "Declaration of Policy" for 1954 and other years; see also NARS 1954a for a State Department response to the Malone Hearings).

In response to such pressures, in October 1953 Eisenhower established a Cabinet Committee to "inquire into national policies affecting the production and utilization of metals and minerals." In his letter to the committee, Eisenhower specifically referred to the depressed state of the domestic lead and zinc mining industries as a subject to be considered (NARS 1954b:2). In submitting its report to the president in November 1954, the Cabinet Committee noted happily that a new stockpile purchase policy, approved by Congress in March 1954, had substantially increased the market prices of both lead and zinc. Based on the objective of being prepared to wage a five-year war (a goal somewhat contradictory to the strategy implied by the "New Look"), the Cabinet Committee urged that stockpile objectives be met as quickly as possible and that selected domestic mineral producers be subsidized in order to fill the stockpile (NARS 1954b:1; Huddle 1976:655).

As Huddle notes (1976:656), the results of this policy were mixed: Some producers benefitted, but "the policy also led to the accumulation of worthless and inaccessible low-grade chromite . . . , procurement of domestic tungsten at four times the world price, and a large accumulation of copper." Furthermore, the purchase of minerals at higher-than-market prices drew domestic production out of competitive private markets, where they were replaced by cheaper, foreign supplies. When the stockpile was filled, buying stopped, prices fell, and many domestic mines went broke (Huddle 1976:656). After stockpile goals were reduced in 1956, in line with the reduction in the expected length of a war, the government found itself not only unable to support producers but also holding enormous surpluses of various materials that "overhung" the market.

In 1958 the director of the Office of Defense Mobilization, Gordon Gray, asked an advisory committee of private citizens to review the goals of the stockpiling program (DDEL 1958i). In general, the committee had little to recommend in terms of what to do with the actual stockpiles, but made suggestions relating to the selection of materials, the problem of excess supplies, and the appropriate function of the stockpile. Among the committee's recommendations was one proposing that materials useful in the aftermath of a *nuclear attack* be acquired (such as food and medicine), thereby acknowledging that "in nuclear warfare the original purpose of stockpiling metals and other materials, viz., their use in production of military goods, would have vanished" (Bidwell 1958:51). The committee also concluded that certain stockpiling activities, such as barter, had been carried too far but warned against using either purchases or sales from the stockpiles as a mechanism for trying to stabilize commodity markets.

The problem of surpluses went unresolved, for the committee was unable to propose a means of getting rid of them without adversely affecting markets (and, hence, the economic and political stability of allies) (Bidwell 1958:52–53). Subsequent administrations found this dilemma equally difficult to deal with. The economic vision of trade in materials as a means of supporting allies and hurting enemies was one that, over the long run, could not be sustained because of the economic costs involved. Material constraints put limits on ideal objectives.

SOME INSIGHTS FOR THE PRESENT

The foreign policy issues associated with access to strategic materials have not changed greatly over the last forty years. U.S. dependence on foreign sources of raw materials is as great as it has ever been. Periodically, crises in areas such as the Persian Gulf or southern Africa make the strategic materials problem salient once again. Sometimes, the issue is used to generate political capital in election campaigns (CENS 1981; U.S. House 1981); at other times, enterprising individuals see opportunities for making money (Posner and Goldberg 1983). Policy papers recommend political, economic, and technical strategies for reducing sensitivity and vulnerability (U.S. CRS 1981; U.S. OTA 1985). Eventually, however, the problem goes away, and its political salience declines. This cycle of increasing and decreasing visibility suggests that strategic material dependence is not a "problem" in the usual sense of the word; rather, it is an issue that is used for other purposes.

Perhaps those purposes can be found by considering the role of raw materals policies within the strategic policy "trinity" described above. Although the United States has less room to maneuver in international arenas than was once the case, and less ability to influence outcomes, the trinity of policy objectives remains largely the same. The strategic arguments, evinced in U.S. policy toward Iran and southern Africa under successive Presidents, still focus on territorial geopolitics. (See, for example, three very pertinent articles published in 1986 in the *New York Times* — Gordon 1986, Reagan 1986, Rostow 1986; the Tower Commission Report (1987); and the testimony of Lt. Col. Oliver North before the Congressional Hearings on the Iran-Contra Affair in July 1987.) The political arguments, although less focused on the economic underpinnings of liberalism, continue to present U.S. security and prosperity as dependent on the support of pro-Western governments, whether democratic or not (Rule 1986; Shipler 1986). The economic arguments also focus on liberal markets and free trade as the *sine qua non* of prosperity and security (Wendt 1985).

Conceptually, the policy trinity is not as tightly unified as it was three or four decades ago. Even so, U.S. foreign policy remains rooted in a curious mixture of ideal and material interests. A poorly defined but richly articulated ideology informs the world view underlying the policy trinity, but implementation is also driven by a recognition of real material interests. The contradictions between the two, far from acting in a dialectical fashion, remain in opposition, because the two core strategic syntheses—autarky and interdependence—are, in practice, difficult to reconcile. U.S. policymakers would still like to remake the world—it would be a safer place for the United States—but such a task requires global involvement with inevitable and incalculable costs. The tools available for such involvement no longer match the vision, if they ever did.

6 MANY UNPLEASANT TRUTHS
Raw Materials and British Foreign Policy

In October 1951 Lord Cherwell, the British paymaster-general and a close advisor of Winston Churchill, jotted down a few thoughts regarding the brewing crises in the Middle East and sent them on to the prime minister. Cherwell (PRO 1951e) wrote:

> In considering whether we should accept large commitments in the Middle East, the following points seem relevant.
>
> Now that we have lost India and Burma the freedom of the Suez Canal is an international rather than a specifically British interest. In any event to sail through the Mediterranean will be difficult with enemy aircraft operating from Bulgaria unless fighter cover is provided. This would mean bases in Africa, Crete and Cyprus all of which would have to be defended against air-borne landings and bombings. It is doubtful whether this would be worth while merely in order to shorten the voyage from Britain to Australia by a couple of weeks.
>
> Middle East oil is an immensely valuable asset. But we have already abandoned our Persian oil and the remainder is largely in American hands. Is it not for America rather than Britain to defend it?
>
> The only other reason for holding the Middle East is to prevent another large accession of territory and manpower to the Communists. This falls under the Truman doctrine and as such is more an American than a British responsibility.
>
> For these reasons it would seem that the U.S. should undertake the defence of the Middle East. With such grave danger nearer home the U.K.

in my view should not accept such a strain on its resources of manpower and shipping.

For a few days, Churchill mulled over Cherwell's minute. He then replied (PRO 1951e):

> I am keeping your paper about the Middle East which contains many unpleasant truths. I have had to agree to Anthony's [Eden, the Foreign Minister] proposals [on Suez]. They will probably lead to a deadlock. It is of utmost importance to get America in.

The correspondence between Cherwell and Churchill was symptomatic of the basic dilemma facing the United Kingdom as early as the end of World War I: How to maintain a far-flung and costly empire with limited and dwindling resources (Gallagher 1982; Kennedy 1983a). Unfortunately for Britain, it could not be done. But the vision of a global Empire/Commonwealth had a great deal of appeal to many British policymakers throughout the 1940s and 1950s. Britain's strategy during this time was oriented to keeping together an heterogenous melange of states and territories, in one form or another, even as it struggled to survive. Raw materials were not central to the strategy, but they were important because they provided important sources of income with which to maintain the vision.

The relationship of raw materials to broader strategic goals can best be seen in three, somewhat distinct areas. First, British policy in the Middle East was focused on oil and the Suez Canal. Second, policy in the Far East rested on the rich colony of Malaya and the trading entrepôts of Hong Kong and Singapore. Third, British economic relations with the United States revolved heavily around the exchange of raw materials for badly needed dollars. The ideal interest of Britain in all of this was to maintain its position as a world power and to be accorded respect. The material constraints, as shall be shown, made this impossible.

The purpose of this chapter is to investigate the role of raw materials policy in broader British strategy during the height of the Cold War (roughly 1946 to 1956). This chapter begins with a discussion of Britain's position during the interwar period, followed by a description of the "organizing principles" of British postwar foreign policy. Finally, it addresses the effect of these organizing principles on Britain's policies and actions in the Middle East and the Far East, and on its economic condition during the period 1946 through 1956.

SIC TRANSIT GLORIA

Great Britain emerged from World War I with control over a greater expanse of territory than it (or any other state, for that matter) had ever commanded. Yet in economic terms, it had never been weaker, a consequence of the great costs of prosecuting the war (Kennedy 1981, 1983c). Thus, Britain appeared immensely powerful, with its train of Dominions, colonies, protectorates, and mandates, but at the same time, it was losing the ability to influence what really counted in a time of peace—the international economy—and hence to exercise meaningful control over its domestic well-being. Territory was important, but for economic and not military reasons. Territory could be an important source of the foreign exchange needed to pay off war debts and could provide critical markets for British manufactures. But territory so far removed in physical terms could not protect the home islands, as World War II eventually demonstrated.

Economic issues were never very far below the surface throughout the interwar period, and the Treasury's influence over foreign policy was not insignificant (Kennedy 1983c). At the same time, the maintenance of empire was never as much an economic issue as it was a political one. The notion of British responsibility to the far-flung territories—more of an ideal than a material interest (and related to the idea of the "white man's burden"; Kennedy 1983b:200)—remained paramount. Proponents of a true "Little England"—a country restricted to the British Isles—were generally ignored (Taylor 1957; Kennedy 1983b:203–06). From the outside, the weakness of the Empire was not readily apparent, and the other Great Powers of the time continued to measure themselves against the British standard. Even more, the vast territorial extent of the Empire, and the associated perception that power flowed from sovereignty over the industrial resources that went with the control of territory, created widespread suspicions of British intentions.

Because Great Britain was *the* major colonial power of the period, opprobrium for the apparent state of affairs with respect to raw materials tended to fall on it (as described in Chapter 4). Furthermore, because London was a center for commodity markets of various kinds, efforts to remedy the cyclical gluts and shortages of raw materials, in the form of cartels and agreements, often originated there. Even so, direct control of raw materials by the British government was limited, although British investors did control significant shares of world production of a few materials, such as rubber, tin, chromite, and manganese (Rawles 1933) (see Table 6–1). Most of this production was located outside of colonial territories, in the British Dominions (such as Canada, Australia, and South Africa) and elsewhere (RIIA 1936:33; Henderson 1939:4). Only in the case of rubber and tin did colonial sources predominate (RIIA 1941).

Of equal concern to the Axis powers, as well as to the United States, were the various international commodity control schemes pursued throughout the 1920s and 1930s in an effort to regulate production and price. As the effect of unregulated markets on prices and production became clearer in the early 1920s — most notably in the case of rubber, but also for tin and oil, among others — control efforts were begun. One of the most contentious was the "Stevenson Plan," implemented by the British government, which sought to raise rubber prices through restrictions on production in British Malaya (in 1923 the source of more than 50 percent of the world's rubber) (Hurstfield 1953:12). The

Table 6–1.   Nationality of Commercial Control of World Minerals, 1929 (% of control)

Mineral	American	British	French	German	Swiss	Brit./Fr. /Amer.	Russian	Other
Bauxite	43	7	12	10	8	—	—	—
Aluminum	52	8.5	10	12	9	5	—	—
Chromite	16.5	68	3.7	3	—	—	5	—
Manganese	20.4	35.4	—	—	—	—	34.4	4.3
Crude oil[a]	70	5.5	0.45	0.16	—	—	NA	~13.5
Refined oil[a]	71	5.3	1.1	0.19	—	—	NA	~14
Tin mines	3	33(+17[b])	1.5	4.5	—	—	—	38
Tin smelter	0.5	41(+44[b])	—	2.3	—	—	—	12.2

Source: [Rawles 1933].
a. Data for 1930.
b. Anglo-Bolivian ownership.
NA Not available.

scheme succeeded in raising prices by a factor of three between 1923 and 1925 (from 14.3d per pound to 43.3d/lb; 1d = 1 penny.) This, in turn, triggered increased production from other sources and led to decreased consumption, resulting in a tenfold drop in price between 1925 and 1930 (to 16.6d/lb. in 1927 and 4.3d/lb. in 1930) (Hurstfield 1953:11).

Notwithstanding the collapse in rubber prices by 1930 (a phenomenon not restricted solely to the rubber market), the Stevenson Plan was considered a great success and was emulated in a number of other commodities.[1] In 1937, as a result, there were as many as thirty-seven such control schemes, effected either through national monopolies, inter-governmental agreements, or intra-industrial collusion (Staley 1937:251–318). Furthermore, during the 1930s, commodity control came to be seen as much a tool of economic warfare as a means of regulating markets.

The Depression had two other wide-ranging economic effects that were to have political repercussions during the 1930s. First, the virtual collapse of international trade in manufactured goods meant that it was increasingly difficult for raw material-importing states to acquire foreign exchange. This, combined with the artificially high exchange rates maintained by Germany and Italy, led to the conundrum of their not being able to purchase raw materials in a world that was, apparently, awash in them.

Second, the Depression led to the imposition of protectionist measures by both the United States and the British Empire. The Hawley-Smoot tariff in the former made it much more difficult for countries to obtain dollars (Hoselitz 1943:3), while Imperial preference and the Sterling Bloc in the latter tended to direct trade to and from Great Britain and away from traditional markets and sources outside of the Empire (RIIA 1938:9). Again, these measures aggravated the foreign exchange positions of various states, Britain included. The general economic conditions of the 1930s have been treated and analyzed at length elsewhere (see, e.g., Kindleberger 1973); what was critical at the time was the resulting perception of the causes of the economic collapse and the intense economic nationalism that developed.

Two overwhelming problems confronted British policymakers and strategic planners during the interwar period, problems that continued

---

[1]Some of which had been cartelized prior to World War I. According to one source, in 1897 there had been forty cartels in industries such as chemicals, iron and steel, and glass products (Domeratzky 1928:2).

to be of great importance during the decade following the end of World War II. The first was the slow but inexorable decline in Britain's economic position relative to other states, which made the defense of empire an increasingly difficult and expensive proposition. The second was that, after seeing to the protection of the British Isles, the Empire had to be defended, not because it was necessarily important for its materials and markets but because it was *the* Empire (Kennedy 1983b:205–206). To be sure, certain territories were essential to Britain's economic health (such as British Malaya for its tin and rubber), but only insofar as their maintenance allowed the Empire to be maintained. There thus emerged a paradox that could not be resolved except by the Empire's dissolution: The Empire was needed to provide the resources to protect the Empire, but Britain could not afford to maintain the Empire even with those resources. Needless to say, the thought of dissolution commanded little consideration until it *was* too late to halt the Empire's decline (In his essay on the decline of the Empire, Gallagher 1982 captures rather clearly the concatenation of dilemmas facing British policymakers).

Throughout the 1930s, efforts were made by British strategic planners to develop an imperial defense plan in which the dominions and colonies would play major roles should war break out. But because the problems of the 1930s came to be seen overwhelmingly in economic terms — at least, until the final years of the decade — more attention was focused on economic problems than on the developing military threat on the Continent and in the Far East. The broad assumption was, of course, that were the apparent economic demands of Germany, Japan, and Italy to be met, the security of the Empire and hence the security of the British Isles would be ensured (RIIA 1936:12; Kennedy 1983c:102–03). As late as 1937, therefore, the defense priorities of Great Britain were, according to the Chiefs of Staff, as follows (quoted in Kennedy 1981:272):

1. Maintenance of the security of the United Kingdom;
2. Protection of the trade routes on which the country depended for essential imports of food and raw materials;
3. Maintenance of forces needed to defend British territories overseas;
4. Co-operation in the defense of the territories of allies in war.

When war finally did break out in Europe in 1939 and in the Pacific in 1941, most of Britain's economic and trade links to the Empire were severed and the threat from the Continent proved to be the most serious one.

Nonetheless, the hierarchy of defense priorities *following* the war was not changed greatly from the prewar list. A June 1945 report by the Post-Hostilities Planning Staff, entitled "The Security of the British Empire," considered the essentials of Imperial security to be (PRO 1945b:3)

(a)   To maintain the integrity of the British Empire against both internal and external threats;
(b)   To keep secure world-wide sea and air communications on which depend the cohesion of the Empire, and access to essential raw materials and industrial capacity.

A report prepared the following year by the Chiefs of Staff, on the "Strategic Position of the British Commonwealth," emphasized the extent to which British military planners thought the international situation to be essentially unchanged. The Chiefs wrote (PRO 1946b:6) that

Our main strategic requirements are based principally upon facts of geography and the distribution of man-power and natural resources which do not change. We consider that the basic principles of our strategy . . . will not be radically altered by new developments in methods or weapons of warfare.

To some degree they were correct—atomic weapons would not have made it any easier to hold on to the Empire—but at the time they could not have foreseen the importance that the basic cost of empire would come to play in its future.

RAW MATERIALS AND THE ORGANIZING PRINCIPLES OF BRITISH FOREIGN POLICY

In some ways, organizing principles were less central to the formulation of British foreign policy than was true of its U.S. counterpart. In particular, the cause-effect relationships that lay at the core of the U.S. principles seem to have been much weaker for the British. This might have been due to the relative power positions of Britain and the United

States, or it might be that British policymakers operated with a more subtle hand than the Americans. They had had, after all, much more experience in international politics.

The British and U.S. perceptions of the factors underlying international friction in the 1930s led to two conclusions regarding the onset of World War II. First, as noted in Chapter 4 and above, Axis demands for raw materials had a significant effect on subsequent interpretations of the causes of World War II. Second, the apparent strength and successes of Germany in the early days of the war caused analysts in the United States and Britain to look for the theoretical basis of this phenomenon. They found it in the German school of *geopolitik* (Strauss-Hupè 1942; Gyorgy 1944), even though the influence on Hitler of this school of thought remains debatable (see Mattern 1942). The penetration of geopolitical thinking into the formulation of Allied politics and strategy followed closely behind.[2]

The experiences of the 1930s and World War II thus led to the emergence of two major themes in the British policy documents of the postwar period. The first was a geopolitical theme, not too dissimilar from that fancied by U.S. policymakers. But whereas U.S. geopolitical doctrine was premised on the idea that the security of the United States was intimately bound up with events in all parts of the world, British geopolitics was much more focused on territorial possession and threats to the Empire. To be sure, these lands were global in spread, but not everything was thought to be of equal importance. For example, the British were able to view the collapse of the Nationalist government in China and its consequences for Hong Kong with some equanimity, thinking to pick up the pieces later (PRO 1950d), whereas the U.S. reaction was simple panic. The second theme to emerge was the intimate connection between British interests and the British economy: return on foreign investment became absolutely essential to postwar reconstruction and growth.

The paradox of the 1930s was, therefore, only gradually resolved following World War II, because territorial possession (or, at a minimum, meaningful sovereignty over foreign investments) was considered

---

[2]Writing in 1943, Halford Mackinder (1943:605), the *eminence grise* of Western geopolitical thinkers, encapsulated future trends with a pithy observation on Allied objectives in the war: "A balanced globe of human beings. And happy, because balanced and thus free." In the long run, however, balance turned out not to be enough to bring either freedom or happiness.

vital to the maintenance of the domestic economy. The U.S. policy trinity was gradually absorbed by the British as the latter's foreign policy fell into line with the former, but never as enthusiastically or wholeheartedly. Indeed, the British viewed the U.S. faith in the virtue of spreading economic and political liberalism as a bit naive, if not stupid (see, for example, PRO 1951b:17; Louis 1984:71).

For the British, as for the Americans, World War II appeared to validate geopolitical determinism. Certainly, in time of war, shipping routes, sources of raw materials, and points of industrial concentration could be thought of as strategic objectives to be captured, blockaded, or destroyed. After 1945, therefore, the lessons of the war were applied with a vengeance. Much planning went into the tactical aspects of achieving such goals, even though their applicability to Cold War conditions was doubtful. The wisdom of carrying geopolitical doctrine appropriate to war into peacetime planning must be questioned, for operationalizing such a theory requires the attribution to the enemy of intent to act in every location that one deems important, to impute importance to places that may not be critical, and to require an equivalent response at those points, an expensive endeavor even in the best of times (Staley 1937:19–20).

Geopolitical doctrine was not new to British thinking. The "Great Game" between Russia and Britain, played out in Central Asia in the nineteenth century, and again in the 1920s, was predicated on Russia's expansion into Central Asia and its supposed desire for a warm-water port on the Indian Ocean as opposed to the Britain's need to protect lines of communication to India and the Far East (PRO 1946c:2; Monroe 1981:159).[3] Examples of geopolitical thinking abound in the British records of the interwar period. For example, in a 1919 report the British Military Attaché in Peking wrote to British Foreign Minister Lord Curzon (PRO 1919, quoted in Louis 1971:25) that

Mongolia is of great natural wealth in every way, but as it is undeveloped it is often looked upon as of minor importance. If however the schemes of the Japanese General Staff should ever be realised, and railways open up the country, an enormous transformation will occur. A glance at the . . . map shows the central position of Mongolia and the importance it might

---

[3]It remains one of the curiously unnoticed phenomena of the present century that the Russian desire to strike southward seems to have vanished with the signing of the Triple Entente in 1907, if only to reemerge after 1939.

have both in a political and in a military sense. The Power which controls this region should be in a position to control the Far Eastern Continent.[4]

For postwar British planners, the focus of geopolitical strategy was the Near East (or Middle East, as it later came to be called). Until 1947 the Near East was the keystone in Britain's "lifeline" to India and after Indian independence to the remaining colonies in the Far East and the Commonwealth. The central element in the lifeline was the Suez Canal, owned and operated by the British, and British territory by virtue of a treaty concluded with (actually, forced on) Egypt in 1936. Following the war, years of British domination and Britain's failure to observe the terms of the treaty came to rankle the Egyptians, who finally abrogated the agreement in 1951 and forced their tormentors to leave. But in justifying the continuing violation of the 1936 Treaty by Britain, the Minister of Defence wrote to Foreign Minister Ernest Bevin (PRO 1947b:2) that

> The geographical situation of the Commonwealth demands a British base in the Middle East to protect their interests and sea communications. The best location for this base has been determined by geography and is in the vicinity of the Canal Zone.[5]

Bevin, himself, seems to have been influenced strongly by geopolitical theory, in particular that of Halford Mackinder (Mackinder 1943; Parker 1985: ch. 2–3). In a 1948 memorandum to the Cabinet, on "The Threat to Western Civilization," Bevin warned that the Soviet Union was (PRO 1949a:2)

> [A]ctively preparing to extend its hold over the remaining part of continental Europe and, subsequently, over the Middle East and no doubt the bulk of the Far East as well. In other words, physical control of the Eurasian land mass and eventual control of the whole World Island is what the Politburo is aiming at — no less a thing than that.

---

[4]Contrast this with an excerpt from a memo on the civil war in the Congo fifty years later, written by a U.S. State Department official (DD 1960d):

> [W]ithout wishing to be a geopolitician, a glance at the map shows the importance of the Congo to Africa. It addition to its central local [sic] astride the waist of Africa, the Congo possesses resources such as cobalt, copper and uranium of great importance to us. It seems essential therefore that this area not fall in Communist hands.

[5]What a coincidence! Especially in light of a footnote to a report by the Post-Hostilities Planning Staff that observed, "The shortest sea route from the United Kingdom to New Zealand is through the Panama Canal, the shortest air route via British Honduras (PRO 1945b:14n.).

(On this point, see also the views of the British Chiefs of Staff in PRO 1949a:2.) For those left gasping at the implications of this program, Bevin added, "The immensity of the aim should not betray us into believing in its impracticability" (PRO 1948a:2). In an annex, Bevin outlined the Soviet strategy and its implications (PRO 1948a:5):

> [I]f the Soviet Union secure control of France and French North Africa, of Italy and of Greece, and particularly if they could undermine our position in the Middle East, they would effectively dominate the Mediterranean and could (if they so wished) deprive us of access to extensive markets of raw materials, especially oil, without which our economic recovery would be difficult or impossible and the strategic position of ourselves and of the United States greatly jeopardised.

Bevin's last point got to the heart of the matter. Without oil from the Middle East, the British economy would be in trouble. The same was true for sources of other raw materials, such as Malaya, which produced rubber and tin, and central and southern Africa, from whence came gold and copper, not to mention uranium. And a weak economy would make it impossible to defend these areas.[6]

More important to Britain than the raw materials from the colonies and concessions, however, were dollars. These were needed to purchase commodities and manufactures from the United States. Britain's inability to maintain the convertibility of the pound sterling in 1946, due to the run on its foreign exchange reserves, meant that it had to acquire dollars in place of the sterling it might have otherwise used for reconstruction (HSTL 1949d). Indeed, it might be said that *dollars* were the strategic material most in demand in the postwar period, and no end of methods were devised to get dollars circulating in the international economy.[7]

---

[6]Bevin, however, seemed to have a somewhat skewed idea about the relative raw materials positions of the Empire and the United States and the extent to which the latter would collaborate with Britain in order to obtain those materials. In 1948, he told Hugh Dalton (quoted in Gallagher 1982:146)

> [I]f we only pushed on and developed Africa, we could have the United States dependent on us, and eating out of our hand, in four or five years. . . . The United States is very barren of essential minerals and in Africa we have them all.

Sic transit gloria!

[7]In a 1949 minute to Prime Minister Attlee on "Dollars and Colonial Development," Herbert Morrison mused, "I have been wondering what new and acceptable outlet might be found to enable the Americans to go on financing the world with dollars as Marshall Aid tapers off" (PRO 1949b).

Britain could obtain the required foreign exchange in three ways: (1) through loans, such as the one provided by the United States in 1945, (2) through foreign aid and purchase programs, such as the Marshall Plan, which, among other things, encouraged the sale of raw materials to dollar and gold surplus countries (such as the United States), and (3) through sales of manufactured goods to dollar and gold surplus countries. Only the first two methods were really practical during the first few years following the war, and with the end of the Marshall Plan in the early 1950s, the second assumed greater importance.

At the same time, the Empire was gradually being transformed into the Commonwealth. This inevitably, led to changes in defense strategy. In January 1947, the Overseas Defence Committee of the Chiefs of Staff wrote (PRO 1947c:1):

> The concept of Imperial defence as it affected the Colonies was founded upon command of the sea, and of the air over the sea, the exercise of which required a chain of firmly held bases, and implied the ability to move reserves at will, and to deny to potential enemies the opportunity for launching and sustaining overseas expeditions.

But the committee recognized that there now existed a fundamental contradiction in the concept of Imperial defense. Prior to the war, the role of the colonies in defense was to supply materials and manpower. The loss of India, the major source of soldiers for the defense of the territories east of Suez, meant that other colonies would have to take up the slack in any future war, and the military planners intended colonial troops to be used from the very outset of any future war (PRO 1949c:2). As the Defence Committee noted, however, "In some [colonies] there is a direct conflict between service in military forces and the maintenance in wartime of the production of commodities of great economic value" (PRO 1947c:2). Even in peacetime, Britain lacked the soldiers and resources to sustain the necessary network of bases (Monroe 1981; Abadi 1982; Gallagher 1982; Kennedy 1983b).

Nonetheless, a concerted effort was made to maintain the system of colonies and dominions in some working form, and the foreign policies of the postwar Labor government led by Clement Attlee (1945–52) and the subsequent Conservative governments led by Churchill and Anthony Eden (1952–56) were both aimed toward this end (Louis 1984: 396). It was not easy to let go an empire for, as noted earlier, Eden's sentiment was widely held: "[O]nce the prestige of a country has started to slide there is no knowing where it will stop" (PRO 1952a:2).

The Chiefs of Staff echoed him on this: "[W]hether we like it or not, we are a Great Power with world-wide responsibilities. British commitments cannot be case aside like an outworn coat" (PRO 1952c:2). They warned that "All over the world we are under the greatest pressure to hand over our responsibilities and our possessions. Any evidence of readiness to quit will start a landslide which we shall be quite unable to control" (PRO 1952c:3), and added " [I]t is unthinkable that we should throw away the fruits of all our toil, effort, and sacrifice in Malaya over the past five years—and with them *abandon our greatest dollar-earner*—on what may be the brink of success" (PRO 1952c:2, emphasis added).

Thus, the two central organizing principles of postwar British foreign policy were intertwined and, to some degree, contradictory. The maintenance of empire required men and materiel, but the costs of empire were beyond the means of the Imperial master. As a result, the British were nickled and dimed—mostly by themselves—out of an empire. In 1952, Sir Roger Makins, a Treasury official, told a meeting in the Economic Relations Department of the Foreign Office that Britain was a "world power operating on a shoestring" (PRO 1952d:5). Alas, shoestrings break.

RAW MATERIALS IN BRITISH FOREIGN POLICY

In order to explore the contradictions between the territorial/diplomatic strategy (the "ideal" interest) pursued by Britain after World War II and the economic constraints on it (the "material" interest), this section looks in greater detail at the interaction of these interests in three specific cases: Middle East oil, raw materials from the Far East, and the problem of obtaining adequate supplies of commodities in world markets.

Middle East Oil

Following the end of World War II, British policy in the Middle East was oriented toward maintaining its preeminent position there. For the first few years after the war, the geopolitical rationales with respect to the importance of the Middle East to the Empire were prominent, but these gradually lost their objective force as British commitments in

Asia and the Far East declined. Eventually, the British attachment to
the oil resources of the region, and secondarily to Africa, came to
supplement the purely geopolitical argument. This attachment was as
much sentimental as it was strategic or economic, as the original reason
for underwriting the development of the Persian fields in the early part
of the century was to provide fuel oil for the Royal Navy (PRO 1951f).
After World War II, the economic arguments became increasingly
important, as Britain found it in its interest to maximize both oil
consumption and oil revenues from Middle East sources.

Even so, geopolitical arguments remained prominent, for it became
increasingly difficult to justify a military policy predicated on the need
to protect oil sources.[8] The maintenance of the security system rested
on the existence of a threat, and the most obvious threat was, of course,
the Soviet Union and its imputed desire for the oil of the Middle East.
But geography was the essential determinant of geopolitics. As George
McGhee, U.S. Assistant Secretary of State for Near Eastern, South
Asian, and African Affairs, told a group of petroleum engineers in 1951
(PRO 1951g; a copy of the speech was apparently passed around the
British Foreign Office)

> Without an [oil-bearing] anticline, the Middle East would still be the most
> important piece of the earth's crust. It lies athwart the air, land, and sea
> crossroads of three continents. It contains the Suez Canal, a vital artery
> which keeps the free world connected and communicating. Every major
> international airline connecting Europe, Asia, and Africa passes through
> the Middle East. Even its vast deserts and barren wastes of lava and
> limestone are strategically important. They have historically constituted
> one of the greatest natural defensive areas in the world.

To the official British mind, the Middle East beckoned the Soviets into
the vacuum that would be left if Britain withdrew (PRO 1946c:2).
Beyond the Canal stood Africa. After that, who knew where Soviet
expansion might stop!

The British strategy for the defense of the Middle East was,
consequently, extensive. It was based primarily on what was called the
"Outer Ring" strategy, which envisioned a line of defense through
Turkey, along the eastern frontier of Iraq, and into Iran so as to protect
the oil fields. An alternative and less attractive strategy in the event of
war was that of holding an "Inner Ring," which would protect parts of

[8]On this point, Gallagher (1982:126) notes that the British "did not need to rule a country to
suck out its oil, as Persia shows."

Turkey, Syria, and Jordan. The worst contingency would leave the British on the "Lebanon-Jordan line." This would offer protection only to the Suez Canal (PRO 1951h:8–11; see also the map appended to this document). But these three strategies were quite specifically for prosecuting a war.

For *peacetime* planning purposes, the region was defined somewhat more broadly by the British Defence Co-ordination Committee, Middle East. Included in the Middle Eastern zone were Morocco, Algeria, Libya, Egypt, Sudan, Eritrea, Abyssinia (Ethiopia), Somaliland, Uganda, Kenya, Tanganyika, Rhodesia, Mozambique, Madagascar, the Indian Ocean along the Tropic of Capricorn to Sumatra, India, Afghanistan, Persia, Saudi Arabia, Syria, Transjordan, Palestine, Turkey, the Black Sea (to the northern shore), Bulgaria, Greece, Cyprus, Yugoslavia, Italy, and the Mediterranean Sea (PRO 1949d; see also the map in PRO 1949e). As is discussed later, British efforts to incorporate even a very few of these states into a collective security organization to defend its interests in the Middle East were fraught with problems.

Even as early as the final years of World War II, the primary British interest in the Middle East was economic. In 1944 the British and Americans began to negotiate an agreement to ensure the orderly development of oil production in region. This, it was thought, would prevent the development of surplus production capacity after the war that might drive down prices and generate friction between the two allies. A second, less apparent reason was to allow U.S. companies to obtain access to British markets (Painter 1986:59–74). This latter U.S. objective soon emerged as a central British concern. The agreement between the two countries was cast in the traditional language of the Open Door and guaranteed equal access for both to all oil-producing territories. The British worried that this might let the U.S. majors get a foot in the door in such traditionally British preserves as Iran and Iraq, that this might only be a first step in an attempt by the United States to break up the Empire, and that it could put Britain at an economic disadvantage following the war.

The first round of talks ended in 1944 with a draft agreement, but prior to the resumption of negotiations in 1945, Ernest Shinwell, the Minister of Fuel and Power, warned Prime Minister Attlee of hidden dangers in the agreement. There were two points on which Britain must stand firm, he insisted (PRO 1948b):

[T]hat there could be no alteration of the definition of the words "country" or "territories" in the Agreement which would have the effect of breaking up the cohesion of the British Empire; and that it was of highest importance to safeguard our foreign exchange position.

Attlee scribbled "I agree" on Shinwell's minute.

In the event, the agreement was never ratified by the U.S. Senate, which tended to see the agreement as a *British* effort to corner Middle East sources. Thus, Shinwell's concerns were rendered moot. They nonetheless provide evidence of the extreme importance of the territorial and economic issues. Years later, in 1951, the agreement was revived — or an attempt was made to resurrect it — in yet another effort to ensure the orderly marketing of Middle East oil as part of a potential solution to the Anglo-Iranian crisis (see Chapter 3 below) (PRO 1951i:4–5). Both the Foreign Office and the Ministry of Fuel favored such an agreement (PRO 1951i:1, 1951j:2), but once again, domestic forces in the United States — the oil companies and oil state representatives in Congress — saw to it that the agreement was buried.

In the years following the end of World War II, the dubious strategic reliability of Middle East oil — and, in particular, Iranian oil — became increasingly obvious. Given the delay in the Soviet evacuation of Iran after the end of World War II, and Soviet demands for an oil concession in northern Iran (Kuniholm 1980: ch. 5; Louis 1984:54–73), British concerns over Soviet intentions mounted. Did the Soviets need Iranian oil? Would they try to seize the Anglo-Iranian Oil Company (AIOC) fields? In early 1947, the Official Oil Committee of the Cabinet noted that (PRO 1947d:1)

> The oil position of the British Commonwealth is precarious, depending as it does on the Middle East and South American supplies. There are strategic hazards connected with the former and political hazards connected with the latter.

A February 1947 memo on "Russian Oil Production," written in the Foreign Office, was very suggestive of what these hazards might be, pointing out that, due to depletion and wartime destruction, *"Russia has now more oil refining capacity* [due to U.S. lend-lease] *than the necessary crude oil to supply them* [sic] *with"* (PRO 1947e:2, emphasis in original). Several weeks later, the Official Oil Committee received a memo prepared by the Future Planning Section of the Joint Planning

Staff, which noted that "No firm reliance can be placed on the defensibility in war of the Middle East oil areas," although attached to this was the *caveat* that "It should be borne in mind . . . that this view has no official validity since the memorandum . . . has not been considered by the Chiefs of Staff" (PRO 1947f).

The economic, as opposed to the strategic, importance of the oil *was* recognized by the British Chiefs of Staff. A memo written in October 1947, entitled "Middle East – Brief for Discussions" (with the U.S. Joint Chiefs of Staff), noted (PRO 1947g, emphasis added) that

> It is, in any case, abundantly clear that quite apart from the question of the Middle East in war, both the Americans and the British have so many economic interests, especially oil, in the Middle East that we must maintain our position and prestige continuously in peace and ensure that *we deny the advantages we enjoy to economic rivals and potential enemies.*

This point of view continued to develop throughout the British government, so that by April 1948 the Joint Secretaries of the Official Oil Committee, in a memo on the "Strategic Importance of South Persian Oil," could write "[T]he continued supply of oil from South Persia is essential to our peacetime needs but . . . it [is] not entirely clear whether we must depend on this source of supply in war time" (PRO 1948c). The Secretaries therefore supplied another reason for maintaining the British position in the Middle East: "[I]t was held that the main reason for retaining a firm hold on the Middle East was not for the purpose of safeguarding the oil fields but to prevent an enemy gaining access to Africa" (PRO 1948c). The shift in strategic purpose is, in and of itself, interesting, for in subsequent years defense of Africa came to figure prominently as a reason for remaining in the Middle East (see, for example, PRO 1950e:2).

With respect to Persian oil, the military rationale for a British presence in the region continued to weaken. A May 1948 report by the Commanders-in-Chief, Middle East, concluded that "The successful defence of the PERSIAN GULF is not in itself vital to the defence of the MIDDLE EAST" (PRO 1948d:3). A July 1948 directive to the Commanders-in-Chief Committee, Middle East, on "Defence of the Middle East," indicated one of the subsidiary tasks of British forces in the region to be the "neutralization as necessary of the Persian and Iraq oilfields to deny their use to the enemy" (PRO 1948e:4) (for a brief discussion of the plans, see PRO 1948f, and for the plans themselves, see PRO 1953a). Thus, by the time the Anglo-Iranian confrontation over the oil concession reached its nadir in 1951, the strategic rationale for remaining in Iran no longer held.

Consequently, faced with recurrent balance-of-payments and sterling crises, the British were forced to relegate strategic concerns to the bottom of their list of political goals in the Middle East during the confrontation with Iran. In order of priority, therefore, British objectives were (PRO 1951b:16–17; see also PRO 1951k, 1951*l*:1)

(i)   The maintenance of a non-Communist Persia;
(ii) The maintenance of oil supplies through control by a United Kingdom company;
(iii) Safeguarding the United Kingdom balance of payments;
(iv) Settlement innocuous to United Kingdom interests in other concessionary countries.

From a reading of various files in the British archives, it is difficult to say which of these objectives *were* the most important. The total cost per annum of the loss of Iranian oil was estimated to be about £100 million from loss of sales plus $350 million to replace AIOC by dollar sources of oil (PRO 1951b:17). Thus, the economic cost was substantial, but it probably would not have been fatal (see also the U.S. calculation and view on this in HSTL 1951a, 1951d, and p. 58, above).

Generally speaking, the British were not happy with the U.S. approach to resolving the impasse with Iran. The British were less concerned than the U.S. about grand strategy, viewing Iranian Prime Minister Mossadeq, and not his advisors, as the primary danger to British interests. Hence, for British policymakers, keeping Iran "non-Communist" came to mean the replacement of Mossadeq by someone more amenable to reaching a settlement (PRO 1951m, 1951n:3–4). British prestige, and the effect of Iranian defiance on British foreign relations, also emerged as major issues (PRO 1951*l*:2–3, 1951m:1, 1951n:1–3).

In February 1952 the authors of a memorandum of the Persia (Official) Committee of the Cabinet complained that (PRO 1952e:4)

> The Americans appear to view the [Iranian] problem solely in terms of fighting Communism and, in the light of their assessment [of the situation], are prepared to take great risks at our expense. We too wish to fight Communism in Persia, but for us it is a question of balancing the risk of

Persia going Communist against the risk of making a settlement which will cause us great and possibly fatal damage in other directions.

Such damage could, as noted above, include loss of both prestige and income, not to mention oil. As Herbert Morrison, Bevin's replacement, warned during a meeting of the Persian Oil Committee of the Cabinet called in May 1951 to discuss the possibility of military intervention in Iran (PRO 1951m:1; see also PRO 1952e:3):

> Apart from the immense financial and material losses we should suffer if we were deprived of the oilfields, acquiescence in their expropriation by the Persian Government would destroy our prestige in the Middle East with disastrous results in Egypt and elsewhere.

The Commanders-in-Chief, Middle East, were more explicit about the costs of giving in to Iranian demands. In mid-1951 they told the War Office (PRO 1951o:2) that

> Our failure to stand firm in PERSIA would be interpreted throughout this area as a sign of fundamental weakness and give immediate impetus to widespread neutralist and nationalist influences throughout the area. We do NOT believe that there is any single government in the MIDDLE EAST, possibly excluding JORDAN alone, which would be able to withstand the political pressure to withdraw from our defence associations which such a situation [as giving in] will produce.[9]

In order to prevent the loss of the Iranian oil fields, as well as British prestige, the Chiefs of Staff favored "large-scale" operations if they were the "only alternative to surrendering the oilfields," and even though "entry of foreign troops into Persia might well be a signal for the overthrow of the present Government and its replacement by a Government more favourably disposed to the U.S.S.R." (PRO 1951m:2). This was, of course, the eventuality most feared by the United States, fear of which led to its involvement in the crisis.

During the summer of 1951, the British chose finally not to intervene with force, although Morrison, among others, thought that the results of such action could only be positive. In a paper published for the Cabinet in July 1951, he noted that military occupation of the Abadan refinery and the oilfields would not only keep them operating

---

[9]Ironically, Jordan was the state most dependent on British military and economic aid for its existence and security (Louis 1984: pt. III, ch. 9).

but would also demonstrate British determination and provide good public relations. Intervention, wrote Morrison, "might be expected to produce a salutary effect throughout the Middle East and elsewhere, as evidence that United Kingdom interests could not be recklessly molested with impunity" (PRO 1951p:1). Throughout the crisis, the British continued to hope for a new Iranian government that would be more amenable to negotiations. Ultimately, a new prime minister did take office, but only as the result of the coup engineered by the British and U.S. intelligence services (Roosevelt 1979). Even that did not help the British, for they were forced to accept a restructuring of the Iranian concession within which the AIOC's holdings, and the visibility of the British presence in Iran, were greatly reduced (Painter 1986: ch. 8).

The Anglo-Iranian crisis must also be understood in the broader context of British policy in the Middle East over this period. During the interminable conflict with the Iranian government, the British were simultaneously engaged in negotiations with Egypt over the future of the Suez Canal and their occupation of the Canal Zone. The 1936 Treaty that allowed a major British military base in the Zone was due to expire in 1956, and renegotiation was complicated by Egypt's resentment of the high-handed way in which Britain had treated it ever since the nineteenth century (Louis 1984: pt. III, ch. 6). Britain's reluctance to yield any measure of sovereignty over the Canal Zone, and its repeated attempts to manipulate domestic Egyptian politics, culminated in the coup that deposed King Farouk in 1952 and led to the rise of Gamal Abdul Nasser as well as the Suez debacle in 1956 (Louis 1984: pt. V, ch. 4–5).

The logic of maintaining control of the Canal was partly economic but primarily geopolitical. The cost of shipping oil through the Canal was much lower than sending it around the Cape, and there was some fear that shipping might be halted arbitrarily by the Egyptians at some indefinite time in the future. But more generally, the Canal Zone was seen as a "barrier" to potential Soviet expansion and as a base from which to attack the Soviet Union in the event of war (PRO 1949f:1). British policymakers realized that Britain alone could neither defend the Middle East in time of war nor keep it firmly in the Western camp in time of peace, and that it would have to enlist the help of others in this effort, in particular, the United States. This was no easy task, as things turned out.

Throughout the late 1940s and early 1950s, U.S. policymakers remained emphatic about the strategic importance of the Middle East to Western security, but they were curiously reluctant to commit significant resources to its defense (FRUS 1951c:9–10). The British found themselves frustrated by this reticence and were determined to do something about it. The apparent solution was a military alliance of Middle Eastern states, known variously as the "Middle East Command" (MEC) or "Middle East Defence Organization" (MEDO).

One of the earliest mentions of such an alliance appears in a memorandum dated September 12, 1949, prepared by the chief of the Imperial General Staff for the upcoming meeting of the Western Union Defence Committee. It was entitled the "United Kingdom Contribution to Western Europe" (PRO 1949g). In the memo, the author noted that, due to the U.S. atomic monopoly,[10] the chances of war were remote and therefore the economic risks of rapid rearmament could not be justified. Taking a cue from the last war, he wrote (PRO 1949g) that

> Should war by any chance break out unexpectedly, the Allied cause would not in any way benefit from the hasty throwing in of United Kingdom Forces into the land battle for Western Europe, where they would be destroyed to no purpose .... We propose therefore to concentrate on the defence of the Middle East, a course which we consider would result in a shorter war and hence offer more prospect of an early liberation of occupied Europe.

The Middle East Defence Organization was the proposed British contribution to this plan. The MEDO was conceived broadly to be similar to the North Atlantic Treaty Organization (NATO), as an alliance of local states and also outside powers with interests in the region.[11] Members of MEDO might, according to British thinking on the subject, include the United Kingdom, France, and South Africa, as well as Egypt, Iraq, and Turkey. The rationale behind such a regional alliance, rather than a NATO Middle East Command, was

[10]Observe closely the date of the memorandum. The first Soviet atomic test had taken place on August 29, 1949.

[11]Initially, some thought was given to extending membership in NATO to Middle Eastern countries (see FRUS 1949c:31). This idea was dropped in favor of the MEDO, but planning continued within NATO for some type of associated command based in the Middle East (NARS 1953c).

identical to that which had informed British Imperial defense: The regional members would provide the manpower to be commanded by British or Western officers (Louis 1984:106).

This was necessary because, on the one hand, the United States was reluctant to send more than token forces to the region during peacetime, for domestic reasons as well as from fear of alienating local regimes (FRUS 1951d; NARS 1952a:1). Furthermore, by its own analysis, during the first two years of a general war the United States would be unable to send troops to the Middle East (FRUS 1951c:9; NARS 1951f:1). On the other hand, the depth of anti-British sentiment in the Middle East made it extremely difficult to cobble together a force composed wholly of men from NATO states to be placed in the region. An alliance of regional and outside states would circumvent this problem it was thought, especially if the local regimes were seen to have some authority and a significant role within the alliance (FRUS 1949c; NARS 1952d).

The British recognized the monumental difficulties involved in establishing the MEDO. A February 1953 paper by the Defence Co-Ordination Committee Middle East, entitled "Defence of the Middle East — An Analysis of Future Prospects," extolled the virtues and goals of an MEDO, but added, almost parenthetically (PRO 1953b:9–10),

> So great are the difficulties that some have concluded that a scheme of defence for the Middle East in war is not possible in our day; yet, it is argued, we must maintain a facade of intention to defend it in order to prevent its loss to communism in the Cold War....
>
> As a Defence Committee for the Middle East, we are bound to limit ourselves to real solutions of the problem of defending this important area, and to exclude those which are only "make-believe". If, however, it is decided that we cannot, for economic or political reasons, afford a real solution, but that, for political reasons again, we must put forward a facade, then we submit the following comments:
>
> (a)   Even if we feel that we must try to deceive others, we should not deceive ourselves or the Americans;
>
> (b)   Our bluff may be called one day and British soldiers and airmen may again find themselves committed to a hopeless situation....
>
> (c)   The facade must not be so transparent that it fails to deceive.

The British task was complicated further by the fact that most Arab regimes simply did not believe in the "Soviet threat." This remained a continual source of frustration to both British and U.S. officials. In a November 1950 Cabinet paper on "Egypt," Foreign Minister Bevin complained that (PRO 1950f:2)

> [T]he Egyptian Government . . . are far more afraid of Israel than the Soviet Union, [and] are still only dimly aware of the danger of the [sic] Soviet aggression; they have categorically refused to consider the concept of joint defence in peacetime.

E.S. Crocker, the U.S. Ambassador to Iraq, cogently described the problem in an October 1951 cable to the U.S. State Department. He reported on a conversation about the MEDO with an official of the Saudi Arabian government (NARS 1951g):

> I . . . asked what steps in his view might be taken by the Arab countries to defend themselves against the threat of Soviet expansion and he replied that he did not consider such a threat to be comparable to the threat of zionism and Israel. This of course is a familiar thesis but its familiarity should not lead us into the error of discounting its acceptance as a basic Arab tenet. It is reiterated with such frequency and earnestness and with such disregard for the facts that the West has a tendency to brush it aside as puerile if not inconsequential . . . . Nothing could lead us into a more serious error than failure to recognize this tenet as the controlling factor in Arab thinking, reactions and policy, above and beyond all other considerations.

(A similar report can also be found in FRUS 1947a:1335–40.) Perhaps the best encapsulation of Arab feelings on the question of Middle East defense was communicated by the British Ambassador to Iraq, J.M. Troutbeck, in a 1951 letter to Foreign Minister Herbert Morrison. Troutbeck quoted a passage from an Iraqi newspaper that read (PRO 1951q:3, also quoted in Louis 1984:713):

> The call of the West finds no echo in our hearts. We do not understand them because we do not feel ourselves to be part of the socalled "free world" which they say they are defending. We are part of the oppressed world which is struggling against them to achieve its freedom and throw off their yoke.

Indeed, it was the apparent inability or unwillingness of the Americans and British to differentiate nationalism from Communism that ultimately confounded their efforts to establish a coordinated defense of the Middle East. The Baghdad Pact that was signed in 1955 did include Britain, Iraq, Pakistan, and Turkey, but neither the United

States nor Egypt nor Israel nor any of the more important oil-producing states joined. The relevant question to ask in retrospect is therefore: What was being defended? As Lord Cherwell pointed out in 1951, India was gone. By 1954, so was Iranian oil and, after 1956, the Suez Canal, too. To be sure, the United Kingdom continued to retain a very strong *economic* interest in Middle East oil, and its economic security was tied to the continued flow of that oil, but experience seemed to suggest that military defense was not needed to keep the oil flowing (Gallagher 1982:126). This realization dawned on British policymakers only very slowly, and it was one that was not fully recognized until after the Suez debacle.

By 1956, the perceived Soviet threat to British interests in the Persian Gulf apparently had vanished, to be replaced by the more local problem of Egyptian nationalism. A Cabinet paper written by Foreign Minister Selwyn Lloyd at the time stated the main British purpose in the Gulf to be "to ensure fair access to the oil and stable conditions for its production" (PRO 1956a:3). Thus, the list of possible threats to the British position in the Gulf included those posed (PRO 1956a:4)

(a)   by the Rulers [of the Gulf states] and their Governments succumbing to the xenophobic influences of Arab nationalism, particularly from Egypt, and turning against us;

(b)   by the degeneration of administration in the hands of an irresponsible ruling family into misgovernment of the kind prevailing in Saudi Arabia;

(c)   by the Rulers (upon our individual relations with whom our position depends) losing their authority to reformist or revolutionary movements which might, on gaining power, reject the British connection;

(d)   by the encroachment upon, or absorption of, the territories [of the Gulf States] by their neighbors, particularly Saudi Arabia.

The Suez Crisis exposed the shallowness of the ideal rationale for a continued British military presence in the region and the territorial/diplomatic strategic synthesis pursued by Britain. Although the joint military venture with France and Israel might be counted a success, to the extent that it achieved its strategic goals (Cooper 1978: chs. 8–9), the U.S. threat to veto a loan by the International Monetary Fund to Britain, enmeshed in yet another balance-of-payments crisis, demonstrated how stringent were the economic constraints on it (Cook 1981:189–90). After Suez, any allusions to "global responsibilities" were simply pretense, and the government of Anthony Eden's successor, Harold Macmillan, engaged in the rapid liquidation of what remained of the British Empire. That Britain *could* continue to survive without a major military commitment to either the Middle East or its oil was demonstrated by its eventual withdrawal of virtually all troops from east of Suez (Abadi 1982).

The history of British postwar policy in the Middle East is obviously far more complex than that recounted here (see, for example, Lowe and Dockrill 1972: ch. 3; Cooper 1978; Monroe 1981; Abadi 1982; Louis 1984), but the essential points are evident. First, in the Middle East, Britain tried to balance an ideal interest—the maintenance of a territorial/diplomatic strategy—against a material one—survival in the face of stringent economic constraints—and failed. Second, although raw materials—in this case, oil—were critical to economic survival because they were so important to Britain's balance of payments, the rhetorical association of the resource with the strategy actually undermined its economic position. This paradox arose because the "protection" of the oil came to be seen as a strategy of political imperialism and an effort to suppress local nationalism. As a result, Britain was pushed out of the region not by what she feared most—Soviet communism—but rather by what she discounted most—indigenous nationalisms. The ultimate weakness of the ideal interest—pursued long after both the oil and the Canal were "lost"—does not obscure the fact that it pushed Britain to the brink of bankruptcy. A similar, although perhaps less dramatic, conflict between ideal and material interests may be seen in British postwar policy in the Far East.

Raw Materials and British Policy in the Far East

Whereas the rationale for the British presence in the Middle East had heavy geopolitical overtones as well as economic objectives, British policy in the Far East was driven primarily by the latter. Prior to World War II, Far East trade had represented an important source of foreign exchange for Britain because a considerable portion of the tin and rubber produced in British Malaya was purchased by the United States. China, as well, was considered an important and potentially large market for British goods (Louis 1971). In order to encourage growth in its trade with China, and to counter growing Japanese influence following the invasion of Manchuria in the 1930s (and after the outbreak of war), the British set about negotiating the return to

Chinese sovereignty of the various commercial concessions obtained by force during the nineteenth century (Luard 1962:38–39, 50–51; Gallagher 1982:130–31).[12] At the same time, British strategists wished to retain certain territories in the region in order to protect British economic interests there, even though the economic constraints on military spending during the 1930s made it difficult, if not impossible, to provide for the defense of those territories (Kennedy 1983a:27–28, 1983c:100–01). In the event, they were quickly overrun by the invading Japanese armies in 1941.

Following the end of World War II, many of the reasons for maintaining a Far East territorial strategy vanished as independence came to India and Burma. Yet the British held on to its Southeast Asian colonies, arguing that they were not yet ready for independence (Stockwell 1984). It was also argued with impeccable domino-theory logic that the British position must be maintained throughout Southeast Asia (PRO 1946d:4):

> The political (both foreign and internal) strategic and economic interests of the Commonwealth in the area are interlocking and ought to be treated as such. What happens in one part of the area is of interest to all other parts of the area. A reversion to the pre-war situation of handling these problems in watertight compartments and penny packets would be a fatal step.

An effort was made to reestablish trade with China, which had been halted during the war, and to restore the British position in the Asian colonies. This was complicated by general political unrest in the region, another consequence of the war. Not long after they returned to Malaya, the British found themselves confronted by a Communist-led insurrection that threatened their control of the colony. This uprising was not suppressed completely until after Malayan independence in 1957 (Short 1975).

A primary reason for maintaining a toehold in Southeast Asia was economic. In a 1949 report to the Cabinet, the Far East (Official) Committee observed (PRO 1950g:2) that

> Traditionally, this area in Asia has played a most important part in the pattern of world trade — thus Malaya and Indonesia were markets for European manufactures while their exports were not only of direct value to the European economy but were also part of the triangular trade

---

[12]This can be seen as part of the British tradition of "appeasement" practiced during the nineteenth and twentieth centuries (Kennedy 1983a).

structure which enabled Europe to obtain many of its requirements from the Western Hemisphere.

The loss of Britain's Asian territories might lead to the virtual elimination of its trade position in the region. In 1949 the China and South East Asia Committee warned (PRO 1949h:4) that

> If Hong Kong were lost to us, the one remaining oasis of stability among the prevailing chaos on the China coast would have disappeared. . . . If we lose Hong Kong Japan will, undoubtedly, acquire a dominating position in the commerce of the Far East.[13]

Furthermore, the Far East continued to be a critical source of dollar earnings for the Commonwealth (PRO 1949i:11). In terms of the balance of payments with respect to dollar earnings of the colonial territories, from 1948 to 1950 Malaya provided between 62 and 76 percent of the dollar surplus (PRO 1951r:8).

But, as was the case in the Middle East, there was no way to make a good case for retaining the colonies in the Far East without reference to military concerns. A February 1948 paper on "The Strategic Position of Malaya," by the Commanders-in-Chief Committee, Far East, laid out the military significance of the colony to the British position, and noted further (PRO 1948g:3) that

> South East Asia is an important source of supply to the British Commonwealth of such materials as rubber, oil, tin, coconut oil and oil palm products and, to an increasing degree, of hemp. There are deposits of bauxite, tungsten and coal. Because of its position on the sea and air routes Singapore is a focal point in the expansion of trade in this area.

The Committee also deduced that "continuing uncertainty in world conditions will encourage the spread of Communism and prejudice Commonwealth influence with the peoples of South East Asia" (PRO 1948g:3). Therefore, they concluded that Malaya, "as a centre of Commonwealth influence in the Far East," was the main "long-term" objective for "Communist and other disruptive elements" (PRO 1948g:3).

The Committee's prediction was directly tied to the growing strength of Communist forces in China. A Chiefs of Staff Committee report on China, written at the end of 1948, gloomily assessed the

---

[13]Curiously, U.S. policy gradually became oriented toward just this end of Japan achieving economic preeminence in the region (see Cumings 1987–88).

changing situation there and commented that British interests were "in a bad way" due to the increasing chaos (PRO 1948h:6–9). This, in and of itself, was not too important as trade with China was minor, investment there fairly small, and imports largely nonessential. The major problem, in the Chiefs' view, was the probable effect of a Communist victory on the rest of Southeast Asia. The Committee saw the likelihood of increased labor disturbances, refugee and immigration problems, and detrimental effects on rice production as the consequences of such an eventuality. The last effect was thought particularly critical because (PRO 1948h:9)

> A decrease in rice consumption will provide fertile ground for Communist agitation. This—together with general disturbances in other South-East Asia industries—would cause further disruption of the economy of the area with consequent adverse effects on the production of such vital commodities as rubber, tin, edible oils, &c., which are of such importance to world economic recovery.

This last comment provides a useful insight into British Far East policy in the late 1940s and early 1950s. Although the geopolitical implications of a Communist Southeast Asia were thought ominous for Australia, New Zealand, and Southeast Asia, for the purposes of British planning it was the economic importance of the region that came first. This was evidenced further by the rapidity with which the United Kingdom recognized the People's Republic of China in 1950, in the face of strong U.S. opposition (Luard 1962:79; Boardman 1976: ch. 3).

In fact, it was the British view that the economic stringencies binding Britain had decided advantages in Southeast Asia, for they weakened the influence on British policymakers of the ideal interests so evident in U.S. policy. In a Cabinet paper in which he was highly critical of U.S. policy in the Far East, written in August 1950, Foreign Minister Bevin argued (PRO 1950h:2) that

> This comparatively negative policy of the United Kingdom which was dictated by our post-war weakness and our many commitments elsewhere has meant that while on the one hand we were unable to exercise much influence upon the course of events, we were, on the other hand, less immediately involved in the debacle in China and Korea and are therefore to-day to some extent freer than the United States to determine our policy for the future in the Far East.

Even though British trade and economic interests in China were comparatively minor at the time, the latter's economic potential as well as its future political influence in Southeast Asia were deemed of major concern. Therefore, between 1946 and the final Communist victory in 1949, Britain attempted to pursue a policy of accommodation with the conflicting parties in China. In the view of the Foreign Office, the West would possess significant economic leverage over China for some time for, as was noted in a March 1949 draft Cabinet paper, "China will be almost entirely dependent on non-Communist sources for supplies of rubber, oil, and fertilisers. She will be deficient in raw cotton. The most serious mineral deficiencies will be the ferroalloy metals" (PRO 1949j:5). The omnipresent dollar shortage provided another reason to maintain trade with China. The Foreign Office noted (PRO 1949j:6) that

> [O]n economic grounds it would be regrettable to cut ourselves off from a potentially vast market for British goods and a potentially important soft-currency source of supply of essential imports (including eggs, tea, broad beans, bristles, soya beans and flour, and tung oil).

The British were, therefore, philosophically prepared to ride out the trouble in China. As another Foreign Office memorandum observed (PRO 1949k:3)

> There are few grounds for optimism as to the future; but British trading communities abroad have weathered many storms in the past, and we are by no means convinced that we should be wise to abandon what remains of our position in China until it becomes abundantly clear that it is untenable.

Nonetheless, as time passed, the British were gradually coming around to the U.S. position on the consequences of a Communist government in China, and beginning to speak the same language as the Americans. It was argued that withdrawal from China would eliminate whatever residual influence Britain had there and would "leave the door wide open to the Russians" (PRO 1949l:4). An April 1950 memorandum by the Foreign Office nonetheless pleaded the case for retaining ties with China as follows (PRO 1950d:8):

> The domination of China by a Communist regime is repugnant to the Western powers, but it is nevertheless a fact which cannot and should not be ignored. Here we have a vast country containing nearly a quarter of the

population of the world, ruled for the time being by a government in alliance with Moscow. To boycott it would certainly strengthen ties between Moscow and Peking; to attempt to create a sanitary cordon around it is beyond the powers of either the United States or the United Kingdom. The present policy of His Majesty's Government is therefore to try to maintain contacts with China for the reason that in the maintenance of contacts with the West lies the only hope of influencing China not to commit herself finally and irrevocably to the Kremlin. If this course is pursued, it will be a hard one from which we must expect to derive no early or material benefits. But the stake is a big one, since the alternative would be to write China off as irretrievably lost to Western democracy and to invite her open hostility.

Not until the outbreak of the Korean War, and Britain's involvement in the military action there, was its Far East policy finally and irrevocably coopted by the United States. Even then, the British remained reluctant to isolate China completely.

In a curious way, the British turned upside down the U.S. reasoning regarding the relative importance of military and economic issues in Southeast Asia, arguing that the failure to pay attention to the economic facts of life might be more important than the practice of containment (but see Cumings 1987–88 on this point). If the economies of the Southeast Asian states were allowed to deteriorate, the region would become prey to Communist destabilization. Such deterioration could result directly from interference with the normal flow of trade in various commodities, particularly rubber and tin. In addition, the disruption of Western trade with China for political purposes was seen as highly threatening to the future of the British territories. Although by 1950 Malaya had declined somewhat in value as a source of rubber and tin for the United States, due to the wartime development of synthetic rubber and new sources of tin in Bolivia, the two materials retained their strategic importance for other countries, both East and West. It was trade in these materials with the East that particularly concerned the Americans.

In the wake of the the Chinese Communist victory and the outbreak of the Korean War, the United States attempted to impose controls on the export of various commodities and goods to the Soviet Union, mainland China, and North Korea. One of the materials on the export control list was natural rubber, and the British reluctance to restrict shipments of rubber to mainland China was a particular source of irritation to the Americans (NARS 1950d; HSTL 1951p; FRUS

1952–54f:944). In April 1951 the Western allies agreed to limit exports of rubber to the Soviet Union to amounts considered "adequate for normal consumption" (PRO 1952f:1). This action, it was thought, would make it difficult for the Soviets to transship rubber to China and North Korea.

For the British, the problem with such restrictions was that they would lead to a surplus of rubber production, with concomitant effects on price. As a result, according to a May 1952 memo by the Foreign Secretary and the President of the Board of Trade (PRO 1952f:3):

> [T]here will be a serious danger to political stability in South-East Asia, and especially in Malaya, where the lower grades [of rubber], demand for which is most likely to be affected, are mainly produced by small holders. So long as we restrict the market for rubber by prohibiting exports to China and North Korea and by refusing on security grounds to allow the Soviet *Bloc* to buy all they could use, the result of further cuts in such shipments as are allowed is likely to be a sharp fall in the market price for natural rubber and one which is likely to be accentuated by the time its effects reach the smallholder. Since the smallholders and their dependents in Malaya form 20 per cent. of the population, the effect of a further fall in the market price therefore might have extremely serious political consequences under present conditions.[14]

A side effect of trade restrictions would be the impact on the London Rubber Market, whose invisible earnings made a significant contribution to the British balance of payments.

The British were also worried that the imposition of stringent economic sanctions on China might provoke it into an attack on British territories in the Far East. Although the Chiefs of Staff thought that the short-term effects of sanctions would be "negligible," they agreed that "a complete cessation of all China's seaborne imports would slow down its war- making capacity" over the longer term (PRO 1951s:2). Until then, however, Hong Kong, Malaya, Indochina, Burma, and Siam would be at increased risk of Chinese military action. Of particular concern was the situation with respect to Hong Kong (PRO 1951s:4):

> There is a grave danger that an overt Chinese attack on Hong Kong might lead to a general war. Appeal would be made to the United Nations which, even if collective military action were agreed upon, could not provide

As a journalist noted at the time in *The Observer* (London) (PRO 1952g), "Malaya's ability to keep people better off than those of any neighbouring State depends to an alarmingly great extent on the United States not discovering a really cheap substitute for rubber."

effective forces for the defence of the colony in time. The necessary forces are not at present available from United Kingdom or Commonwealth sources without denuding vital areas. Since economic sanctions may lead to an attack on Hong Kong we must be prepared for such an attack which at best could only end in a fighting withdrawal.

In general, therefore, the Chiefs opposed a total embargo (PRO 1951s:6), as did the Working Party on Economic Sanctions Against China of the Far East (Official) Committee of the Cabinet (PRO 1951t:1). The Chiefs concluded that "[W]e have no evidence that China is determined upon a general war with the West . . . and we should gain time and not get embroiled in a major war in Asia" (PRO 1951s:6).

In the event, Britain went along with the U.S. insistence on controls on trade with China, although the degree of restriction never reached the level of the total economic embargo demanded by the United States in the early days of the Korean War. Nonetheless, the more limited program of controls was still quite extensive, covering a broad range of metals, minerals, and their manufactures; chemical and petroleum equipment; miscellaneous machinery and equipment; rubber and rubber products; electronic and scientific equipment; arms, ammunition, and implements of war; and atomic energy materials and equipment (PRO 1951u). The objectives of the embargo lists as finally formulated were twofold, according to the Far East (Official) Committee (PRO 1951v:2):

> [F]irst to limit the Chinese war potential as far as possible and to remove any basis for criticism of United Kingdom policy both in the country and the United States; and secondly and the most important . . . to bring the conflict in Korea to an end.

But the Committee continued to express concern over the consequences of even this limited program and the "possibility that the initial reaction to the additional embargo, if any, would be to widen the conflict" (PRO 1951v:2).

As events turned out, the feared effects of trade controls on the British territories did not materialize, nor did China launch an attack against any of them. Still, the British remained generally unhappy with the export controls and throughout the 1950s agitated periodically for their elimination. Between 1956 and 1958, matters finally came to a head, but for reasons apparently having nothing to do with the British economy, as we shall see.

Raw Materials and British Economic Policy

A third area in which raw materials played a central role in British foreign policy was in direct relation to the British economy. Policy in the Middle East and with respect to the colonies of the Far East was influenced by both ideal and material objectives, albeit to differing degrees. But the high level of British dependence on imports of certain raw commodities, as well as the reliance of the economy for its health on the sale of other materials, were inescapable material facts of life in the 1940s and 1950s. The voluminous files of the Ministries of Supply (1945–51), Materials (1951–54) and Trade (1954–on) in the U.K. Public Record Office provide ample evidence of this ever-present concern. Furthermore, the raw materials issue entered into British relations with the United States and confounded economic planning in a way that is today scarcely imaginable.

As always, the key to the problem was dollars, which were in chronically short supply. Dollars were needed for the purchase of those materials not available from the Sterling Bloc area, to replace those that had come traditionally from Eastern Europe but could no longer be obtained there for one reason or another, and to finance the purchase of machinery and goods needed for post-war construction.

At the same time, the dependence of Britain on imported raw materials meant that, inevitably, it would be competing with the United States for certain essential commodities. Although shortages arising from high levels of demand did not develop until after the outbreak of the Korean War, for Britain the long-term implications of high levels of U.S. demand were clear. As the Chancellor of the Duchy of Lancaster noted in September 1952, after reading *Resources for Freedom*, the report of the Paley Commission (PRO 1952h:2),

> [T]he prospective increase in the demands of the United States for raw materials [as projected by the report] is not without serious dangers for the United Kingdom. If the expansion of supplies fails to keep pace, the superior purchasing power of the United States is likely to force up prices and suck in supplies at our expense.

But high prices were not the only potential hazard. Uncontrolled fluctuations in price posed a problem, as well. Wrote Sir Arthur Salter, the Minister of Materials, in 1953 (PRO 1953c):

> A much more serious danger [than excessive cheapness of raw materials, followed by scarcity] arises from the fact that, while the UK is an importer,

the rest of the Commonwealth and Sterling Area is an exporter of raw materials. Our foreign exchange reserves (which of course serve the whole Sterling Area) are therefore reduced by a fall in price.

Finally, the U.S. insistence on controls on trade with the Eastern Bloc was not without its effects on the economies of Britain and other territories and countries within the Sterling area. Each of these points is discussed in turn below.

Sterling and the Dollar Shortage.   The nonconvertibility of sterling led British economic planners to maximize dollar income and minimize dollar expenditures whenever possible. This meant that they were very cautious about purchasing goods from so-called dollar sources (such as the United States and various other countries outside the Sterling Bloc). At the same time, concerted efforts were made to maximize trade in certain goods available from within the Sterling Bloc and from nonsterling, "soft-currency" sources (such as the Netherlands, Soviet Union, and China) in order to economize on the outflow of dollars (see for example PRO 1947h). The U.S. insistence on controls on trade with the Eastern Bloc led to a sort of tightrope act by Britain as it tried to balance its material needs against the ideal interests of the United States.

There was, in the final analysis, no ignoring these latter interests. In an analysis of the $4 billion postwar stockpiling program legislated into being by the U.S. Congress in 1946, an official with the British Military Mission in Washington, D.C., worriedly communicated to the Ministry of Supply in London almost every concern that would arise over the following decade (PRO 1946e:2):

> Questions will arise as to the effect of such a huge program on the markets for strategic materials particularly so far as European producers are concerned. Over what period of time will the Americans attempt to build their stockpiles? Will they buy in the cheapest materials or will they attempt to support certain areas for particular political reasons, e.g., South America? Will they use their purchases to attempt to stabilize prices by buying in bad times and slacking off in good? Will there be any attempt to co-ordinate purchasing policy with other countries such as the United Kingdom to avoid competitive bidding? What safeguards will there be against using "strategic" stockpiles to manipulate world prices, e.g., to keep the price of tin down? Will large Government stockpiles hang over markets and cause uncertainty among producers? Will the U.K. have a strategic stockpiling policy?

Not infrequently, the answers to these questions were not what the British had hoped for, even though U.S. actions that negatively affected the economies of Britain and the Sterling area were not the result of deliberate maliciousness but, rather, bureaucratic conflict within the U.S. government. The fact remained that the economy of the United States was so big relative to the rest of the world that its every action had some effect on international markets. As a 1954 Foreign Office memorandum put it (PRO 1954b:6),

> U.S. purchases of certain important commodities are so large as to deter-
> mine their price in the world market. These commodities are therefore
> subjected to violent price movements in accordance with changes in U.S.
> demand. Unfortunately the economies of the countries which produce
> such commodities as tin and rubber are almost wholly dependent on the
> sale of these commodities at a reasonable price. Some of these countries
> are in the sterling area, and are highly vulnerable to Communist penetra-
> tion. It is therefore in the interest of the U.S. as well as ourselves to
> co-operate in arrangements whereby the sale of these commodities is
> cushioned from violent price fluctuations which alternately cause inflation
> and extreme poverty.

Although U.S. policymakers were not insensitive to the effects of U.S. purchases on world prices, they generally refused to become involved in market stabilization efforts unless such action was absolutely de-manded by the situation. As a result, it was left to the British to try to cushion the effects of these violent price fluctuations on Sterling Bloc countries.

Not only was the United States a vital source of dollars through trade, loans, and the European Recovery Program (ERP — the Marshall Plan), as noted above it was also a major purchaser of materials for the strategic stockpile. One of the objectives of the ERP, as legislated by the U.S. Congress, was to obtain foreign minerals for U.S. defense needs. Among the funds available from the Economic Cooperation Administration (ECA), the agency running the ERP, were some to be used for the direct purchase of strategic materials for the U.S. stockpile and others to expand materials production in European colonies (PRO 1948i; Pollard 1985:202). But transfer of materials to the United States tended to compete with European requirements, particularly as post-war reconstruction led to an increase in European demand for the same materials. As a result, the ECA spent very little — only $161 million — on acquisitions for the stockpile (NARS 1950e).

The ERP goal of funding colonial development found itself, at times, caught between the U.S. ideal interest of encouraging decolonization and its material interest in acquiring colonial raw materials (NARS 1952e; Pollard 1985:202). Depending on circumstances, which had as much to do with geopolitics as economics, funding for colonial development was provided rather willingly. The Americans and Europeans, however, tended to view each other's intentions with suspicion. The Europeans feared that the United States might be trying to take over their markets, while the Americans were always on the lookout for what they considered efforts by the Colonial powers to close the Open Door in favor of their own nationals. Thus, commenting on an article in the *Mining Journal* (Moyal 1952), a U.S. official noted (NARS 1952e) that

> All of the beneficiaries of ECA funds named in the attached appear to be enterprises of the ruling colonial power. It is questionable whether this is consistent with the desire of Congress as expressed in the pending Mutual Security Bill to encourage private investment in under-developed areas. The practice of making U.S. public funds available on a non-equity basis to enterprises protected by discriminatory regulations would seem to be in direct opposition to the intent of Congress. On the other hand, the availability of these funds could be used to support negotiations for the elimination of discriminatory barriers to investment and trade.

The British remained cautious about unregulated American investment in colonial territories. In a 1949 memorandum entitled "Investment of Foreign Capital in the Colonies," the Secretary of State for the Colonies wrote (PRO 1949m:2) that

> A statement on this subject is clearly one which has to be very carefully balanced. On the one hand it must, unless offence is to be given to American sentiment, seek to show that we are not placing and do not intend to place undue obstruction on foreign private investment, and that in fact our attitude is one of positive welcome. On the other hand it must have regard to the need to ensure that foreign private enterprise, like British or local enterprise, conforms not only with the social and economic interests of the Colonial territories, but also is in harmony with the general economic policies of the sterling area.

For the British, utilization at home of Sterling Bloc and soft currency raw materials and food was one way to minimize dollar expenditures. At the same time, the sale of Sterling Bloc raw materials for dollars was also of interest. Because Britain was, in effect, the "banker" for the Sterling area (PRO 1952d:3), all dollars resulting from such sales flowed through London. To the extent that Britain was able to sell commodities and goods produced within the Sterling area to dollar-earning territories and countries, it would then be able to use the dollars for its direct needs. Thus, there was always a great deal of currency juggling going on.

For example, out of a desire not to destabilize markets, the United States periodically went to noncommercial sources for supplies of rubber and tin for the strategic stockpile beyond what could be supplied in world markets. Because a major fraction of world rubber production was located in British-administered territories, a U.S. search for rubber always provided a great opportunity to earn some extra dollars. In 1947, the U.S. National Security Resources Board began to explore the possibility of acquiring rubber for the stockpile from Britain. It so happened that Britain was holding surplus stocks of rubber, and this, as noted in a minute by C.T. Crowe, an official in the Foreign Office, would enable Britain to rid itself of part of the stockpile and earn some dollars (PRO 1947i). But it would have to move fast. As Crowe wrote in early January 1948 (PRO 1948j):

> We shall be paid in dollars if we act quickly enough and if the Americans want to go ahead fast themselves. There is a danger if matters drag in that this deal might get involved with the Marshall plan & that we would have to use this rubber to repay part of the aid. But this would not be too bad.

Ultimately, the deal was consummated successfully. But dependence on U.S. purchases led to dependence on U.S. good will. As a Foreign Office official cabled to Washington, in the midst of yet another British balance-of-payments crisis in 1952 (PRO 1952i),

> We are hunting everywhere to find the means to restore dollar-sterling balances and balance of trade. It is vital we should get maximum results in first half year. It would be enormous help if United States would buy substantial amount of rubber from our stockpile.

Competition for Raw Materials.   Until 1950, world commodity markets were generally able to accommodate global demand for raw materials. Problems did not really materialize until 1950 and 1951, when demand began to exceed supply on the heels of the outbreak of the Korean War and the initiation of Western rearmament programs (Mason 1952). At that time, Britain found itself priced out of the market for some materials and unable to acquire others that it had been purchasing from the United States. The reasons for these shortages, it was generally agreed, were the policies of the United States. As the Economic Steering Committee of the Cabinet reported on December 2, 1950 (PRO 1950i:1),

> The causes of the shortages differ in different cases but, by and large, they are all derivatives of the present world situation. On the top of a rapid rise in production all over the world, and particularly in the U.S.A. (where the index of production has increased by 20 per cent since January), and in Japan and Germany, is now superimposed a large increase in armament production and increased buying for defence stockpiles particularly by the U.S.A. To this is added increased commercial buying for stock and to meet increased civilian demand resulting from general nervousness.

In a meeting of the Economic Policy Committee of the Cabinet on December 5, 1950, the Chancellor of the Exchequer, the president of the Board of Trade, and the Minister of Supply all agreed that U.S. stockpiling policy was responsible for the "grave" shortage of raw materials (PRO 1950j:1). The Economic Steering Committee therefore went so far as to ask (PRO 1950k:1)

> Should we try in agreement with Commonwealth countries to get control over Commonwealth raw materials, so as to have some power to bargain with the Americans? The biggest possibility is (as in the last war) to buy the wool clip of the Southern Dominions, but sisal, tin, rubber, and possibly other materials could become involved in such a policy.

Indeed, the problem of adequate supply of raw materials for Britain was a major topic of discussion at the summit meeting between President Truman and Prime Minister Attlee in December 1950 (HSTL 1951q). One outcome of these discussions was the formation of the International Materials Conference, whose purpose was, as noted in Chapter 5, the allocation of raw materials in short supply among the Western consuming nations (Liebhafsky 1957).

In the British view, there was a tendency for the United States to enter commodity markets without much regard for the needs of other countries or the effect of its actions on prices, and to indiscriminately cease purchases when the price went too high. For example, in March 1951, when the price of tin reached £1,600 per ton, a price regarded as too high by the Americans, the Reconstruction Finance

Corporation withdrew from the market. Consequently, according to a Cabinet memo (PRO 1951w:1),

> As well as losing us dollars, this [action] has been the cause of a good deal of ill-feeling which may increase in the very near future if, as is likely, the United States is soon forced to resume tin purchases through exhaustion of commercial stocks.

Notwithstanding the allocation system set up by the International Materials Conference, and the barter deals in various metals negotiated between the United States and Great Britain during the period of shortage (Fleischmann 1952), the British remained fairly contemptuous of the American approach to stockpiling. A report by the Economic Committee (Washington) on "US Strategic Stockpiling" asserted that (PRO 1951x:4)

> What is perhaps more important [than effects on price] is that increases in the American objectives and an accelerated rate of buying for the stockpile (caused in part by genuine concern on the part of the administration and in part by the goading of the Johnson Committee which, on one occasion, reported that the administration was conducting its stockpiling affairs with the efficiency and acumen usually devoted to the running of charity bazaars) have contributed greatly to the general shortage and increased prices of the very raw materials needed so urgently for current military production programmes, for manufactures for export and for manufactures needed to maintain in the U.K. and in other allied countries economies healthy enough to support major re-armament programmes.

The shortages, as British policymakers never tired of reminding whomever would listen, were of particular concern to the United Kingdom because it was so dependent on exports for its prosperity (PRO 1951y:2) and because

> The U.K.'s capacity to import, and therefore its capacity to survive, normally depends upon its ability to pay for imports by exporting goods and services in exchange. The export trade is therefore an indispensible foundation of the whole economy.

This meant, therefore, that "the objective of U.K. policy must be to retain maximum freedom of action with regard to the use of the resources at its disposal" (PRO 1951y:1).

Even with international agreements in place, U.S. practices continued to annoy the British. In early January 1951 the British ambassador to the United States, Oliver Franks, reported to the Foreign Office on the precipitous U.S. decision to try to corner the market on rubber and tin from Southeast Asia (see p. 140). Franks reported that late on January 6, Willard Thorp of the State Department had spoken to an official of the British embassy, telling him that (PRO 1951z:1)

> During past week United States authorities have been reviewing both stockpile and availabilities of rubber and reassessing on the military side the position in South East Asia. On this latter point the conclusion they reached was that while they could not predict how the situation would develop it must be considered hazardous.

The decision was therefore made, according to Franks, to purchase and remove as much rubber, tin, and other strategic materials from the area, as quickly as possible, regardless of price.

This policy was maintained for only about twenty-four hours, when it was recognized by the State Department that "A policy of unrestricted buying would have bad political effects as it would be regarded as hoisting the flag of pessimism about the area" (PRO 1951z:1). Furthermore, according to a Foreign Office telegram to Washington several days later (PRO 1951aa:2),

> [The] United Kingdom Government strongly objected on political grounds to a procedure which seemed to indicate that United States expected all rubber which had not been evacuated from Malaya by the end of January to be lost to the free world.

But the precise U.S. motivation for this remarkable program remained elusive. Did the Americans know something? Were they trying to corner the market for the stockpile? Or as Franks continued, was the United States "anxious to stop supplies of rubber to Russia and China" and therefore prepared to engage in preclusive buying (PRO 1951z:3)? The impression of embassy officials was that "someone in the United States administration went out on a panic line without any coordination" (PRO 1951z:3).

The final note on the British position with respect to U.S. raw materials policy was best expressed, perhaps, by reactions to the publication of *Resources for Freedom* in 1952. A minute sent to Prime Minister Churchill from the "Treasury Chambers" (presumably from the Chancellor of the Exchequer) noted (PRO 1952j) that

> Shortages of raw materials is the one thing which can really frustrate our economic future. It is no good having an expanding industrial production here, if we cannot feed it with raw material . . . .

I think the potential danger to our raw material supply which is implicit in the Paley Report's analysis is great, and in my view we should set on foot a really serious examination of long-term raw material policy. If the Americans think they need one, we need one much more. For the dangers which confront us are very much greater than those which confront them.

There is no indication that such a study was ever undertaken and, in any event, the problem of shortage soon disappeared to be replaced, once again, by one of surplus.

Raw Materials and East-West Trade.   With the deterioration of East-West relations after 1946, Britain's continuing trade in its traditional markets in Eastern Europe came to be perceived by the United States as a problem. For American policymakers, export controls on East-West trade were considered a vital element in the struggle to contain the Soviet Union (Adler-Karlsson 1968; Mastanduno 1985). For the British, economic issues were paramount and of greater import than political or military containment. As a 1947 memorandum written for the Overseas Economic Policy Committee put it (PRO 1947a:1),

[We] should not . . . wish to press on political grounds that his Majesty's Government should itself engage, or should encourage firms or individuals to engage, in such trade [with Eastern Europe] unless it is justified by commercial considerations. We should not in our present financial and economic situation take, for political ends, steps which might prove costly in themselves.

The newly established Soviet Bloc was not only a producer of certain vital commodities but also a soft-currency source only too willing to engage in barter trade or accept sterling in payment for goods. Furthermore, raw materials produced in the Sterling Bloc and purchased by the Soviet Union and Eastern Europe helped to keep surpluses from flooding the market. Somewhat ironically, Soviet Bloc purchases had other positive effects, too (PRO 1949m:2):

There is the general consideration that Russian purchases of rubber and wool have helped to keep prices of these commodities high and have thus assisted indirectly in maintaining our dollar earnings. If we could give the Russians some assurance about tin their purchases would help to maintain the demand and the price for tin and this would not be without its effect on the political situation in Malaya.

The implementation of export controls by the United States in early 1948, and its extension to Western Europe through the so-called Paris Group (PRO 1950*l*), came to pose real problems for the British economy, as the United States pressured its allies to restrict exports of certain key commodities to the Soviet Bloc. Rubber was one such material, as noted earlier. Tin was another. Tin, as it turned out, was a strategic material that neither the United States nor the Soviet Union possessed domestically, although the bulk of world tin production was in Western hands. This fact, it was thought in the United States, might provide useful leverage over the Soviet economy (PRO 1949o:3).

Because tin had been in short supply during World War II, an international allocation system, called the Combined Tin Committee (CTC), had been set up to distribute supplies among consumers (Knorr 1945; Fox 1974). The CTC continued to operate after the war and became one of the mechanisms whereby tin sales to the Soviet Union were restricted. One of the requirements for obtaining an increase in a country's tin allocation was provision of information on national production and consumption, data that the Soviet Union consistently refused to provide (PRO ND). As a consequence, Britain, under prodding from the United States, continually sought to limit sales of tin to the Soviets to levels considered "adequate" for civilian consumption (whatever this meant).

Several different techniques were used to control sales. During the years 1948 to 1951, the United Kingdom and the Soviet Union conducted annual negotiations over trade. Each year, the Soviets would ask for an extra allotment of tin. Each year, the British would refuse. The United States remained adamant that, unless the Soviet Union joined the CTC, such an allocation could not be made. The Americans thought that the tin would be used for military and strategic purposes (PRO 1949o:3); the Russians insisted that it was to be used for civilian applications such as canning fish (PRO ND). But as was explained in a June 1948 telegram to the British Ministry of Supply (PRO 1948k),

> Any allocation to the U.S.S.R. without proper application will be impossible to defend before Congress who will resent the diversion of a most important strategic raw material at a time when U.S.A. are trying to accumulate a strategic stock pile and are just about to forbid use of tin in U.S.A. for non essential tin-plate in beer and other cans. They also suggest it might have unfavorable effect on E.R.P. discussions.

The United States was intent on using the CTC as a means for denying tin to Russia (PRO 1949p:3) and warned that, were the tin allocation system to be abolished, she would press for tin to be included in the export control lists (PRO 1949p:5). The British found themselves caught in the middle, because on the one hand, as noted above, they had a decided interest in meeting the Soviet request while, on the other, they were unsure of U.S. motives in demanding controls on tin sales — were they strategic or economic? As a Foreign Office official lamented in a telegram to Washington in November 1949 (PRO 1949q:2–3),

> We do not know what importance United States attaches to preventing Russia stockpiling tin. No steps are taken to prevent her buying rubber which we should regard as not less important strategically.[15] For our part, although we agree that it is desirable to prevent Russia stockpiling tin, we are disposed to attach much more importance strategically to preserving the Malayan economy from the effects of a collapse in tin prices due to conditions of surplus. Such a collapse would also have a serious economic effect on dollar earnings of sterling and other areas. In our view it is more urgent and important to remove the surplus than worry about Russian purchases.

Nonetheless, the British did cooperate with the Americans on restricting tin sales and, with the abolishing of the CTC in 1949 and the return to free market conditions, the problem became one of how to maintain control over sales of tin to the Soviet Union. Because periodic surpluses were endemic in the tin industry, there was international sentiment for the setting-up of a stabilization agreement; this was eventually realized in the establishment of an "International Tin Agreement" (Fox 1974). Anticipating the formation of such an agreement, a Treasury memorandum drafted in November 1948 suggested that "[T]he proposed new tin agreement . . . be drafted in such a way as to make it sufficiently obnoxious to the Russians to make them refuse to sign it and join the allocating organisation" (PRO 1948*l*:3). In the event, the Soviet Union seems to have had little trouble in finding alternative sources of tin. Furthermore, they may have gotten their revenge on the United States and Britain later in the 1950s, when they began to dump Chinese tin on international markets, wreaking havoc on prices (see pp. 228–29, below).

---

[15] Controls on rubber were not implemented until after the outbreak of the Korean War.

Generally speaking, the British seem not to have been altogether comfortable with the American insistence on export controls. Not only did the restrictions cause economic difficulties for Britain, but it was also not altogether clear that they could be effective. As the Economic Warfare Sub-Committee observed in 1948 (PRO 1948m:3),

> It is our opinion that the old concept of blockade cannot be applied in a war against such a country as Russia, rich in raw materials and still under-industrialised. This large, amorphous, land mass sprawling across half the world and in physical contact with other areas especially rich in raw material cannot be isolated by physical means.

It was the considered opinion of the Committee that, short of direct military action against the Soviet Union, there was little that could be accomplished in limiting its war-making potential (PRO 1948m:1). If this were true during war, how much more so in a time of peace! A report by the Chiefs of Staff at the same time asserted (PRO 1948n:2) that

> There is at present no economic objective outside the borders of the Soviet Union, or beyond her control, which she is likely to regard as essential for the fulfillment of her plans. The Soviet Union's economic condition does not appear to be, in itself, such as to impel her to use methods which might lead to a major war in order to acquire external resources.

The British regarded the American program of export controls as tantamount to an effort to implement an economic blockade. In a discussion of U.S. proposals to widen the lists of goods prohibited from export following the outbreak of the Korean War, the president of the Board of Trade, Harold Wilson, stated (PRO 1950m:1) that

> The United States authorities clearly wanted to institute a blockade, by denying to Eastern Europe all materials which could contribute to the development of the Soviet economy, while the object of our restrictions, which had been agreed with other Western European countries, was to prevent them from obtaining materials directly useful for war. The effect of the wider restriction on the United States economy would be negligible, but if we agreed to them our attempt to achieve economic viability would be gravely prejudiced. We should be deprived of all our imports from the U.S.S.R. and possibly also of those from the satellites, and would be obliged to incur heavy additional dollar expenditures.

Wilson went on to warn (PRO 1950o:2) that

> The complete denial of raw materials to the U.S.S.R. from our overseas territories would seriously affect their economies, and, since we should wish to secure a common line with other Western European countries, the economies of their countries.

Although the Paris Group was eventually able to agree on extending the trade restrictions, the British were never happy with the extent of their coverage and agitated for changes in the lists throughout the 1950s.

In 1957 and 1958, they proposed the elimination of many items from the lists (DDEL 1958j, 1958k), but for reasons that were other than economic. As Douglas Dillon, a U.S. official, told the British Deputy Undersecretary of State, Mr. Gore-Booth, in a February 1958 discussion at the State Department on the subject of strategic controls (DDEL 1958*l*:2),

> [R]emarks had shown that there is a real difference of opinion between the U.S. and UK regarding the level, nature, and purpose of controls. We had originally thought that the entire pressure for modification of controls within the British Government originated in the Board of Trade for commercial reasons, but we were interested to learn that the British position was based on the position of the Ministry of Defense.

As it turned out, the British Joint Chiefs of Staff had also come around to the opinion that trade controls were likely to have little impact on the warmaking abilities of the Soviet Bloc. First, they concluded, a nuclear war would be brief, and second, unlike the Americans who thought the notion of limited war in Europe to be quite plausible, the British Chiefs believed that war in Europe was unlikely to remain conventional or even "semi-conventional" (DDEL 1958m:3). As a result of British pressure, therefore, the lists were revised, but only in a cosmetic sense. The conflict would arise, again and again.

SUMMARY AND CONCLUSIONS

Over the ten years between 1946 and 1956, the British found themselves in an increasingly untenable position with respect to international commodity markets and international politics. Because they exerted a measurable degree of control over the trade of only a very few raw materials, they were forced to compete with larger consumers when supplies were scarce. Because the currency of preference at the time was dollars, the British had to engage in practices they might have otherwise eschewed so as to acquire funds. Finally, because they were relegated increasingly to the role of junior partner in the Atlantic Alliance, the British found it necessary to accede to the demands of their senior partner, so as not to alienate the Americans. The struggle to maintain the Empire represented an effort to retain at least some modicum of influence in international affairs. In the end, the effort proved very costly, as Britain was forced to surrender one territory after another to the new force of national self-determination.

The logic of maintaining the Empire had two aspects: a material one and an ideal one. First, by arguing that raw materials and markets were essential to the home economy and that without certain pieces of property, such as the Suez Canal and the Anglo-Iranian Oil Company (AIOC) concession, trade would be impossible, the Empire was deemed essential to British survival. Second, the argument continued, without the Empire, Britain would no longer be great (although it might still be Great), and no one would respect it. At least if it controlled a scattering of territories around the world, other states would have to acknowledge its hegemony there.

In both cases, the logic proved false. Raw materials and markets could be acquired without the control of territory, as the Japanese and West Germans have proven so admirably, and the British lost the respect not so much of the Great Powers as of its colonial subjects, who made empire too expensive to maintain. Without the power to support the pursuit of its ideals, the effort finally collapsed at Suez. Everything that occurred thereafter was epilogue.

7 BOMBS AND BUTTONS
Raw Materials and Soviet Foreign Policy

While on the campaign stump in Kalinin in 1963, Premier Khrushchev made the following observation (quoted in Stent 1981:93):

> Of course, anything one pleases can be regarded as strategic material, even a button, because it can be sewn onto a soldier's pants. A soldier will not wear pants without buttons, since otherwise he would have to hold them up with his hands. And then what to do with his weapon? If one reasons thus, then buttons also are a particularly strategic material. But if buttons really had such importance and we could find no substitute for them, then I am sure that our soldiers would even learn to keep their pants up with their teeth, so that their hands would be free to hold weapons.

In some sense, these sentiments reflect the Soviet tendency toward autarky and the general attitude toward the strategic materials question in particular: One does best to have *both* bombs and buttons, but one is better off doing without than relying on others to supply either. As was observed in Chapter 4, autarky has ideal as well as material roots, and this complicates the analysis of the raw materials policies of any state.

Consequently, when one turns to an analysis of Soviet raw materials policy, one encounters what might be called the "Soviet paradox." This paradox centers on what appears to be a sharp contradiction between Soviet ideal interests and material ones. On the one hand, the Soviet Union possesses a well-developed ideology that purports to provide definitive guidance to action. On the other hand, the Soviet

Union faces many of the same constraints with which any modern state must cope: the need for security, satisfaction of the material wants of the population, the limits of the natural environment, and so on. If one accepts the notion that ideology does direct action (see, for example, George 1969; Sartori 1969; Schurmann 1974), then it might be possible to divine intentions from rhetoric, and Soviet goals might be inimical to Western well-being. But this approach would remain problematic because Marxism regards ideology as superstructure and itself as a "scientific" discipline based on material factors. For the purposes of this analysis, do we therefore regard Marxist-Leninist doctrine as ideology or "science"? The answer is not clear. Any action may be interpreted from either an ideal or a material perspective, and the two need not coincide. The difficulty is which perspective to accept as "real" from the policymakers' points of view.

The study of Soviet raw materials policy is also handicapped by a paucity of solid information on the subject. Although there is a relatively rich body of case studies of Soviet "resource diplomacy" — the manipulation of resource flows for political ends — these have been, for the most part, reported by the targets of Soviet action and analyzed by third parties. They are not based on reports and studies by Soviet scholars, nor can they be regarded as the final word on an event. There are, to date, no open archives that can be used to divine thoughts, patterns, or processes. The most that can be done is to extrapolate from the case studies and other sources of information as are available.

As a result of these problems, the structure of this chapter differs from that of the previous two. It begins with a general discussion of the place of the Soviet Union in the international system as understood by Soviet scholars and then turns in the second section to a discussion of what Soviet analysts have had to say about strategic materials and the relationship of Soviet trade policy to material and ideal interests. The third part of the chapter presents a set of case studies of Soviet resource diplomacy. The final section attempts to offer some insights into whether ideal or material interests stand foremost in Soviet raw materials and foreign policies as they have been practiced over the past four decades.[1]

---

[1]The reader should be aware, of course, that Soviet foreign policy is undergoing a major reassessment and that major shifts from what is described here are possible.

THE PLACE OF THE SOVIET UNION IN THE INTERNATIONAL SYSTEM

As was noted in Chapter 4, the relationship of the Soviet Union to the international economic and political system has been an ambivalent one for many decades. For Soviet leaders, involvement with the world has promised great returns in terms of power and prestige even as it has threatened to allow hostile outside forces to penetrate and weaken the state. Hence, contradictory objectives have been the norm, rather than the exception. As is true of the United States and the United Kingdom, these mixed goals can be explained in terms of both material and ideal interests.

Until the death of Stalin in 1952, Soviet interaction with the world economy was relatively small. Subsequently, even though the volume of economic transactions with the nonsocialist world did increase, for largely political reasons, the basic insulation of the socialist from the world economy did not. For a variety of reasons, some of which will be discussed in this chapter, this era of relative independence of world markets could be coming to an end. The customary Soviet approach to economic growth—both material and capital-intensive—has proved less and less effective (Jensen 1983:3). At the same time, the costs of obtaining raw materials have greatly increased due to depletion of domestic sources, obsolescing technology, and problems of accessibility (Lipschutz 1986b:25). Although during the past twenty years, Soviet planners have become more conscious of concepts such as scarcity value and the cost of inputs into industrial processes, this consciousness has not been translated effectively into policy on any broad scale due to the structure of the Soviet economic system (Lipschutz 1986b:27–28).

Beginning in the early 1970s, the terms of trade with the West in raw materials—particularly petroleum—turned decisively in favor of the Soviet Union and provided a relatively easy means of earning the hard currency needed to purchase wheat and advanced technology abroad. This, as well as the promise of détente with the United States, provided an impetus to greater interdependence with world markets. More recently, the policies of Party Chairman Gorbachev seem designed to wean the Soviet economy even further from its ingrained tendencies toward self-sufficiency (see, e.g., Hough 1986a; *PlanEcon*

1986). Whether these policies will have the intended effect remains to be seen.

The shift to greater economic interdependence has not been wholly welcome in the West, accustomed as it is to regard the Soviet Union as an aggressive and expansionist power. Increased Soviet activity in various parts of the world during the 1970s and early 1980s led many analysts to warn of a long-term strategy aimed at undermining the international economic and political system (see, for example, Rees 1977; Thomas 1985a). A particular focus of this strategy was thought to be the flows of petroleum and minerals from the Middle East and southern Africa to Europe and the United States, The concept of the "Resource War," as it has been called, has lost much of its currency over the last several years (Maull 1984:290–99). Furthermore, the Soviet Union has always been relatively cautious in its use of resource diplomacy, and it is likely to remain relatively cautious in this respect in the future.

A residual question remains as to whether potential domestic deficiencies in various minerals may, at some time in the future, impel the Soviet Union to become a major purchaser of raw materials in international markets (Coker 1984a). Such a trend could have both positive and negative effects on commodity supplies and prices, and increase competition for minerals such as cobalt. Although the past cannot be used precisely to predict the future in this regard, and notwithstanding *perestroika*, there is little reason to think that Soviet policies in the raw materials area will undergo significant structural change in the coming years, even though some domestic sources of raw materials may well be depleted during that time. In any event, if it does develop, greater interdependence with the outside world would be likely to increase Soviet sensitivity to international economic fluctuations instead of giving it greater leverage over others.

It is possible, of course, that greater Soviet participation in the world economy, if it were to come about, might have as its goal the creation of a new world order, although the process through which this new order would emerge is not altogether clear. But this new international system is not seen as one that necessarily will be beset by conflict. David Holloway (1984:107), citing the work of M. Maksimova, has written that

> Soviet globalists argue that the postwar order created by the United States has now collapsed, and that a new international order—economic, political,

and military—must be created. They maintain there are global problems that require international cooperation for their solution, but that at present these problems are a source of conflict between East and West. A solution can be found only through a restructuring of international relations. Because of growing Soviet power, a new order cannot be created without the participation of the Soviet Union, and the creation of a new world order provides a goal for Soviet power to pursue. Soviet writings do not give a clear picture of such an order, but they do indicate a more subtle vision than is provided by the pattern of domination in Eastern Europe.

Pursuit of a new world order—whether or not it is built around socialism and headed by the Soviet Union—does not require possession of strategic minerals, acts of war, or even absolute control of global affairs. According to Marxist theory, such a society will come about from the contradictions inherent in capitalism itself (Holloway 1984:82) and, in the meantime, as Holloway (1984:92) puts it, "The Soviet Union is indeed an important actor on the international stage, but it does not devise the plot, write the script, set the scene, and direct the play as well."

For the purposes of this study, therefore, the critical question is: Where do raw materials fit into Soviet global strategy? What, for that matter, *is* Soviet global strategy? A clear understanding of Soviet objectives is constrained by the lack of information regarding the beliefs and intentions of Soviet leaders. Thus, we are left to extrapolate and infer those beliefs and intentions from announced ideology, speeches, quotes, and journal articles, and publicized acts. As always, "non-events" and "non-decisions" (Jentleson 1986:32)—the "dog that does not bark," if you will—are counted for very little in the assessment of Soviet intentions and goals.

This chapter utilizes secondary sources as well as the publications of Soviet academics as a guide to perspectives and possible changes in policy. Valkenier (1983:ix) and Hough (1986b: ch. 2) argue that, in the Soviet Union, policy debates are often conducted in the specialized publications of various academic institutes of the USSR Academy of Sciences, such as the Institute of World Economics and International Relations (IMEIMO) and the Institute of the USA and Canada. Even if these discussions do not provide conclusive evidence of influence over policymakers, they do provide a guide, at least, to current schools of thought within the Soviet Union regarding certain problems and issues.

The Strategic Perspective

What constitutes the Soviet "strategic synthesis," and where do strategic raw materials fit into the picture? From his reading of Soviet literature and his analysis of Soviet behavior, George Breslauer (1983) suggests that Soviet leaders see four major roles for their state within the international political system: continental power, global power, superpower, and leader of the world Communist movement. Each of these roles leads to somewhat different policies, depending on the region involved and its proximity to Soviet borders. David Holloway (1984:106) describes four tendencies in Soviet thinking: autarkist, disposed toward detente, activist (looking for opportunities to expand power and influence), and globalist (working for the creation of a new world order that will include the Soviet Union as a major actor). As is true of the United States, the Soviets seek influence and like-minded friends around the world and are prepared to do many things in pursuit of these ends. Such actions include the provision of aid and assistance to ideologically friendly regimes.

What is the role of strategic raw materials in this picture? Marxist-Leninist doctrine recognizes the importance of raw minerals to material and technical progress but tends to focus on the acquisition of raw materials as an impetus to *imperialist* (and not socialist) expansion (Papp 1982). The classic formulation of this idea is to be found in the works of Lenin. In his book, *Imperialism: The Highest Stage of Capitalism*, Lenin argued that capitalism added the struggle for the sources of raw materials to its other colonial motives (Lenin 1943, quoted in Wright 1976:50):

> The more capitalism is developed, the more the need for raw materials is felt, the more bitter competition becomes, and the more feverishly the hunt for raw materials proceeds throughout the world, the more desperate becomes the struggle for the acquisition of colonies.

Some have seen this as indicating that the Soviet Union would seek to employ for its own ends the competitive struggle for raw materials between capitalist states, and many Soviet actions have been interpreted in the West as efforts to exploit this tendency.

In the 1970s, in particular, official pronouncements by Soviet leaders in public and at Party Congresses drew attention to Western dependence on imported raw materials, particularly petroleum (see, for example, Rees 1977:3; Thomas 1985a, 1985b:5–17), and the possibility that, under certain circumstances, this dependence might lead to local or regional war. In the West, such statements were taken as indicative of Soviet objectives in the Third World. This led to the formulation of the "Resource War" thesis that posited a Soviet strategic plan to seize control of those raw materials most critical to the West.[2] The Soviet intent in this regard was extrapolated from three observations: (1) The Soviet Union periodically acted as a major supplier of certain strategic minerals to the West, (2) it was providing military and financial support to fledgling socialist regimes in Ethiopia, Angola, and Mozambique, all countries astride oil shipping routes from the Persian Gulf to Western Europe and the Americas (Kaltefleiter 1983), and (3) it might be running short of certain critical materials available from such unstable regions such as southern Africa (Papp 1982).

Hard evidence to support this hypothesis is scanty. In most cases, intentions have been difficult to divine, and Soviet support for resource-rich states (such as Angola) or those in geopolitically-sensitive areas (such as Mozambique and Ethiopia) has failed to yield significant gains in either an economic or strategic sense. Furthermore, Soviet analyses of the question of access to raw materials tend to recognize that such competition, should it occur in an unregulated fashion, might well embroil the Soviet Union in conflict with the United States, even against its wishes. In addition, the gradual shift from a position of high self-sufficiency within the Eastern Bloc as a whole, to one of greater dependence on outside sources of raw materials (see Coker 1984a), has made Soviet analysts of international politics much more sensitive to the possibility of inadvertent conflicts in the Third World. As a result, according to Elizabeth Valkenier (1983:149), some Soviet specialists:

---

[2]The "Resource War" thesis can actually be traced back, at least, to the late 1950s or early 1960s (see JFKL 1961b; Huddle 1976; pp. 128–29 above).

[C]onsider access to raw materials [a] destabilizing factor [in international politics] and advocate global regulations to assure the legitimate interest not only of the producing Third World countries but also of the consuming industrial states, socialist and capitalist, alike.

The roots of Soviet ideology in material development, and the history of the Soviet Union, have made Soviet analysts conscious (some might say "hyperaware") of the role of raw materials in the process of world economic development. For example, in an article drawn from a collective monograph published in 1980 by the Institute of World Economics and International Relations of the USSR Academy of Sciences (IMEIMO), S. Glebov (1980:8) wrote:

As an integral part of the natural resources of society, minerals are linked directly to the history of the development of its productive forces. The composition and qualitative and quantitative characteristics of raw material and energy sources have changed as a function of change in the needs of human society and the opportunity for it to purposefully influence nature.

As the natural resource endowments of individual states differ greatly, he continues (Glebov 1980:9–10, emphasis added)

In combination with disproportionality in the development of individual parts of the world economy, unevenness in the distribution of mineral resources results in a sharp incongruity between the resources of many countries and the level of productive forces they have achieved and the level of demand of social production for raw material and fuel. This is often a source of serious difficulties and conflicts, *including those of an international nature.*

According to Glebov (1980:11, 15), the energy and materials "crisis" of the early 1970s was not the consequence of an "absolute lack of individual types of fuel and raw material" but, rather,

[T]he coinciding of an exacerbation of the conflict between the developed capitalist countries and the developing countries based on the destruction of the traditional relations of domination and subordination, including in the energy and raw material sector of the world capitalist economy, with cyclical tremors in the economy.

In a 1983 issue of the IMEIMO journal, *Mirovaya Ekonomika I Mezhdunarodnye Otrosheniya,* Academician O. Bogomolov (1983a:17) wrote that the growing dependence of Western states on imported sources of energy and material was a consequence of depletion of their own resources, combined with the rapid growth in consumption and rising costs of production. Although means were available for managing such dependence, according to Bogomolov (1983a:17),

> The rationalization of consumption, technical innovations geared to the substitution of metals and minerals in particularly short supply and the fuller development of their own resources [that is, those of the Western countries] have not yet halted the trend toward an increase in this dependence.

(For a detailed Soviet assessment of U.S. mineral problems, see Sitnikov 1979.) Consequently, continued Bogomolov (1983a:17, emphasis added),

> The threat of a raw material and energy crisis has not passed, despite a certain lessening of its seriousness. *The struggle for access to mineral raw material markets is increasing.* The depletion of their own natural resources and an endeavor to preserve the customary way of life demand, prominent Western specialists believe, an "uninterrupted influx" of these resources from the developing countries.

Given this perspective, and the actions of successive U.S. administrations over the last fifteen years, Soviet analysts have drawn certain conclusions regarding the importance of strategic materials in international politics. For example, in a *Moscow APN Daily Review* "digest" of a 1983 article in *SShA: Ekonomika, Politika, Ideologiya*, the journal of the Institute of the USA and Canada, G.I. Rubinshteyn (1983:42) wrote

> In the 1970's [sic] the United States started to display a heightened interest in the import of mineral fuel. African oil became more advantageous for the United States compared with oil from the Middle East because of the known events in the latter region. The U.S. military-industrial complex also revealed great interest in some strategic raw materials plentiful in Africa.

(For a similar analysis, see also Kondrashov 1982.) The Reagan administration's strategic mineral supply policy was thus seen as a means of asserting (or reasserting) U.S. hegemony in Third World areas both for military reasons (by virtue of "national interests") (Tabarin 1982), and in order to provide "American monopolistic capital . . . [with] much cheaper foreign raw materials" (Sitnikov 1982:33).[3]

---

[3]To what degree Soviet academics might have been influenced by the torrent of U.S. analyses of the resource problem during the 1970s and early 1980s is unclear, but they were undoubtedly familiar with much of the literature.

These perspectives tell little about Soviet policy with respect to strategic fuels and materials, but they do suggest several important factors relevant to the formulation of that policy. First, Soviet strategists and analysts are keenly aware of the extent of Western dependence on imported raw materials (Sitnikov 1982:33), and the as-yet much lower level of import dependence of the Soviet Union and other Eastern Bloc states taken together (Bogomolov 1983a:16; see also Lipschutz 1986b). Second, notwithstanding polemics about monopolies and imperialism, these analysts are also cognizant of the strategic sensitivity to the United States of such areas as southern Africa and the Persian Gulf (Tabarin 1982). Third, they believe that conflict over materials is a very real possibility that must be avoided in the interests of both East and West (Bogomolov 1983a:17).

From a military planning perspective, it appears that certain resource-rich regions, and the sea lanes providing access to them, are as important to the Soviets as they are to the West (perhaps even more so; see Gordon 1986). Consequently, the imperatives of military-strategic planning, combined with the long-standing Soviet policy of a high level of self-sufficiency in mineral production, might indicate a long-term, peacetime strategy of resource denial in the pursuit of world domination. It is equally likely, however, that other factors of a more political nature are of greater importance in determining Soviet policy in the Third World. In addition, economic pragmatism as well as economic opportunism may underlie some Soviet actions in resource-producing regions because the Soviet Union is not immune from the problem of relative economic costs and the benefits to be gained from importing lower-cost raw materials. These points, when combined with known facts about the operation of the domestic minerals production system (Lipschutz 1986b), suggest not a coherent strategy regarding raw materials, but more of a policy of incremental coping or, in the words of Charles Lindblom (1959), "muddling through."

The Economic Perspective

In terms of the analytic schemes introduced in Chapters 2 and 4, there is no question but that Soviet raw materials policy has tended toward the autarkic end of the spectrum. Although the apparent commitment to autarky has been interpreted by some Western analysts as part of an expansionist strategy (see, for example, Strauss 1979), the reasons for this policy have their origins in both history and ideology, as discussed in Chapter 4. It is clear that the type of state-directed trading engaged in by centrally planned economies is more geared toward the fulfill-ment of national objectives than is the case with market-oriented states, but it is much less obvious that any sort of planned *global* strategy lies behind Soviet trading patterns. Marshall Goldman (1983a:122), in commenting on the sale of titanium sponge by the Soviet Union to the United States (which bans the sale of the same to the Soviets), has observed that trade policy is often driven by expe-diency, rather than strategy, and "In a sense, the Soviet need to earn the hard currency which the sale of such strategic items makes possible, suggests that at times, the Soviets are prepared to sell us the rope we may someday use to hang them."

Four basic principles underlie the Soviet attitude toward trade in general and raw materials in particular. First, trade is used to bolster national objectives. According to Raymond Vernon (1984:9),

> The USSR conducts its foreign trade on the principle that no trade is justified unless it makes a contribution to the nation's objectives. The economies of Western Europe and North America [by contrast] conduct their trade on the principle that any trade is permissible unless it is explicitly adjudged harmful to the nation's objectives.

Although Vernon may overstate the case in both directions, his point is generally accurate. The Soviet approach to trade does reflect a general philosophical or ideological difference, but it also arises as a consequence of the process of decision-making and resource allocation in a centrally planned economy. Not only are the objectives of the state given priority over the requirements of individuals in this type of planning, but it is also much easier to control inputs into state-run enterprises than into individually run operations.

A second principle, as noted earlier, is that of self-sufficiency or autarky. Some Soviet scholars have argued for a higher degree of self-sufficiency for economic and political reasons (see Shabad 1985 for an example of this with respect to aluminum). There are other obvious advantages to such a strategy, including conservation of hard currency and lower exposure to international market fluctuations (but, see pp. 208–09, below). Although it is generally believed that the Soviet Union strives for complete self-sufficiency, this has never been official Soviet policy (Shmelev 1985:12–13). Rather, the goal has been to rely on selective trade in order to build Communism but to strive for autarky as a higher ideological goal (rather like the U.S. objective of pursuing "freedom" around the world) (Ulam 1981).

A third principle, and one of the most important objectives, is maximization of hard currency earnings, as this is required for purchases of goods such as grain and advanced technology from the West. Finally, a fourth is the use of trade to maintain the standard of living of the Soviet population. The most conspicuous example this principle in practice is the purchase of grain in order to feed livestock for meat production.

The relationship of the Soviet Union to the global political economy is, from the perspective of Soviet analysts, an evolving one. Until Stalin's death, the traditional doctrine regarding the inevitability of conflict between capitalism and socialism was adhered to, and the Stalinist theory of "two world markets" or "systems" posited an inevitable and irreconcilable division between them. (Indeed, Stalin gave credit for this division to the Western economic blockade conducted against the Socialist Bloc in the late 1940s and early 1950s) (Valkenier 1983:40).

Capitalism was regarded, in true Leninist fashion, as an exploiter of the raw material resources of the underdeveloped world, and the latter was seen as a mere appendage of the former. Although the Soviet Union did conduct trade with the developing world throughout the 1940s, this was primarily in goods that were domestically in short supply. In 1948, for example, Soviet imports from Egypt totaled almost $50 million (Smith 1973: 229), most of which was cotton. This level was not reached again until the late 1950s. Only in 1953, however, did there begin an active courtship of specific developing countries for both political and economic reasons and, even then, the volume of trade with those countries remained low in global terms.

During the height of the Cold War — between 1953 and 1964 — economic relations were utilized as a political tool, in a deliberate effort to wean developing countries from their involvement with global capitalism. The Soviet "economic offensive" launched by Khrushchev in 1955 was thus seen in the West as a deadly threat to international markets. But as Valkenier (1983: ch. 1) notes, the impact of Soviet economic activities in the Third World never fulfilled either the fantasies of Soviet policymakers or the nightmares of Western ones.

The reasons for this were that trade and assistance were often provided to states seen as ideologically promising (such as Guinea and Mali) rather than those with substantial economic potential (such as Nigeria). Poor countries were of little interest to the West and lacked the real or latent power to affect Western markets by their withdrawal. The fatal defect in the Soviet strategy, as demonstrated many times over the following decades, was that "radical" regimes, often unable to deliver the goods to their populations, derived little stability from high levels of economic support provided by the Soviet Union.[4] The failure of Khrushchev's economic offensive and the fact that recent adherents to "scientific socialism" have been, almost without exception, very weak states,[5] have led to a definite evolution in thought about the relationship between socialism, capitalism, and economic development. Recent articles on the nature of the global economy indicate that a reevaluation of the relationship of the Soviet economy to the rest of the world is underway.[6] For example, in the *MEIMO* article cited earlier, Academician O. Bogomolov (1983a:14) writes:

> Economic life in the modern world has been internationalized to a far greater extent than ever before. The degree of this internationalization is such that the future of each country is conditioned by the normal development of international economic relations and the need for the removal of the conflicts and contradictions undermining the world economy.
>
> The internationalization of economic life is expressed in the existence and functioning of the world economy. As a reality of our times, it represents a complex and far from homogeneous system of relations. Given the existence of two opposite social systems — socialism and capitalism and the industrially developed and developing states — the world economy appears as a contradictory but integral system.

(The same perspectives can also be found in Bogomolov 1983b.).

[4]The relative staying power of "Marxist-Leninist" regimes in Third World states may be more a consequence of the military assistance provided to governments than the result of economic support. During the next several years, events in Afghanistan and Angola may provide empirical evidence with respect to this hypothesis.

[5]The roster of states brought into the socialist sphere between 1975 and 1981 reads like a list of international basket cases. According to Jeanne Kirkpatrick (1984), speaking to the 1984 Republican National Convention, these included Laos, Cambodia, Angola, Ethiopia, Mozambique, South Yemen, Libya, Syria, Aden [sic], Congo, Madagascar, Seychelles, Nicaragua, and Grenada (and let us not forget South Vietnam).

[6]Tentative Soviet exploration of the possibility of joining GATT, the IMF, and the World Bank are also suggestive of major changes in this regard; (see Hough 1986a; *PlanEcon* 1986).

Similarly, in a more recent article in *International Affairs* (Moscow), a Soviet journal published in English which ordinarily includes academic articles as well as polemical ones, Professor N. Shmelev (1985:13), an economist at IMEIMO, writes that

> The ability to utilize the potentialities of the international division of labour, to improve the country's position in the system of world economic exchange is an increasingly important criterion of the efficiency of the national economy as a whole and of its various branches. The growing links between Soviet industry and the foreign market provide effective incentives for economic, scientific, and technical progress, for improving product quality, raising the technical level of production, and perfecting the work of every unit of economic administration and management.

Interestingly, Shmelev (1985:18–19) invokes a variant of the "Open Door" in justifying the need for greater Soviet access to and involvement in the world economy:

> Naturally, the socialist countries are ever more interested in free and stable access to the world markets. In order to buy, one must sell; in order to sell, one must compete; and in order to compete successfully, one must have equal terms of competition.

In the view of some Western analysts, to the extent that a shift in the Soviet attitude toward trade has taken place (and it remains to be seen just how significant that shift really will be), this may reflect weaknesses in the Soviet economy rather than the pursuit of a grand design. According to Arthur Wright (1983:618), for example,

> This shift has little to do with a desire for greater contacts with the outside world *per se*. Rather, it seems to stem from attempts to cope with lagging labor force growth, capital-goods saturation in many industries, and the continued domestic inability to develop and introduce improved methods of production. One way to acquire modern technology is to import it. To do that . . . a nation must export domestically produced goods to obtain the necessary foreign exchange.

Another general observation should be made here. Although it is often thought that a centrally planned economy offers great advantages in terms of allocating resources for trade, as well as providing an assured market for the commodities of producing countries, such an economy can be affected seriously by unanticipated downturns in the market price of raw commodities. I. Korolev (1982:83) has thus observed that

In the sphere of foreign economic relations, the Soviet Union encounters beyond the confines of the socialist community the uncertainty of the capitalist market and inflation, which are capable via export-import relations of influencing the planned economy and price system.

(A similar point can be found in Bogomolov 1983a:25.) This has come as something of a surprise to Soviet economists who, for many years, assumed that a planned economy could circumvent such uncertainties. In 1960, for example, A.S. Kodachenko (1960:43, quoted in Neuberger 1963:2) wrote that

> The development of trade relations with socialist countries assures a guaranteed market for the export products of underdeveloped countries, and creates a stable market not subject to economic fluctuations. The planned character of the economy of socialist countries presupposes the conclusion of long-term trade agreements in which the conditions of delivery are firmly fixed: their volume, time period, prices, etc. This alone eliminates the tremendous instability which exists in the demand for and the prices of export products of underdeveloped countries as a result of the cyclical character of capitalist production.

By and large, this has not turned out to be the case.

The Soviet Union has the international trade pattern of a developing country — in the early 1980s, about 80 percent of hard currency earnings came from the export of raw materials (Wright 1983:617) — and cyclical instabilities in the prices of export commodities, such as the collapse in the price of oil in 1985–86, must have a significant effect on the planning process (even though foreign trade planning is done on a yearly, and not long-term, basis; Stern 1987a).

As is true of any other producer of raw materials, the Soviets seek to obtain the best possible prices for exports and imports — that is, high prices for their commodities and low prices for the materials they purchase from others. This economic strategy is pursued, at best, in an *ad hoc* and somewhat dialectical fashion. On the one hand, the Soviets have expressed qualified support for efforts to stabilize and support commodity prices in international markets (Lavigne 1984:16–17). On the other hand, at the same time they have criticized efforts by raw material producers (particularly OPEC) to force prices upward (Valkenier 1986:423; see also Bogomolov 1983a:22–23 and Vasil'yev 1982:70).

The process of trade and exchange is complicated by the inconvertibility of the ruble. As a result, it is difficult to calculate precisely either the exact price of a commodity (in dollars, for example) or the cost to the Soviet economy of selling or purchasing raw materials (in terms of opportunity costs).[7] To complicate matters further, a good deal of Soviet foreign trade is conducted on the basis of barter deals, either with specific foreign firms or on a government-to-government basis. Although the ruble value of total trade between countries — including barter deals — is published in the annual compendium of foreign trade, *Vneshniaia torgovlia*, the appropriate exchange rates are not. Precisely *what* gains the Soviet Union has realized from upward pressure on commodity prices is unclear, although some Western analysts do argue that major economic benefits have been achieved (Hewett 1985:173–77).

What is clear is that the ability of the Soviet Union to intentionally affect international markets and prices is, for the most part, not very great. It has a dominant position in only a few commodities and can play only a marginal role in most others (although even a small role can have major effects in some situations, such as purchases of wheat in the 1970s) (Vernon 1984:7). Finally, the desire of the Soviet Union to use trade for political purposes is probably limited. Although it has engaged in such practices in the past, with a few exceptions it has been very selective in wielding the weapons of sanctions and restrictions on exports, aiming these mostly at recalcitrant members of the socialist community (see Goldman 1983a; Thomas 1985a:79; Stern 1987b:48–50 and pp. 218–24, below).

Notwithstanding their posture on trade, the Soviets have generally proven to be reliable trading partners, with a few exceptions (see Goldman 1983a for an illuminating discussion of East-West trade and politics). There is broad agreement that they have rarely tried to "challenge . . . the rules of the market" (Stern 1987b:46; see also Coker 1984b:43; Hannigan and McMillan 1984:79). Thane Gustafson (1985:14) writes that

> [The Soviet] style of behavior in foreign markets . . . has long been familiar to the Soviets' trading partners: episodic, sometimes opportunistic to the point of predatoriness . . . , frequently overbearing and devious in relations with prospective trading partners, yet punctilious in observing bargains once concluded and often strikingly loyal to established customers.

---

[7]For example, Professor Gregory Grossman (1986) has suggested that at various times, if calculated in terms of opportunity costs, seven tons of oil have been been traded for one ton of wheat.

Generally speaking, three distinct sets of Soviet trading partners can be distinguished: the CMEA countries (Council on Mutual Economic Assistance: Eastern Europe plus Vietnam, Cuba, and Mongolia), the developing countries of nonsocialist (such as Argentina) and socialist "orientation" (such as Angola and Mozambique), and the industrialized West (Western Europe, the United States, and so forth). Each is discussed in turn below.

CMEA. Since the formation of the CMEA in the late 1940s, trade between the Soviet Union and the states of Eastern Europe has been conducted in practice, if not in theory, on the basis of comparative advantage.[8] For the most part, the Soviet Union supplies Eastern Europe with raw materials, in exchange for machinery, consumer items, and other finished goods, and every effort is made to balance trade on a bilateral basis, with the exchange of hard goods for hard goods and soft goods for soft goods (Marrese and Vanous 1983:103; Vernon 1984:9).[9] These arrangements may involve the exchange of raw materials, such as bauxite or alumina, for processed or semifinished goods, such as aluminum, or it may be based on the trade of minerals (such as petroleum) for finished goods (such as machine tools and foods).

A sizable fraction of Soviet-CMEA trade has been conducted on the basis of joint investment and production agreements. Under such arrangements, which have been common throughout the CMEA, consumers of raw materials extend investment credits to producers in exchange for some portion of the output of a project (Csaba 1985:232; Gillette 1986). Thus, for example, in the late 1950s and early 1960s, Czechoslovakia and East Germany granted credits to the Soviet Union, Poland, and Bulgaria in exchange for such raw materials as oil, gas, iron, nonferrous metals, and asbestos (Csaba 1985). More recently, bilateral deals have been replaced by "multilaterally coordinated joint projects enjoying political priority" (Csaba 1985:234). For the most part, these joint ventures have involved the development of new

[8]Csaba (1985:228) asserts that "International economic intercourse among CMEA countries has never been based on considerations of comparative advantage. Even the theory of comparative advantage has been emphatically refuted as aimed at conserving structural dependencies established under imperialism" (but see pp. 213–14, below).

[9]"Hard" goods are those that can be sold in international markets for convertible currencies; "soft" goods cannot be sold for hard currency.

resource extraction projects in Siberia. This approach has been pre-ferred because "the impact of the oil shock brought supply security considerations to the fore in the East European countries, who favored long-term agreements as a guarantee of a planned way of meeting . . . strategic needs" (Csaba 1985:234). These ventures have not been as successful as anticipated due to capital shortages and the difficulties of working in the Siberian environment. In addition, in the past the East Europeans disliked these arrangements because they became locked into inefficient, impractical projects that offered no flexibility in prices. But there is some suggestion that joint ventures may be coming back into fashion (Stern 1987b).

Some Western analysts have suggested that the Soviets have used trade with Eastern Europe to "soften" the impact of Soviet hegemony by offering both advantageous prices and markets for goods (Marrese and Vanous 1983), although this notion is disputed by others (Csaba 1985:227). According to Marrese and Vanous (1983:104), for example, during the period from 1960 to 1980, the Soviet Union provided implicit trade subsidies of up to $87 billion through underpricing of raw materials. But they observe (1983:106) that

> The presence of these subsidies does not indicate that the Soviet Union has been irrational or that it is squandering gains from trade. Rather, it suggests to us that the Soviet political leadership may be maximizing a utility function that incorporates military, political, ideological, and certain special economic variables in addition to conventional gains from trade.

(On the question of the economic aspects of Soviet hegemony in Eastern Europe, see also Bunce 1985.) Whether this subsidy (if, indeed, it did exist) has been the result of a rational utility function, or simply a consequence of hegemonic behavior in a relatively closed trading system, is not altogether clear.[10] What is clear is that, as prices of raw materials rose during the 1970s, it became more disadvanta-geous for the Soviets to maintain below-market prices for raw material exports to the CMEA, particularly with respect to oil. In 1975, therefore, a new pricing system was introduced, based on a five-year moving average, that was intended to slowly bring CMEA raw

---

[10]It is interesting to note in this regard that the liberal model of hegemonic stability suggests that a hegemon will concede certain advantages to allies in order to gain benefits elsewhere (see Keohane 1984: ch. 3).

material prices to world market levels (this new pricing system did not, however, anticipate the collapse in the price of oil during the 1980s). In 1982, perhaps in response to declining production, the Soviet Union announced that oil supplies to Eastern Europe would be reduced by 10 percent over a three-year period (Gillette 1986), along with cutbacks in supplies of other raw materials. The uncertainty about future supplies has apparently triggered a search abroad by the CMEA countries for alternative sources (Coker 1984a; 1984b).

Developing Countries.   Until the mid-1950s, the Soviet Union tended to pay little attention to the developing world (Sawyer 1966; Smith 1973:225–26; Valkenier 1983: ch. 1). Beginning at that time, there was a growing Soviet belief that the destinies of the Third World and the socialist states were linked, and it was thought that a natural economic progression toward socialism would take place in every newly independent country. During the latter half of the 1970s, as revolutions swept through various parts of Africa, there was a great deal of optimism regarding the future of states of so-called socialist orientation. For example, R. Ulyanovsky (quoted in Coker 1984a:84 n. 65) announced that:

> On the whole the course of events has confirmed that the tendency towards a socialist orientation arises from amidst the liberation struggle of the peoples of Africa and is reproduced again and again — despite a great many difficulties and sometimes even temporary defeats.

But the 1980s have tempered this attitude and introduced greater pragmatism into Soviet relations with many Third World states. Where it was previously assumed that lasting political and economic relationships would grow out of such fraternal linkages, it is now recognized that Third World states with a "socialist" orientation are among the least developed and have the least to offer in terms of trade (Valkenier 1983:27, 1986). Many Soviet scholars have come to recognize that only the West can supply these states with the capital needed for economic development (Gorman 1984:178) and that their participation in a worldwide division of labor is a necessary element for overcoming "economic backwardness" (Valkenier 1983:83).

Valkenier has found, perhaps ironically, that some Soviet economists and development specialists are coming to sound more and more like their Western counterparts. She writes (1983:81) that since 1974

[Recognition of the existence of a] single world market and pressing global problems have brought a reinterpretation of development in a wider context, wherein elements of interdependence or universalism often predominate over those of competition and exclusiveness.

Furthermore, these specialists advocate "the expansion of international trade as largely conditioned by an appropriate specialization among all countries" in which developing nations would maximize the use of their own natural resources rather than rely on foreign aid in order to achieve eventual industrialization (Valkenier 1983:122). Thus, L. Zevin (1985:47) writes that

Given the considerable growth of the volume of relations with the socialist countries, the developing states concerned can embark on the formation . . . of a rational national economic complex on a modern basis with regard for the possibility of the organization of a stable division of labor with this group of countries.

And according to Professor Shmelev (1985:17)

[A]ssistance to the developing countries is gradually becoming a major factor in the formation of a stable and lasting division of labor between the two groups of countries, a standing and planned source for meeting mutual requirements in machinery, energy, raw materials, and consumer goods.

Development requires participation in the capitalist market, even for radical states, and the avoidance of trade restrictions imposed for noneconomic reasons (Valkenier 1983:100, 116; see also Shedlov and Podtserob 1983:60; Shmelev 1985:18–19). The long-term prospect for these states, it is asserted, remains a transition to socialism and a decoupling from the capitalist system (Gorman 1984:179), but the process cannot be short-circuited (on this point, see also U.S. CRS 1985:39–43).

In terms of trade, certain developing states, such as Argentina, have become favored sources of particular commodities (such as grain) due to advantageous prices. In other instances, the Soviet Union has established joint mining ventures in order to acquire certain raw materials that are in short supply domestically (such as bauxite from Guinea). To an increasing degree, therefore, the Soviet Union is looking to the nations of the Third World, including nonsocialist ones, as potential partners in economic collaboration (Valkenier 1983:32–33). For example, of the $2.7 billion in aid to Africa provided by the Soviets between 1974 and 1979, almost 75 percent went to

Morocco to develop phosphate deposits for export to the USSR, whereas only about $330 million was directed to the possessors of several strategic materials, the socialist states of sub-Saharan Africa (Valkenier 1983:33). Over the thirty-year lifetime of the Moroccan project, the total cost will be $9 billion, much of which will apparently be supplied by the Soviet Union (Shedlov and Podtserob 1983:61).

According to Soviet authors, approximately 12 percent of CMEA foreign trade takes place with developing countries, and this trade is growing at the rate of 15.4 percent per year. CMEA countries have assisted ninety-seven developing countries in the construction of some 3,500 projects in basic extraction and processing industries (Shmelev 1985:16–17; Zevin 1985:47), with a view toward establishing an ongoing relationship in raw materials and manufactures (see also Hannigan and McMillan 1984). Writes Academician Bogomolov (1983b:26),

> The long-term target-oriented cooperation programmes to meet the economically justified needs of the CMEA countries in fuel, energy, raw materials, foodstuffs and the main types of modern equipment envisage an opportunity for developing countries to take part in the integrational measures.

The Soviets have also acquired some commodities through barter, in repayment for various types of assistance offered to Third World countries (Gorman 1984:181). But compared to trade taking place between developing countries and the West, the level of Soviet trade with the Third World—a few states such as India excepted—still remains fairly limited.

Industrialized West. The subject of Soviet trade with the West in raw materials has been addressed in great detail by many analysts, particularly over the last ten years (for discussions focused on energy trade, see Wulf 1982; Braathu 1982; Frost and Stent 1983; Stern 1987b). Two primary concerns have developed in the West with regard to this trade. First, with respect to the purchase of raw materials, there has been a long-term fear that dependence on Soviet sources might open consumers up to price manipulation and blackmail. The flap over natural gas pipeline construction and sales in the early 1980s was only the most recent manifestation of this (the literature on this episode is extensive; good analyses can be found in Stent 1981; Jentleson 1984, 1986; Gustafson 1985; Stern 1987b).

Second, there has been concern, dating back to the late 1940s, that sales of high-technology equipment to the Soviets, such as that required to develop oil and natural gas resources, might enable them to develop more quickly their military capabilities than would otherwise be possible (on this, see Mastanduno 1985; Jentleson 1986; for earlier analyses, see DDEL 1953f, 1953g). The data in support of these beliefs are inconclusive (Tran 1987), but both fears have had enormous influence over the pattern of East-West trade. The first has generated periodic pressure, mostly by the United States on its European allies, to not rely too heavily on imports from the Soviet Union. The second concern has resulted in ongoing efforts to impose export controls limiting the sale of strategic goods to the Eastern Bloc (Adler-Karlsson 1968; Mastanduno 1985; Jentleson 1986).

The Soviets, too, have been reluctant to become too dependent on Western technology. David Holloway cites a Soviet economist (N. Inozemstev, quoted in Holloway 1984:106) to the effect that the Western sanctions imposed in the early 1980s led to the inescapable conclusion that

> [N]o important sectors of the Soviet economy should become dependent on imports of machinery from the capitalist countries, but . . . at the same time, the Soviet Union should not forego the benefits of international economic and scientific-technical collaboration.

From the Soviet perspective, therefore, trade with the West has had mixed benefits. Patterns of trade have been more consistent with those states geographically close to Eastern Europe, and more varied with those farther away (Smith 1986:5), and they have fluctuated in response to the state of East-West relations at any given time.

Nonetheless, the USSR has made consistent attempts to acquire and maintain customers in the West in order to obtain hard currency, technology, and goods. Ed Hewett (1983:643) asserts that the Soviets have "decided to exploit their abundant resource endowments and create export industries for key primary products" (see also Shmelev 1985:19). Thus, for example, the pattern of trade with the West during the early 1980s was heavily tilted toward exports of fuels and raw materials and imports of machinery, equipment, and food. In 1980, the Soviet Union exported $20.2 billion (1 ruble = $1.50) in raw materials to the West, of which 75 percent was oil and gas (Hewett 1983:624–25).

In addition to deals made through contracts with Western states, the Soviets have also tried to establish market positions in oil sales in Western Europe. In the late 1950s and early 1960s, the Soviets sought to increase trade relations with Western Europe through the sale of petroleum at competitive prices (Stent 1981; Jentleson 1984:641, 1986; see also pp. 230–31, below). The Soviets failed to capture a significant share of the aggregate market in Europe, in part due to an aggressive reaction by the Western majors. They did, however, establish a number of wholesale and retail companies, owned by *Soyuznefteksport*, in the United Kingdom, Belgium, Denmark, Finland, Italy, and Switzerland (Goldman 1983b; Hannigan and McMillan 1984:77) and achieved a respectably large market share in several of these countries.

THE USE OF "RESOURCE DIPLOMACY" BY THE SOVIET UNION, 1945–87

The trade relationships established between the Soviet Union and the three groups of states (East, South, and North) have had political as well as economic ends. Over the years, the political functions have shifted in response to changes in international politics and economics. The failure of the tide of socialist revolution to sweep over much of the Third World, and the stagnation of the Soviet economy relative to other industrialized states, has demonstrated that the propagation of a revolutionary ideology may, over the long run, be more successful if its advocates are capable of "delivering the goods." (This may be true in the industrialized world as well as the developing one.) The Soviets seem to recognize that, although it is possible to manipulate the "correlation of forces" in one's favor through aid and assistance, one cannot "rush" history or short-circuit the path to socialism. This has made them more cautious in the use of economic tools such as the manipulation of resource flows—that is, "resource diplomacy"—to achieve political ends.

A survey of the practice of resource diplomacy by the Soviet Union suggests a variety of motives. In almost every case, the use of this tool has involved the disruption of existing trade relationships, rather than the application or threatened use of force to interdict flows of resources to third parties. Hence, there may be cause to regard with some trepidation the establishment of trade with the Soviet Union.[11] Although the Soviets have not hesitated to use resource diplomacy in situations where they have judged that it might be effective, they have nonetheless been relatively careful in choosing their targets. In particular, in their dealings with the West, the Soviets have engaged in this practice only in reaction to political or economic provocations by Western states.

Table 7–1 page lists twenty examples of resource diplomacy by the Soviet Union. In virtually all of the cases considered, one motive — ideological, political, or economic — was dominant. Ideological actions were directed against other states of the Communist Bloc, in an effort to bring them back "into line." Political actions were generally taken in reaction to events outside the Communist Bloc and were intended to express disapproval. Economic actions were a reflection of the need to balance trade flows or of economic opportunism. There were also a set of cases in which the "dog did not bark," that is, in which the Soviet Union failed to or decided not to apply resource diplomacy. As always, it is impossible to make a clean and clear distinction between the three types of motives. In the following sections, the incidents listed in Table 7–1 are discussed in detail.

Ideological Actions

It is often assumed that the Soviet Union has used its patron-client relationships with other "Marxist-Leninist" states to influence the policies and doctrines of those states. Although a number of examples exist of such manipulation, I have been able to find only five in which the control of a strategic resource was used in furtherance of ideological objectives: against Yugoslavia in 1948, the People's Republic of China (PRC) during the 1960s, Albania from 1961–65, Cuba in 1967,

---

[11]But a study of the use of economic sanctions since the end of World War II suggests in fact that trading with the United States is a much riskier proposition. The study found that of ninety-nine cases, the United States was involved as the "sending" party in sixty-two, the United Kingdom in eighteen, and the Soviet Union in ten (most of which were directed against ideological allies). Only two episodes were initiated by developing resource-producing states or cartels (by AOPEC in 1967 and 1973–74) (Hufbauer and Schott 1985:8). This suggests that commonly expressed fears about "economic blackmail" by the Soviet Union may be largely misplaced.

Table 7–1.   Case Studies of Soviet Resource Diplomacy

Dominant Motive	Target of Action	Date	Resources Involved	Stated or Apparent Reason for Action
Ideological	Yugoslavia	1948–55	Oil, minerals	Ideological conflict
	People's Republic of China	1960s	Oil	Ideological conflict
	Albania	1961–65	Grain, oil	Ideological conflict
	Cuba	1967–68	Oil	Ideological conflict
	Nicaragua	1987	Oil	Reduce ideological fervor?
Political	United States	1948	Minerals	Response to U.S. trade sanctions
	Australia	1954	Wool	Response to asylum for defector
	Israel	1956	Oil	Punishment for Suez conflict
	Iran	1956	Rice	Signing of Baghdad Pact
	Finland	1958	Oil, metals	Displeasure with government
Economic	Britain, others	1950s	Tin	Balance of payments with United Kingdom
	Britain	1957–58	Aluminum	Balance of payments with United Kingdom
	Western Europe	1960–64	Oil	Competition for market share
	Zaire, Zambia	1977–78	Cobalt	Economic opportunism?
	World	Ongoing	Diamonds	Collaboration to support price
Cases in which the "dog did not bark"	Iran	1944–46	Oil	Demand for oil concession
	Czechoslovakia	1968	Oil	Ideological conflict
	Poland	1981	Oil	Ideological conflict
	Egypt	1955	Cotton	Replacement market
	Cuba	1960	Sugar, oil	Replacement market

and Nicaragua in 1987.[12] In each instance (except, possibly, the last), the Soviet Union reduced or halted oil deliveries as part of a more comprehensive set of economic and political sanctions designed to bring a wayward ideological ally or client back into line.

Yugoslavia, 1948–55.   The rift between the Soviet Union and Yugoslavia had its origins in the circumstances of the latter's liberation from occupation by Nazi Germany in 1945. Following the end of the war, Prime Minister Tito attempted to pursue what has been described as a "nationalist" foreign policy, independent of the Soviet Union, rather than one that was Communist (or Soviet-led) (Ulam 1952; U.S. State Department 1952; Campbell 1967; Clissold 1975). In response, the Soviet Union and its CMEA allies initiated a political and economic offensive against Yugoslavia, with the intent of forcing it back into the fold. Because most of Yugoslavia's trade was conducted with the Eastern Bloc, and because its Five-Year Plan was predicated on Soviet and Eastern European assistance (including the provision of financial and technical aid as well as raw materials), it was relatively easy for the Socialist Bloc to implement such an offensive.

During most of 1948, the USSR refused to sign a trade agreement with Yugoslavia and applied a series of increasingly harsh economic sanctions against it. When, in December 1948, an agreement for 1949 was finally signed, it provided for trade at levels greatly reduced from those of 1948 (Yugoslavian Ministry of Foreign Affairs 1951:293). In explaining the agreement, the Ministry of Foreign Trade of the Soviet Union (quoted in Clissold 1975:228) asserted that

> Owing to the hostile policy of the Yugoslav Government towards the Soviet Union, in consequence of which it is impossible to maintain large-scale economic exchange between the USSR and Yugoslavia, the [trade] protocol provides for reduced exchange of goods between the USSR and Yugoslavia for 1949. This exchange of goods will be reduced by 8 times as compared with 1948.

Romania ceased supplying oil to Yugoslavia (Yugoslavian Ministry of Foreign Affairs 1951:288–91) and other Eastern European states halted shipments of raw materials as well (Hufbauer and Schott 1985:205).

---

[12]Although the Soviets suggested that they might use resource diplomacy against Czechoslovakia in 1968 and Poland in 1981, they did not do so (Stern 1987b:50). These two instances are discussed below under the heading "Cases in Which the Dog Did Not Bark."

The supply of oil from the Soviet Union to Yugoslavia was cut by 50 percent in 1948, and dropped to zero by 1950 (Goldman 1980:59). Yugoslavia managed to make up many of the resulting shortfalls in the supply of aid and materials by striking deals with the West, but the economic and political pressures did not really begin to diminish until after Stalin's death. Subsequently, relations between Yugoslavia and the Soviet Union when through a number of ups and downs (Hufbauer and Schott 1985:206).

Broadly speaking, in applying sanctions and pressures against Yugoslavia, the goal of the Soviet Union was to assert leadership in the international Communist movement. A geopolitical motive may also have been involved, as Stalin might have feared the complete "defection" of Yugoslavia from East to West, leading to an opening in the band of buffer states separating the Soviet Union from Western Europe. But as noted above, resource diplomacy was only one element in the economic and political offensive. In more general terms, the Soviets gained only marginally from sanctions against Yugoslavia, and the overall effectiveness of the economic offensive was limited. Yugoslavia was able to maintain a relatively high degree of independence from Moscow by playing off East against West.

People's Republic of China (PRC), 1960s. The rift between the PRC and the Soviet Union developed for two, somewhat unrelated reasons. First, throughout the latter half of the 1950s, the Chinese leadership periodically criticized the Soviets for revisionism, particularly with respect to the policy of reconciliation with Yugoslavia and the pursuit of coexistence with the United States. In 1960 these attacks became particularly sharp (Hufbauer and Schott 1985:308). Second, the Soviet Union apparently reneged on an agreement to supply China with a "sample" atomic bomb as well as technical information about its manufacture (Clemens 1968:15–24; Hufbauer and Schott 1985:308). When a Soviet demand for control over China's atomic development program was rebuffed, the Soviets cancelled the agreement on atomic cooperation.

In 1960, *all* Soviet technicians (not only nuclear scientists) were withdrawn from China, taking with them blueprints for many Soviet-built or financed installations (Hufbauer and Schott 1985:308–09). Along with the elimination of technical and financial aid, the Soviets also began to reduce oil supplies to the PRC. In the 1950s and throughout early 1960s, as much as one-third of China's crude and refined oil was supplied by the Soviet Union (Klinghoffer 1977:197; Goldman 1980:58). After 1960, shipments of crude oil to the PRC ceased entirely and, as the PRC found other foreign and domestic sources, shipments of refined products from the Soviet Union declined, too (Klinghoffer 1977:196).

Again, resource diplomacy comprised only a small part of a much broader political, economic, and ideological offensive conducted by the Soviet Union against the PRC. The Soviet Union, under Khrushchev and his successors, Brezhnev and Kosygin, sought to assert its leadership of the international Communist movement and, from time to time, to gain approval from other states of the Socialist Bloc for efforts to improve relations with the United States. The effort to bring the PRC back into line can be judged to have been a failure, as it must have been a major factor in the eventual rapproachment between the PRC and the United States. The use of resource diplomacy only encouraged the Chinese to seek out alternative sources of oil, of which many were available, and to develop their own domestic resources.

Albania, 1961–65.   The Soviet split with Albania also had its roots in Khrushchev's efforts at reconciliation with Tito. In 1960, several months after Albania and the PRC publicly opposed this policy at a meeting of party leaders in Bucharest, the Soviets began to initiate a program of economic sanctions by refusing to ship grain to Albania. In 1961, they withdrew technical assistance to the Albanian oil industry, as well as other industries, attempted to instigate a coup against the Albanian leader, Enver Hoxha, halted all economic aid, and eventually broke all diplomatic and trade relations and ejected Albania from the CMEA. All of these efforts had little effect, as the PRC agreed to supply Albania with the aid and trade lost from the Soviet Union and Eastern Europe (Hufbauer and Schott 1985:329–31). Once again, the effort to impose ideological rigor on a Communist state was stymied by the availability of an alternative source of support and supplies. This made the cumulative impact of sanctions, among which was included resource diplomacy, relatively minor.

Cuba, 1967–68.   The ideological conflict between the Soviet Union and Cuba arose out of disagreement over the appropriate role of the latter in fostering revolution in the Third World. Castro was critical of Soviet attempts to establish relations with "imperialist" regimes in Latin America, such as those in Chile and Brazil, and believed that

Cuba should encourage and support revolutionary movements in the Third World (Shearman 1987:17–20). The Soviets, in the aftermath of the Cuban Missile Crisis, and in pursuit of improved relations with the United States, opposed such open support for revolution.

In late 1967, the Soviets began to apply economic pressures against Cuba in an effort to get Castro back into line (Stern 1987b:49–50; Shearman 1987). During 1967, Cuba's oil requirements rose by 8 percent while Soviet shipments to Cuba rose by only 2 percent. At the same time, Soviet oil exports to Brazil and Argentina were increased (Shearman 1987:21). But Cuba was relatively powerless in this situation. Raul Castro, Fidel's brother, reported a Soviet diplomat's warning that were Cuba to give any consideration to breaking with the Soviet Union, "[A]ll we have to do is tell the Cuban government that repairs are going to be made in the port of Baku that will last for three weeks" (quoted in Shearman 1987:21).

In the trade agreement for 1968, the level of increase in trade was lower than that for 1967. This was interpreted by Castro as an effort by the Soviets to apply pressure on Cuba (Shearman 1987:21). Ultimately, Castro seemed to back down on his advocacy of an independent line, possibly in support of or as a response to the Soviet invasion of Czechoslovakia. In a recent study of Cuban-Soviet relations, Peter Shearman has argued that it was not the economic pressures applied by the Soviet Union that caused Castro to repent but, rather, fear of the United States as well as the potentially pernicious effects of the "Prague Spring" on Cuban citizens (Shearman 1987:23).

Nicaragua, 1987.   The most recent apparent use of resource diplomacy by the Soviet Union has been aimed at Nicaragua. According to published reports, in mid-1987 the Soviets reduced oil shipments to Nicaragua by some 60 percent, forcing it to turn to elsewhere for replacement supplies (Chace 1987:26, 28; Golub 1987; Rohter 1987). Somewhat ironically, in this case the Soviets may have wished to induce the Sandinista leadership to soften its "Marxist-Leninist" stance in the hope that this might lead to a reduction in U.S. pressure on the regime (Chace 1987:28; Golub 1987). Whether this was actually the Soviet goal is unclear, but Soviet experience (as well as that of the United States) would suggest a low probability of success. Although Nicaraguan government may have been pushed, in part, into peace talks with the *Contras* by such pressures, a hardening of Sandinista resistance to the entreaties of both superpowers, or even a turn to suppliers such as Libya or Iran could not have been ruled out.

In four of the five cases recounted above, resource diplomacy played a small, mostly marginal role in Soviet efforts to force wayward Communist regimes back into Marxist-Leninist "orthodoxy." The potential for effective economic and political sanctions would seem great, given the extent of ties between the states of the Communist Bloc, but this has not proved to be the case. In all five cases, furthermore, the Soviet Union has lacked a sufficiently commanding global market position to allow it to back up its ideal objectives. Only with respect to Cuba, which was in a very weak geostrategic position relative to the United States, did such efforts achieve notable success. At this writing, the actual effect of Soviet pressures on Nicaragua remains unclear.

Political actions

Whereas the Soviet Union has used resource diplomacy in a negative sense against its ideological allies and clients, it has used the same tool in both a positive and negative sense with respect to non-Communist countries. I use the term "negative" to refer to sanctions and "positive" to refer to situations in which the Soviets have agreed to act as replacement purchasers of commodities produced by developing countries. I have been able to identify five cases of negative resource diplomacy with political motivations — against the United States in 1948, Australia in 1954, Israel in 1956, Iran in 1956, and Finland during 1958 and 1959. The two most conspicuous cases of positive resource diplomacy occurred with respect to Egypt in 1955 and Cuba in 1960. One indeterminate case involved a demand for an oil concession in northern Iran in 1944. These latter three cases are discussed elsewhere in this chapter (pp. 232–33). There are also a number of examples of Soviet trade agreements with developing countries that may have had political as well as economic rationales, but these are not discussed here (see Smith 1973: ch. 7 for details).

United States, 1948.   As was noted in Chapter 5, in late 1947, in response to pressure from Congress, the U.S. Department of Commerce promulgated regulations to control the export of sensitive and strategic goods to the Soviet Union. The implementation of export controls began in early 1948.[13] At the time, the United States still imported a significant fraction of its chromium and manganese requirements from the Soviet Union, a residual trading relationship left over from the wartime alliance. U.S. policymakers were well aware that one consequence of the imposition of trade controls might be a Soviet embargo on the export of strategic minerals (NARS 1948b). In fact, there was little else in the way of economic retaliation available to the Soviets. They duly halted the export of both manganese and chromium to the United States, but only toward the end of 1948 (NARS 1949a). Because the United States was prepared for such a stoppage and was able to find alternative sources of supply in fairly short order, the Soviet action had little material effect. It did serve to underline symbolically the growing rift between East and West.

Australia, 1954.   In April 1954, the third secretary and consul at the Soviet Embassy in Canberra, Vladimir Petrov, defected to the West, bringing with him information about Soviet espionage in Australia. Petrov's wife, who charged initially that he had been kidnapped, subsequently asked for asylum, too. When the Soviet demand for Petrov's return was rebuffed by the Australian government, the Soviet Union broke diplomatic relations and embargoed imports of wool. The two countries did not reestablish diplomatic relations until 1959. The embargo resulted in an annual loss of approximately $50 million to Australia. Nonetheless, the Soviet sanctions had no effect on Australian policy, and Petrov and his wife remained in Australia (Hufbauer and Schott 1985:240–43). Again, resource diplomacy was applied largely as a symbolic act.

Israel, 1956.   Information on the Soviet embargo of oil shipments to Israel in response to the Suez invasion is limited; only Klinghoffer (1977:355 n. 166) seems to know anything about the episode because, he claims, the Israeli government has tried to keep it a secret. Israel first imported oil from the Eastern Bloc in 1948, when supplies were not available from neighboring sources (Klinghoffer 1977:146). The first oil shipments from the Soviet Union were made in 1952, and by 1954

---

[13]Initially, the controls had nothing to do with the Berlin Crisis but were part of an evolving policy of economic containment (Adler- Karlsson 1968; Mastanduno 1985; Jentleson 1986). Deteriorating relations between the United States and Soviet Union, exacerbated by the Berlin Crisis, the Korean War, and other events, contributed to the expansion of controls between 1948 and 1950.

Israel was receiving some 300,000 to 400,000 tons per year. In May 1956 Israel and the Soviet Union signed a new contract stipulating delivery of 700,000 tons during that year and up to 1 million tons per year in 1957–58 (Klinghoffer 1977:148–49). At the same time, the Soviets also began to provide various forms of economic and political support to Egypt.

After the start of the Suez campaign in October 1956, Soviet political support shifted to the Arab states. At that point, reports Klinghoffer, *Soyuznefteksport*, the Soviet oil export company, cabled the Israeli national oil company that export licenses from the Ministry of Foreign Trade had been cancelled. This action voided the contract signed shortly before between the two countries. As a result, according to the company, no more oil would be delivered. Israel protested and filed suit in a Soviet court, but it lost the case (Klinghoffer 1977:151–52). Direct oil shipments stopped, although the Soviets apparently continued to supply oil to Israel via Turkey, Italy, and Yugoslavia. Israel was also able to find alternative suppliers. Hence, the Soviet action had little effect in comparison with the pressures applied against Israel at the time by other countries.

Iran, 1956.   According to papers in the Public Record Office of the United Kingdom, in 1956 the Soviet Union halted purchases of rice from Iran as an expression of displeasure over the latter's adherence to the Baghdad Pact (PRO 1956b:3). I have been unable to find any other information about this episode.

Finland, 1958–1959.   The Finnish "Nightfrost Crisis" is perhaps the most interesting of the cases discussed here in that it has both a political and an economic explanation. There seems to be general agreement among analysts that the origins of the crisis had to do with a shift in Finnish domestic politics, and that the Soviet Union expressed displeasure with these developments through the application of economic and political pressure. As one author put (Allison 1985:114) it,

> The strong political colouring of Finnish-Soviet trade in the Soviet frame of reference has led to Soviet leaders using trade relations to demonstrate the Soviet comprehension of an unsatisfactory state of political relations between the neighbour states.

The formation of a center-right government in Finland in mid-1958, after months of political uncertainty, raised fears in the Soviet Union that a change in Finnish foreign policy was underway (Allison 1985:137–39). At approximately the same time, decisions were made by the Finnish government to free import trade from licensing requirements and to devalue the Finmark. These two steps led to a major expansion in trade with Western Europe.[14] This, in turn, resulted in a drop in the volume of imports from the Eastern Bloc, which meant that Finland was unable to meet the agreed-on annual import quota for Soviet goods. Because of the bilateral nature of Finnish-Soviet trade, a large surplus of rubles built up in the trade clearing account, to the disadvantage of the Soviets (Forster 1960:148; Vayrynen 1969:211; Skully 1973:20–21).

The Soviets began to express displeasure at the general trend of events in Finland through both diplomatic and economic actions. The Soviet ambassador left Helsinki, ostensibly for health reasons (Vayrynen 1969:211). Various agreements and discussion of credits were delayed. Power plant construction was halted. Trade and other negotiations were postponed, metal deliveries were curtailed, imports from Finland to the Soviet Union were suspended, and payments by the Soviets to Finland were not made on time (Vloyantes 1975:96–97). According to Klinghoffer (1977:24), oil deliveries from the Soviet Union to Finland were halted after November 28, 1958. The cumulative pressures finally led to the collapse of the Finnish government in December 1958 and to its replacement by one more acceptable to the Soviets (Vloyantes 1975:98–99) — and, writes one analyst, after the signing of the 1959 bilateral trade agreement, crude oil shipments to Finland from the Soviet Union apparently doubled (Vayrynen 1969:229). The Soviets, according to Vloyantes (1975:95), *"perceived* that Finland was moving away from its traditional foreign policy line" (1975:95) and toward the West, and reacted accordingly, with great success.

Four of the five cases of resource diplomacy applied for political reasons must be judged to have failed. In the case of Finland, geographic proximity to and the volume of trade relations with the Soviet Union gave the latter the leverage necessary to influence the former. In

---

[14]Whether the shift in economic policy had anything to do with the change in government is unclear from the secondary sources I consulted.

all other cases, the Soviet action was, at best, a symbolic expression of Soviet displeasure and, at worst, a nuisance for the targeted state.

Economic Actions

The case studies of resource diplomacy in which economic motivations were involved have to do with Soviet activities in international commodity markets, that is, either apparent Soviet dumping in markets (tin, 1950s; aluminum, 1957–58; oil, 1960–64) or economic opportunism (cobalt, 1977–78; diamonds, ongoing). In the first three cases, the Soviets sold commodities at prices below those prevailing in international markets. In the West, these actions were interpreted frequently as efforts to depress prices, destabilize markets, or supplant competitors. A more plausible explanation may lie with the Soviet need to balance hard-currency imports with exports. In the last two cases listed, Soviet activities have been aimed at taking advantage of high commodity prices, when they have occurred.

Tin, 1950s.   In the late 1940s and early 1950s, the Soviet Union was a net importer of tin. During this period, Soviet purchases of tin from Western sources were limited, due largely to the U.S. desire to restrict Soviet consumption to what the U.S. judged were "reasonable" quantities.[15] In the mid-1950s, the Soviet Union finally found an alternative source and began to import large quantities of tin from the People's Republic of China — as much as 94,000 tons between 1956 and 1960, according to one estimate (Fox 1974:285).[16] This quantity was far in excess of Soviet needs, and so, in 1957, the Soviets began to export the surplus. Coupled with weak demand due to a global economic recession, the Soviet sales had a disastrous effect on world prices (Fox 1974:81).

In an effort to stabilize the market, the International Tin Committee approached the Soviet government with proposals to limit these sales,

---

[15]There was some suspicion in U.S. circles that the Soviets were stockpiling tin for military purposes. But why not? So was the United States.

[16]Soviet tin purchases from the PRC may have been an example of positive resource diplomacy, as Western markets were presumably closed to Chinese tin during the 1950s.

but the Soviets were reluctant to do so. As William Fox (1974:295) analyzed the situation,

> No one knew whether . . . [Soviet] sales of tin at a time of world crisis in the industry had been actuated by malice to destroy economically an industry of flagrant colonial character or had arisen from the stupidity of a bureaucracy which, told to sell massive accumulated stocks of tin, sold them at the worst time and price for itself. There seems to have been little, if any, actual price cutting, in spite of the market rumors.

Eventually, after Western countries imposed import restrictions on tin from the USSR, the Soviets agreed to stop sales in order to support prices (Fox 1974: 296–97). In the 1960s, Soviet tin sales were halted entirely, presumably because it had gotten rid of its surplus or, possibly, as a result of the cessation of purchases from the PRC.

Aluminum, 1957–58. At almost the same time as they dumped tin, the Soviets also began to sell aluminum on world markets. Because of the economic recession of 1957–58, the aluminum market was very soft. Therefore, the Soviets sold the metal in Britain at 2 cents a pound below the world price. In doing so, they were able to capture part of the British market from Alcan, which had cut production in an effort to support prices (Smith 1973:22). Although this activity was viewed as another attempt to destabilize markets, the explanation for Soviet activities apparently had to do with the need, once again, to balance exports and imports.

In 1957 Soviet purchases from the British Commonwealth — especially of raw materials such as rubber — led to a severe balance-of-payments problem with the Sterling Bloc. The inconvertibility of sterling at the time made it necessary for the Soviets to increase sales of goods and commodities to the United Kingdom so as to balance bilateral trade (Smith 1973:22, 23). Thus, from 1956 to 1957, Soviet exports of raw commodities to Britain — petroleum, timber, manganese, ferroalloys, aluminum, and tin — increased by 185 million rubles. Aluminum and tin accounted for 87 million rubles, and the Soviets underpriced these commodities in order to obtain customers (Smith 1973:23). But in response to Canadian complaints, they did limit voluntarily the volume of aluminum shipments to Britain (Pisar 1970:236). As Samuel Pisar (1970:236) analyzed the episode in retrospect,

This pattern [of sales] is hardly consistent with an effort to become a stable, dependable source of export to a permanent market expected to yield maximum economic advantage. More persuasive is the hypothesis of a one-shot directive to dispose of an unplanned, sizable surplus of aluminum metal.

Oil, 1960–64. The Soviet effort to penetrate Western European oil markets in the early 1960s is, by far, the most celebrated example of economically motivated resource diplomacy, and it has been treated in varying degrees of detail by a number of authors (Smith 1973:23–24; Klinghoffer 1977:216–23; Goldman 1980:67–72; Stent 1981: ch. 5.; Jentleson 1984, 1986). Soviet actions in this area generated a strong Western response, led by the United States, that included a pipeline embargo.

Between 1955 and 1960, Soviet oil sales to Western Europe rose from 116,000 barrels per day (bpd) to 486,000 bpd, of which a significant fraction went to Italy and West Germany (Stent 1981:98). In particular, ENI (*Ente Nazionale Idrocarburi*), the Italian national oil company, desired to free itself from its dependence on the major oil companies for crude, and was especially eager to acquire Soviet supplies. As a result, by 1962–63, ENI obtained 38 percent of its crude requirements from the Soviet Union (Goldman 1980:69). Furthermore, in comparison to the official posted price of about $2.50 per barrel (bbl) of crude, the Soviets sold to West Germany at $1.71/bbl (Stent 1981:98) and to Italy at $1.15/bbl (Goldman 1980:69).[17] The majors regarded these sales as a potentially serious market threat, and in order to limit Soviet market penetration, they engaged in price cutting competition, but they did this without consulting the governments of the oil-producing states.[18]

The oil companies also raised the specter of Soviet economic warfare and of a security threat to Western Europe in order to induce the U.S. government to act (Goldman 1980:70–71; Stent 1981:99; Jentleson 1984, 1986). The U.S. strategy to deal with the Soviet "oil threat" was to coerce its NATO allies into embargoing sales of forty-inch steel pipe to the Soviet Union, on the grounds that such

---

[17]Whether this actually constituted "price-cutting" is unclear because the posted price of crude from the Middle East bore no relationship whatever to its cost of production. The majors were, as a result, able to meet and beat Soviet prices when necessary.

[18] As noted earlier, it was this move that led directly to the establishment of the Organization of Petroleum Exporting Countries in 1961 (Jentleson 1984:641).

sales constituted a security threat to the West (Stent 1981:100; Jentleson 1986: ch. 4). Even so, by 1965 Soviet exports to the West had increased to more than 1 million bpd (Stent 1981:98).

Although the Western tendency was to see the Soviet sales in terms of the so-called Soviet economic offensive (DDEL 1958e), the explanation was probably, according to Glen Smith (1973:24), less diabolical:

> As in the case of aluminum and tin, the [oil] markets were tightly held by producers that maintained artificially high prices. To enter these markets the Soviets were forced to use the only tool available to them— price concessions . . . . [T]he stiff price competition gave the Soviets what they needed, the wherewithal to pay for needed imports . . . . The major oil producers probably cried "dumping" because they were forced to make overdue cuts in price to meet Soviet competition. They used the security issue as Pavlov used a bell.

The three case studies recounted above all suggest a certain degree of economic opportunism by the Soviet Union with respect to world commodity markets. Where long-term contracts are concerned, the Soviets have generally proved to be reliable and observant; when market opportunities arise, they have been less restrained. Two other cases bear brief mention here: cobalt and diamonds.

Cobalt.   Toward the end of the 1970s, reports emerged that the Soviet Union had engaged in the purchase of large quantities of cobalt just prior to the 1977 and 1978 invasions of the Shaba province (formerly Katanga) of Zaire by Katangan exiles (Severin 1981:50; Papp 1982:163; see also the accusations in Mott 1981:19–20). This, along with reports that the exiles had been trained by East Germany, led some observers to deduce Soviet involvement in the invasion and an effort to destabilize the Mobutu government in Zaire (see, for example, the discussion in Mangold 1979:108–09).

No credible evidence has ever emerged to support these contentions, but there is an alternative explanation, more in keeping with previous Soviet behavior. The Soviet Union is a net importer of cobalt (Severin 1981:45; Lipschutz 1986b:17), a mineral in great demand in electronic and alloying applications, many of them military-related. In 1977, prior to the Shaba invasion, cobalt markets were very soft, partly as a result of sales from the U.S. strategic stockpile. It is therefore plausible to suggest that the purchases were made in order to take advantage of the low price.

Diamonds.   The Soviet Union is also one of the world's largest producer of gem-quality diamonds, second only to the Republic of South Africa. Although one might expect the Soviets to make every effort to sell in volume on the open market, such is not the case. There are obvious advantages to a seller in maintaining high diamond prices. Thus, the Soviets cooperate in marketing their stones with the the so-called diamond cartel or Syndicate based in London and South Africa (Campbell 1986:72–75). Although this cooperation has been adduced by some as evidence that the Soviets might well collude with South Africa in order to control flows of other minerals, such as chromium and manganese (Severin 1981:51), the evidence in support of such a proposition is uncertain. In any case, a more likely explanation of Soviet cooperation with the diamond syndicate is that the orderly marketing of diamonds enables the Soviets to obtain the highest and best possible prices. In any event, were they to engage in price-cutting in diamond markets, the Soviets could be easily undercut by the Syndicate, which controls a much larger volume of gem-quality stones.

Cases in Which the "Dog Did Not Bark"

There are at least five cases of resource diplomacy that do not fall precisely within any of the previous three categories. These are instances in which the Soviets seem to have acted in pursuit of a resource (Iran, 1944–46), threatened but did not apply resource diplomacy (Czechoslovakia, 1968; Poland, 1981), or acted as a replacement market for commodities (Egypt, 1955; Cuba, 1960). In each case, the motivation for action (or non-action) was slightly different.

Iran, 1944–46.   In 1944 the Soviets demanded an oil concession in the Azerbaijan province of Iran as a *quid pro quo* for evacuating wartime occupation troops. The general Western suspicion was that the Soviets intended to annex the province, and indeed, they apparently aided and abetted the establishment of a pro-Soviet government there (Kuniholm 1980:304–50). But under some pressure from the United States and Britain, and after obtaining agreement on an oil concession from the Iranian prime minister, the Soviets withdrew their troops in March 1946. Eventually, the concession agreement was submitted to the

Iranian *Majlis*, which rejected it, and no more was heard of a Soviet oil concession in Iran.

The reasons adduced for the Soviet demand vary from analyst to analyst. The most common explanations rest on the supposed Soviet desire to establish a buffer state between itself and Iran, which was considered to be within the British sphere of influence (see Kuniholm 1980), the "traditional" Russian drive for a warm-water port (PRO 1946d), or a felt need to balance the British presence in southern Iran (see Louis 1984: pt. II). An alternative explanation, put forth in British policy circles at the time, rested on the supposed Soviet wish to find crude oil to supply the excess refining capacity built up in the Soviet Union during World War II (PRO 1947e).

Czechoslovakia, 1968, and Poland, 1981.   In 1968 and 1981, the Soviets apparently warned its two allies that it might cut off oil supplies if the internal political situation in both countries deteriorated markedly. In neither case did the Soviet Union follow through on the threat, although it did invade Czechoslovakia. Whether the threat had any effect on the domestic politics of both satellites is unclear. In any event, the threats were certainly motivated by ideological considerations (Klinghoffer 1977: 200; Stern 1987b:50).

Egypt, 1955, and Cuba, 1960.   In both of these cases, the Soviet Union acted as an alternate purchaser of commodities when Western markets were closed off. In the Egyptian case, the reduction in Western purchases of cotton was related to the Soviet-Egyptian agreement on construction of the Aswan Dam (Meyer 1980: ch. 6). The Soviet Union had traded with Egypt for many years, but after 1955 became a major purchaser of Egyptian cotton. In the case of Cuba, the Soviets agreed to buy sugar in 1960 after President Eisenhower eliminated the Cuban quota for sugar sales to the United States. The Soviets also became the major supplier of oil to Cuba at the same time (Klinghoffer 1977:21–22). The motivation in both cases can be considered political, rather than economic or ideological because, while both Egypt and Cuba were regarded as increasingly radical by their former customers (primarily the United States), neither had openly declared itself to be socialist or "Marxist-Leninist." In addition, it is unlikely that the Soviet Union realized any significant economic advantage at the time by purchasing Egyptian and Cuban commodities.

SUMMARY AND CONCLUSIONS

This chapter has described the political and economic positions of the Soviet Union with respect to international raw materials flows and the Soviet use of "resource diplomacy" against allies as well as "enemies." In the past, these positions have reflected a mixture of material and ideal interests, and they continue to do so. Undoubtedly, Soviet decisionmakers possess a cognitive map, or follow a set of organizing principles, just as do U.S. and British policymakers (although the principles themselves are quite different in some respects). Lacking the necessary archival documentation, it is difficult to specify precisely what these principles might be, but it is possible to make some generalizations.

First, Soviet leaders do appear to follow certain geopolitical principles having to do with the position of the Soviet Union as a land power and the United States as a maritime power. Consequently, Soviet leaders are well aware of the role which shipping lanes play in world politics. But these principles do not seem to apply in the same sense for the Soviet Union, at least as long as the principle of autarky remains prominent. Second, in the past the Soviets have tried to make use of what was long assumed to be an advantage of socialist markets — namely, stability in demand and price, in establishing political and economic relations with Third World states. Khrushchev's economic offensive, announced in 1955, was an admission that Soviet leaders recognized they could not depend on the attraction of ideology or example alone to realize their ideal goal of an international socialist system; market power as well as political leverage was also needed (Christensen 1977). In practice, this power and leverage was not realized to a significant degree and, much to the disappointment of the Soviets and their customers, the realities of economic relations with the Soviet Union failed to match the theory.

Ultimately, the ability of the Soviets to influence or manipulate resource trade aimed at recalcitrant partners has been limited for at least two reasons. First, the tradition of self-sufficiency means that Soviet purchasing power in world commodity markets has been minimal, and the threat of import embargoes or sanctions against other countries has been a relatively empty one. Second, the Soviet Union is a relatively minor seller of most commodities, and in those materials where it does command a significant fraction of the market (for example, petroleum), alternative sources usually exist. Although the Soviets do possess the military power to interdict flows of raw materials, in general the potential costs of such actions have been seen as incommensurate with the risks. Consequently, the effectiveness of the "resource diplomacy" practiced by the Soviet Union has been rather limited. Finally, in recent years—particularly since the accession to power of Chairman Gorbachev—there seems to have been a growing concern over the extent to which it is safe to manipulate others in the pursuit of ideal interests, as reflected in recent pronouncements on relations with Eastern Europe (Taubman 1987).

8 THE SHATTERED MIRROR
Some Conclusions and Their
Implications for U.S. Foreign Policy

The mirror lies at our feet. It is time to pick up the pieces. But where do we start? At the beginning of this book, two questions were posed: (1) Do states go to war in order to gain access to strategic resources? (2) Are the foreign policies of states influenced significantly by efforts to gain access to such resources? This study has shown that there are no unequivocal answers; one's conclusions depend on which pieces of the mirror one picks up.

The conventional wisdom is that states *do* go to war in pursuit of strategic raw materials (see, for example, Choucri and North 1975). If the sources of basic national power are threatened, according to this view, the state has no choice but to move to restore or recapture those sources. The analytical literature builds on this basic realist thesis but fails to take it too much farther. Liberal theorists are forced to fall back on interest-based arguments to explain the outbreaks of war, while Marxists continue to invoke economic arguments — whether based on domestic class structure or dominance/dependency relationships — to explain conflicts over raw materials. All three schools are correct, but their explanations are incomplete (see Lipschutz 1987: ch. 3 for a survey and critique of the literature).

The conventional wisdom on resources and conflict is not, however, completely wrong; it is correct, although only up to a point. It is, however, precisely at that point that things begin to get interesting. We can see how states behave, but state actions are merely the visible consequences of human behavior; to understand the reasons for actions, we must dig more deeply. If we are to understand actions, we must understand rules, too. To quote Bruce Andrews (1975:525): "If a domestic rule 'stands there like a signpost,' then a rule-guided action will stand there like a signpost as well". And rules have meaning. Only by looking at the "rules" and their origin—and even the anarchic international system has some rules—do we gain greater insight into the forces that push states, and policymakers, into action. This study represents an effort to find and interpret those rules and to relate them to material and ideal interests. Therefore, this final chapter summarizes my findings and conclusions about those rules and includes some thoughts about the implications of these conclusions for U.S. foreign policy.

INTERESTS AND RULES IN THE INTERNATIONAL REALM

On March 30, 1961, not too long after John F. Kennedy took office, his national security advisor, McGeorge Bundy, penned the following note (JFKL 1961c, emphasis in original):

> The other day in talking with Dean Acheson you asked about a quotation, and he skillfully covered his ignorance by saying that he thought it worthy of himself. Now he has sent me the whole sentence to send on to you, together with its source, and here it is:
>
> "The pursuit of *a remote and ideal object, which captivates the imagination by its splendor and the reason by its simplicity*, evokes an energy which would not be inspired by a rational, possible end, limited by many antagonistic claims, and confined to what is reasonable, practicable and just."
>
> "An Essay on Nationality"
in
"A History of Freedom and Other Essays"
by
John Emerich Edward Dalberg-Acton
(Lord Acton) 1834–1902

Having come into office on a wave of Cold War sentiment, one is forced to wonder whether Kennedy was being devious or rueful in raising the question. Whatever his reason, the point is well-made: For policymakers—and, by extension, for the foreign policies of states—

the interplay between material realities and ideal interests is critical. Material realities define the limits of the possible, while ideal interests define the limits of the preferable. Sometimes, the two coincide; often, they do not.

In Chapter 1, it was suggested that the raw materials policies of states, and the relationship of these policies to broader foreign policy goals, should provide us with a great deal of insight into the linkages between the material and ideal "realities" of international politics. On the one hand, raw materials are physical, measurable inputs into the industrial base of a state and, presumably, are somehow related to a state's military and economic power. As was shown in Chapter 6, in describing the postwar raw materials policies of the United Kingdom, the availability and flows of raw materials can impose real constraints on the freedom to make policy and can even influence the direction of that policy. On the other hand, except under infrequent and dire conditions, raw material flows function more commonly as intervening or dependent variables in the formation of a foreign policy that may have both material and ideal objectives.

The nature and strength of the linkage between material and ideal interests is therefore not irrelevant to the analysis presented in this book. Indeed, it is critical to our understanding of history, as well as our planning for the future for, as Mary Tétreault and Charles Abel (1986:4) point out in a recent monograph on international political economy: "[I]t is ideology that makes policy, and policy has the power to constrain the normal interplay of material forces." As they put it (1986:3),

> There are two realities in modern international political economy. One is material and the other is ideological. Both are absolutely real and occupy the same space at the same time; neither is destined to predominate nor to direct unequivocally the future of that order. The material reality is based upon the distribution of raw materials; technology; economic, political, and social development; population; purchasing power; knowledge; economic and political alliances; and the cost of labor, investment, and land. The ideological reality is too often based upon nationalism and its seemingly inevitable concomitants: misperception, insecurity, and the need to establish power and prestige.

They overstate, perhaps, the separation between the material and the ideal, but they do begin to get at an essential feature of the foreign policies of states and the international political system: the central role of ideology—often in the form of nationalism—in influencing international politics. To consider either "reality" in isolation leads to, in the words of Kenneth Waltz, a form of "reductionism" that fails to fully explain the operation of that system (Waltz 1979: ch. 2).

Unfortunately, many efforts to get at the "black box" of ideology, in the words of Giovanni Sartori (1969:398), are not successful (see Lipschutz 1987: ch. 9 for more details on this point). For example, in his statist analytical approach to U.S. foreign policy, Stephen Krasner (1978) identifies the long-standing and repeated preferences of "central decisionmakers" with the "national interest" of a state. In his view (1978:338), these preferences are informed by an ideological framework—in the case of the United States, Lockean liberalism—that cannot be unambiguously linked to material goals. In fact, Krasner explicitly rules out material goals—security of resource supplies—as the primary motivator of U.S. foreign policy in the post-World War II period. He argues, instead, that the "totalitarian hold" of Lockean liberalism—a notion propounded by Louis Hartz (1955)—is responsible for the primacy of ideological and "nonrational" behavior (Krasner 1978:335). But as John Ruggie points out in a review of Krasner's study, liberalism is quite clearly an ideology with ideal as well as material components (Ruggie 1980:298). The material components have to do with property rights, in the narrow sense, and the ideal components with the relationship of men to each other, to society, and to the world (that is, property rights in a broader sense). Krasner's effort to relegate ideology to the realm of the "irrational" simply fails to explain the function of ideology in foreign policy.

In this study, therefore, I have posited the existence of what I have called "property rights" to explain why, when, and where conflicts over raw materials take place. Property rights, according to this framework, represent the fusing of material and ideal interests; in a sense, they are the outcomes of the interplay between ideology and material realities. Property rights are not laws—although they can be—and they are not regimes—although they often are embedded in regimes. To repeat an earlier passage in this book (p. 16, above),

> Property rights can . . . be defined in terms of systems of rules, customs, norms, and laws that specify relationships between actors . . . and between actors and their political, economic, and physical environments. Property rights express an idealized version of the relationship of actors to the material conditions of their environment.

Property rights incorporate both the material and ideal interests of a state; they rationalize the order of things and act as instrumental rules for maintaining that order. Property rights — which may or may not be constitutive of an international regime — are in no small part a reflection of domestic social structure and the norms and rules operative within a particular state.

In an article entitled "Social Rules and the State as a Social Actor," Bruce Andrews (1975:521) considers the "relationship between the state and the domestic social structure" in a way that begins to provide some insight into the problem at hand. He writes (1975:523) that

> Most of a state's significant (or signifying, meaningful) foreign policies can be thought of [as] ... guided and constrained by an array of domestic expectations which are considered legitimate, and by social conventions which both define and delimit those broader social purposes. If "meaning is use," then these social rules are rules of usage — for domestic society. They are both defining and constitutive (in that they suggest which ends the government must aim at if a particular domestic "act" or purpose is to be effected) as well as constraining (in that they regulate conduct by ruling out certain international ends which would jeopardize those social purposes).

We can identify Andrew's "array of legitimate domestic expectations" with the material *and* ideal components of a society's ideology. His "rules of usage" that are both "defining and constitutive" are not too dissimilar in this sense from "organizing principles," as developed in this study. According to Andrews (1975:525, emphasis in original),

> Domestic norms make up one of the *referential dimensions* of a state policy. They are patterns (outside the regularities provided by the actions themselves) which those actions both point to and implicate — in a symbolic or representative guise, for example. They take on their importance not as causal antecedents or background conditions in a deductive generalization, but as a setting of constraint and guidance for both the aims and the reasons of the actors.

Furthermore, Andrews (1975:525) writes that

> If a domestic rule "stands there like a signpost," then a rule-guided action will stand there like a signpost as well. It refers back not only to the rules but to the domestic social purposes which underlie them. In this respect, state actions resemble language. The significance (or "motivation") of words, for example, is not intrinsic. It derives from their place within a framework of governing rules and expectations.

In other words, the system of rules that directs and constrains state behavior — that is, the behavior of central decisionmakers — obtains its meaning from the purposes and expectations of a society. Those purposes and expectations are reflected, I would assert, in what we ordinarily call "ideology."

Property rights are Bruce Andrew's "domestic rules" projected into the international arena. Their successful propogation is, of course, a function of state power, among other things, but their application often comes about only as the result of a process of negotiation among and incremental "muddling through" by states and policymakers. This leads to the establishment of regimes. When an internationally accepted regime exists in an issue area (and, as noted earlier, regimes may be implicit, as well as explicit), conflict is muted, and war does not occur. When a state tries to impose its own idiosyncratic set of property rights in an international arena, in the face of opposition from other states, conflict is likely to occur, and war is possible.

None of this, however, explains the sources of ideological behavior. From whence come the beliefs and organizing principles that are so prominent in the behavior of decisionmakers? To look for the roots of ideological behavior, we must look to the historical evolution of states, both internally and with respect to their external environment. As was suggested in Chapter 1, history plays an important role in the formation of these beliefs and principles.[1] They evolve over extended periods of time, and reflect the "rationalized national myths" of nations-states that provide the "framework for social action" (Haas 1986:709) in the domestic as well as the international sphere. Moreover, ideology, and the accompanying principles of action, establish constraints on the freedom of actors. Not all choices are possible; only those consonant with the national myth may be pursued. Leaders who violate this rule do so at their own physical or electoral risk.[2] Property rights and organizing principles can therefore be seen as part of process or part of structure. They change only very slowly, albeit not as slowly as geography or, for that matter, natural endowments of resources.

For states in the international system, ideologies — or nationalisms — continue even today to play a central role in the formulation of policies.

---

[1]In *Ideology and U.S. Foreign Policy* (1987), Michael Hunt suggests, moreover, that an understanding of "real" history requires going back centuries, and not mere decades.

[2]To paraphrase Franz Schurmann (1974:35), a leader who loses vision may also lose his or her constituency.

Ideologies both differentiate between states and provide cohesion to societies that may otherwise be economically, ethnically, and politically fragmented (Haas 1986). An ideology, however odious it might be, helps to integrate society and to sustain its cohesiveness. Ideology is therefore not the "vector sum" of individual or group interests. But, it may be similar to a "force field" in that it pushes or pulls states, and central decisionmakers, as Weber might have it, in a given direction. In this sense, therefore, ideals and ideology become crucial to the formulation of foreign policy.

Sometimes, one state comes to dominate an international political system. The ideology developed by that state rationalizes its position relative to others. The organizing principles followed by that state's decisionmakers, formulated in such a way as to legitimate the explanatory ideology, become the rules of the system. A system of rules imposed unilaterally or maintained as a result of the power of a single state cannot, it seems, be maintained indefinitely. As long as the constraints imposed by ideology are not so far out of synch with the constraints imposed by material facts of international life, the decline or downfall of the state may be postponed. But as demonstrated by the cases of Japan and Germany in the 1930s and 1940s and Great Britain in the 1940s and 1950s, when faced with choices that may lead to decline or defeat, ideal interests may prove more compelling than material realities in determining foreign policies and actions.

IDEAL INTERESTS, MATERIAL INTERESTS, AND THE FOREIGN POLICIES OF STATES

Let us turn now to the second question developed in this book: What is the relationship of ideal and material interests to the foreign policies of states? It has been suggested throughout this study that raw materials policies, which may be construed as one of the material interests of a state, cannot be considered in isolation from either ideal interests or foreign policies. Chapters 5, 6, and 7 presented three case studies of the relationship between the raw materials policy and the foreign policy of a state. Although each of the three states could be considered as a Great Power in its own right, the material constraints on each and the opportunities afforded to each were quite different. But the constraints and opportunities did not lead to quite the behavior one might expect from a simple power or material-interest analysis.

A power analysis would have predicted the decline of British influence in the Middle East after World War II, but it could not have predicted British behavior there in the face of such decline. A material-interest analysis would have suggested the U.S. stake in Iran in 1951 to be minor; it could not have foreseen the extent to which Iran would become a national obsession with the United States. Something would be missing from both types of analysis: an understanding of the ideal interests involved. Here I will address the missing element and consider the relationship of organizing principles, or "rules," to material interests, on the one hand, and systemic structure and state capabilities, on the other.

Raw materials are, of course, basic inputs into the capabilities of states. Conversely, denial of raw materials can threaten the security of states. It is from these two facts that assumptions are derived about the likelihood of conflict over strategic materials. But as suggested above, behavior in the international system is tempered by a variety of factors and rules, both structural and instrumental. Although systemic structure as a function of capabilities can tell us about the relative material interests of states — such as security, wealth, and power — it tells us nothing about the values held by states and decisionmakers that also constitute interests that may be deemed worth fighting for.

In his book *Theory of International Politics*, Kenneth Waltz (1979) uses the image of the competitive market as an analogue to the anarchic realm of international politics. According to this image, firms in the marketplace seek to maximize profit, as states in the international system seek to maximize security. Firms are constrained in their freedom by laws inherent in the structure of markets. Similarly, states are constrained by structural features of the international system. The structure of markets is a function of the number and size of firms. The structure of the international system is a function of the number of and the distribution of capabilities among states. Hence, in a somewhat tautological fashion, the relationship between the units making up a system determines the structure of the system. In both cases, the system is anarchic — that is, there is no superior authority to impose rules of behavior on the units making up the system.

Waltz fails, however, to carry the metaphor to its logical conclusion. Markets are not static; they are prone to oligopoly. Firms merge and grow and drive other firms out of business. In this fashion, they engage in a form of warfare — in a *process* — in order to establish a secure business environment. But warfare is not the only means to achieve security. Other processes are available. Competitive markets are often not completely anarchic—in Barry Buzan's (1983:96) terms, they can be immature or mature anarchies (on this point, see also Ruggie 1983). Rules evolve, understandings are reached, practices are standardized, territories are delineated, all without written agreements or the presence of a superior authority.[3] This is part of "process." Although it is true that unwritten rules do not have the force of law or the punitive content of unfriendly takeovers, they establish a degree of security in the market environment and do so at a cost lower than that of unrestrained warfare.

States do not have quite so free a hand in the international system but if we accept the image as a useful heuristic model, their behavior can be characterized in terms similar to that of firms in a competitive market. Waltz's focus on the structure of the market—and his general contempt for process—allows no space for the pursuit of goals other than those related to security and survival. Consequently, the kinds of behavior described in the earlier chapters of this book are largely irrelevant to his model of international politics.

The introduction of rules (and regimes) into that system, however they are established, shifts the center of gravity of a system from structure to a mixed one of structure and process. Rules and regimes alter the *perception* of systemic structure, even if the structure itself is left unaffected. Rules and regimes introduce expectations and regulate the behavior of states (Krasner 1983a). Furthermore, the actions of states do not take place in a vacuum. Relative capabilities are not assessed on an instantaneous basis. Past behavior affects future behavior. In other words, the behavior of states, and the actions of decisionmakers, are determined not by actual material capabilities of other states but, rather, by perceptions of those capabilities at present and in the future and anticipation of other states' acceptance of rules

---

[3]The microeconomist would ascribe this process to the natural operations of a "free market," citing such factors as "efficiency," "economies of scale,", and so forth. (Or, he might invoke the notion of "iterated cooperation" which has become so popular in game theory.) In fact, unwritten collusion between firms is often important in determining the ground rules of competition in a market. A good historical example of this is the old petroleum cartel of the "Seven Sisters," in which agreements were generally oral so as not to run afoul of U.S. antitrust laws (see, e.g., Sampson 1976).

and regimes. Neither of these latter factors, however, can be assessed in any "objective" sense.

Raw materials are, as noted earlier, basic inputs into the capabilities of states. Furthermore, raw materials do have a certain degree of salience for the pursuit of foreign policy goals, both material and ideal. How, then, can the two goals be connected? The study of process and its rules provides the means. The way in which states use capabilities — as tools — to influence process can tell us what they value most in addition to security. Thus, we should look at raw materials as direct inputs into capabilities, and as indirect inputs into process, in order to understand the pursuit of ideal interests.

Foreign policy goals themselves are not purely ideal or material; rather, they can be seen as the external manifestation of societal fears and desires (Andrews 1984). Nor do these goals comprise a world view or ideology; if anything, they are the shadows cast by those world views. Therefore, if the world view is the independent variable in the equation, and the interests or goals the dependent variables, the organizing principles operate as the intervening variables, providing a means to an end (Lipschutz 1987:313). The manipulation of material factors provides a way to operationalize the organizing principles. In other words, material factors, such as raw materials flows, provide the tools that central decisionmakers have to work with in pursuit of broader foreign policy objectives. This can be seen clearly in the case studies of U.S., British, and Soviet raw materials policies.

What the case studies of the United States, Great Britain, and the Soviet Union suggest, therefore, is that raw material flows can be seen as inputs to general capabilities in three senses. They are directly relevant to military power and the use of force, both of which are material interests. They provide a direct economic connection between the material world and ideal interests through influence over markets, and they can be used indirectly for political purposes to support or undermine governments and states. But for each of the three states, the salience of raw materials flows to each of these three levels was historically different (Table 8–1.) The differences were partly a consequence of environmental factors and partly the result of a differing hierarchy of material and ideal interests (Table 8–2). The ability of each state to act on these interests was, in turn, partly a function of each one's market position in raw materials (Table 8–3). Here we have the means to explore the interaction between material and ideal interests.

Table 8-1. Salience of International Raw Material Flows to State Capabilities.

State	Military	Economic	Political
United States	Low	Medium-high	High
Great Britain	High	High	Medium
Soviet Union	Low	Low	Low

Table 8-2. Relationship of International Raw Material Flows to State Interests.

State	Direct Material Interests	Indirect Material Interest	Ideal Interests
United States	Security of supply	National security	Containment of radicalism
	Price	Security of investments	Promotion of stability
		Economic prosperity	Promotion of liberalism
Great Britain	Balance of payments	Protection of territory	Maintenance of Empire
	Security of supply	Economic prosperity	British prestige
	Price and adequacy	Security of investment	
Soviet Union	Hard currency	Security of borders	Ideological fidelity
		Internal stability	Promotion of communist doctrine

Let us begin with the Soviet Union. Throughout the past forty years, with a few telling exceptions, the Soviet Union has been almost wholly independent of international commodity markets. It also has been an exceptionally powerful state possessing a considerable

Table 8–3.   Position of Three States in International Commodity Markets.

State	As Purchaser	As Seller/Supplier
United States	Monopsonist for most materials	Oligopolist for some materials; monopolist for dollars
United Kingdom	Mostly small or marginal for all materials	Marginal, except in oil, tin, rubber
Soviet Union	Marginal, except for tin, rubber	Marginal, except for Socialist Bloc

domestic resource base. These factors would seem to imply a significant degree of influence through the use of "resource diplomacy." Yet the case studies presented in Chapter 7 suggest quite the opposite conclusion. Why?

In a wartime environment, with uncertain territorial control, autarchic policies are desirable. In a peacetime situation — even during a Cold War — in which rules of process are important, autarky not only reduces the influence of external forces on the domestic realm, it also minimizes external influence. To be sure, the Soviets have used their considerable military capabilities to good effect in many parts of the world but, with the exception of Eastern Europe and Afghanistan, which are in some sense special cases, only as a tool of influence and not of direct conquest. With respect to raw material flows, the Soviets have lacked historically a sufficient degree of involvement in the international political economy to be able to wield resource diplomacy as a meaningful tool. Even in military terms there are no resources of sufficient importance in allied countries to warrant direct military involvement if denial is threatened.

The Soviets *have* wielded the resource weapon, usually in conjunction with other tools, in the pursuit of ideological goals. But in virtually no case, except perhaps Cuba in 1967, can resource diplomacy be judged to have been of significant effect. The same conditions continue to hold true today. The Soviet Union remains largely autarchic in terms of resource consumption, and there are enough alternative suppliers of critical resources so that Soviet allies, deprived of resource flows by their patron, can find replacements. Only if the Soviet Union were to become a significant consumer or seller in world commodity markets (as it has, for example, in wheat), might it be able to use resource diplomacy to some advantage in the pursuit of ideal interests. This does not imply that the Soviet Union has not engaged in ideological behavior — only that it has not been very successful in using resource diplomacy to pursue ideal ends.

The case of Great Britain is somewhat different. Except for a very few commodities, Britain was a marginal supplier and consumer of raw materials in the Western world, and so it remains today. Following the end of World War II, it found itself in a position of military debilitation with little structural power in markets. It also was challenged in these markets by the economic power of the United States, which not only occupied a monopsonist/oligopolist position with respect to many commodities, but also exercised monopoly over the supply of dollars. Holding on to Empire, it was thought by some, would enable Britain to regain the position in markets that it had occupied prior to 1939. At least, as Ernest Bevin suggested to Hugh Dalton, it would provide Britain with some leverage over the United States (Gallagher 1982:146; see also p. 159, above).

The British position was undermined, however, by some of the same factors that affected the Soviet Union. First, the decreasing utility of military force meant that other means had to be found to maintain influence. Second, its marginal position in most markets meant that it had few material tools with which to pursue ideal ends. Finally, even in those markets where it did occupy a relatively strong position — oil, rubber, tin — only the latter two proved sufficiently critical or scarce to impel it to apply military force in order to hold on to territory. But this was not an example of using material resources to pursue ideal interests; it was pure economic interest that kept Britain in Malaya.

The futile attempt to hold on to the Middle East was, in the final analysis, not connected integrally to the oil resource. Although it was recognized that the prosecution of a war would be difficult without oil from the Persian Gulf, well-developed plans existed to destroy those resources in the event of general war. And even though the economic importance of Middle Eastern oil to Britain cannot be gainsaid, in the final analysis this did not provide a sufficient rationale to justify military intervention in Iran in 1951. Only the imagined geopolitical threat of a Soviet sweep across the land bridge into Africa remained to explain the British obsession with the Suez Canal, and this idealized fear could not be maintained under the threat of either U.S. market power or economic disaster. Again, the lack of structural power explains failure; not the reasons for ideological behavior.

Finally, there is the United States. Ironically, for all the talk of resource insecurity, throughout the period in question the United States found itself in a reasonably secure position with respect to raw material supplies. Although there existed some uncertainty about the reliability of sources of supply in time of war, there were few, if any, raw materials essential to national defense that could not be easily obtained in a time of peace. Furthermore, the United States occupied a dominant position in most commodity markets as both buyer and/or seller. As a result, it was able exercise significant influence over the behavior of a number of mineral markets and to use this influence in the pursuit of ideal objectives. As a supplier of certain minerals, it was also influential, although this, by itself, would not have been sufficient to pursue economic and political goals.

It was as the balance wheel of the world economy that the United States was most important (and remains, to a lesser extent, today, as events in 1987 and 1988 in the stock and currency markets remind us). As the major manufacturer of finished goods, it was indispensible to the reconstruction of Europe and to the economic development of newly independent colonial territories. As the only global source of hard currency — other than gold — it was essential to oiling the wheels of international commerce. Finally, because raw material flows were of low salience to the military security of the United States — which was to a large degree, dependent on the threat of nuclear weapons — it was able to use its economic and political influence to engage in ideological behavior.

All of this more or less follows on Stephen Krasner's (1978:340) observation that only the very strong and very weak are ideological. But it does go further: only the very strong can pursue ideal interests without suffering significant costs. Those that are not so strong — such as Great Britain between 1945 and 1956 — chase ideal interests at their own risk. And even those that are quite powerful — such as the Soviet Union — may find it difficult to pursue ideological goals if they do not possess the appropriate tools to do so.

This conclusion leads to one further point: Even for a state possessing the power to behave in an ideological fashion, the costs of pursuing ideal interests may, over the long run, prove too great to sustain. There is a danger implicit in the successful pursuit of ideals: too much success may breed complacency and conviction that one's path is the "true one." The "habit-driven actor," in James Rosenau's (1986) words, may find it difficult to change his or her behavior until it is too late to do so without great material costs. Then one is forced to pay the piper.

The irony of this conclusion should not be lost on U.S. policymakers. All three victors in World War II — the United States, the United Kingdom, and the Soviet Union — found themselves in a position to pursue ideal interests following the end of the war and did so at considerable long-term cost to themselves. The losers — Japan and West Germany — have had less freedom to pursue ideal interests, and today they may be the better off for it.

SOME IMPLICATIONS FOR U.S. FOREIGN POLICY

This study has focused on a period that is now twenty-five years or more in the past. What relevance do its findings have for the formulation of foreign policy in the coming decades? Does ideology remain an important force in international politics or is it, as Schumpeter (1919/1951, quoted in Wright 1976:77–78) would have put it, simply an atavism? Is conflict over raw materials — whether real or imagined — a thing of the past, or will it return in the future to haunt us? Fortunately, we do not have to look very far to find a recent example of such ideological behavior: the Persian Gulf.

The direct U.S. involvement in the affairs of the Persian Gulf in 1987 came about as the consequence of a conjunction of several factors. Ostensibly, the initial mission of U.S. naval forces posted to the region was to remain neutral in the conflict between Iran and Iraq and to guard reflagged Kuwaiti oil tankers (and, subsequently, other vessels) in transit through the Gulf and the Straits of Hormuz against Iranian attacks — in the naval vernacular the "protection of SLOCs", or sea lines of communication. The contradictions inherent in this policy were many — the generally low level of U.S. dependence on Persian Gulf oil, the Kuwaiti alliance with Iraq against Iran, the significant Iraqi role in the "tanker war," and so on (these manifest and multiple oddities were cogently addressed in an article by Theodore Draper 1987; for a more recent, albeit briefer, pre-cease fire assessment, see Powell 1988), but the fundamental problems were obvious.

U.S. policymakers chose to emphasize two objectives in the Persian Gulf: maintaining the oil "lifeline" in the face of local threats, and preventing the Soviet Union from "gaining a foothold" in the Gulf. That the first did not require the sort of high-visibility operation staged by the United States was demonstrated by the discomfiture of its European allies, who generally preferred to conduct a low-profile operation (although they eventually went along with the United States; see Markham 1987).

That the second objective became important enough to provoke action only *after* seven years of the Iran-Iraq war, during which the Soviets had many opportunities to gain influence in the Persian Gulf, only serves to indicate that U.S. policymakers were falling back on traditional geopolitical organizing principles to validate their actions. It may be simple luck that there were no "liberal" or "democratic" regimes in the area to further obfuscate the issues (although the Iran-Contra connection might have provided this necessary element).

Even until the cease fire of August 1988, after a year of a reasonably quiescent situation, there remained the possibility that U.S. involvement in the Persian Gulf might "blow up," so to speak, as did the U.S. Marines' mission in Lebanon (and as it might have over the shooting down of the Iranian airbus). In a sense, the United States established such high standards for this operation, that even so small an event as a tanker hitting a mine came to be seen as a "blow" to U.S. credibility (Cowell 1987; Powell 1988). In the event that a Persian Gulf state — let us say, just as an example, Iran — had launched some type of action against U.S. vessels, leading to loss of life, a proportionate U.S. response — such as an attack on an oil platform — would, by itself, have been unlikely to have much deterrent effect. A disproportionate response might well have evoked a stronger counterreaction by Iran. In all of this, there was little or nothing that the United State could have done to protect the integrity of the Persian Gulf oil fields, should someone have decided to start attacking them in earnest.[4]

---

[4]Claims by officials of the Reagan administration (including President Reagan himself) that the demonstration of U.S. power in the Gulf represented a triumph of policy because it finally brought home to the Iranian government the futility of continuing the war with Iraq *and* remaining an antagonist of the United States are generally nonsensical. The shooting down of a civilian airliner may have convinced the Iranians of the risks of not dealing with the United States but, whatever its effect, it can hardly be called a triumph of policy planning. To describe it as such is an insult to policy planners and strategists in Washington.

Left unprovoked, it is unlikely that the Iranians would have engaged in unlimited warfare against the petroleum infrastructure in the Persian Gulf. Iran, after all, is much more dependent on the sea lanes for the transport of oil than is Iraq. Why should the United States have gotten involved in the Gulf at so late a date? In this instance, the old fear of Soviet intentions in the region came, once again, to the fore.[5] Did the Soviets see an agreement to lease tankers to Kuwait as a way to get their warships into the Gulf, or as a means of gaining influence with the Kuwaitis and, ultimately, the Saudis? The Soviet deal with Kuwait was, after all, a commercial one, and the Soviets were doing no more than the British or French in a similar situation. The entire episode is characterized by a sort of cloudy clarity, in which the logic appears clear for a moment, only to become lost as another inconsistency appears. The contradictions between the protection of a material interest and the pursuit of an ideal one are apparent, even if the outcome of the policy is not.

Is it too much to hope for a match between ideal desires and material constraints? Perhaps. Ideal interests are not irrelevant; they constitute an important facet of individual and national life. The problem is how to recognize when the pursuit of such interests can become crippling. Unfortunately, the United States remains much too big and powerful to recognize *these* limits to power. As long as U.S. policymakers feel the pressures of history and the electorate, they will probably continue to ignore material realities whenever possible.

The conundrum is not, of course, a new one. Many years ago, in a moment of apparent frustration, Gordon Merriam, the director of the Division of Near Eastern Affairs in the Office of Near Eastern and African Affairs of the U.S. State Department, complained to his superior, Loy Henderson (NARS 1946a) that

> One could write a book on these JCS comments. It is evident that they don't understand our work.
>
> We have to meet situations as they arise, and we should be prepared to meet contingencies. They would have it that our foreign policy should be geared completely with our state of military preparedness at any given time, which is ridiculous.

[5]Warnings from various quarters that we must initiate a "dialogue" with Iran because of its geopolitical importance and proximity to the Soviet Union simply demonstrate the continuing allure of the old myths and doctrines.

We write foreign policy only in the most superficial sense. In the real sense, our foreign policy is written for us by the aggressive plans, or other designs, of foreign countries in the international field touching our overall as well as immediate interests.

It is, therefore, events which count, not what the State Department puts down on paper. We can have control over events only if we have the means to control them. In the lack of such means, events will control us, as they have in the past, with disastrous and expensive results.

BIBLIOGRAPHY

Abadi, J. 1982. *Britain's Withdrawal from the Middle East, 1947–1971: The Economic and Strategic Imperatives.* Princeton: The Kingston Press.

Adler-Karlsson, G. 1968. *Western Economic Warfare, 1947–1967 — A Case Study in Foreign Economic Policy.* Stockholm: Almqvist & Wiksell.

Alexander, R.J. 1958. *The Bolivian National Revolution.* New Brunswick, N.J.: Rutgers University Press.

Allison, R. 1985. *Finland's Relations with the Soviet Union, 1944–84.* London: Macmillan.

Anderson, I.H., Jr. 1981. *Aramco, the United States and Saudi Arabia: A Study of the Dynamics of Foreign Oil Policy, 1933–1950.* Princeton: Princeton University Press.

———. 1975. *The Standard-Vacuum Oil Company and United States East Asian Policy, 1933–1941.* Princeton: Princeton University Press.

Andor, L.E. 1985. *South Africa's Chrome, Manganese, Platinum and Vanadium — Foreign Views on the Mineral Dependency Issue, 1970–1984.* Braamfontein: South African Institute of International Affairs, Bib. Series No. 13.

Andrews, B. 1984. "The Domestic Content of International Desire." *International Organization* 38, #2 (Spring):321–27.

———. 1975. "Social Rules and the State as a Social Actor." *World Politics* 27, #4 (July):521–40.

Angell, J.W. 1933. *Financial Foreign Policy of the United States.* Report to the Second International Studies Conference on "The State and Economic Life," London, May 29–June 2, 1933. New York: Council on Foreign Relations.

Aron, R. 1966. *Peace and War — A Theory of International Relations.* Garden City, N.Y.: Doubleday.

Ascher, W. 1978. *Forecasting — An Appraisal for Policy-Makers and Planners.* Baltimore: Johns Hopkins University Press.

Ashley, R.K. 1980. *The Political Economy of War and Peace.* London: Frances Pinter.

Avery W., and D. Rapkin, eds. 1982. *America in a Changing World Political Economy.* New York: Longman.

Baldwin, D.A. 1985. *Economic Statecraft.* Princeton: Princeton University Press.

———. 1966. *Economic Development and American Foreign Policy, 1943–62.* Chicago: University of Chicago Press.

255

Balsier, C. 1985. *The Hovering Giant — U.S. Responses to Revolutionary Change in Latin America 1910–1985*. Pittsburgh: University of Pittsburgh Press.

Barnet, R. 1980. *The Lean Years — Politics in the Age of Scarcity*. New York: Simon & Schuster.

———. 1972. *Roots of War*. Baltimore: Penguin Books.

Bendix, R. 1984. *Force, Fate, and Freedom — On Historical Sociology*. Berkeley: University of California Press.

———. 1962. *Max Weber — An Intellectual Portrait*. Berkeley: University of California Press.

Bernstein, B.J. 1970. "American Foreign Policy and the Origins of the Cold War." In B.J. Bernstein, ed., *Politics and Policies of the Truman Administration*, pp. 15–77. Chicago: Quadrangle Books.

Bidwell, P.W. 1958. *Raw Materials — A Study of American Policy*. New York: Council on Foreign Relations/Harper & Brothers.

Bilder, R.B. 1977. "International Law and Natural Resource Policies." In P. Dorner and M.A. El-Shafie, eds., *Resources and Development — Natural Resource Policies and Economic Development in an Interdependent World*, pp. 385–421. Madison and London: University of Wisconsin Press and Croom Helm.

Block, F.L. 1977. *The Origins of International Economic Disorder — A Study of United States International Monetary Policy from World War II to the Present*. Berkeley: University of California Press.

Boardman, R. 1976. *Britain and the People's Republic of China*. London: Macmillan.

Bobrow, D.B., and R.T. Kudrle. 1987. "How Middle Powers Can Manage Resource Weakness: Japan and Energy." *World Politics* 39, #4 (July):536–65.

Bogomolov, O. 1983a. "Interdependence, Structural Changes and Conflicts in the World Economy." *MEIMO* #10 (Oct.):11–22. Translated in JPRS-UWE-84–002, pp. 14–28.

———. 1983b. "CMEA and Global Problems." *International Affairs* (Moscow) #5 (May):21–31.

Bohi, D.R. and M. Russell. 1978. *Limiting Oil Imports: An Economic History and Analysis*. Baltimore: Johns Hopkins University Press for Resources for the Future.

Boulding, K.E., and T. Mukerjee, eds. 1972. *Economic Imperialism — A Book of Readings*. Ann Arbor: University of Michigan Press.

Boutin B. 1964. Oral History Interview of Bernard Boutin, Head of the General Services Administration, June 3. Washington, D.C. JFKL.

Braathu, J. 1982. "Unilateralism and Alliance Cohesion: The United States, Western Europe, and the Regulation of Energy-Related Trade with the Soviet Union." *Cooperation and Conflict* 18, #1:24–41.

Breslauer, G. 1983. "The Dynamics of Soviet Policy Toward the Arab-Israeli Conflict: Lessons of the Brezhnev Era." Berkeley: Department of Political Science, University of California. Working Paper #3.

Brooks, L.F. 1986. "Naval Power and National Security: The Case for a Maritime Strategy." *International Security* 11, #2 (Fall):58–88.

Browne, M. 1986. "Fearing Instability, West Seeks to Replace Minerals from Africa." *New York Times*, July 15, pp. 17, 20.

Bruce, J.W. 1986. *Land Tenure Issues in Project Design and Strategies for Agricultural Development in Sub-Saharan Africa*. Madison: Land Tenure Center, University of Wisconsin. March.

Bueno de Mesquita, Bruce. 1981. *The War Trap*. New Haven: Yale University Press.

Bullis, L.H., and J.E. Mielke. 1985. *Strategic and Critical Materials*. Boulder: Westview Press.

Bunce, V. 1985. "The Empire Strikes Back: The Evolution of the Eastern Bloc from a Soviet Asset to a Soviet Liability." *International Organization* 39, #1 (Winter):1–46.

Buzan, B. 1983. *People, States & Fear — The National Security Problem in International Relations*. Brighton, Sussex: Wheatsheaf Books.

Calleo, D.P., and B.M. Rowland. 1973. *America and the World Political Economy, Atlantic Dreams and National Realities*. Bloomington: Indiana University Press.

Campbell, J.C. 1967. *Tito's Separate Road — America and Yugoslavia in World Politics*. New York: Published for the Council on Foreign Relations by Harper & Row.

Campbell, K.M. 1986. "The Soviet-South African Connection." *Africa Report* 31, #2 (March-April):72–75.

Center for Economic and National Security. 1981. "Introduction: What is the Resource War?" In *Strategic Minerals: A Resource Crisis*. New York: National Strategy Information Center.

Chace, J. 1987. "The End of the Affair?" *New York Review of Books* 34, #15 (Oct. 8):24–30.

Choucri, N., and R. North. 1975. *Nations in Conflict*. San Francisco: W.H. Freeman.

Christensen, C. 1977. "Structural Power and National Security." In K. Knorr and F.N. Trager, eds., *Economic Issues and National Security*, pp.127–59. Lawrence, Kansas: Regents Press of Kansas.

Clayton, W. 1946. "The Importance of International Economic Relations to World Peace." Address to the Academy of Political Science, New York, April 11, 1946. *Department of State Bulletin* 14 (April 21):677–81.

Clemens, W.C., Jr. 1968. *The Arms Race and Sino-Soviet Relations*. Stanford: Hoover Institution Press.

Cleveland, H. 1963. "Immediate and Future Problems in the Congo." Testimony before the Subcommittee on Africa of the House Committee on Foreign Affairs, 88th Cong., 1st Sess., March 14.

Clissold, S., ed. 1975. *Yugoslavia and the Soviet Union 1939–1973 — A Documentary Survey*. London: Published for the Royal Institute of International Affairs by the Oxford University Press.

Clough, M. 1983. *The United States and Revolutionary Conflict in Southern Africa*. Ph.D. dissertation. Berkeley: Department of Political Science, University of California-Berkeley.

Coase, R. 1960. "The Problem of Social Cost." *Journal of Law and Economics* 3:1–44.

Coker, C. 1984a "The Soviet Union and Eastern Europe: Patterns of Competition and Collaboration in Southern Africa." In R.C. Nation and M.V. Kauppi, eds., *The Soviet Impact in Africa*, pp. 59–85. Lexington, Mass.: Lexington Books.

———. 1984b. *The Soviet Union, Eastern Europe, and the New International Economic Order*. New York: Praeger. The Washington Papers #111.

Commissariat on Foreign Trade, USSR. 1935. "Foreign Trade up to the 7th Congress of the Soviet of the USSR." Moscow: Vneshtorgizdat.

Conybeare, J.A.C. 1980. "International Organization and the Theory of Property Rights." *International Organization* 34, #3 (Summer):307–34.

Cook, B.W. 1981. *The Declassified Eisenhower — A Divided Legacy*. Garden City, N.Y.: Doubleday.

Cooper, C.L. 1978. *The Lion's Last Roar — Suez, 1956*. New York: Harper & Row.

Cotman, J.W. 1978. "South African Strategic Minerals and U.S. Foreign Policy, 1961–1968." *Review of Black Political Economy* 8, #3 (Spring):277–301.

Cowell, A. 1987. "A Mine Sends Shock Waves through U.S. Policy in Gulf." *New York Times*, July 26, section 4, p.1.

Cox, R.W. 1983. "Gramsci, Hegemony and International Relations: An Essay in Method." *Millenium: Journal of International Studies* 12, #2 (Summer):162–75.

Craib, I. 1984. *Modern Social Theory from Parsons to Habermas*. Brighton, Sussex: Wheatsheaf Books.

Csaba, L. 1985. "Joint Investments and Mutual Advantages in the CMEA — Retrospection and Prognosis." *Soviet Studies* 37, #2 (April):227–47.

Cumings, B. 1987–88. "Power and Plenty in Northeast Asia: The Evolution of U.S. Policy." *World Policy Journal* 5, #1 (Winter):79–106.

———. 1984. "The Origins and Development of the Northeast Asian Political Economy: Industrial Sectors, Product Cycles, and Political Consequences." *International Organization* 38, #1 (Winter):1–40.

d'Arge, R.C. 1981. "On Managing the Global Commons." Chapel Hill, N.C.: The Institute for Environmental Studies, University of North Carolina.

DD. 1960a. "U.S. Policy toward the Congo." Briefing Note for the NSC Meeting, 8/1/60 (NSC 6001). Attached study by the Joint Chiefs of Staff. In DD 1960(81)484A.

———. 1960b. "Meeting of Patrice Lumumba with Members of the Communist Party of Belgium." CIA Report, no date (circa Feb. 1960). In DD 1960(76):8C.

———. 1960c. Report in *CIA Current Intelligence Weekly Summary*. June 30. In DD 1960(76):8D.

———. 1960d. Satterthwaite, J. to the Secretary of State. "Briefing for the NSC on the Situation in the Congo." July 14, 1960. DDEL. In DD 1960(81)526A.

———. 1961a. U.S. State Department Deptel 1160 to Leopoldville, 12/28/61. In DD 1961(R):401E.

———. 1961b. U.S. State Department Deptel 3505 to London, 12/29/61. In DD 1961(R)402E.

———. 1962a. Telegram, Brussels A-254, MacArthur to Secretary of State Rusk, 1/4/62. In DD (62):405B.

———. 1962b. U.S. Embassy Brussels 1378 to U.S. State Department, 1/30/62. In DD1962(R)412G.

DDEL. ND. Memoranda in Records of the Council on Foreign Economic Policy. Policy Paper Series, Box 12. Folder: CFEP 566, US Economic Defense Policy (2), (9).

———. 1960a. Briefing Note for NSC Meeting, July 7, 1960 (revised). Initialed: PJH/llw, July 6, 1960. "U.S. Policy toward the Near East (NSC 5820/1)." National Security Assistant Records, Special Assistant Series, Presidential Subseries. Box 5. Folder: 1960-Meetings with the President-Vol. 2 (10).

———. 1960b. Memorandum for General Persons from A.J. Goodpaster, Staff Secretary, White House. March 7, 1960. White House Central Files, Confidential Files, Subject Series. Box 47. Folder: Office of Civil and Defense Mobilization.

———. 1960c. Letter to Gordon Gray, Special Assistant to the President for National Security Affairs, from Admiral Arleigh Burke, Chief of Naval Operations. 19 November 1960. National Security Council Series, Briefing Notes. Box 14: Petroleum (1960).

———. 1959a. Minutes of the Eisenhower Cabinet. Meeting on April 24, 1959. "Copper Stockpile." Whitman Files, Cabinet Series. Box 13.

———. 1959b. Minutes of the Eisenhower Cabinet. Meeting on April 24, 1959. Whitman Files, Cabinet Series. Box 13.

———. 1959c. Memorandum for Mr. Randall from J. Rand. Nov. 22, 1959. Files of the Council on Foreign Economic Policy, Chairman, Staff Series. Box 5. Folder: E-W Trade (1).

———. 1958a. NSC-5818: "US Policy toward Africa South of the Sahara

Prior to Calendar Year 1960." Records of the White House Office of the Special Assistant for National Security Affairs, NSC Series, Policy Paper Subseries. Box 25.

———. 1958b. Twining, N.F., Chairman, Joint Chiefs of Staff. Memorandum for the Secretary of Defense. Subject: "Briefing Paper for Presidential Use in Discussions with the Shah of Iran (U)." June 9, 1958. "Top Secret." Whitman Files, International Series. Box 29: Iran, 1953–1959 (5).

———. 1958c. Gray, G. Letter to C.B. Randall, Special Assistant to the President from Director of Office of Defense Mobilization. March 6, 1958. Council on Foreign Economic Policy Chairman, CFEP Papers Series. Box 4: CFEP 567 (2).

———. 1958d. Memorandum for Mr. Randall from J. Rand. Subject: "The Effect of Nationalism on Foreign Economic Policy." Jan. 8, 1958. Files of the Council on Foreign Economic Policy, Rand Series.

———. 1958e. Memorandum on Soviet Economic Penetration. April 21, 1958. No author. White House Office, Cabinet Secretariat Records. Box 7. Folder: Soviet Economic Penetration (2).

———. 1958f. Minutes of the Eisenhower Cabinet. Meeting on Jan. 10, 1958. Whitman Files, Cabinet Series. Box 10.

———. 1958g. Minutes of the Eisenhower Cabinet. Meeting on July 25, 1958. Whitman Files, Cabinet Series. Box 11.

———. 1958h. Draft letter from J. Randall, CFEP, to M.G. Peter, Chairman, International Tin Council. No date (circa July 1958). Files of the Council on Foreign Economic Policy, Chairman, Randall Series, Subject Subseries. Box 7: International Tin Agreement.

———. 1958i. U.S. Office of Defense Mobilization. *Stockpiling for Defense in the Nuclear Age.* A Report to the Honorable Gordon Gray, Director of ODM, by the Special Stockpile Advisory Committee, Jan. 28, 1958. Council on Foreign Economic Policy, Chairman, Randall Series, Agency Subseries. Box 3: OCDM (1).

———. 1958j. Memorandum from Joseph Randall, Council on Foreign Economic Policy, to Governor Adams, Jan. 31, 1958. CFEP Records, Policy Paper Series. Box 12. Folder: CFEP 566, U.S. Economic Defense Policy (9).

———. 1958k. Memorandum from Paul H. Cullen to CFEP, Feb. 13, 1958. Subject: "CFEP 566 – U.S. Economic Defense Policy." CFEP Records, Policy Paper Series. Box 12. Folder: CFEP 566 – U.S. Economic Defense Policy (2).

———. 1958l. Memorandum of Conversation, U.S. Department of State, Feb. 18, 1958. "Strategic Controls." CFEP Records, Policy Paper Series. Box 12. Folder: CFEP 566, U.S. Economic Defense Policy (9).

———. 1958m. Memorandum of Meeting, Office of the Secretary of Defense, Jan. 16, 1958. "Criteria for Trade Control Based on Strategic Concepts."

CFEP Records, Policy Paper Series. Box 12. Folder: CFEP 566 – U.S. Economic Defense Policy (3).

————. 1957a. Minutes of the Eisenhower Cabinet. Meeting on Feb. 1, 1957. Whitman Files, Cabinet Series. Box 8.

————. 1956a. Memorandum: "Gains in Trade, Expressed in Dollars, Which Might Follow from the Virtual Elimination of all Controls on Trade with the Bloc." No date, circa 1956. Files of the Council on Foreign Economic Policy, Chairman. Dodge Series, Subject Series. Box 2. Folder: E-W Trade (5).

————. 1956b. Eisenhower Diary. Entry, Jan. 11, 1956. Whitman Files, Papers as President of the United States, 1953–61. Box 12: January 1956 Diary.

————. 1956c. Discussion at the 272nd meeting of the National Security Council, Jan. 12, 1956. Dated 1/13/56. Subject 1: "Defense Mobilization Planning Assumptions Applicable to Stockpiling," pp. 1–10. Whitman Files, National Security Council Series. Box 7.

————. 1956d. Paper: "Trends and Prospects in East-West Trade." April 13. Files of the Council on Foreign Economic Policy, Chairman. Dodge Series, Subject Series. Box 1. Folder: East-West Trade (3).

————. 1955a. Cabinet Committee Report. "Energy Supplies and Resources Policy." Jan. 19, 1955. Draft & Final. White House Office, National Security Assistant Series, Briefing Note Subseries. Box 14. Folder: Petroleum Policies and Issues (1) [1953–60].

————. 1955b. Office of Defense Mobilization. "The Exchange of Surplus Agricultural Commodities for Strategic Materials." CFEP-517/2, ODM 10879. Circa February, 1955. Records of the Council on Foreign Economic Policy, Policy Paper Series. Box 3: CFEP 517.

————. 1955c. Preliminary Summary of Paper to be Delivered by Mr. G. Nebolsine, 9/7/55. "East-West Trade: Threat or Promise?" Council on Foreign Economic Policy, Chairman, Dodge Series, Subject Series. Box 1: Bilderberg Conference (1).

————. 1954a. NSC 5414/1. Note by the Executive Secretary to the National Security Council. "Defense Mobilization Planning Assumptions." April 30, 1954. National Security Council Series, Policy Papers. Box 10: NSC 5414/1-Defense Mobilization.

————. 1954b. Notes of Meetings of Eisenhower Cabinet (Minnich notes). White House Office, Office of the Staff Secretary, Records. Cabinet Series. Box 2. Folder C-12(3). March 12, 1954.

————. 1954c. Minutes of the Eisenhower Cabinet. Meeting on March 12, 1954. Whitman Files, Cabinet Series. Box 3.

————. 1954d. Minutes of the Eisenhower Cabinet. Meeting on March 5, 1954. Whitman Files, Cabinet Series. Box 3.

————. 1954e. Minutes of the Eisenhower Cabinet. Meeting on Nov. 5, 1954. Whitman Files, Cabinet Series. Box 4.

————. 1953a. U.S. Commission on Foreign Economic Policy (Randall Commission). Papers of the Commission.

————. 1953b. Minutes of the National Security Council, Meeting 178, December 30, 1953. Discussion of NSC 176 (NSC 26 Series). White House Office, National Security Assistant, NSC Series, Administrative Subseries. Box 1: NSC Agenda and Minutes. Folder: 1953 (10).

————. 1953c. Eisenhower, D.D. Statement to Cabinet on FY 1954 Budget. Thursday prior to May 1, 1953. White House Central Files, Confidential File, Subject Series. Box 45. Folder: National Security (1).

————. 1953d. Vernon, R. "The Economic and Political Role of United States Trade Policy." Dec. 4, 1953. Records of the Commission on Foreign Economic Policy (Randall Commission). Box 44. Folder: Drafts of Report, Area 3, No. 7-Vernon.

————. 1953e. Sham, D., and H.O. Rogers. "Mineral Raw Materials in Defense and Foreign Trade Policies. Dec. 12, 1953. Staff Report: Area 8-No. 6. Papers of the Commission on Foreign Economic Policy (Randall Commission). Box 47: Drafts of Report, Area 8, No.6.

————. 1953f. U.S. Commission on Foreign Economic Policy. "The Implications of East-West Trade." Paper prepared by Raymond Vernon, Nov. 10, 1953. In Files of Joseph Randall, Commission on Foreign Economic Policy. Box 47. Folder: "Drafts-Area 8, No. 2."

————. 1953g. U.S. Commission on Foreign Economic Policy. "Trade Policy and Defense." Paper prepared by Raymond Vernon, Dec. 11, 1953. In Files of Joseph Randall, Commission on Foreign Economic Policy. Box 47. Folder: "Drafts-Area 8, No. 3."

————. 1951a. Eisenhower, D.D. Letter to E.J. Bermingham, Feb. 8, 1951. Bermingham Papers—Correspondence with D.D. Eisenhower, Oct. 1948–Feb. 1958.

————. 1951b. Eisenhower, D.D. Letter to E.J. Bermingham. "Personal and Confidential." February 28, 1951. Bermingham Papers—Correspondence with D.D. Eisenhower, Oct. 1948–Feb. 1958.

Deese, D. 1981. "Oil, War, and Grand Strategy." *Orbis* (Fall):525–55.

Demsetz, H. 1967. "Toward a Theory of Property Rights." *American Economic Review* 62, #2 (May):347–59.

DeNovo, J.A. 1963. *American Interests and Policies in the Middle East 1900–1939.* Minneapolis: University of Minnesota.

Domeratzky, L. 1928. *The International Cartel Movement.* Washington, D.C.: U.S. Department of Commerce, Bureau of Foreign and Domestic Commerce. Trade Information Bulletin No. 556.

Dowie, M. 1986. "Showdown at Site 300." *Image (Sunday San Francisco Examiner and Chronicle)* (June 15):20–24.

Dowty A., and R. Kochan. 1976. "The 'Stakes of Conflict': Examination of a Concept." *Jerusalem Journal of International Relations* 1, #4 (Summer):11–49.

Draper, T. 1987. "American Hubris: From Truman to the Persian Gulf." *New York Review of Books* (July 16):40–48.

Dulles, F.R. 1946/1967. *China and America — The Story of Their Relations since 1784*. Port Washington, N.Y.: Kennikat Press.

Eisenhower, D.D. 1948. *Crusade in Europe*. New York.

Eisenhower, M. 1953. "Report of M. Eisenhower on His Trip to Latin America, Nov. 18." *Department of State Bulletin* (Nov. 23).

Emeny, B. 1934. *The Strategy of Raw Materials*. New York: Macmillan.

Epstein, J.M. 1987. *Strategy and Force Planning — The Case of the Persian Gulf*. Washington, D.C.: Brookings Institution.

Etzold, T.H., and J.L. Gaddis, eds. 1978. *Containment: Documents on American Policy and Strategy, 1945–1950*. New York: Columbia University Press.

Falk, P. 1987. "Cuba in Africa." *Foreign Affairs* 65, #5 (Summer):1077–98.

Feis, H. 1950. *The Road to Pearl Harbor — The Coming of the War between the United States and Japan*. Princeton: Princeton University Press.

Fischer, L. 1927. *Oil Imperialism — The International Struggle for Petroleum*. London: George Allen & Unwin.

Fisher, A.C. 1981. *Resource and Environmental Economics*. Cambridge: Cambridge University Press.

Fleischmann. M. 1952. "An International Materials Policy for a Free World." *Department of State Bulletin* (Feb. 25):297–302.

Forster, K. 1960. "The Finnish-Soviet Crisis of 1958–1959." *International Journal* 15, #2 (Spring):147–50.

Fox, W. 1974. *Tin — The Working of a Commodity Agreement*. London: Mining Journal Books.

Frank, A.G. 1982. "Crisis of Ideology and Ideology of Crisis." In S. Amin, G. Arrighi, A.G. Frank, and I. Wallerstein, *Dynamics of Global Crisis*, pp. 109–66. New York and London: Monthly Review Press.

Frost, E.L., and A.E. Stent. 1983. "NATO and East-West Trade." *International Security* 8, #1 (Summer):179–200.

FRUS. 1952–54a. Memorandum by the Executive Secretary (Lay) to the National Security Council. Subject: "Source of U.S. Aluminum Supply in Time of War." Oct. 16, 1953. Enclosure A: NSC Staff Study, Prepared by the Office of Defense Mobilization. "Reliance to be Placed by the United States on Kitimat Facilities of ALCAN in Canada as Wartime Aluminum Supply Source." In I: 1020–26.

———. 1952–54b. Letter from the Secretary of State (Dulles) to the Secretary of the Treasury (Humphrey). Oct. 5, 1953. RG 59, Records of the U.S. State Department. Decimal file number 824.2544/9–2153. In I:1016–17.

———. 1952–54c. U.S. Economic Defense Advisory Committee. "Report on

Organized and Coordinated Program of Preclusive Buying." June 12, 1952. In I:854–57.

———. 1952–54d. Memorandum by the Secretary of State to the President, "Tariff Commission Recommendation on Lead and Zinc." June 7, 1954. In I:201–02.

———. 1952–54e. Memorandum by the President to the Director of Office of Defense Mobilization (Flemming). Subject: "Establishment of 'Long-Term' Mineral Stockpile Objectives." April 14, 1954. In I:1145–47.

———. 1952–54f. Memorandum of Conversation, by the Chief of the Economic Defense Staff (Goodkind), March 20, 1953. "Subject: Discussion of East-West Trade with Staff of Senate Permanent Subcommittee on Investigations." In I:943–45.

———. 1951a. NSC 100. Report to the National Security Council by the Chairman of the National Security Resources Board (Symington). "Recommended Policies and Actions in Light of the Grave World Situation." Jan. 11, 1951. In I:7–18.

———. 1951b. NSC 114/2. "U.S. Programs for National Security " Oct. 12, 1951. In I:208–23.

———. 1951c. Paper Drafted in the U.S. Department of State. No author, undated. "Reevaluation of US Plans for the Middle East." In V:6–11.

———. 1951d. Draft Study by the U.S. National Security Council. "The Position of the United States with Respect to the General Area of the Eastern Mediterranean and the Middle East." Dec. 27, 1951. PPS Files: Lot 64D 563: "Villard." In V:257–64.

———. 1950a. "Editorial Note." In V:1842.

———. 1950b. NSC 68. "United States Objectives and Programs for National Security." April 14, 1950. In I: 234–92.

———. 1950c. U.S. State Department. "Regional Policy Statement on Africa South of the Sahara." Bureau of Near Eastern, South Asian, and African Affairs. Dec. 29, 1950. In V:1587–99.

———. 1949a. Letter from the Assistant Secretary of State for Economic Affairs to the Director of the Staff of the Munitions Board, March 16. In I:268–69.

———. 1949b. SANACC 360/11. Subcommittee for Rearmament. "Military Aid Priorities." In I:259–67.

———. 1949c. Memorandum by G.P. Merrian of the Policy Planning Staff, U.S. Department of State, June 13, 1949. PPS Files, Lot 64D563, Record Copies. In VI:31.

———. 1948a. Memorandum by the Policy Planning Staff. "French North Africa." March 22, 1948. PPS-25. S/S-NSC Files, Lot 63 D351, NSC 12 Series, NARS. In III:684.

———. 1947a. Telegram from the Minister in Saudi Arabia (Childs) to the Secretary of State, Dec. 4, 1947. "Audience with His Majesty, King Azul Aziz." In V: 1335–38.

————. 1912. Memoranda by Secretary of State Philander Knox Regarding U.S. Investment and Involvement in Honduras in 1911, pp. 581–95.

Gaddis, J.L. 1982. *Strategies of Containment—A Critical Appraisal of Postwar American National Security Policy*. Oxford: Oxford University Press.

Gallagher, J. 1982. "The Decline, Revival and Fall of the British Empire." In J. Gallagher, *The Decline, Revival and Fall of the British Empire—The Ford Lectures and Other Essays*, pp. 73–153. Cambridge: Cambridge University Press.

Gallagher, J., and R. Robinson. 1953. "The Imperialism of Free Trade." *Economic History Review* 6, #1 (2nd Series):1–15.

Gardner, R.N. 1980. *Sterling-Dollar Diplomacy in Current Perspective—The Origins and the Prospects of Our International Economic Order*. New York: Columbia University Press.

Geertz, C. 1964. "Ideology as a Cultural System." In D.E. Apter, ed., *Ideology and Discontent*, pp. 46–76. New York: Free Press.

George, A.L. 1969. "The 'Operational Code': A Neglected Approach to the Study of Political Leaders and Decision-Making." *International Studies Quarterly* 13, #2 (June):190–222.

Gerth, H.H., and C.W. Mills, eds. 1946. *From Max Weber: Essays in Sociology*. New York: Oxford University Press.

Gillette, R. 1986. "Soviets Demand More of East Bloc." *Los Angeles Times*, Aug. 8, pp. 1, 14–16.

Gilpin, R. 1981. *War and Change in World Politics*. Cambridge: Cambridge University Press.

————. 1977. "Economic Interdependence and National Security in Historical Perspective." In K. Knorr and F.N. Trager, eds., *Economic Issues and National Security*, pp. 19–66. Lawrence, Kansas: Regents Press of Kansas.

————. 1975. *U.S. Power and the Multinational Corporation*. New York: Basic Books.

Glebov, S. 1980. "Problem of Providing Mankind with Raw Material and Energy." *MEIMO* #10 (Oct.):30–43. Translated as "Global Raw Materials, Energy Problems Viewed." JPRS 77475, pp. 8–21.

Gleick, P.H. In press. "Global Climatic Changes and Geopolitics: Pressures on Developed and Developing Countries." In *Climate and Geo-Sciences: A Challenge for Science and Society in the 21st Century*. Dordrecht: D. Reidel.

Goldman, M.I. 1983a. "Interaction of Politics and Trade: Soviet-Western Interaction." In selected papers submitted to the Joint Economic Committee, U.S. Congress, *Soviet Economy in the 1980s: Problems and Prospects*, Dec. 31, 1982, pp. 117–28. Washington, D.C.: U.S. Government Printing Office.

————. 1983b. "The Changing Role of Raw Material Exports in Soviet Foreign Trade." In R.G. Jensen, T. Shabad, and A.W. Wright, eds., *Soviet Natural Resources in the World Economy*, pp. 623–38. Chicago: University of Chicago Press.

————. 1980. *The Enigma of Soviet Petroleum — Half-full or Half-empty?* London: Allen & Unwin.

Goldstein, J. 1986. "Ideas, Institutions and American Trade Policy." Paper presented to the Conference on the Political Economy of Trade Policy, Endicott House, Dedham, Mass., Jan. 10–11. Cambridge, Mass.: National Bureau of Economic Research. Photocopy.

Golub, D. 1987. Report on cessation of Soviet oil supplies to Nicaragua, "Morning Edition," National Public Radio. July 20.

Gordon, M.R. 1986. "Reagan's 'Choke Points' Stretch From Sea to Sea." *New York Times*, Feb. 13, 1986, p. 6.

Gorman, R.F. 1984. "Soviet Perspectives on the Prospects for Political and Economic Development in Africa." *African Affairs* 83, #331 (April): 163–88.

Govett, M.H., and G.J.S. Govett. 1978. "The New International Economic Order and World Mineral Production and Trade." *Resources Policy* (Dec.):230–41.

Gowing, M., with L. Arnold. 1974. *Independence and Deterrence: Britain and Atomic Energy, 1945–1952*. U.K. Atomic Energy Authority. Vol. 1. New York: St. Martin's Press.

Grossman, G. 1986. Lectures in Economics 260c: "The Soviet Economic System." Department of Economics, University of California-Berkeley. Spring semester.

Gustafson, T. 1985. *Soviet Negotiating Strategy — The East-West Gas Pipeline Deal, 1980–1984*. Santa Monica: RAND Corp.

Gyorgy, A. 1944. *Geopolitics — The New German Science*. Berkeley: University of California Press.

Haas, E.B. 1986. "What is Nationalism and Why Should We Study It?" *International Organization* 40, #3 (Summer):707–44.

————. 1985. Lectures in Political Science 222: "Nationalism and Imperialism." Department of Political Science, University of California-Berkeley. Fall semester.

Hall, C.T. 1988. "President Hails 'Reaganomics'." *San Francisco Chronicle*, Feb. 20, p.1

Halloran, R. 1980. "Brown Warns That a Persian Gulf War Could Spread." *New York Times*, Feb. 15, p.A3.

Halperin, M.H. 1974. *Bureaucratic Politics and Foreign Policy*. Washington, D.C.: Brookings Institution.

Hamilton, W.R., Jr. 1963. *The President's Materials Policy Commission (Paley Commission): A History and Analytical Inquiry into Policy Formation by a Presidential Commission*. Ph.D. dissertation. College Park, Md.: University of Maryland, Department of Political Science.

Hancock, W.K. 1943. *Argument of Empire*. London: Penguin Books.

Hannigan, J.B., and C.H. McMillan. 1984. "The Soviet Union and World

Trade in Oil and Gas." In M.M. Kostecki, ed., *The Soviet Impact on Commodity Markets*, pp. 68–99. London: Macmillan.

Hartz, L. 1955. *The Liberal Tradition in America*. New York: Harcourt Brace Jovanovich.

Hawtrey, R.G. 1930/1952. *Economic Aspects of Sovereignty*. London: Longmans, Green.

Helmreich, J.E. 1986. *Gathering Rare Ores—The Diplomacy of Uranium Acquisition, 1943–1954*. Princeton: Princeton University Press.

Henderson, H.D. 1939. *Colonies and Raw Materials*. Oxford: Clarendon Press. Oxford Pamphlets on World Affairs, No. 7.

Hermann, M.G. 1976. "When Leader Personality Will Affect Foreign Policy: Some Propositions." In J.N. Rosenau, ed., *In Search of Global Patterns*, pp. 326–33. New York: Free Press.

Hewett, E.A. 1985. "Soviet Economic Relations with the West: Economic Options." In H. Sonnenfeldt, ed., *Soviet Politics in the 1980s*, pp. 171–81. Boulder: Westview Press.

———. 1983. "Soviet Primary Product Exports to CMEA and the West." In R.G. Jensen, T. Shabad, and A.W. Wright, eds., *Soviet Natural Resources in the World Economy*, pp. 639–58. Chicago: University of Chicago Press.

Hirschmann, A.O. 1945/1980. *National Power and the Structure of Foreign Trade*. Berkeley: University of California Press.

Hobbs, E.H. 1954. *Behind the President—A Study of Executive Office Agencies*. Washington, D.C.: Public Affairs Press.

Holdren, J.P. 1986. "Energy and the Human Predicament." In F. Fesharaki, J.P. Holdren, and K. Smith, eds., *Earth and the Human Future: Essays in Honor of Harrison Brown*, pp. 124–60. Boulder: Westview Press.

Holloway, D. 1984. *The Soviet Union and the Arms Race*. New Haven: Yale University Press.

Holsti, K.J. 1986. "Politics in Command: Foreign Trade as National Security Policy." *International Organization* 40, #3 (Summer):643–71.

Hoopes, T. 1973. *The Devil and John Foster Dulles*. Boston: Atlantic-Little, Brown.

Hoselitz, B.F. 1943. "British Trade Policy and the United States: A Survey of Recent Discussion in Great Britain on Post-War Commercial Policy." New Haven: Yale Institute of International Studies. Oct. 8. Mimeo, "For Private Circulation Only."

Hoskyns, C. 1965. *The Congo Since Independence—January 1960 to December 1961*. London: Oxford University Press.

Hough, J.F. 1986a. "Soviet Union's Turn toward Capitalism." *San Francisco Chronicle*, Oct. 1, p.F1.

———. 1986b. *The Struggle for the Third World: Soviet Debates and American Options*. Washington, D.C.: Brookings Institution.

Howland, C.P. 1929. *Survey of American Foreign Relations*. New Haven: Published for the Council on Foreign Relations by Yale University Press.

HSTL. ND. "Chronological List of Policies Developed through the National Security Council." President's Secretary's Files-NSC. Box 194: Memoranda-Reports-1.

———. 1952a. Mendershausen, H. "Review of Strategic Stockpiling (Security & Market Section)." Circa 1952. Box 4. Folder: Stockpiling, Files of the Executive Secretary, Administrative Files, President's Materials Policy Commission.

———. 1952b. NSC 29. "Security of Strategically Important Industrial Operations in Foreign Countries." Oct. 3, 1952. President's Secretary's Files — NSC Meetings. Box 219: Meeting 124.

———. 1952c. Truman, H.S. "Negotiating Paper, Indochina." TCT D-5/3c. Jan. 2, 1952. President's Secretary's Files — General File. Box 116: Churchill-Truman Meetings (Jan. 1952). Folder: negotiating papers (1).

———. 1952d. Minutes of the Truman Cabinet. Meeting on April 25, 1952. Papers of Matthew J. Connelly, Set II, Box 2 (Cabinet Meeting notes).

———. 1952e. Progress Report by the Undersecretary of State on "The Implementation of U.S. Policies and Programs in the Economic Field Which May Affect the War Potential of the Soviet Bloc" (NSC 104/2). Discussed in NSC Meeting 111, Jan. 16. President's Secretary's Files — NSC Meetings.

———. 1951a. Embtel (Paris) 2808 from David Bruce to Secretary of State, 11/10/51. President's Secretary's Files, Subject File. Box 180: Foreign Affairs. Folder: Iran.

———. 1951b. Statement by Dean Acheson, as reported in Cabinet Meeting Notes, June 22, 1951, Matthew Connelly Papers, Set II, Box 2.

———. 1951c. Memorandum of Conversation, U.S. State Department, "Iranian Oil Problem", 10/10/51. Acheson Papers. Box 66: Memoranda of Conversations, 1951. Folder: Oct. 1951.

———. 1951d. U.S. Central Intelligence Agency. "The Importance of Iranian and Middle East Oil to Western Europe under Peacetime Conditions." NIE-14. President's Secretary's Files. Box 253: Intelligence.

———. 1951e. Office Memo. To: Mr. Mikesell, President's Materials Policy Commission. From: Hollis Peter, Technical Cooperation Administration, U.S. Department of State. Draft Report: "Point 4 and Raw Materials Development." July 31, 1951. Files of the President's Materials Policy Commission, Foreign Resources Section. Box 125: General Subject File, P–Z; Reading File. Folder: Project-TCA-Exploration.

———. 1951f. Minutes & Decisions of the National Security Council, Meeting 100, Aug. 22, 1951, NSC 26/2. President's Secretary's Files — NSC Meetings.

———. 1951g. Notes on National Security Council Meeting, Aug. 22, 1951,

Discussion of NSC 26/2. Acheson Papers. Box 66: Memoranda of Conversations, 1951. Folder: Aug. 1951.

———. 1951h. Memorandum of Conversation, O. Endler, NSRB; Mr. Nash, NSRB; W.T. Phillips, PMPC; W.S. Hunsberger, PMPC. Subject: "Materials Security." Oct. 3, 1951. Records of the President's Materials Policy Commission. Box 128: Security & Market Policy. Folder: Materials Security (II).

———. 1951i. Memorandum of Conversation, April 27, 1951. Secretary Acheson, Paul Nitze, and Sir Oliver Franks. Acheson Papers. Box 66: Memoranda of Conversation, 1951. (Subject: AIOC). Folder: April 1951.

———. 1951j. Memorandum of Conversation, July 5, 1951. Secretary Acheson, Max W. Thornberg, and Mr. Rountree (CTI). Acheson Papers. Box 66: Memoranda of Conversation, 1951. (Subject: AIOC). Folder: July 1951.

———. 1951k. NSC Staff Study on Proposed Transfer of the Point IV Program from the Department of State to the Economic Cooperation Administration. Draft. Aug. 9, 1951. President's Secretary's File, Subject File, NSC. Box 198: (Reports-S-Souers). Folder: Senior NSC Staff-Point Four.

———. 1951l. Knorr, K., and W.S. Runsberger. "Security and Political Assumptions." June 28, 1951 (dated 7/28, but 2nd draft dated 7/2/51). 1st draft. Papers of the President's Materials Policy Commission, Foreign Resources Section. Box 128: Security and Market Policy Section-Drafts of Chapters in PMPC Report dealing with Market Policy and Material Security. Folder: Assumptions, Security.

———. 1951m. Memorandum of Conversation, Secretary of State Acheson, with S. Symington, RFC, and others. July 9, 1951. Acheson Papers. Box 66: Memoranda of Conversations, 1951. Folder: July 1951.

———. 1951n. Memorandum to Mr. Teets from W.S. Runsberger. "Security Assumptions and Conclusions." July 2, 1951. Second Draft. Records of the President's Materials Policy Commission. Box 128: Security and Market Policy. Folder: Assumptions, Security.

———. 1951o. Ames, E. "The Materials Position of the Soviet Bloc." June 19, 1951. "Confidential (Early) Draft." Records of the President's Materials Policy Commission. Box 10: Preliminary Drafts of Report. Folder: The Materials Position of the Soviet Bloc.

———. 1951p. Discussion of Progress Report on NSC 104/2, Meeting 107 of the NSC, Nov. 29, 1951. "U.S. Policies and Programs in the Economic Field Which May Affect the War Potential of the Soviet Bloc." President's Secretary's Files—NSC Meetings—memos. Box 220. Folder: 1951.

———. 1951q. NSC 93/1. "Results of the Conversations Between the President and the British Prime Minister." Jan. 4, 1951. President's Secretary's Files—NSC Meetings. Box 211: Meeting 82.

————. 1950a. Memorandum from the U.S. Joint Chiefs of Staff to the Secretary of Defense, Subject: The Philippines. Sept. 9, 1950. In NSC 84, "Secretary of Defense on the Position of the United States with Respect to the Philippines." Sept. 14, 1950. President's Secretary's Files—NSC Meetings. Box 210, Meeting 71, 11/9/50.

————. 1950b. Memorandum on Meeting 57 of the National Security Council, May 18, 1950. President's Secretary's Files—NSC Meetings—memos. Box 220. Folder: 1949.

————. 1950c. Acheson, D. Memorandum of Conversation between Secretary Acheson and Secretary Sawyer. Nov. 29, 1950. Acheson Papers. Box 65: Memoranda of Conversation, 1950. Folder: Nov. 1950.

————. 1950d. Meetings of the National Security Council. Memorandum on Meeting 66, Aug. 25, 1950. "Export Controls and Security Policy." Remarks of Secretary Acheson. President's Secretary's Files—NSC Meetings—memos. Box 220. Folder: 1950.

————. 1950e. Memorandum for the President from Secretary Acheson. "Position of the Administration on the Reciprocal Trade Agreements Program and the ITO Charter in the 82nd Congress." Nov. 20, 1950. President's Secretary's File, Subject Files. Box 159: Cabinet (State 1). Folder: State, Secretary of (Folder 2).

————. 1950f. "Raw Materials Problems—Summary." Records of Truman-Atlee Talks, Dec. 1950. President's Secretary's Files, Subject, Conferences. Box 163. Folder: Truman-Attlee Talks, Dec. 1950 (I).

————. 1950g. Note by Standard Oil Company (New Jersey). "Dollar-Sterling Oil Problem." Jan. 26, 1950. New York. President's Secretary's Files, General Files. Box 132. Folder: Oil.

————. 1950h. Memorandum to President Truman from W. Stuart Symington. "Petroleum Imports." June 26, 1950. President's Secretary's Files, General Files. Box 132: (Nor–P). Folder: Oil.

————. 1949a. NSC 54. "The Position of the United States with Respect to Iran." President's Secretary's Files—NSC Meetings. Box 206, Meeting 44, 8/4/49.

————. 1949b. Memorandum on 31st Meeting of the National Security Council, Jan. 7, 1949. President's Secretary's Files-NSC Meetings. Box 220. Folder: 1949.

————. 1949c. Memorandum of Conversation, Congressmen (Texas) W.R. Poage, E. Worley, E. Gossett, G.H. Mahon, A. Thomas, O.C. Fisher, W.H. Lucas, with Secretary Acheson, Mr. Eakens, Mr. Thorp. Subject: "Oil Imports." Aug. 31, 1949. Acheson Papers. Box 64: Memoranda of Conversation, 1949. Folder: Aug.–Sept. 1949.

————. 1949d. U.S. Central Intelligence Agency. "U.S. Security and the British Dollar Problem." ORE 79–49. Aug. 31, 1949. President's Secretary's Files. Box 257: Intelligence. Folder: ORE 1949 (76–89).

————. 1948a. U.S. Central Intelligence Agency. "The Breakup of Colonial Empires and Its Implications for U.S. Security." ORE 25–48. Sept. 3, 1948. President's Secretary's Files. Box 255: Intelligence. Folder: ORE 1948 (21–30).

————. 1948b. Hargrave, T.J. Letter to Truman, re: "Stockpiling." Sept. 20, 1948. Folder 1075 (1945–49): Stockpiling. White House Central Office Files.

————. 1948c. U.S. Central Intelligence Agency. "The Strategic Value to the USSR of the Conquest of Western Europe and the Near East (to Cairo) prior to 1950." Appendix to ORE 58–48. Oct. 27, 1948. President's Secretary's Files, Intelligence, CIA Reports. Box 254, Central Intelligence Group.

————. 1948d. Comment of Mr. Lovett. Memorandum on 12th Meeting of the National Security Council, June 4, 1948. President's Secretary's Files — NSC Meetings. Box 220. Folder: 1948.

————. 1948e. Comments by A. Harriman, Cabinet Meeting, Friday, March 26, 1948. Papers of Matthew J. Connelly. Set II, Box 2 (Cabinet Meeting Notes). Notebook 4.

————. 1948f. U.S. Central Intelligence Agency. "Vulnerability to Sabotage of Petroleum Installations in Venezuela, Aruba, and Curaçao." May 14, 1948. ORE 31–48. President's Secretary's Files. Box 255: Intelligence. Folder: ORE 1948 (30–39).

————. 1947a. Clifford, C.M. "Speech to Congress on Greece" (Truman Doctrine Speech), March 12, 1947. Second draft of March 9, Suggested Draft, Revised, March 9, 1947. Papers of Clark M. Clifford, Presidential Speech File, 1935–April 5, 1947. Box 28.

————. 1947b. Clifford, C.M. "Speech to Congress on Greece" (Truman Doctrine Speech), March 12, 1947. Draft of March 10, Papers of Clark M. Clifford, Presidential Speech File, 1935–April 5, 1947. Box 28.

————. 1947c. NSC 46. "Report by the National Security Council on Control of Exports to the U.S.S.R. and Eastern Europe." Appendix A. Dec. 17, 1947. President's Secretary's Files — Meetings. Box 206: Meeting 39 (NSC 46).

————. 1946a. "Statement by the President in approving S752." Press Release, July 23, 1946. Records of the President's Materials Policy Commission. Box 58: Executive Director-Correspondence. Folder: Stockpile.

Huddle, F.P. 1976. "The Evolving National Policy for Materials." *Science* 191 (Feb. 20):654–59.

Hufbauer G.C., and J.J. Schott, with K.A. Elliot. 1985. *Economic Sanctions Reconsidered: History and Current Policy.* Washington, D.C.: Institute for International Economics.

Hunt, M.H. 1987. *Ideology and U.S. Foreign Policy.* New Haven: Yale University Press.

Hurstfield, J. 1953. *The Control of Raw Materials.* London: Her Majesty's Stationery Office & Longmans, Green.

Immerman, R.H. 1982. *The CIA in Guatemala – the Foreign Policy of Intervention*. Austin: University of Texas Press.

Iriye, A. 1967. *Across the Pacific – An Inner History of American-East Asian Relations*. New York: Harcourt, Brace & World.

Janis, I. 1982. *Groupthink: Psychological Studies of Policy Decisions and Fiascoes*. Boston: Houghton-Mifflin.

Jensen, R.G. 1983. "Soviet Natural Resources in a Global Context." In R.G. Jensen, T. Shabad, and A.M. Wright, eds., *Soviet Natural Resources in the World Economy*, pp. 3–7. Chicago: University of Chicago Press.

Jentleson, B.R. 1986. *Pipeline Politics: The Complex Political Economy of East-West Energy Trade*. Ithaca: Cornell University Press.

———. 1984. "From Consensus to Conflict: The Domestic Political Economy of East-West Energy Trade Policy." *International Organization* 38, #4 (Autumn):625–60.

Jervis, R. 1978. "Cooperation under the Security Dilemma." *World Politics* 30, #2 (January):167–214.

———. 1976. *Perception and Misperception in International Politics*. Princeton: Princeton University Press.

JFKL. 1963a. Research Memorandum from INR-T.L. Hughes to The Secretary, U.S. Department of State. Subject: "U.S. and South African Economic Leverage on Each Other." Aug. 12, 1963. Bureau of Intelligence and Research. RAF-30. National Security Files. Box 159: Countries: South Africa, 8/7–8/12/63.

———. 1963b. Note for Mr. Bundy from S.E. Belk, National Security Council. "Data on Importance of U.S.-South Africa Economic Relations." July 11, 1963. National Security Files. Box 3: Countries: Africa, 7/63.

———. 1962a. "NSC Numbered Documents That Have not Been Rescinded." 8/8/62. National Security Files, Departments and Agencies. Box 283. Folder: National Security Council, General, 1/62–11/63.

———. 1962b. E.A. McDermott, Acting Director, OEP, Chairman. "Report of the Executive Stockpile Committee to the President." March 19, 1962. National Security Files, Meeting and Memoranda, NSAM 126, Box 333: Stockpiling of Strategic Materials.

———. 1962c. Outgoing Telegram from U.S. Department of State. Action: circular 1361, 1/31/62. National Security Files, Meeting and Memoranda, NSAM 126, Box 333: Stockpiling of Strategic Materials.

———. 1962d. Memorandum from E-W.M. Blumenthal to ARA-Mr. May, FE-Mr. Peterson, AF-Mr. Tasca, Subject: "The Future of the U.S. Surplus Tin Disposal Program." Nov. 20, 1962. National Security Files, Kaysen Series. Box 372: Economic Policy: Strategic Materials, 8/62–12/62.

———. 1962e. Letter to Joseph Kasavubu, Chief of State, Republic of the Congo (Leopoldville) from J.F. Kennedy. July 25, 1962. National Security Files. Box 28a: Countries: Congo, Congo General, 7/1/62–7/27/62.

————. 1961a. Memorandum for Mr. Bundy from Carl Kaysen. Subject: "Tin." Aug. 7, 1961. National Security Files. Box 321: Meetings and Memos: Staff Memos. Kaysen, 6/61–8/61.

————. 1961b. Memorandum to Gov. Williams from H.J. Tasca, Bureau of African Affairs, U.S. Department of State. "An American Economic Posture Towards Africa: Some Reflections." National Security Files-Countries: Afghanistan, 1/20/61–Africa, 8/61. Box #2. Folder: Africa 2/1/61–3/20/61.

————. 1961c. Memorandum for the President from McGeorge Bundy, March 30, 1961. President's Office Files. Box 62. Folder: Staff Memoranda, M. Bundy (2/61–4/61).

Just, E. 1951. "If West Fights East . . . Victory or Stalemate? Minerals Can Decide." *Engineering Mining Journal* (June).

Kalb, M. 1982. *The Congo Cables—The Cold War in Africa from Eisenhower to Kennedy.* New York: Macmillan.

Kalberg, S. 1980. "Max Weber's Types of Rationalization: Cornerstones for the Analysis of Rationalization Processes in History." *American Journal of Sociology* 85, #5 (March):1145–79.

Kaltefleiter, W. 1983. "The Resource War: The Need for a Western Strategy." *Comparative Strategy* 4, #1:31–49.

Kapp, K.W. 1941. "The League of Nations and Raw Materials—1919–1939. (Geneva Research Centre). *Geneva Studies* 12, #3 (Sept.)

Kapstein, E.B. 1983. "The Sterling-Dollar Oil Problem." Medford, Mass.: Fletcher School of Law and Diplomacy, Tufts University. May. Unpublished paper.

Karber, P.A., with A.R.W. Menzel. 1975. "In Defense of Fortress America: Autarky as an Alternative to Isolation and Interdependence." In M.A. Kaplan, ed., *Isolation or Interdependence? Today's Choices for Tomorrow's World*, pp. 59–80. New York: Free Press.

Kaufman, B.I. 1982. *Trade and Aid—Eisenhower's Foreign Economic Policy, 1953–1961.* Baltimore: Johns Hopkins University Press.

Kaysen, C. 1986. Interview with author, June 3, Massachusetts Institute of Technology, Cambridge, Mass.

Keddie, N.R. 1981. *Roots of Revolution—An Interpretive History of Modern Iran.* New Haven: Yale University Press.

Kennedy, P. 1987. *The Rise and Fall of the Great Powers—Economic Change and Military Conflict from 1500 to 2000.* New York: Random House.

————. 1983a. "The Tradition of Appeasement in British Foreign Policy, 1865–1939." In P. Kennedy, *Strategy and Diplomacy 1870–1945*, pp. 15–39. London: George Allen & Unwin.

————. 1983b. "Why Did the British Empire Last So Long?" In P. Kennedy, *Strategy and Diplomacy 1870–1945*, pp. 199–218. London: George Allen & Unwin.

————. 1983c. "Strategy versus Finance in Twentieth-Century Britain." In P. Kennedy, *Strategy and Diplomacy 1870–1945*, pp. 87–108. London: George Allen & Unwin.

————. 1981. *The Realities Behind Diplomacy: Background Influences on British External Policy, 1865–1980*. London: George Allen & Unwin/Fontana.

Keohane, R.O. 1984. *After Hegemony—Cooperation and Discord in the World Political Economy*. Princeton: Princeton University Press.

Kindleberger, C.P. 1975. "The Rise of Free Trade in Western Europe, 1820–1875." *Journal of Economic History* 35, #1 (March):20–55.

————. 1973. *The World in Depression, 1929–1939*. Berkeley: University of California Press.

King, A. 1972. "Ideas, Institutions and the Policies of Governments: A Comparative Analysis." *British Journal of Political Science* 3:291–313, 409–23.

Kirkpatrick, J. 1984. Speech to the Republican National Convention, reprinted in the *New York Times*, Aug. 21.

Klinghoffer, A.J. 1977. *The Soviet Union and International Oil Politics*. New York: Columbia University Press.

Knorr, K. 1945. *Tin under Control*. Stanford, Calif.: Food Research Institute, Stanford University.

————. 1943. "Access to Raw Materials in the Postwar World." *Harvard Business Review* (Spring). Reprint.

Kobrin, S. 1985. "Diffusion as an Explanation of Oil Nationalization— Or the Domino Effect Rides Again." *Journal of Conflict Resolution* 29, #1 (March):3–32.

————. 1984. "Expropriation as an Attempt to Control Foreign Firms in LDCs: Trends from 1960 to 1979." *International Studies Quarterly* 28, #3 (September):329–48.

————. 1980. "Foreign Enterprise and Forced Divestment in LDCs." *International Organization* 34, #1 (Winter):65–88.

Kodachenko, A.S. 1960. *Sovevrovanie dvhukh sistem i slaborazvitye strany*. Moscow: Sotsekgiz.

Kolko, G. 1969. *The Roots of American Foreign Policy*. Boston: Beacon Press.

Kondrashov, Ye. N. 1982. "United States-Africa: Raw Materials Aspect." *SShA* #7 (July):67–75. Translated as "Africa's Importance to U.S. as Source of Minerals Noted." JPRS (circa #81000), pp. 48–58.

Korelev, I. 1982. "Important Aspect of the Study of the USSR's Foreign Economic Relations." *MEIMO* #10 (Oct.):133–34. Translated as "Role of Foreign Trade in Soviet Regional Economies." JPRS 82867, pp. 82–85.

Krasner, S.D. 1985. *Structural Conflict—The Third World Against Global Liberalism*. Berkeley: University of California Press.

————. 1983a. "Structural Causes and Regime Consequences: Regimes as Intervening Variables." In S.D. Krasner, ed., *International Regimes*, pp. 1–21. Ithaca: Cornell University Press.

————. 1983b. "Regimes and the Limits of Realism: Regimes as Autonomous Variables." In S.D. Krasner, ed., *International Regimes*, pp. 355–68. Ithaca: Cornell University Press.

————. 1978. *Defending the National Interest: Raw Materials Investments and U.S. Foreign Policy*. Princeton: Princeton University Press.

Kuniholm, B.R. 1980. *The Origins of the Cold War in the Near East: Great Power Conflict and Diplomacy in Iran, Turkey, and Greece*. Princeton: Princeton University Press.

LaFeber, W. 1979. *The Panama Canal — The Crisis in Historical Perspective*. Oxford: Oxford University Press.

Laitin, D. 1986. *Hegemony and Culture — Politics and Religious Change among the Yoruba*. Chicago: University of Chicago Press.

Larson, D.W. 1985. *Origins of Containment — A Psychological Explanation*. Princeton: Princeton University Press.

Lasky, S.G. 1945. "The Concept of Ore Reserves." *Mining and Metallurgy* 26 (Oct.):471–74.

Lavigne, M. 1984. "Long-term Commodity Agreements and the USSR." In M.M. Kostecki, ed., *The Soviet Impact on Commodity Markets*, pp. 15–25. London: Macmillan.

Leith, C.K. 1940. "Minerals in the Peace Settlement." From CBS Round Table Discussion. "Mineral Resources and the International Situation," Dec. 29, 1939. Transcript reprinted by Geological Society of America. Feb.

————. 1938. "The Role of Minerals in the Present International Situation." Anniversary Day Address, University of Wisconsin. Dec. *Bulletin of the Geological Society* 50 (March 1, 1939):433–42.

————. 1925. "The Political Control of Mineral Resources." *Foreign Affairs* (July).

Lenin. V.I. 1943. "Imperialism: The Highest Stage of Capitalism." In H. Wright, ed., *The "New Imperialism" — Analysis of Late Nineteenth-Century Expansion*, pp. 44–69. Lexington, Mass.: D.C. Heath, 1976.

Liebhafsky, H.H. 1957. "The International Materials Conference in Retrospect." *Quarterly Journal of Economics* 71, #2 (May):267–88.

Lindblom, C.E. 1977. *Politics and Markets — The World's Political-Economic Systems*. New York: Basic Books.

————. 1959. "The Science of 'Muddling Through'." *Public Administration Review* 19 (Spring):78–88.

Lipschutz, R.D. 1987. *Ore Wars: Access to Strategic Materials, International Conflict, and the Foreign Policies of States*. Ph.D. dissertation. Berkeley: Energy and Resources Group, University of California.

————. 1986a. "Send Danger from the East unto the West — Order, Control and U.S. Policy in the Congo: 1960–1963." Berkeley: Energy and Resources Group, University of California. ERG Working Paper 86–5. May 19.

————. 1986b. "The Soviet Minerals System: Prognosis and Prospects." Berkeley: Energy and Resources Group, University of California. Unpublished paper.

————. 1985. "Energy, Resources and Major Conflict—An Annotated Bibliography." Berkeley: Energy and Resources Group, University of California. ERG Working Paper 85–9. Oct. 1.

Lipson, C. 1985. *Standing Guard—Protecting Foreign Capital in the Nineteenth and Twentieth Centuries*. Berkeley: University of California Press.

Louis, W.R. 1984. *The British Empire in the Middle East, 1945–1951—Arab Nationalism, the United States, and Postwar Imperialism*. Oxford: Clarendon Press.

————. 1971. *British Strategy in the Far East, 1919–1939*. Oxford: Clarendon Press.

Lowe, C.J., and M.L. Dockrill. 1972. "Anglo-Russian Relations and the Middle East." *The Mirage of Power—British Foreign Policy 1902–14*, Vol 1, pp. 59–95. London: Routledge & Kegan Paul.

Luard, E. 1962. *Britain and China*. Baltimore: Johns Hopkins Press.

Mackinder, H.J. 1943. "The Round World and the Winning of the Peace." *Foreign Affairs* (July):595–605.

McBeth, B.S. 1985. *British Oil Policy 1919–1939*. London: Frank Cass.

Mahan, A.T. 1895. *The Interest of America in Sea Power, Present and Future*. Boston: Little, Brown.

————. 1893. *The Influence of Sea Power Upon History*. Boston: Little, Brown.

Mahoney, R.D. 1983. *JFK: Ordeal in Africa*. Oxford: Oxford University Press.

Mangold, P. 1979. "Shaba I and Shaba II." *Survival* (May/June):107–115.

Manners, G. 1978. "The Future Markets for Minerals—Some Causes of Uncertainty." *Resources Policy* (June):100–05.

Markham, J.M. 1987. "Allies Leery of Military Role in Gulf." *San Francisco Chronicle*, Aug. 5, p.13.

Marrese, M., and J. Vanous. 1983. "Soviet Policy Options in Trade Relations with Eastern Europe." In Selected Papers Submitted to the Joint Economic Commmittee, U.S. Congress, *Soviet Economy in the 1980s: Problems and Prospects*. Dec. 31, 1982, pp. 102–16. Washington, D.C.: U.S. Government Printing Office.

Marshall, J. 1975. *The Road to War: Raw Materials and America's Far Eastern Policy, 1940–1941*. Senior thesis. Stanford: Stanford University, Department of History. Oct.

Marx, K. 1926. *The Eighteenth Brumaire of Louis Bonaparte*. New York: International.

Mason, E.S. 1952. "Raw Materials, Rearmament, and Economic Development." *Quarterly Journal of Economics* 46, #3 (August):327–41.

————. 1949. "American Security and Access to Raw Materials." *World Politics* 1, #2 (Jan.):147–60.

Mastanduno, M. 1985. "Strategies of Economic Containment: U.S. Trade

Relations with the Soviet Union." *World Politics* 37, #4 (July):503–31.

Mather, K.F., and H.A. Meyerhoff. 1951. "Mineral Resources and International Understanding." *The Scientific Monthly* (May):295–99.

Mattern, J. 1942. "Geopolitik—Doctrine of National Self-Sufficiency and Empire." *The Johns Hopkins University Studies in Historical and Political Science* 60, #2.

Maull, H.W. 1984. *Raw Materials, Energy and Western Security*. Baltimore: Johns Hopkins University Press.

May, E.R. 1973. *"Lessons" of the Past: The Use and Misuse of History in American Foreign Policy*. New York: Oxford University Press.

Meyer, C.J., and G.A. Riley. 1985. *Public Domain, Private Dominion—A History of Public Mineral Policy in America*. San Francisco: Sierra Club Books.

Meyer, G.E. 1980. *Egypt and the United States—The Formative Years*. Rutherford, N.J.: Farleigh Dickinson University Press.

Milward, A.S. 1977. *War, Economy and Society, 1939–1945*. Berkeley: University of California Press.

Mitchell, B. 1988. "Undermining Antarctica." *Technology Review* 91, #2 (Feb./March):48–57.

Monroe, E. 1981. *Britain's Moment in the Middle East, 1914–1971*. London: Chatto & Winders.

Morgenthau, H.J. 1967. *Politics Among Nations—The Struggle for Power and Peace*. New York: Knopf.

Mott, Adm. W.C., ret. 1981. Testimony before the Subcommittee on Africa of the Committee on Foreign Affairs, U.S. House of Representatives, *The Possibility of a Resource War in Southern Africa*, pp. 8–29. July 8. Washington, D.C.: U.S. Government Printing Office.

Moyal, Dr. Maurice. 1952. "The Role of E.C.A. in the Development of French Africa's Mineral Resources." *The Mining Journal* (London), March 14.

Myers, N. 1987. "Linking Environment and Security." *Bulletin of the Atomic Scientists* (June):46–47.

NARS. ND. RG 304, Files of the U.S. National Security Resources Board. Series 31,34 & 41. K Series: International Mobilization Planning. File K6-9: Preclusive Buying. Modern Military Records Branch.

———. 1954a. Nichols, C.W. Office Memorandum to Mr. Waugh (E). Subject: "Malone Subcommittee Report on the Accessibility of Critical Materials." July 23, 1954. RG 59, Records of the U.S. State Department. Decimal File 711.6/7-2354.

———. 1954b. U.S. Department of the Interior. *Report of the Cabinet Committee on Minerals Policy*, plus attachments. Nov. 5, 1954. RG 59, Records of the U.S. State Department. Decimal File, 711.63/11–554. (Also published as a public document by the DOI on Nov. 30, 1954.)

———. 1953a. NSC 163. "Security of Strategically Important Industrial Operations in Foreign Countries." Oct. 10, 1953. NSC Documents. Judicial, Social, and Fiscal Branch.

————. 1953b. Office Memorandum from OMP-Mr. Evans to E-Mr. Waugh. Subject: "Commodity Policy and ARA." Dec. 11, 1953. RG 59, Records of the U.S. State Department. Decimal File 711.6/12–1153.

————. 1953c. Memorandum from F.F. Everest, Director, Joint Staff of the U.S. Joint Chiefs of Staff to the Secretary of Defense, Aug. 11, 1953. "Defense Arrangements for the Middle East." RG 59, Records of the U.S. State Department. Decimal File 780.5/8–2653 (A/29).

————. 1952a. Foster, A.B. Memorandum to Mr. Perkins and Mr. Bonbright (EUR) from BNA, "Two Lines of Approach in Defining U.S. Policy toward the Defense of the Middle East." May 3, 1952. RG 59, Records of the U.S. State Department. Decimal File 780.5/4–352.

————. 1952b. Memorandum from RA-Mr. Spalding to RA-Mr. Parsons. "NATO and the Arab World." Feb. 25, 1952. RG 59, Records of the U.S. State Department. Decimal File 780.5/2–2552.

————. 1952c. Materials Office, National Security Resources Board. "A Critical Survey of the Organization and Operation of the Stockpile Program." June. NSRB 6587. RG304, Records of the NSRB. Folder: Stockpiling of Strategic and Materials General, 1952. H2–6. Modern Military Records Branch.

————. 1952d. Memorandum from P.C. Jessup, Ambassador-at-Large, to Mr. Matthews. Subject: "Middle East Command." April 28, 1952. RG 59, Records of the U.S. State Department. Decimal File 780.5/4–2852, XR611.80.

————. 1952e. Memorandum from J.K. Remsen for Mr. Stead, Natural Resources Office, National Security Resources Board, 21 May 1952. RG 304, Records of the NSRB. Files of Director W.H. Stead, 1952–53, Natural Resources Offices. Series 168. Folder: African Resources. Modern Military Records Branch.

————. 1951a. NSC-117: "A Report to the National Security Council by the Secretary of Defense on the Anglo-Iranian Problem." Oct. 18, 1951. RG 273, Records of the NSC, Policy Paper Files.

————. 1951b. Gorrie, J. "Current Status of Stockpile Administration." May 18, 1951. RG 304, Records of the National Security Resources Board, Box: Entry 31, Central Files, July 1949–April 1953, Folder: "Stockpiling of Strategic Critical Materials, General 1949–1951, H2–6." Modern Military Records Branch.

————. 1951c. Memorandum of Conversation, U.S. Department of State. "Procurement of Strategic Materials in the Far East," Jan. 5, 1951. RG 59, Records of the U.S. State Department. Decimal File 711.6/1–551.

————. 1951d. Memorandum of Conversation, U.S. Department of State. "Procurement of Strategic Materials in the Far East," Jan. 6, 1951. RG 59, Records of the U.S. State Department. Decimal File 711.6/1–651.

————. 1951e. Memorandum. "Outline of Report." No date, no author. RG

304, Files of the National Security Resources Board, Chairman. Series 3. Box 14. Folder: Defense Mobilization Board. Modern Military Records Branch.

———. 1951f. Memorandum from Mr. McGhee (NEA) to the Secretary of State, Feb. 9, 1951. "Middle East Defense." (Memo not sent.) RG 59, Records of the U.S. State Department. Decimal File 780.5/2–951.

———. 1951g. Foreign Service Despatch from E.S. Crocker, U.S. Ambassador to Iraq to the U.S. Department of State, Oct. 17, 1951. "Saudi Arabian Minister's [Abdullah al Khayal] Views on MEC and Related Matters." RG 59, Records of the U.S. State Department. Decimal File 780.5/10–1751.

———. 1950a. Memo to S/MDA-Mr. Bruce, From: NEA-Mr. McGhee, Feb. 10, 1950. "Military Assistance Program for Fiscal Year 1951 — Establishment of Objectives and Basic Policies to Govern the Selection and Development of Programs. Tab E: Saudi Arabia." Box 1. Folder: MAP-Index. RG 59, Lot 484: Records of the Military Advisor to the Office of Near Eastern, Asian, and African Affairs, U.S. State Department.

———. 1950b. Bradley, Gen. O. Memorandum for the Secretary of Defense from the Chairman, Joint Chiefs of Staff. Subject: "Near Eastern Security." May 4, 1950. RG 59, Records of the U.S. State Department. Decimal File 780.5/5–450.

———. 1950c. Lanphier, T.G. Memo to S. Symington. May 8. (Draft.) RG 304, Records of the National Security Resources Board. Box 17: NSRB-Rubber. Modern Military Records Branch.

———. 1950d. Comments of Stuart Symington, Summary of Minerals Meeting #8, National Security Resources Board, Dec. 4, 1950. RG 304, Records of the NSRB. Symington Files, Box 17. Folder: Secretariat, NSRB Board. Modern Military Records Branch.

———. 1950e. Memorandum from S.S. Shannon, to Mr. Symington, National Security Resources Board, Aug. 21, 1950. "Activities of the Economic Cooperation Administration in obtaining materials for the National Stockpile." RG304, Records of the NSRB. Folder H1–13: Foreign Sources of Strategic Materials. Modern Military Records Branch.

———. 1949a. Winant, F. Memorandum to Mr. R.E. Gillmore, Vice Chairman, National Security Resources Board. "Review of Manganese Situation." Feb. 8, 1949. RG 304, Records of the NSRB, Series 100. Box 13: Foreign Activities Office, Commodity File, 1948–1951. Modern Military Records Branch.

———. 1948a. Report by SANACC, Subcommittee for the Near & Middle East. "Enclosure: Preparations for Demolition of Oil Facilities in the Middle East." May 25, 1948. SANACC 398/4. RG 59, Lot 484: Records of the Military Advisor to the Office of Near Eastern, Asian, and African Affairs, U.S. Department of State. Box 4: Foreign Military Assistance Coordinating Committee, SANACC.

————. 1948b. Winant, F. Memorandum to A.M. Hill, Chairman, National Security Resources Board. Subject: "Plan for *Quid Pro Quo* Trade Negotiations with USSR." May 10, 1948. RG 304, Records of the NSRB, Series 100. Box 13: Foreign Activities Office, Commodity File, 1948–1951. Modern Military Records Branch.

————. 1946a. Memorandum from "GPM" [George P. Merriam] to "LWH" [Loy W. Henderson], Office of Near Eastern and African Affairs, U.S. Department of State, March 15, 1946. RG 59, Lot 484: Records of the Military Advisor to the Office of Near Eastern, Asian, and African Affairs, U.S. Department of State. Box 3. Folder: SWCC — Misc.

Nelson, H.D., and I. Kaplan. 1980. *Ethiopia — A Country Study*. Washington, D.C.: U.S. Government Printing Office.

Neuberger, E. 1963. *The European Soviet Bloc and the West as Markets for Primary Products: Stability, Growth and Size*. Santa Monica: RAND Corp.

Neustadt, R.E., and E.R. May. 1986. *Thinking in Time — The Uses of History for Decision-Makers*. New York: Free Press.

Noble, S.B. 1975. "Resources and the Political Options Facing the United States." In M.A. Kaplan, ed., *Isolation or Interdependence? Today's Choices for Tomorrow's World*, pp. 167–92. New York: Free Press.

North, R.C., and N. Choucri. 1983. "Economic and Political Factors in International Conflict and Integration." *International Studies Quarterly* 27:443–61.

Oakerson, R.J. 1985. "A Model for the Analysis of Common Property Problems." In National Research Council, *Common Property Resource Management*, pp. 13–29. Washington, D.C.: National Academy of Sciences.

O'Brien, D. J. 1974. *The Oil Crisis and the Foreign Policy of the Wilson Administration, 1917–21*. Ph.D. dissertation. Columbia, Mo.: University of Missouri, Department of History.

Odell, J. 1979. "The U.S. and the Emergence of Flexible Exchange Rates: An Analysis of Foreign Policy Change." *International Organization* 33, #1 (Winter):57–81.

Overton, A.J., Jr. 1983. President's Letter. "Gaining Access to a Minerals Base: Soviets Break Ice, but U.S. Assets Stay Frozen." *American Mining Congress Journal* 69, #21: back cover.

Oxman, B.H. 1985. "Summary of the Law of the Sea Convention." In R. Falk, F. Kratochwil, and S.H. Mendlovitz, eds., *International Law: A Contemporary Perspective*, pp. 559–70. Boulder: Westview Press.

Packenham, R.A. 1973. *Liberal America and the Third World: Political Development Ideas in Foreign Aid and Social Science*. Princeton: Princeton University Press.

Painter, D.S. 1986. *Oil and the American Century — The Political Economy of U.S. Foreign Oil Policy, 1941–1954*. Baltimore: Johns Hopkins University Press.

Paley, W. 1979. *As It Happened*. Garden City, N.Y.: Doubleday.

Papp, D.S. 1982. "Soviet Non-fuel Mineral Resources – Surplus or Scarcity?" *Resources Policy* (Sept.):155–76.

Parker, G. 1985. *Western Geopolitical Thought in the Twentieth Century*. London: Croom Helm.

Penn State. 1979. Pennsylvania State University, Department of Mineral Economics. *Report on Phase I: Domestic Policy Review of Nonfuel Minerals; Volume III: Compendium of Issues, Options, and Recommendations Contained in Major Post-War Nonfuel Mineral Policy Studies*. Washington, D.C.: U.S. Government Printing Office.

Petras, J., and M. Morely. 1975. *The United States and Chile: Imperialism and the Overthrow of the Allende Government*. New York: Monthly Review Press.

Pisar, S. 1970. *Coexistence and Commerce – Guidelines for Transactions Between East and West*. New York: McGraw-Hill.

PlanEcon. 1986. "Growing Soviet International Economic Isolation and a Severe Problems [sic] ahead in the Foreign Trade Sector Prompt Top Soviet Economists to Advocate Membership in the IMF, World Bank and GATT." *PlanEcon Report* 2, #31 (July 31).

Polanyi, K. 1957. *The Great Transformation*. Boston: Beacon Press.

Pollard, R.A. 1985. *Economic Security and the Origins of the Cold War, 1945–1950*. New York: Columbia University Press.

Posner, M.J., and P. Goldberg. 1983. *The Strategic Metals Investment Handbook – How to Profit from the International Scramble for Resources*. New York: Holt, Rinehart and Winston.

Powell, S.M. 1988. "U.S. Foreign Policy Adrift in the Persian Gulf." *San Francisco Examiner*, May 15, p. A–8.

President's Commission on Foreign Aid. 1947. *European Recovery and American Aid*. Washington, D.C.: U.S. Government Printing Office. Nov. 7.

PMPC. 1952. President's Materials Policy Commission. *Resources for Freedom*. Washington, D.C.: U.S. Government Printing Office. June.

Prestwich, R. 1984. "Strategic Minerals – A Bibliography." Cambridge: School of Geography, CCAT, December.

Price, R.M. 1984. Lectures in political science course: "The Politics of Modernization." Department of Political Science, University of California-Berkeley. Fall semester.

PRO. ND. Various memoranda in SUPP14/47: Ministry of Supply, Trade with Russia.

———. 1956a. Paper by the Secretary of State for Foreign Affairs (Selwyn Lloyd), CP(56) 122, May 15, 1956. "Persian Gulf – An Analysis of Our Position and Problems." CAB 129/81: Papers for the British Cabinet.

———. 1956b. Report from Mr. Stevens, British Embassy, Teheran to Foreign Office, Jan. 18, 1956. No. 14, 15323/1/56. FO371/120825/UE51171/2: Supplies, 1956 – Middle East Oil Committee. Draft paper for Economic Steering Committee, "The Middle East."

————. 1954a. Eisenhower, D.D. Letter to Prime Minister Churchill on Indochina. April 5, 1954. PREM 11/645: Papers of the Prime Minister.

————. 1954b. Memorandum by Mr. Wakefield, Economic Division, Foreign Office, circa Jan. 1954. "United States Economic Policy." FO371/110148/UEE1007/1.

————. 1953a. Supplement to the War Planning Directive, Commanders-in-Chief Committee, DCC(54)-42, no date. "Delaying and Denial Operations in the Middle East." In Note by the Secretary, Chiefs of Staff Committee, COS(53)247, May 28, 1953. "Defence of the Middle East." DEFE 11/60: Minutes and Memoranda of the British Defence Co-ordination Committee.

————. 1953b. Report by the British Defence Co-Ordination Committee Middle East, DCC(53)-16, Feb. 23, 1953. "Defence of the Middle East—An Analysis of Future Prospects." DEFE 11/58 (#1459): Minutes and Memoranda of the Defence Co-Ordination Committee.

————. 1953c. Personal Note by Sir Arthur Salter, April 29, 1953. "Raw Material Prices." PREM11/521: Files of the Prime Minister, Raw Materials 1953.

————. 1952a. Report by A. Eden, Foreign Secretary. "British Overseas Obligations." C(52)202, June 18, 1952. CAB 129/53: Papers for the Cabinet.

————. 1952b. FO 371/99630. Folder of the Far Eastern Department, U.K. Foreign Office, on tungsten supplies in South Korea, 1952.

————. 1952c. Report by the Chiefs of Staff (Slim, Slessor, McGrigor), D(52)45, Oct. 31, 1952. "Defence Programme." CAB 131/12: Papers of the Defence Committee.

————. 1952d. Minutes of a meeting in the Economic Relations Department of the Foreign Office, June 19, 1952. "The Economic Situation in the Middle East and Sterling Area." FO371/99032/UE/E176/1.

————. 1952e. Report by the Persia (Official) Committee, PO(M)(52)1, Feb. 5, 1952. "Memo: International Bank and State Department Proposals." CAB 134/1143: Minutes and Memoranda of the Persia Committee [PO(M)(51–52)].

————. 1952f. Memorandum by the Secretary of State for Foreign Affairs & the President of the Board of Trade, C(52)38, May 5, 1952. "Rubber Exports to the Soviet *Bloc*, China and North Korea." CAB129/51: Papers for the Cabinet.

————. 1952g. Knox, Rawle. "Malaya's Dangerous Economy." *The Observer*, Feb. 3, 1952. FO371/99150/UES1323/18: Foreign Office, US Rubber Policy, UE, 1952.

————. 1952h. Note by the Chancellor of the Duchy of Lancaster, C(52)314, Sept. 30, 1952. "The Paley Commission." PREM11/306: Papers of the Prime Minister, USA (General) 1952.

————. 1952i. Telegram from Swinton, Foreign Office to Knollys, Washington, D.C., Jan. 22, 1952. No. 441. FO371/99150/UES1323/3: US Rubber Policy, UE, 1952.

————. 1952j. Minute to the Prime Minister from "Treasury Chambers", Oct. 14, 1952. PREM11/306: Papers of the Prime Minister, USA (General) 1952.

————. 1951a. Paper by H. Morrison, Foreign Secretary. "The Oil Dispute with Persia." CP(51)257, Sept. 26, 1951. CAB 129/47: Papers for the Cabinet.

————. 1951b. Memorandum (Secret): "Persia-Instructions to Negotiators." No date. BT 172/44: Board of Trade, Personal Papers of R.R. Stokes, MP (former Minister of Materials and Lord Privy Seal). Folder: Persian Oil Dispute, 1951. Historical Notes, etc.

————. 1951c. Memorandum GEN 363/6: "Persian Oil." June 20, 1951. CAB 130/67: Papers of Cabinet Committee GEN 363, Persian Oil.

————. 1951d. Memorandum: "Note for Lord Privy Seal's Mission [to Persia]." Aug. 2, 1951. BT 172/38: Board of Trade, Personal Papers of R.R. Stokes, MP (former Minister of Materials and Lord Privy Seal). Folder: Persian Oil Dispute, 1951. General-Part I, 6/1–8/3/51.

————. 1951e. Minute, Lord Cherwell to Prime Minister Churchill (Nov. 8, 1951), and reply (Nov. 10, 1951). PREM 11/208: Papers of the Prime Minister, 1952 Middle East (Policy).

————. 1951f. Confidential Annex to PO(O)(51)8th meeting, Nov. 23, 1951. "His Majesty's Government's Shareholding in the Anglo-Iranian Oil Company." CAB 134/1145: Minutes and Memoranda of the Persia (Official) Committee (6.11.51–27.12.51).

————. 1951g. Address by the Honorable George C. McGhee, Assistant Secretary of State for Near Eastern, South Asian, and African Affairs, before the Petroleum Branch of the American Institute of Mining and Metallurgical Engineers, Oklahoma City, Oklahoma, Wednesday, Oct. 3. U.S. Dept. of State Press Release No. 892, Oct. 2. FO 371/92048: Foreign Office.

————. 1951h. Report by Joint Planning Staff, COS(51)93rd meeting, June 6, 1951. "Defence of the Middle East-1951–1954, Confidential Annex." DEFE 4/43: Staff Reports to the Chiefs of Staff Committee.

————. 1951i. Paper by the Foreign Office, Economic Relations Department, for Persian Oil Working Party, 1951. "An Anglo-American Oil Policy for the Middle East." POWE 33/1968: Papers of the Ministry of Fuel and Power, Oil Policy—US/UK.

————. 1951j. Comments on Foreign Office Paper by W.L.F. Nutthall, Ministry of Fuel and Power, Nov. 1, 1951. POWE 33/1968: Papers of the Ministry of Fuel and Power, Oil Policy—US/UK.

———. 1951k. Note by an Official Working Party, GEN 363/7, June 23, 1951. "Economic Pressures on Persia." CAB 130/67: Minutes and Memoranda of GEN 363, Persian Oil Working Party.

———. 1951l. Memorandum by H. Morrison, Foreign Secretary. CP(51)114, April 20, 1951. "Persian Oil." CAB 129/49: Papers for the Cabinet.

———. 1951m. Minutes of GEN 363, 3rd Meeting, May 9, 1951. CAB 130/67: Minutes and Memoranda of GEN 363, Persian Oil Working Party.

———. 1951n. Letter from D. Fergusson, Minister of Fuel and Power, to R.R. Stokes, Oct. 3, 1951. Re: Settlement with Persia. FO371/91599/EP1531/1839G: Foreign Office, Persia.

———. 1951o. Telegram from Commanders-in-Chief, Middle East, to the War Office, July 17, 1951. CIC/18245. Top Secret. GEN 363/9. CAB 130/67: Minutes and Memoranda of GEN 363, Persian Oil Working Party.

———. 1951p. Paper by H. Morrison, Foreign Secretary. CP(51)212, July 20, 1951. "Persia." CAB 129/46: Papers for the Cabinet.

———. 1951q. Letter from J.M. Troutbeck, British Embassy, Bagdad to H. Morrison, June 13, 1951. FO371/91185/E1024/35/G: Foreign Office, Eastern, General, 1951: Anglo-US Cooperation in the Middle East.

———. 1951r. Paper by the Secretary of State for the Colonies, C(51)22, Nov. 19, 1951. "Balance of Payments of the Colonial Territories." CAB129/48: Papers for the Cabinet.

———. 1951s. Memorandum by the Chiefs of Staff Committee, COS(51)63, Feb. 10, 1951. "Strategic Implications of the Application of Economic Sanctions Against China." CAB 134/291: Minutes and Memoranda of the Far East (Official) Committee.

———. 1951t. Synopsis of report by the Working Party on Economic Sanctions Against China, Far East (Official) Committee, FE(O)(51)7, Feb. 3, 1951. CAB 134/291: Minutes and Memoranda of the Far East (Official) Committee.

———. 1951u. Note by the Joint Secretaries of the Far East (Official) Committee, FE(O)(51)22, June 8, 1951. "Simplified List of Prohibited Goods." CAB 134/291: Minutes and Memoranda of the Far East (Official) Committee.

———. 1951v. Minutes of the Far East (Official) Committee, FE(O)(51)6th meeting, June 6, 1951. "Control by the United Kingdom and British Colonial and Dependent Territories of Trade with China." CAB134/291: Minutes and Memoranda of the Far East (Official) Committee.

———. 1951w. Memorandum by the Chancellor of the Exchequer, the Chancellor of the Duchy of Lancaster, and the Minister of Supply, C(51)42, Dec. 11, 1951. "Tin and Steel Negotiations with the U.S.A." CAB129/48: Papers for the Cabinet.

———. 1951x. Report by the Economic Committee (Washington), EC(W)(51)9, Aug. 25, 1951. "U.S. Strategic Stockpiling." FO371/92040/UES 1369/10: Foreign Office, Discussions in Advisory Committee of Central Group on Stockpiling, Feb./March 1951.

———. 1951y. Foreign Office Memo, Feb. 8, 1951. "General line to be taken by the United Kingdom in negotiations with the United States on raw material allocations, with particular reference to export policy." FO371/ 94141: Raw Materials – American Defence Measures. M1012/5.

———. 1951z. Telegram from Sir Oliver Franks, Washington to the Foreign Office, Jan. 6, 1951. (Marked: "This telegram is of particular secrecy and should be retained by the authorised recipient and not passed on.") FO371/94141: Raw Materials – American Defence Measures. M1013/2.

———. 1951aa. Telegram from Foreign Office to Washington, D.C., No. 101, Jan. 9, 1951. FO371/94141: Raw Materials – American Defence Measures. M1013/2.

———. 1950a. U.K. Ministry of Defense. Telegram to BJSM, Washington, Lord Tedder for COS Washington from COS. Oct. 19, 1950. FO371/ 83000/UES1534/57: Foreign Office.

———. 1950b. Moss, E.H. St.G. "Oil Supplies in War." Minute. Eastern Department, Foreign Office. Oct. 16, 1950. FO371/83000/UES1534/55/G.

———. 1950c. Minutes of the Cabinet Economic Policy Committee, EPC (50) 29th Meeting, Dec. 5, 1950. PREM 8/1509: Papers of the Prime Minister, 1951 Raw Materials.

———. 1950d. Memorandum from the Foreign Office [by E. Bevin?] to the Far East (Official) Committee, FE(O)(50)16, April 13, 1950. "China." CAB134/ 290: Minutes and Memoranda of the Far East (Official) Committee.

———. 1950e. Report by the Chiefs of Staff to the Cabinet Defence Committee, DO(50)40, May 19, 1950. "Co-operation with Egypt." Appendix I: "Brief for the Chief of the Imperial General Staff." PREM 8/1359: Papers of the Prime Minister, 1951 Defence (Organisation).

———. 1950f. Paper by E. Bevin, Foreign Secretary, CP(50)283, Nov. 27, 1950. "Egypt." CAB 129/43: Papers for the Cabinet.

———. 1950g. Report by the Far East (Official) Committee to the Official Committee on Economic Development (Overseas), ED(OS)(49)26, Jan. 6, 1950. "Annex: Economic and Social Development in South and South-East Asia and the Far East." CAB134/288: Minutes and Memoranda of the Official Committee on Economic Development (Overseas).

———. 1950h. Paper by E. Bevin, Foreign Secretary, CP(50)20, Aug. 30, 1950. "Review of the International Situation in Asia in the Light of the Korean Conflict." CAB129/41: Papers for the Cabinet.

———. 1950i. Report to the Economic Steering Committee, ES(50)22, Dec. 2, 1950. "Report on the Raw Materials Situation." PREM8/1509: Papers of the Prime Minister, 1951, Raw Materials.

———. 1950j. Minutes of the Economic Policy Committee, EPC(50)29th meeting, Dec. 5, 1950. PREM8/1509: Papers of the Prime Minister, 1951, Raw Materials.

————. 1950k. Memorandum by R.F. Bretherton, EPC(50)125 & 126, Dec. 4, 1950. "Raw Materials." PREM8/1509: Papers of the Prime Minister, 1951, Raw Materials.

————. 1950*l.* Summary of Working Party's Report on East-West Trade, "Restrictions on exports of strategic goods to Eastern Europe." Attached to: Memorandum by the President of the Board of Trade, GEN330/1, July 17, 1950. "East-West Trade." CAB130/62: Papers of GEN 330, Cabinet Committee on East-West Trade.

————. 1950m. Minutes of the Cabinet Committee on East-West Trade, GEN330/1st mtg., July 19, 1950. CAB130/62: Papers of GEN 330, Cabinet Committee on East-West Trade.

————. 1949a. Report by the Chiefs of Staff Committee, COS(49)381, Nov. 10, 1949. "Strategic Implications of an Independent and United Libya." PREM8/478: Papers of the Prime Minister, 1951, Middle East (General).

————. 1949b. Minute from H. Morrison, Office of the Lord President of the Council, to the Prime Minister [Attlee]. "Dollars and Colonial Development." June 20, 1949. PREM 8/977: Papers of the Prime Minister, 1949, Financial Policy.

————. 1949c. Note by the Vice Chief of the Imperial General Staff, COS(49)85, March 9, 1949. "Colonial Forces." DEFE7/413: Papers of the Chiefs of Staff Committee, Colonial Defence Contributions.

————. 1949d. Memorandum by the Chiefs of Staff, DO(49)17, Feb. 16, 1949. "British Defence Coordination Committee, Far East and Middle East— Revised Terms of Reference." CAB 131/7: Papers of the Defence Committee.

————. 1949e. Memorandum by the Chiefs of Staff Committee, COS(49)239, July 18, 1949. "Strategic Background for Diplomatic Representatives from the Middle East. Annex: Middle East Strategy and Defence Policy." Map attached. DEFE5/15:I: Minutes and Memoranda of the Chiefs of Staff Committee.

————. 1949f. Paper by E. Bevin, Foreign Secretary, CP(49)209, Oct. 19, 1949. "The Middle East." CAB 129/37: Papers for the Cabinet.

————. 1949g. Note by the Chief of the Imperial General Staff, COS(49)298, Sept. 12, 1949. "United Kingdom Contribution to Western Europe." DEFE 5/16: Minutes and Memoranda of the Chiefs of Staff.

————. 1949h. Memorandum by the Secretary of State for the Colonies, SAC(49)5, May 18, 1949. "Hong Kong." CAB134/669: Minutes and Memoranda of the South East Asia Committee (1949–1950).

————. 1949i. Report of the Working Party on Malaya, FE(O)(49)50(Revise), No date. CAB134/287: Minutes and Memoranda of the Far East (Official) Committee.

————. 1949j. Draft Cabinet Paper by the Foreign Office for the Far East (Official) Committee, FE(O)(49)8(Revise), March 1, 1949. "The Situation in China." CAB 134/287: Minutes and Memoranda of the Far East (Official) Committee.

———. 1949k. Memorandum by the Foreign Office to the Far East (Official) Committee, FE(O)(49)49, Aug. 8, 1949. "China." CAB134/287: Minutes and Memoranda of the Far East (Official) Committee.

———. 1949*l*. Minutes of the Far East (Official) Committee, FE(O)(49)10th meeting, Aug. 11, 1949. "Control of Exports to China." CAB134/286: Minutes and Memoranda of the Far East (Official) Committee.

———. 1949m. Memorandum by the Secretary of State for the Colonies to the Economic Policy Committee, EPC(49)74, July 5, 1949. "Investment of Foreign Capital in the Colonies." PREM8/977: Papers of the Prime Minister, 1949, Financial Policy.

———. 1949n. Note by the Board of Trade, ON(49)240, July 12, 1949. "Russia." SUPP14/47: Papers of the Ministry of Supply, Overseas Negotiation Committee, Trade with Russia.

———. 1949o. Telegram from Sir F.H. Miller, Washington to the Foreign Office, Aug. 1, 1949, #3788. "Tin for USSR, discussions with State Dept." SUPP14/47: Papers of the Ministry of Supply, Trade with Russia.

———. 1949p. Minutes of the Overseas Negotiations Committee, ON(49)56th mtg., July 14, 1949. SUPP14/47: Papers of the Ministry of Supply, Trade with Russia.

———. 1949q. Telegram from Foreign Office to Washington, Nov. 5, 1949, #10514. "Tin." FO371/75618/UE7061/197/71: Supplies (1949)-Economic.

———. 1948a. Memorandum by E. Bevin, Foreign Secretary, CP(48)72, March 3, 1948. "The Threat to Western Civilization." CAB 129/25: Papers for the Cabinet.

———. 1948b. Memorandum from E. Shinwell, Ministry of Fuel and Power to Prime Minister Attlee, Sept. 13, 1945. Re: "First meeting of Ministerial Oil Committee (MOC), preparation for resumption of talks with Ickes." PREM 8/857: Papers of the Prime Minister, 1948, Oil.

———. 1948c. Note by the Joint Secretaries, Official Oil Committee, OOC(48)4, April 24, 1948. "Strategic Importance of South Persian Oil." CAB 134/588: Minutes and Memoranda of the Official Oil Committee.

———. 1948d. Report by the Commander-in-Chief, Middle East, COS(48)111(O), May 13, 1948. "Staff Study 'Intermezzo'." DEFE 5/11: Minutes and Memoranda of the Chiefs of Staff Committee.

———. 1948e. Directive to the Commanders-in-Chief Committee, Middle East, COS(48)144(O), July 1, 1948. "'PLAN SANDOWN'—Defence of the Middle East." DEFE 5/11: Minutes and Memoranda of the Chiefs of Staff Committee.

———. 1948f. Note by the War Office, COS(48)189(O), Aug. 21, 1948. "Denial of Persian and Iraq Oil and Demolition of the Trans-Persian

Railway." DEFE5/12: Minutes and Memoranda of the Chiefs of Staff Committee.

———. 1948g. Report by the Commanders-in-Chief Committee, Far East, CIC(FE)(48)1(P), Feb. 6, 1948. "The Strategic Position of Malaya." In COS(48)43(O), Feb. 23, 1948. "The Strategic Position of Malaya." DEFE5/10: Minutes and Memoranda of the Chiefs of Staff.

———. 1948h. Memorandum by the Chiefs of Staff, COS(48)200, Dec. 10, 1948. "China." Annex 2. DEFE5/9: Minutes and Memoranda of the Chiefs of Staff Committee.

———. 1948i. Note by the Joint Secretaries, European Economic Cooperation, Strategic Materials and Stockpiling Sub-Committee, ER(STOCK)(48)51, Dec. 7, 1948. "E.C.A. Mission Report: Article V(2) of Bilateral Agreement." CAB134/255: Minutes and Memoranda of the European Economic Cooperation Committee.

———. 1948j. Minute by C.T. Crowe, Foreign Office, Jan. 6, 1948. "Rubber & Strategic Stockpiling." FO371/62778/UE12492: Economic 1947.

———. 1948k. Cypher telegram from BSO NY/Wash. to Ministry of Supply, Jan. 20, 1948, #E44. "Tin for Russia." SUPP14/47: Papers of the Ministry of Supply, Metals Division Commodities, 1948–51, Trade with Russia.

———. 1948l. Treasury memorandum, Nov. 19, 1948. "Export of Strategic Materials to Russia and Eastern European Countries." FO371/68956B/UE8755: Foreign Office.

———. 1948m. Report by the Economic Warfare Sub-Committee, Defence (Transition) Committee, COS(48)201(O), Sept. 9, 1948. "Conduct of Economic Warfare." DEFE5/12: Minutes and Memoranda of the Chiefs of Staff Committee.

———. 1948n. Report by Chiefs of Staff, DO(48)61, Sept. 14, 1948. "Defence Review." CAB131/6: Papers of the Defence Committee.

———. 1947a. Memorandum by the Minister of State, OEP(47)8, Feb. 24, 1947. "Trade with Italy and Eastern and South Eastern Europe." CAB 134/541: Papers of the Overseas Economic Policy Committee (1946–1947).

———. 1947b. Letter from L.C. Hollis, Ministry of Defence, to E. Bevin, Foreign Secretary. Re "Egyptian Complaint to Security Council on British Troops." July 30, 1947. PREM 8/837: Papers of the Prime Minister, 1948, Middle East (Forces).

———. 1947c. Memorandum by the Overseas Defence Committee, ODC 707-M (Draft) Jan. 1947. "The Role of the Colonies in War." DEFE 5/1: Minutes and Memoranda of the Chiefs of Staff Committee.

———. 1947d. Meeting of the Official Oil Committee, OOC (47), Feb. 21, 1947. "Minutes." CAB134/588: Minutes and Memoranda of the Official Oil Committee (1947–49).

———. 1947e. Memorandum by the Foreign Office to Official Oil Committee,

OOC(47)8, Feb. 12, 1947. "Russian Oil Production." CAB 134/588: Minutes and Memoranda of the Official Oil Committee (1947–1949).

———. 1947f. Report by the Future Planning Section of the Joint Planning Staff to the Official Oil Committee, OOC(47)4, Jan. 4, 1947. "Oil." CAB 134/588: Minutes and Memoranda of the Official Oil Committee (1947–1949).

———. 1947g. Memorandum by the Chiefs of Staff, COS(47)209(O)(Revise), Oct. 2, 1947. "Middle East—Brief for Discussions." DEFE 5/6: Minutes and Memoranda of the Chiefs of Staff Committee.

———. 1947h. Memorandum by the Treasury to the Far East (Official) Committee, FE(O)(47)20, April 18, 1947. "Financial and Economic Policy for the Netherlands East Indies." CAB134/283: Minutes and Memoranda of the Far East (Official) Committee.

———. 1947i. Minute by C.T. Crowe, Foreign Office, Dec. 29, 1947. "Rubber & Strategic Stockpiling." FO371/62778/UE12492: Economic 1947.

———. 1946a. Report by the Technical Sub-Committee on Axis Oil, U.K. Chiefs of Staff Committee, AO(46)1, March 8, 1946. *Oil as a Factor in the German War Effort, 1933–1945*. CAB 77/29: Reports to the Cabinet.

———. 1946b. Report by the Chiefs of Staff, DO(46)47, April 2, 1946. "Strategic Position of the British Commonwealth." CAB 131/2: Papers of the Defence Committee.

———. 1946c. Report by the Chiefs of Staff, DO(46)80, June 18, 1946. "British Strategic Requirements in the Middle East." CAB131/3: Papers of the Defence Committee.

———. 1946d. Note by the Chairman, Far East (Official Committee), FE(O)(46)88. "Coordination in South East Asia." Annex: Telegram from Special Commissioner in South East Asia, Lord Killearn, Singapore to Foreign Office, No. 12, June 17, 1946. "Survey of Co-ordination within the Territories of South East Asia." CAB 134/281: Minutes and Memoranda of the Far East (Official) Committee.

———. 1946e. Telegram from BRMM Wash. to M. of Supply, Feb. 18, 1946. "American Stockpiling." Ramat 10338. FO371/58398/UR2988: Foreign Office, Relief, 1946, Supplies.

———. 1945a. "International Control of Atomic Energy: Distribution of Raw Materials." Minutes of Cabinet Committee GEN 75, Oct. 29, 1945. PREM 8/116, GEN 75/10. Papers of the Prime Minister, Correspondence and Papers, 1945–51.

———. 1945b. Report by the Post-Hostilities Planning Staff, PHP(45)29(O) Final, June 29, 1945. "The Security of the British Empire." CAB 81/46: Reports to the Cabinet.

———. 1924. Notes on the Chinese Student by the late Brigadier-General G.E. Pereira. (Received in Foreign Office, July 24, 1924). F 2497/174/10, FO 371/10270.

————. 1919. D.S. Robertson, British Military Attaché in Peking, "Report on Mongolia and Chinese Frontier Questions." Sept. 29, 1919. Enclosed in Jordan to Curzon, No. 446, 1 Oct. 1919. [151590/104499/10]. FO371/3696.

Puxty, A.G. 1979. "Some Evidence Concerning Cultural Differentials in Ownership Policies of Overseas Subsidiaries." *Management International Review* 19, #2:39–52.

Rapoport, A. 1974. *Conflict in Man-Made Environment*. Harmondsworth, U.K.: Penguin Books.

Rathbone, M.J. 1959. "Middle East Nationalism." Speech to the University Club, New York, Feb. 7, 1959. (Sent to Gordon Gray, 3/10/59.) Special Assistant Series, Name Subseries. Box 4. Folder: R-General (3) [1957–59]. DDEL.

Rawles, W.P. 1933. *The Nationality of Commercial Control of World Minerals*. New York: The Mineral Inquiry.

Reagan, R. 1987. "Continuation of Nicaraguan Emergency." Message to the Congress, April 21, 1987. *Weekly Compilation of Presidential Documents: Administration of Ronald Reagan 23, #16 (April 27):407–08.*

————. 1986. "Transcript of Talk by Reagan on South Africa and Apartheid." *New York Times*, July 23, p.6.

Rees, D. 1977. "Soviet Strategic Penetration in Africa." *Conflict Studies* #77 (Nov.): entire issue.

Rohter, L. 1987. "Soviet Supply Cut, Managua to Get Latin Oil." *New York Times*, June 20, p.3.

Roosevelt, K. 1979. *Countercoup — The Struggle for Control of Iran*. New York: McGraw-Hill.

Rosecrance, R. 1985. *The Rise of the Trading State*. New York: Basic Books.

Rosenau, J.N. 1986. "Before Cooperation: Hegemons, Regimes, and Habit-Driven Actors in World Politics." *International Organization* 40, #4 (Autumn):849–94.

Rosenberg, D. 1979. "American Atomic Strategy and the Hydrogen Bomb Decision." *Journal of American History* 66, #1 (June):62–87.

Rostow, E.V. 1986. "Where Will the Libyan Episode Lead? Toward Global Order." *New York Times*, April 27, p. E23.

RIIA. 1941. *World Production of Raw Materials*. London: Royal Institute of International Affairs. Information Department Paper No. 18B.

————. 1938. *Anglo-American Trade Relations*. London: Royal Institute of International Affairs. Information Department Paper. No. 22.

————. 1936. *Raw Materials and Colonies. London: Royal Institute of International Affairs.* Information Department Paper No. 18.

Rubin, B. 1980. *The Great Powers in the Middle East, 1941–1947 — The Road to the Cold War*. London: Frank Cass.

Rubinshteyn, G.I. 1983. "U.S. Trade-Economic Expansion in African Countries." *Moscow APN Daily Review* (in English), Dec. 22, pp. 1–5, digest of article in *SShA* #12 (Dec. 1983). In JPRS-USA-84–002, pp. 42–44.

Ruggie, J.G. 1983. "International Regimes, Transactions, and Change: Embedded Liberalism in the Postwar Economic Order." In S.D. Krasner, ed., *International Regimes*, pp. 195–232. Ithaca: Cornell University Press.

———. 1980. Review of S.D. Krasner, *Defending the National Interest*, 1978. *American Political Science Review* 74, #1 (March):296–99.

Rule, S. 1986. "In Sudan, Tide Turns against the U.S." *New York Times*, April 29, p.4.

Russett, B. 1984. "Dimensions of Resource Dependence: Some Elements of Rigor in Concept and Policy Analysis." *International Organization* 38, #3 (Summer): 481–99.

———. 1983. "Prosperity and Peace, Presidential Address." *International Studies Quarterly* 27:381–87.

———. 1981–82. "Security and the Resources Scramble: Will 1984 Be Like 1914?" *International Affairs* (London) 58, #1 (Winter): 42–58.

———. 1967. "Pearl Harbor: Deterrence Theory and Decision Theory." *Journal of Peace Research* 4, #2:89–106.

Sampson, A. 1976. *The Seven Sisters: The Great Oil Companies and the World They Shaped*. New York: Bantam.

San Francisco Chronicle. 1988. "NCAA Says No to GPA Standards." Jan. 14, p.D5.

Sartori, G. 1969. "Politics, Ideology, and Belief Systems." *American Political Science Review* 63:398–411.

Sawyer, C.A. 1966. *Communist Trade with Developing Countries: 1955–65*. New York: Praeger.

Schumpeter, J.A. 1919/1951. "Imperialism as Social Atavism." In H.M. Wright, ed., *The "New Imperialism"—Analysis of Late Nineteenth-Century Expansion*, pp. 69–87. Lexington, Mass.: Heath, 1976.

Schurmann, F. 1974. *The Logic of World Power—An Inquiry into the Origins, Currents, and Contradictions of World Politics*. New York: Pantheon.

Severin, W.K. 1981. Testimony before the Subcommittee on Africa of the Committee on Foreign Affairs, U.S. House of Representatives. *The Possibility of a Resource War in Southern Africa*, July 8, 1981, pp. 42–51. Washington, D.C.: U.S. Government Printing Office.

Shabad, T. 1985. "News Notes: Potential Uses of Synnyrite Being Studied." *Soviet Geography* 26, #1 (Jan.):64–66.

Shabecoff, P. 1988. "Development seen for the Minerals of All Antarctica." *New York Times*, June 8, p.1.

Shafer, M. 1983. "Capturing the Mineral Multinationals: Advantage or Disadvantage?" *International Organization* 37, #1 (Winter):93–119.

———. 1982. "Mineral Myths." *Foreign Policy* #47 (Summer):154–71.

Shapley, D. 1986. *The Seventh Continent—Antarctica in a Resource Age*. Baltimore: Johns Hopkins University Press.

Shaw, D.J.B. 1983. "Southern Frontiers of Muscovy, 1550–1700." In J.H. Bater and R.A. French, eds., *Studies in Russian Historical Geography*, Vol. 1, pp. 118–42. London: Academic Press.

Shaw, M. 1986. *Title to Territory in Africa — International Legal Issues*. Oxford: Clarendon Press.

Shearman, P. 1987. *The Soviet Union and Cuba*. London: Royal Institute of International Affairs/ Routledge & Kegan Paul. Chatham House Papers 38.

Shedlov, A., and A. Podtserob. 1983. "The Soviet Union and North African Countries." *International Affairs* (Moscow) #6 (June):54–62.

Shipler, D.K. 1986. "Missionaries for Democracy: U.S. Aid for Global Pluralism." *New York Times*, June 1, p.1

Shmelev, N. 1985. "The Soviet Union and World Economic Relations." *International Affairs* (Moscow) #1 (Jan.):12–20.

Short, A. 1975. *The Communist Insurrection in Malaya — 1948–1960*. London: Muller.

Sitnikov, B.P. 1982. "Materials and Minerals Policy of the Reagan Administration." *SShA* #8 (August):56–64. Translated as "Reagan Policies to Insure Raw Materials Supplies Explained," in JPRS 82454, pp. 33–43.

———. 1979. "America's Mineral Materials Problem." *SShA* #2 (Feb.): 77–87. Translated in JPRS 073105, pp. 97–115.

Skully, M.T. 1973. "Finnish-Soviet Trade." Research paper for the International Graduate Seminar on Regional Integration Studies, University of Stockholm. Photocopy.

Smith, A. 1986. *East West Trade, Embargoes and Expectations*. London: Centre for Economic Policy Research. Discussion Paper Series #139.

Smith, G.A. 1973. *Soviet Foreign Trade — Organization, Operations, and Policy, 1918–1971*. New York: Praeger.

Snyder G.H., and P. Diesing. 1977. *Conflict Among Nations — Bargaining, Decision Making, and System Structures in International Crises*. Princeton: Princeton University Press.

Snyder, G.H. 1965. *Stockpiling Strategic Materials — Politics and National Defense*. San Francisco: Chandler.

Soroos, M.S. 1986. *Beyond Sovereignty — The Challenge of Global Policy*. Columbia, S.C.: University of South Carolina Press.

———. 1982. "The Commons in the Sky: The Radio Spectrum and Geosynchronous Orbit as Issues in Global Policy." *International Organization* 36, #3 (Summer):665–77.

Speiser, E.A. 1947. *The United States and the Near East*. Cambridge, Mass.: Harvard University Press.

Spykman, N.J. 1944. *The Geography of the Peace*. H.R. Nicholl, ed. New York: Harcourt, Brace.

Staley, E. 1937. *Raw Materials in Peace and War*. New York: Council on Foreign Relations.

Stein, A.A. 1984. "The Hegemon's Dilemma: Great Britain, the United States, and the International Economic Order." *International Organization* 38, #2 (Spring):355–86.

Steinbruner, J. 1974. *The Cybernetic Theory of Decision.* Princeton: Princeton University Press.

Steiner, M. 1983. "The Search for Order in a Disorderly World: Worldviews and Prescriptive Decision Paradigms." *International Organization* 37, #3 (Summer):373–413.

Stent, A. 1981. *From Embargo to Ostpolitik — The Political Economy of West German-Soviet Relations, 1955–1980.* Cambridge: Cambridge University Press.

Stern, J.P. 1987a. Personal communication. Jan. 15.

————. 1987b. *Soviet Oil and Gas Exports to the West: Commercial Transaction or Security Threat?* London: Gower.

Stivers, W. 1982. *Supremacy and Oil — Iraq, Turkey, and the Anglo-American World Order, 1918–1930.* Ithaca: Cornell University Press.

Stockwell, A.J. 1984. "British Imperial Policy and Decolonization in Malaya, 1942–52." *The Journal of Imperial and Commonwealth History* 13, #1 (Oct.):68–87.

Strange, S. 1983. "*Cave! Hic Dragones*: A Critique of Regime Analysis." In S.D. Krasner, ed., *International Regimes*, pp. 337–54. Ithaca: Cornell University Press.

Strauss, S. 1979. "Mineral Self-Sufficiency — The Contrast Between the Soviet Union and the United States." *American Mining Congress Journal* 65, #11 (Nov.):49–54,59.

Strauss-Hupè, R. 1942. *Geopolitics — The Struggle for Space and Power.* New York: Putnam's.

Summers, H. 1988. "Panama Turmoil is Their Problem." *San Francisco Chronicle*, March 3, p. A20.

Sylvan, D.J. 1981. "The Newest Mercantilism." *International Organization* 35, #2 (Spring):375–93.

Symington, W.S. 1951. "History of the National Security Resources Board." NARS. Document supplied to author by Greg MacLauchlan.

Szuprowicz, B. 1981. *How to Avoid Strategic Materials Shortages — Dealing with Cartels, Embargoes, and Supply Disruptions.* New York: Wiley.

Tabarin, Ye. 1982. "Africa in the Global Strategy of Imperialism." *MEIMO* #2 (Feb.):25–37. Excerpt translated as "United States Seeks Military Bases, Ideological, Economic Influence in Africa." JPRS 80837, pp. 17–27.

Taubman, P. 1987. "Soviets Won't Push Policy on Allies, Gorbachev Says." *New York Times*, Nov. 5, p.1.

Taylor, A.J.P. 1957. *The Trouble Makers — Dissent Over Foreign Policy, 1792–1939 — The Ford Lectures, 1956.* London: Hamish Hamilton.

Tétreault, M.A., and C.F. Abel. 1986. "Dependency Theory and the Return of High Politics." In M.A. Tétreault and C.F. Abel, eds., *Dependency Theory and the Return of High Politics*, pp. 3–21. New York: Greenwood Press.

Thomas, J.R. 1985a "Soviet Global Policy and Raw Materials." In U. Ra'anan and C. Perry, eds., *Strategic Minerals and International Security*. Washington, D.C.: Pergamon-Brassey's. Institute for Foreign Policy Analysis "On the Agenda" #1.

Thomas, J.R. 1985b. *Natural Resources in Soviet Foreign Policy*. New York: National Strategy Information Center. Agenda Paper #15.

Thompson, J. 1984. *Studies in the Theory of Ideology*. Berkeley: University of California Press.

Thompson, J.D., and A. Tuden. 1959. "Strategies, Structures, and Processes of Organizational Decision." In J.D. Thompson, et al., eds., *Comparative Studies in Administration*, pp. 195–216. Pittsburgh: University of Pittsburgh Press.

Tilly, S. 1986. Conversation with Steven Tilly, Judicial, Social and Fiscal Branch, NARS. June 5.

Tower Commission. 1987. *Report of the President's Special Review Board*. Washington, D.C.: U.S. Government Printing Office.

Tramerye, P. l'E. de la. 1924. *The World Struggle for Oil*. New York: Knopf.

Tran, M. 1987. "US 'Hurt' by Soviet Hi-Tech Ban." *The Guardian* (London), Jan. 13, p.26.

Turner, L. 1983. *Oil Companies in the International System*. London: Royal Institute of International Affairs/George Allen & Unwin.

Ulam, A. 1981. "Russian Nationalism." In S. Bialer, ed., *The Domestic Context of Soviet Foreign Policy*, pp. 3–18. Boulder: Westview Press.

———. 1952. *Titoism and the Cominform*. Cambridge, Mass.: Harvard University Press.

U.S. BOM. 1981. U.S. Bureau of Mines. *Mineral Facts and Problems 1980*. Washington, D.C.: U.S. Government Printing Office.

———. 1952. "Tungsten." In *Minerals Yearbook, Vol. 1*. Washington, D.C.: U.S. Government Printing Office.

———. 1940. "Forward." *Minerals Yearbook*. Washington, D.C.: U.S. Government Printing Office.

U.S. Congress, Joint Economic Committee. 1983. *Soviet Economy in the 1980s: Problems and Prospects*, Dec. 31, 1982. Washington, D.C.: U.S. Government Printing Office.

U.S. CBO. 1983a. Congressional Budget Office. *Strategic and Critical Nonfuel Minerals: Problems and Policy Alternatives*. Washington, D.C.: U.S. Government Printing Office. Aug.

———. 1983b. *Rapid Deployment Forces: Policy and Budgetary Implications*. Washington, D.C.: U.S. Government Printing Office. Feb.

U.S. CRS. 1985. Congressional Research Service. *The Soviet Union in the Third World, 1980–85: An Imperial Burden or Political Asset?* Prepared for the Committee on Foreign Relations, U.S. House. Committee Print. Washington, D.C.: U.S. Government Printing Office. Sept. 23.

————. 1981. *A Congressional Handbook on U.S. Materials Import Dependency/ Vulnerability*. Report to the Subcommittee on Economic Stabilization of the Committee on Banking, Finance and Urban Affairs. U.S. House of Representatives. Washington, D.C.: U.S. Government Printing Office. Sept.

U.S. DOI. 1947. Krug, J.A., U.S. Department of the Interior. *Natural Resources and Foreign Aid*. Washington, D.C.: U.S. Government Printing Office.

U.S. House of Representatives. 1981. Hearings Before the Subcommittee on Africa of the Committee on Foreign Affairs, July 8, 1981. *The Possibility of a Resource War in Southern Africa*. Washington, D.C.: U.S. Government Printing Office.

U.S. LRS. 1950. Legislative Reference Service (Library of Congress). *Mobilization Planning and the National Security (1950–1960)*. Washington, D.C.: U.S. Government Printing Office.

U.S. Military Academy. 1947. *Raw Materials in Peace and War*. West Point: Associates in International Relations, Department of Social Sciences.

U.S. NSRB. 1952. National Security Resources Board. *The Objectives of United States Materials Resources Policy and Suggested Initial Steps in Their Accomplishment*. Washington, D.C.: U.S. Government Printing Office.

U.S. OTA. 1985. Office of Technology Assessment, U.S. Congress. *Strategic Materials: Technologies to Reduce U.S. Import Vulnerabilities*. Washington, D.C.: U.S. Government Printing Office. May. OTA-ITE-248.

U.S. Senate. 1959. Minerals, Materials, and Fuels Subcommittee of the Committee on Interior and Insular Affairs. *Mineral Resources of and Background Information on the Eastern Hemisphere including the Soviet Union and Satellite Countries*. Washington, D.C.: U.S. Government Printing Office.

————. 1954. Metals, Materials and Fuels Economic Subcommittee of the Committee on Interior and Insular Affairs, Hearings, 1953–54. *Stockpile and Accessibility of Strategic and Critical Materials to the United States in Time of War*. 83rd Cong. Washington, D.C.: U.S. Government Printing Office.

U.S. State Department. 1952. "Yugoslavia: Titoism and U.S. Foreign Policy." *Background* (June). Washington, D.C.: Office of Public Affairs.

Valkenier, E. 1986. "Revolutionary Change in the Third World: Recent Soviet Assessments." *World Politics* 38, #3 (April):415–34.

————. 1983. *The Soviet Union and the Third World—An Economic Bind*. New York: Praeger.

Vasil'yev, V. 1982. "The Developing Countries in the System of the International Capitalist Division of Labor." *MEIMO* #11 (Nov.):91–106. Excerpt translated as "Third World Trapped in Role Importing Manufactures, Supplying Raw Materials." JPRS 83011, pp. 61–72.

Vawter, R.L. 1983. *Industrial Mobilization—The Relevant History*. Washington, D.C.: National Defense University Press.

Vayrynen, R. 1969. "A Case Study of Sanctions: Finland-USSR 1958–59." *Conflict and Cooperation* 3:205–33.

Vernon, R. 1984. "Soviet Commodity Power in International Economic Relations." In M.M. Kostecki, ed., *The Soviet Impact on Commodity Markets*, pp 6–14. London: Macmillan.

———. 1983. *Two Hungry Giants — The United States and Japan in the Quest for Oil and Ores*. Cambridge, Mass.: Harvard University Press.

———. 1977. *Storm over Multinationals: The Real Issues*. Cambridge, Mass.: Harvard University Press.

Verrier, A. 1986. *The Road to Zimbabwe — 1890–1980*. London: J. Cape.

Vloyantes, J.P. 1975. *Silk Glove Hegemony — Finnish-Soviet Relations, 1944–1974*. Kent, Ohio: Kent State University Press.

Waltz, K.N. 1979. *Theory of International Politics*. Reading, Mass.: Addison-Wesley.

Webster's. 1970. *Webster's Seventh New Collegiate Dictionary*. Springfield, Mass.: Merriam.

Weissman, S.R. 1974. *American Foreign Policy in the Congo, 1960–1964*. Ithaca: Cornell University Press.

Welch, R.E., Jr. 1985. *Response to Revolution — The United States and the Cuban Revolution, 1959–1961*. Chapel Hill: University of North Carolina Press.

Welles, S. 1942. "Address by the Acting Secretary of State to the Twenty-Ninth National Foreign Trade Convention, Oct. 8." *Department of State Bulletin* 7 (Oct. 10):808–13.

Wellington Koo, Dr. V.K. 1939. "The Open Door Policy and World Peace." Eleventh Richard Cobden Lecture. Oxford: Oxford University Press.

Wells, S.F., Jr. 1981. "The Origins of Massive Retaliation." *Political Science Quarterly* 96, #1 (Spring):31–52.

Wendt, E.A. 1985. "Energy Trade: Problems and Prospects." Address by Deputy Assistant Secretary of State for International Energy and Resources Policy, before the Oxford Energy Seminar, Oxford, England, Sept. 5. *Current Policy* #741. Washington, D.C.: U.S. Department of State, Bureau of Public Affairs.

Westing, A.H. 1986. "Introduction." In A.H. Westing, ed., *Global Resources and International Conflict — Environmental Factors in Strategic Policy and Action*, pp. 1–2. Oxford: Oxford University Press.

Whyte, Sir F. 1941. *Japan's Purpose in Asia*. London and Oxford: Royal Institute of International Affairs and Oxford University Press. Nov.

Wijkman, P.M. 1982. "Managing the Global Commons." *International Organization* 36, #3 (Summer):511–36.

Williams, W.A. 1972. *The Tragedy of American Diplomacy*. New York: Delta.

Wolanin, T.R. 1975. *Presidential Advisory Commissions — Truman to Nixon*. Madison: University of Wisconsin Press.

Wright, A.W. 1983. "Soviet Natural Resource Exports and the World Market." In R.G. Jensen, T. Shabad, and A.W. Wright, eds., *Soviet Na-*

tural Resources in the World Economy, pp. 617–22. Chicago: University of Chicago Press.

Wright, H., ed. 1976. *The "New Imperialism" — Analysis of Late Nineteenth-Century Expansion*. Lexington, Mass.: Heath.

Wulf, H. 1982. "East-West Trade as a Source of Tension." *Journal of Peace Research* 19, #4:301–21.

Young, C. 1965. *Politics in the Congo: Decolonization and Independence*. Princeton: Princeton University Press.

Yoshpe, H.B. 1953. *A Case Study in Peacetime Mobilization Planning — The National Security Resources Board, 1947–1953*. Washington, D.C.: Executive Office of the President. April 30.

Yugoslavian Ministry of Foreign Affairs. 1951. *White Book on Aggressive Activities by the Governments of the USSR, Poland, Czechoslovakia, Hungary, Rumania, Bulgaria and Albania towards Yugoslavia*. Beograd.

Zevin, L. 1985. "The CMEA Countries' Economic Cooperation with the Developing States — Inventions and Reality." *MEIMO* #7 (July): 60–72. Translated as "Cooperation between CMEA Countries, Third World Discussed." JPRS-UWE-85–011, pp. 44–58.

Zhirmunski, M.M. 1935. *Organization and Technique of Soviet Exports*. Moscow: Vneshtorgizdat.

Zoppo, C.E., and C. Zorgbibe. 1985. *On Geopolitics: Classical and Nuclear*. Dordrecht: Martinus Nijhoff, in cooperation with NATO Scientific Affairs Division.

Index

Names

Subjects

property rights and, 66, 240–241
strategic syntheses and, 32–33, 82–94
United States foreign policy and, 97–148
use of term, 2
war and conflict and, 1–2, 3, 237–238
World War II causes and, 156
Reagan administration, 129, 252
Realist-mercantilist model in political
science, 8–9
Reconstruction Finance Corporation,
186–187
Regimes
international structure and, 245–246
political property rights and, 18
property rights at international level and,
21–22, 240
use of term, 16–17
Resource diplomacy, and Soviet Union,
217–233
Resources, *see* Natural resources
Resources for Freedom (Paley Commission),
98, 99, 100, 142, 181
Romania, 220
Roosevelt (Franklin) administration, 71
Royal Dutch Shell, 51, 55
Rubber
United Kingdom policy on, 152–153,
178–179, 249
United States policy on, 188, 190
Rules of access
dyadic conflicts over property rights and,
42–43
intercollegiate sports example of, 19
property rights and, 17–18, 39–40
strategic syntheses and, 86
Rules of eligibility
Congo crisis (1960–63) and, 65
dyadic conflicts over property rights and,
42–43
intercollegiate sports example of, 19
international economic institutions and,
71
land ownership and, 19
property rights and, 17–20, 39–40, 66
struggle for hegemony in Asia (1931–41)
and, 56
World War II and, 71
Russia, *see* Soviet Union

Saudi Arabia, 107, 108, 171
Singapore, 150
South Africa, 232
South America, and raw materials policy,
126

Southeast Asia
defense mobilization and, 115–116
geopolitical determinism and, 103
Soviet Union
China and, 177–178, 221–222
Congo crisis (1960–63) and, 64–65
Council on Mutual Economic Assistance
(CMEA) and, 211–213
defense mobilization and, 112, 114
developing countries and, 213–215
economic issues and, 134–136, 197–198,
204–217, 228–232, 231
export controls on, 92, 131–134, 159, 189,
190, 192–193
expropriation of foreign property by, 49
geopolitical determinism and, 103, 104
ideological actions of, 218–224
international raw material flows and
interests of, 246–249
international system and, 197–217
oil policy of, 128–129, 136, 164–165, 197,
198, 209
paradox between ideal and material
interests in policies of, 195–196
political actions and, 224–228
property rights and, 70
raw materials and foreign policy of, 5, 6,
32, 81, 195–235
resource diplomacy of, 217–233
strategic syntheses and foreign policy of,
90–94, 200–204
Third World and, 206–207
trade and objectives of, 205, 215–217
United Kingdom and, 158, 159, 162, 173,
179
United States and, 224–225
Western export controls on, 92, 131–134
Spheres of influence, and raw materials
strategies, 81
Sports, and rules of eligibility, 19
Standard Oil of New York (Socony), 51
State
definition of interests by, 3–4
dyadic conflicts over property rights
between, 42–49
economic property rights and, 20–21
evolution of property rights and, 68–69
ideological behavior of, 241–243
organizing principles and ideas and, 4–5,
6
political property rights and, 20
raw materials as input to, 244, 246

ABOUT THE AUTHOR

Ronnie D. Lipschutz has degrees in Physics from the University of Texas — Austin and the Massachusetts Institute of Technology, and a Ph.D. from the Energy and Resources Group at the University of California — Berkeley. He has worked on the scientific staffs of the Union of Concerned Scientists, the Massachusetts Audubon Society, and the Lawrence Berkeley Laboratory. He has been a Research Fellow of the Institute of International Affairs at U.C. Berkeley (1985–86), a Visiting Research Fellow of the Royal Institute of International Affairs in London (1986–87), and a Postdoctoral Fellow of the U.C. Berkeley MacArthur Interdisciplinary Group in International Security Studies and the Energy and Resources Group (1988). In 1985 he received a two-year Social Science Research Council Predoctoral Fellowship in International Peace and Security Studies, funded by the John D. and Catherine T. MacArthur Foundation. He is the author of *Radioactive Waste: Politics, Technology and Risk* (Ballinger, 1980), a contributor to *Energy Strategies: Toward a Solar Future* (Ballinger, 1980), and the co-author of *The Energy Saver's Handbook for Town and City People* (Rodale Press, 1982) and a number of studies on energy conservation published by the Lawrence Berkeley Laboratory. He is presently the President and Executive Director of the Pacific Institute for Studies in Development, Environment, and Security in Berkeley, California.